Indus Script deciphered

-- Rosetta stones, *Mlecchita vikalpa*, 'meluhha cipher'

S. Kalyanaraman
Sarasvati Research Center
2015

ISBN 978-0-9911048-4-0

Library of Congress Control Number 2015912104

First Published in the United States of America

Mlecchita Vikalpa, 'meluhha cipher', is an ancient Prakritam language writing system which is identified in Indus Script Corpora of ca. 7000 inscriptions.

The cipher is composed of hieroglyph multiplex hypertexts of metalwork.

Meluhha people who created the Sheffield of Ancient Near East in Chanhu-daro, invented and used writing in the River Valleys of Sarasvati, Indus (Sindhu) rivers and Indo-Iran borderlands.

This work corroborates with select samples of inscriptions, a trilogy which has demonstrated that the Indus Script Corpora constitute *catalogus catalogorum* of metalwork of the Bronze Age:

1. I*ndus Script Cipher -- Hieroglyhphs of Indian Linguistic Area*(2010)
2. *Indus Script: Meluhha metalwork hieroglyphs* (2014)
3. *Philosophy of Symbolic forms in Meluhha cipher* (2014)

[S. Kalyanaraman, Herndon, Sarasvai Research Center.]

Rosetta stone is a metaphor for decipherment of a writing system. It refers to a stone found in a town called Rosetta (Rashid), carved in 196 BCE with writing on it in two languages (Egyptian and Greek) and three scripts then in use in Egypt (hieroglyphic, demotic and Greek). Three scripts were used to enable priests, government officials and rulers of Egypt to read the message. Champollion could read both Greek and Coptic scripts, traced them back to hieroglphic signs. Rosetta stone validated Jean-Francois Champollon's decipherment in 1822, of Egyptian hieroglyphs -- that is, determining what the hieroglyphs stood for.

Now, for the tough problem of Indus Script, the following Rosetta stones have been found. Six Rosetta stones of Indus Script which validate the Indus Script Cipher are detailed; a seventh stone hints at the underlying language to be Meluhha. Hundreds of Punch-marked coins from ca. 6th century BCE display select Indus Script hieroglyphs.

1. A circular seal reported by Gadd displayed what he identified as a hieroglyph: 'water-carrier' which is a commonly deployed sign on Indus script.

Seal impression, Ur (Upenn; U.16747); dia. 2.6, ht. 0.9 cm.; Gadd, PBA 18 (1932), pp. 11-12, pl. II, no. 12; Porada 1971: pl.9, fig.5; Parpola, 1994, p. 183; water carrier with a skin (or pot?) hung on each end of the yoke across his shoulders and another one below the crook of his left arm; the vessel on the right end of his yoke is over a receptacle for the water; a star on either side of the head (denoting supernatural?). The whole object is enclosed by 'parenthesis' marks. The parenthesis is perhaps a way of splitting of the ellipse

(Hunter, G.R., *JRAS*, 1932, 476). An unmistakable example of an 'hieroglyphic' seal. kuṭi 'water-carrier' (Telugu); Rebus: kuṭhi 'smelter furnace' (Santali) kuṛī f. 'fireplace' (H.); krvṛI f. 'granary (WPah.); kuṛī, kuṛo house, building'(Ku.)(CDIAL 3232) kuṭi 'hut made of boughs' (Skt.) guḍi temple (Telugu) मेढ (p. 662) [mēḍha] 'polar' star'
Rebus: mẽṛhẽt, meḍ 'iron' (Ho.Munda)

2. A fragment of a relief 'The spinner' made of Bitumen mastic of Neo-Elamite period (8th cent. BCE - middle of 6th cent. BCE) was found in Susa. This fragment displayed a well-coiffured woman being fanned by an attendant while the woman wearing bangles on both arms -- seated on a stool with feline legs -- held what may be a spinning device before a table with feline legs with a bowl containing a whole fish with six blobs assembled on top of the fish.

Hieroroglyph: aya 'fish' Rebus: aya 'iron' (Gujarati) ayas 'metal' (Rigveda)
kola 'tiger' Rebus: kolle 'blacksmith' kol 'working in iron'; kolhe 'smelter' kole.l 'smithy, temple'; kolimi 'smithy, forge' Hieroglyph: bhaTa 'six' Rebus: baTa 'furnace'. kAtI 'spinner' Rebus: kAtI 'wheelwright'

3, 4, 5. Three pure tin ingots were discovered from a shipwreck in Haifa, Israel, now held in the Museum of Ancient Art of the Municipality of Haifa (#8252); the three ingots displayed hieroglyphs of Indus Script.

Tin ingots in the Museum of Ancient Art of the Municipality of Haifa, Israel (left #8251, right #8252). The ingots each bear two inscribed Cypro-Minoan markings. (Note: I have argued that the inscriptions were Meluhha hieroglyphs (Indus writing) denoting ranku 'tin' dhatu 'ore'. See: The Bronze Age Writing System of Sarasvati Hieroglyphics as Evidenced by Two "Rosetta Stones" By S. Kalyanaraman in: *Journal of Indo-Judaic Studies* Volume 1: Number 11 (2010), pp. 47-74.) (Appended)

ranku 'liquid measure'; *ranku* 'antelope' Rebus: *ranku* 'tin' (Santali) *dhatu* 'cross' Rebus: *dhatu* 'mineral ore' (Santali).

- Hieroglyph: *ran:ku* = liquid measure (Santali) Rebus: *ran:ku* = tin (Santali)
- Hieroglyph: *ran:ku* a species of deer; *ran:kuka* (Skt.)(CDIAL 10559).
- Hieroglyph: *dāṭu* = cross (Telugu) Rebus: dhatu = mineral (Santali)
- Hindi. *dhāṭnā* 'to send out, pour out, cast (metal)' (CDIAL 6771).

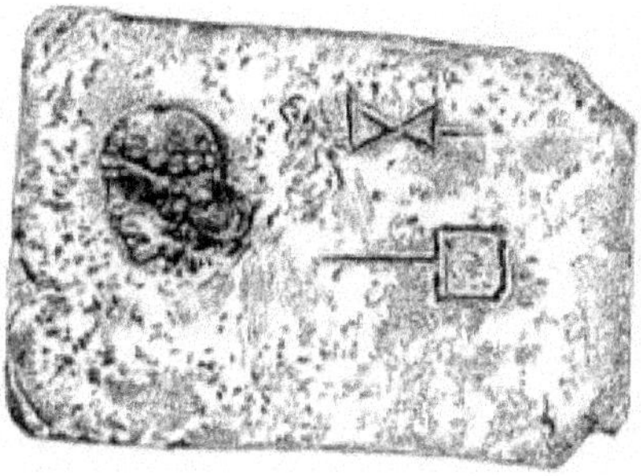

These two hieroglyphs were inscribed on two tin ingots discovered in port of Dor south of Haifa from an ancient shipwreck.

Inscribed tin ingot with a moulded head, from Haifa (Artzy, 1983: 53). (Michal Artzy, 1983, Arethusa of the Tin Ingot, Bulletin of the American Schools of Oriental Research, BASOR 250, pp. 51-55) An additional hieroglyph on this third tin ingot is : human face. Hieroglyph: mũhe 'face' (Santali) Rebus: mũh 'ingot' (Santali). mũh opening or hole (in a stove for stoking (Bi.); ingot (Santali) mũh metal ingot (Santali) mũhā̃ = the quantity of iron produced at one time in a native smelting furnace of the Kolhes; iron produced by the Kolhes and formed like a four-cornered piece a little pointed at each end; mūhā mẽṛhẽt = iron smelted by the Kolhes and formed into an equilateral lump a little pointed at each of four ends; kolhe tehen mẽṛhẽt ko mūhā akata = the Kolhes have to-day produced pig iron (Santali).

6. A clay storage pot was discovered in Susa (Acropole mound), Old Elamite period, ca. 2500-2400 BCE (H. 20 1/4 in. or 51 cm.) now in Musee du Louvre, Paris which displayed a fish hieroglyph on the rim. The pot which also had a lid, contained metal tools, and weapons. Hieroglyph: aya 'fish' Rebus: aya 'iron' (Gujarati) ayas 'metal' (Rigveda)

Sb 2723 (After Harper, Prudence Oliver, Joan Aruz, Francoise Tallon, 1992, The Royal city of Susa: Ancient Near Eastern Treasures in the Louvre, Metropolitan Musem of Art, New York.)

Hundreds of Rosetta stones of punch-marked coins from 6th cent. BCE

In addition to these 6 Rosetta stones of Indus Script, hundreds of punch-marked coins have been found from many mints extending from Gandhara (Afghanistan) to Anuradhapura (Sri Lanka) displaying hieroglyphs from Indus Script.

What unites the hieroglyphs on these Rosetta stones are the metalwork catalogues of Indus Script Corpora, validating what the hieroglyphs stood for: metalwork. In what language was the metalwork signified? Prakritam.

Another Rosetta stone which may relate to Indus Script is an Akkadian cylinder seal of Shu-ilishu, a Meluhha interpreter. This shows a Meluhha merchant carrying his signature hieroglyph: goat. mr..eka, mlekh 'goat' Rebus: meluhha, milakkhu ! This seventh Rosetta stone eliminates Akkadian as the language of Indus Script and hints that the underlying language of the Indus Script Cipher is Meluhha.

Overview of Indus Script Cipher

Rebus-metonymy layered reading in Prakritam: *sal karṇī* 'workshop supercargo' (from) *bhāṛ* 'furnace'.

Text 4305. Harappa. Three-sided prism tablet. A standing warrior with a raised club, horns and bovine features (hoofed legs and/or a tail)(After Asko Parpola, Fig. 6.3, p.91). Mahadean Pict-90. Identical hieroglyphs on another Harappa tablet: h714 A and B.

Hieroglyph: kárṇaka m. ' projection on the side of a vessel, handle ' ŚBr. [kárṇa --]Pa. kaṇṇaka -- ' having ears or corners '; Wg. kaṇə ' ear -- ring ' NTS xvii 266; S. kano m. ' rim, border '; P. kannā m. ' obtuse angle of a kite ' (→ H. kannā m. ' edge, rim, handle '); N. kānu ' end of a rope for supporting a burden '; B. kāṇā ' brim of a cup ', G. kānɔ m.; M. kānā m. ' touch -- hole of a gun '.(CDIAL 2831) karṇín ' having ears ' AV., karṇika -- W. [kárṇa --]N. kāne, Or. kāniā̃; -- ext. with -- la -- : S. kaniru.(CDIAL 2850) Rebus: M. kārṇī m. ' prime minister, supercargo of a ship ', kul-- karṇī m. ' village accountant '. karaṇika m. ' teacher ' MBh., ' judge ' Pañcat. [kā- raṇa --]Pa. usu -- kāraṇika -- m. ' arrow -- maker '; Pk. kāraṇiya -- m. ' teacher of Nyāya '; S. kāriṇī m. ' guardian, heir '; N. kārani ' abettor in crime '; M. kārṇī m. ' prime minister, supercargo of a ship ', kul -- karṇī m. ' village accountant '.(CDIAL 3058)

Hieroglyph: sal 'splinter': śalá1 m. ' staff ' TBr., ' dart, spear ' lex. [~ śará -- 1: cf. śilī --]S. sarī f. ' a stick forming part of a waterwheel '; Or. saḷa ' pin, thorn '; Bi. sar ' sticks used in setting up the warp ', Mth. sarkā; H. sal m. ' stake, spike, splinter, thorn, difficulty '; G. saḷī f. ' small thin stick ', saḷiyɔ m. ' bar, rod, pricker '; -- Kho. šoḷ ' reed '(CDIAL 12343) Rebus: sal 'workshop' (Santali): śā́lā f. ' shed, stable, house ' AV., śālám adv. ' at home ' ŚBr., śālikā -- f. ' house, shop ' lex. Pa. Pk. sālā -- f. ' shed, stable, large open -- sided hall, house ', Pk. sāla -- n. ' house '; Ash. sal ' cattleshed ', Wg. šāl, Kt. šål, Dm. šâl; Paš.weg. sāl, ar. šol ' cattleshed on summer pasture '; Kho. šal ' cattleshed ', šeli ' goatpen '; K. hal f. ' hall, house '; L. sālh f. ' house with thatched roof '; A. xāl, xāli ' house, workshop, factory '; B. sāl ' shed, workshop '; Or. sāḷa ' shed, stable '; Bi. sār f. ' cowshed '; H. sāl f. ' hall, house, school ', sār f. ' cowshed '; M. sāḷ f. ' workshop, school '; Si. sal -- a, ha° ' hall, market -- hall ' (CDIAL 12414)

Hieroglyph: bhaṛ m. ' warrior (Gujarati): Rebus: *bhāṛ* 'furnace': *bhaṭa* -- m. ' hired soldier, servant ' MBh. [√bhr̥] 1. Ash. 3 sg. pret. bəṛə, f. °ṛī ' brought ', Kt. bṙå; Gaw. (LSI) bṛoet ' they begin '.2. Pa. bhata -- ' supported, fed ', bhataka -- m. ' hired servant ', bhaṭa -- m. ' hireling, servant, soldier '; Aś.shah. man. kāl. bhaṭa -- ' hired servant ', kāl. bhaṭaka -- , gir. bhata -- , bhataka -- ; Pk. bhayaga -- m. ' servant ', bhaḍa -- m. ' soldier ', bhaḍaa -- m. ' member of a non -- Aryan tribe '; Paš. buṛī́ ' servant maid ' IIFL iii 3, 38; S. bhaṛu ' clever, proficient ', m. ' an adept '; Ku. bhaṛ m. ' hero, brave man ', gng. adj. ' mighty '; B. bhaṛ ' soldier, servant, nom. prop. ', bhaṛil ' servant, hero '; Bhoj. bhar ' name of a partic. low caste '; G. bhaṛ m. ' warrior, hero, opulent person ', adj. ' strong, opulent ', ubhaṛ m. ' landless worker ' (G. cmpd. with u -- , ' without ', i.e. ' one without servants '?); Si.beḷē ' soldier ' < *baḷaya, st. baḷa -- ; -- Pk. bhuaga -- m. ' worshipper in a temple ', G. bhuvɔ m. (rather than < bhūdēva --).S.kcch. bhaṛ ' brave '; Garh. (Śrīnagrī dial.) bhɔṛ, (Salānī dial.) bheṛ ' warrior '.(CDIAL 9588)*bhr̥takarman ' soldier -- work '. [bhr̥ta -- , kárman -- 1]Si. *baḷām* ' warfare '.(CDIAL 9589)

Rebus: bhráṣṭra n. ' frying pan, gridiron ' MaitrS. [√bhrajj]Pk. *bhaṭṭha* -- m.n. ' gridiron '; K. *büṭhü* f. ' level surface by kitchen fireplace on which vessels are put when taken off fire '; S. *baṭhu* m. ' large pot in which grain is parched, large cooking fire ', *baṭhī* f. ' distilling furnace '; L. *bhaṭṭh* m. ' grain -- parcher's oven ', *bhaṭṭhī* f. ' kiln, distillery ', awāṇ. *bhaṭh*; P. *bhaṭṭh* m., °*ṭhī* f. ' furnace ', *bhaṭṭhā* m. ' kiln '; N. *bhāṭi* ' oven or vessel in which clothes are steamed for washing '; A. *bhaṭā* ' brick -- or lime -- kiln '; B. *bhāṭi* ' kiln '; Or. *bhāṭi* ' brick -- kiln, distilling pot '; Mth. *bhaṭhī,bhaṭṭī* ' brick -- kiln, furnace, still '; Aw.lakh. *bhāṭhā* ' kiln '; H. *bhaṭṭhā* m. ' kiln ', *bhaṭ* f. ' kiln, oven, fireplace '; M. *bhaṭṭā* m. ' pot of fire ', *bhaṭṭī* f. ' forge '. -- X bhástrā -- q.v.S.kcch. *bhaṭṭhī keṇī* ' distil (spirits) '.*bhraṣṭrapūra ' gridiron -- cake '. [Cf. *bhrāṣṭraja* -- ' pro- duced on a gridiron ' lex. -- bhráṣṭra -- , pūra -- 2 P. *bhaṭhūhar*, °*hrā*, *bhaṭhūrā*, °*ṭhorū* m. ' cake of leavened bread '; -- or < **bhṛṣṭapūra* - *bhraṣṭrāgāra ' grain parching house '. [bhráṣṭra -- , agāra --]P. *bhaṭhiār*, °*ālā* m. ' grainparcher's shop '.(CDIAL 9656-9658) bhrāṣṭra m. ' gridiron ' Nir., adj. ' cooked on a grid- iron ' Pāṇ., °*ka* -- m. (n.?) ' frying pan ' Pañcat. [NIA. forms all < eastern MIA. **bhāṭha* -- , but like Pk. none show medial aspirate except G. with -- *ḍ* -- poss. < -- *ḍh* -- . -- bhráṣṭra -- , √bhrajj] Pk. *bhāḍa* -- n. ' oven for parching grain '; Phal. *bhaṛ*<-> ' to roast, fry ' (NOPhal 31 < *bhṛkta* -- with ?); L. *bhāṛ* ' oven '; Ku. *bhāṛ* ' iron oven, fire, furnace '; Bi. *bhār* ' grain -- parcher's fireplace ', (N of Ganges) *bhaṛ* -- *bhū̃jā* ' grain -- parcher '; OAw. *bhārū*, pl. °*rā* m. ' oven, furnace '; H. *bhāṛ* m. ' oven, grain -- parcher's fireplace, fire '; G.*bhāḍi* f. ' oven ', M. *bhāḍ* n. *bhrāṣṭraśālikā ' furnace house '. [bhrāṣṭra -- , śā´lā --] H. *bharsārī* f. ' furnace, oven '.(CDIAL 9684, 9685)

Allograph: back to back: <Al-kAnDoG>,,<Ar-kAnDoG>(L) {IND} ``^back to back". #4431. <Al-kAnDoG.kAnDoG>(L) {ADV} ``back to back". #4042 (Munda etyma)

Allograph: <kanda>(A) {N} ``^saddle (between two ^hills)" (Munda etyma) WPah.kṭg. (kc.) *kaṇḍɔ* m. ' thorn, mountain peak ',(CDIAL 2668)

Terracotta female adorned with 'dotted circles'; Period Namazga II; Yalangach Tepe, Geoksyur (Weiner, 1984, Fig. 183) Hieroglyph: buttock, rump: *kaṇṭa3 ' backbone, podex, penis '. 2. *kaṇḍa -- . 3. *karaṇḍa -- 4. (Cf. *kāṭa -- 2, *ḍākka -- 2: poss. same as káṇṭa -- 1]1. Pa. *piṭṭhi* -- *kaṇṭaka* -- m. ' bone of the spine '; Gy. eur. *kanro* m. ' penis ' (or < káṇṭaka --); Tir. *mar* -- *kaṇḍḗ* ' back (of the body) '; S. *kaṇḍo* m. ' back ', L. *kaṇḍ* f.,*kaṇḍā* m. ' backbone ', awāṇ. *kaṇḍ*, °*ḍī* ' back '; P. *kaṇḍ* f. ' back, pubes '; WPah. bhal. *kaṇṭ* f. ' syphilis '; N. *kaṇḍo* ' buttock, rump, anus ', *kaṇḍeulo* ' small of the back '; B. *kā̃ṭ* ' clitoris '; Or. *kaṇṭi* ' handle of a plough '; H. *kā̃ṭā* m. ' spine ', G. *kā̃ṭɔ* m., M. *kā̃ṭā* m.; Si. *äṭa* -- *kaṭuva* ' bone ', *piṭa* -- *k*° ' backbone '.2. Pk. *kaṁḍa* -- m. ' backbone '.3. Pk. *karaṁḍa* -- m.n. ' bone shaped like a bamboo ', *karaṁḍuya* -- n. ' backbone '.(CDIAL 2670) <kanDuD>(Z) {NB} ``^vagina, female ^sex_organ". *So.<kAnDoD>(Z)/<DoD> `frog'. #15920.(Munda etyma)

<kanDae>(MK),,<kanDai>(P) {N} ``^old ^woman". *Kh.<kanDaebo'>, ~<kaR~aebO'>, ~<kanRaebO'>, ~<ka~Raybo?>(B); Kh.<kaNDae>(P), ~<kaR~ae>,

~<kaNRae>, ~<ka~Ray>(B) `wife, bride'. %16211. #16101.<kaN-Dae-ki>(M) {N} ``^female ^elders''. |<-ki> `plural'. %7613. #7543.(Munda etyma)

Rebus: kiln: kándu f. ' iron pot ' Suśr., °uka -- m. ' saucepan '.Pk. kaṁdu -- , kaṁḍu -- m.f. ' cooking pot '; K. kõda f. ' potter's kiln, lime or brick kiln '; -- ext. with -- ḍa -- : K. kãdur m. ' oven '. -- Deriv. Pk. kaṁḍua -- ' sweetseller ' (< *kānduka -- ?); H. kãdū m. ' a caste that makes sweetmeats '. (CDIAL 2726) *kandukara ' worker with pans '. [kándu -- , kará -- 1]K. kãdar, kãduru dat. °daris m. ' baker '. (CDIAL 2728)

Copper tablets: 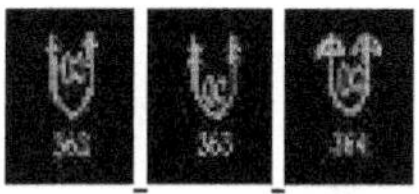 Hieroglyph multiplexes as 'text' hieroglyphs. Hieroglyph: loa 'ficus religios' Rebus: *loh* 'copper'. Hieroglyph: *kamaḍha* '**crab**' Rebus: *kammaṭa* 'mint, coiner' Hieroglyph: *baTa* 'widemouthed pot' Rebus: *bATa* 'furnace'. Inscribed bronze weapon h380A Hieroglyph: *doḷā, ḍoḷā* ' pupil of eye ' (Or.); M. ḍoḷā m. ' eye ' (CDIAL 6582); rebus: *dul* 'cast metal'.

Incised miniature tablet.
Object in the shape of a
double-shield or double-axe

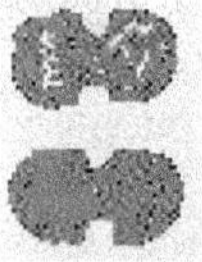
.

h326A

h326B

h818A
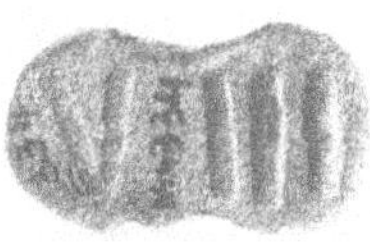
h818B

h233A
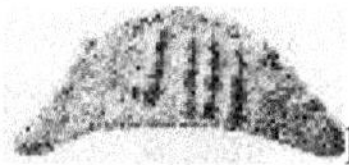
h233B Sickle-shaped tablet

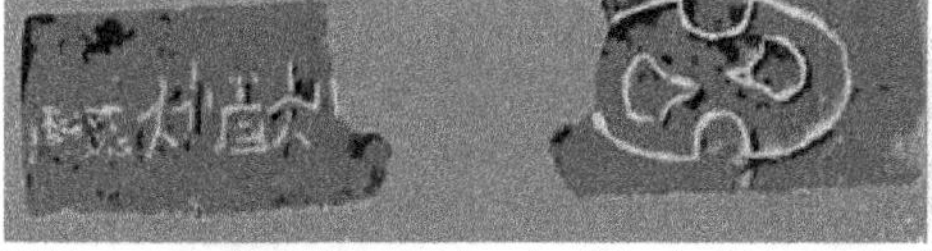
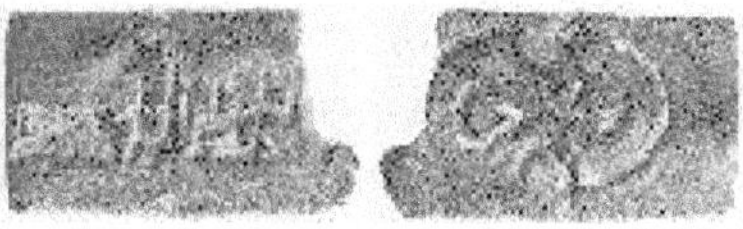

Weaponry in Mesopotamia (Early Dynastic levels at Sumerian sites 2500-2016 B.C.): "(The products of metalsmiths), in the form of weapons, implements and utensils, have survived in great numbers, side-by-side with pictorial representations of the purposes for which they were used. In a well-known relief, spears, shields and helmets of copper are to be seen; in another battle-axes; 'guardian' figures in seal designs wield daggers with crescent-shaped handles; 'rein-rings' with their animal mascots appear on chariots in battle-scenes; and at a 'banquet' copper 'drinking-tubes' are used.")

Mohenjo-daro Copper tablet. m592A and B with broken inscription. Side B shows double-edged battle-axe.

Crescentic battle-axe unearthed from an Ur tomb (Seton Lloyd, The Archaeology of Mesopotamia, London, Thames and Hudson, p. 126.

Fillet around the forehead: Mes kalam dug (helmet) and lady made of diorite. Fillet is leadership.

Hieroglyph: **paṭṭa** 1 m. ' slab, tablet ' MBh., *°ṭaka* -- m., *°ṭikā* -- f. Kathās. [Derivation as MIA. form of *páttra* -- (EWA ii 192), though very doubtful, does receive support from Dard. **paṭṭa* -- ' leaf ' and meaning ' metal plate ' of several NIA. forms of páttra --]Pa. *paṭṭa* -- m. ' slab, tablet '; Pk. *paṭṭa* -- , *°ṭaya* -- m., *°ṭiyā*<-> f. ' slab of stone, board '; NiDoc. *paṭami* loc. sg., *paṭi* ' tablet '; K. *paṭa* m. ' slab, tablet, metal plate '(CDIAL 7699)

Rebus: *Ta.* paṭṭaṭai, paṭṭaṟai anvil, smithy, forge. *Ka.* paṭṭaḍe, **paṭṭaḍi** anvil, workshop. *Te.* paṭṭika, paṭṭeḍa anvil; paṭṭaḍa workshop(DEDR 3865)

Sumerian electrum helmet from the Royal Cemetery at Ur; early Dynastic III Period, ca. 2400 B.C.; After Prichard 1969b: 49, no.160; Parpola, 1994, p. 254. This helmet was made of beaten gold, in the form of a wig with a most elaborate hair-style. There is a knot of hair tied at the back, a twisted plait and a headband, and there are guards for ears and cheeks. It belonged to Mes-kalam-dug, the 'Hero of the Good Land'; he was perhaps a prince; a cylinder-seal with his name was later found in a queen's grave.

Gold dagger with lapis lazuli hilt and filigree sheath, Ur. Mes-kalam-dug's grave chamber had: a shield, two gold-mounted daggers, chisels and other tools, copper jugs, silver bowls and a set of arrows. He wore a broad silver belt from which hung a gold dagger and a whetstone of lapis lazuli. The coffin had been covered with a mass of beads of gold and semi-precious stones. Golden bowls were placed between the corpse's hands, near his feet elbow and behind his head, and by the right shoulder there was a double axe-head of electrum.

A woman's head in diorite found in Nin-Gal temple at Ur, ca. 2150 B.C.; note the engraved modulations of the hair, elaborate bun at the back of the head and the fillet around the forehead. Indus Inscriptions seem to occur in almost every household in the entire population of Mohenjo-daro as Janam, 'metalcaster folk'. Findspots:

[House I, HR-A area, Mohenjo-daro: Find spots of twelve seals together with many prestige objects, all from one house; Wheeler assumed that this was a temple; the house has rooms immediately adjacent to the exit, transit rooms having more than one door, terminal rooms with just one door; seals were found in all these rooms. After Jansen, Michael, 1986, *Die Indus-Zivilisation: Wiederentdeckung einer fruhen Hochkultur*, Cologne, 200f., fig. 125]

Seals have been found in almost every exposed room excavated in Mohenjodaro. In room 85 in house IX of the HR-area in Mohenjodaro were found five unicorn selas. In this room 'a mass of shell-lay was found…along with…many waste pieces of sea-shells' indicating this to be a shell-cutter's room (Mackay, 1931a: I, 195).

Possible use of the messages conveyed through inscriptions in trade

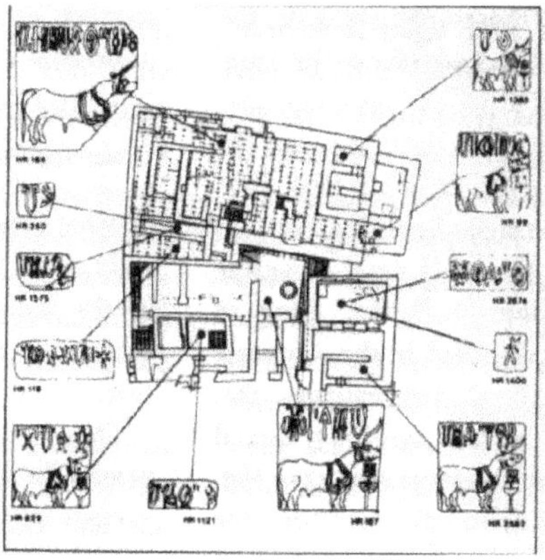

In addition to the field symbol, the texts of the inscriptions are composed of an average of five signs. The longest inscription has 26 signs (found on two identical three-sided tablets: M-494 and M-495 of Parpola corpus).

There are over 25 inscriptions with only pictorial motifs, 40 inscriptions with only one sign (in addition to the field symbol); about 110 inscriptions have only two signs; and nearly 150 inscriptions have only 3 signs. (See also: Sepo Koskenniemi et al., 1973, p. x)

This is a remarkably cryptic (economical) use of graphemes and an indication that the graphemes (or signs) and (perhaps, also pictorials) may refer to physical objects and numbers.

Among the ashes on a warehouse floor in Lothal were found a hundred clay tags, bearing inscriptions created by seal impressions on one side and of packing materials (bamboo, mattings, woven cloth, cords, reeds) on the other.

It has also been noted by earlier attempts at decipherment that many seals with inscriptions have cord holes, suggesting that the seals might have been worn by their owners.

Inscribed pottery, ball and stone-slab

ns4A Nausharo: Terracotta ring with two signs inscribed

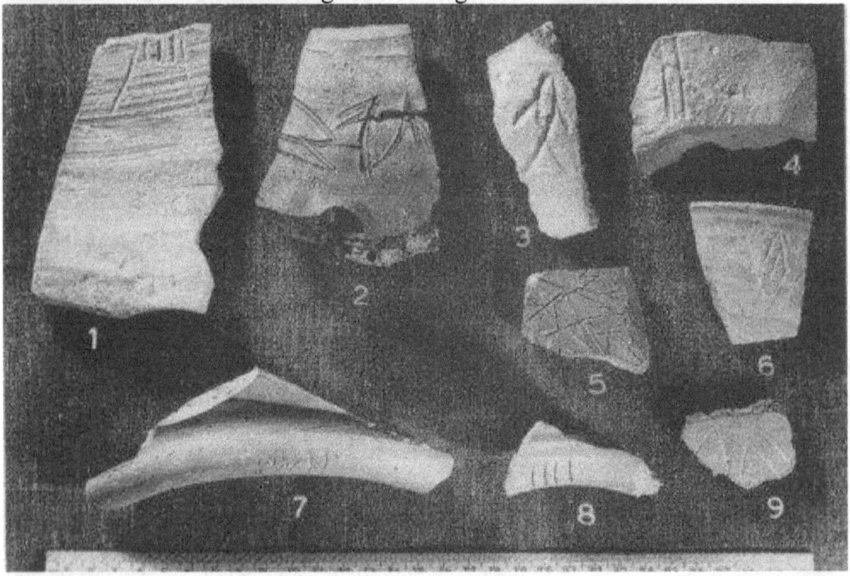

Inscribed pottery (pre-firing inscription), Bahawalpur; province; 2:Rappwala Ther; 3 and 9:Guddal; Mughal, M.R., 1997, Pl. 62.

Inscribed ball and pottery, Harappa (After Vats, Pl. CI)

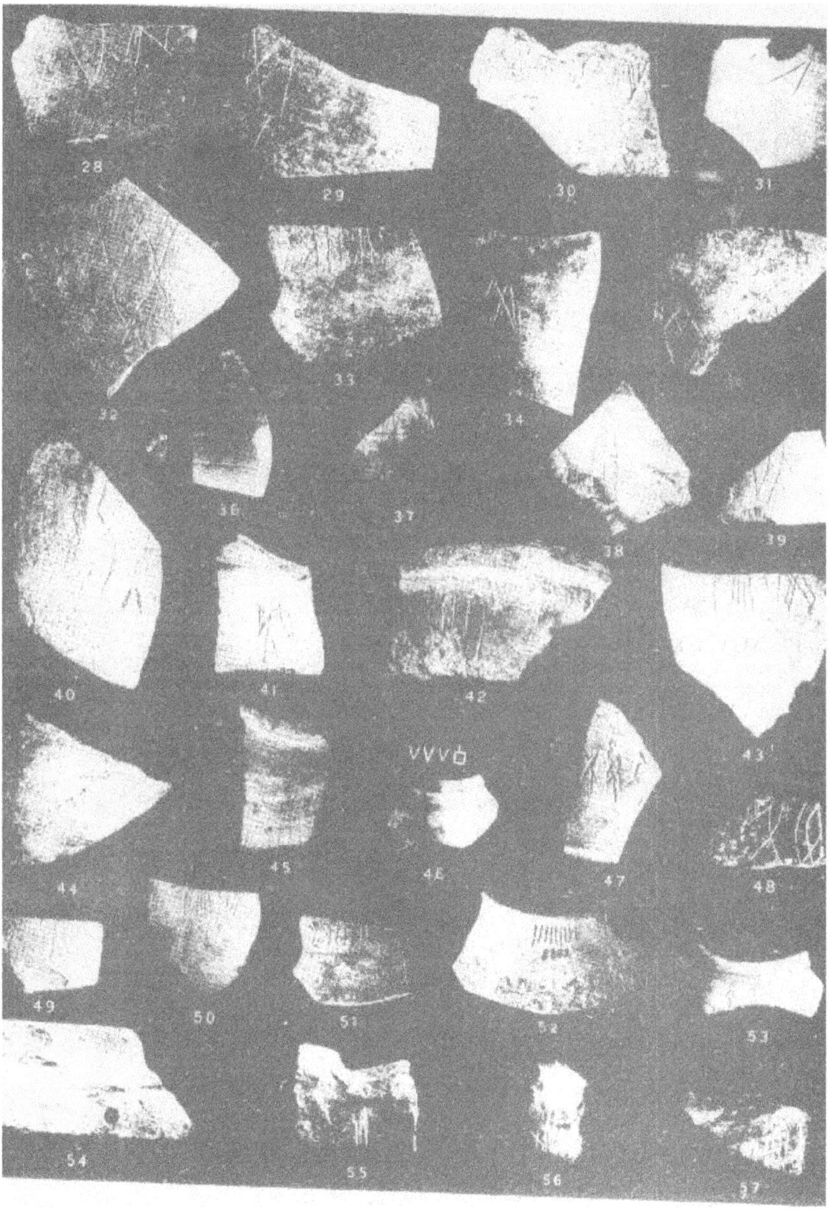

Inscribed pottery, Harappa (After Vats, Pl.CIII).

Inscribed stone slab, Harappa (After Vats, Pl. XCVIII).

Inscribed pottery, Harappa (After Vats, Pl. CII).

Out of about 3000 inscriptions recorded in Mahadevan corpus, over 1990 inscriptions contain 'field symbols'. An object may have many sides and each side may feature a different field symbol with or without accompanying inscriptions. Thus, field symbols constitute the major message component of the corpus of inscriptions. 'Reading' these pictorials is an imperative to successfully interpret the 'underlying language' and 'meaning' of the inscriptions. There will be continuing disagreements on the 'orthographic values' to be assigned to some 'images' or pictorials. For example, is the 'unicorn' an imaginary construction of a single horn on an ox or did such an animal, in fact, exist? Is the 'image' of a 'bat' a ligatured fish? If the fish sign a variant of a 'loop'?

There are, however, many images, which are emphatically deciphered orthographically, for example in such motifs as, elephant, tiger, bison, rhinoceros. A start can be made for the decipherment effort with such images with emphatic, orthographic clarity. Such a beginning will provide valuable clues to categorize the life-activities connoted by the texts and pictorials in inscriptions contained in the inscriptions.

Many pictorials are mostly calligraphically definitive. For example, a bull is a bull is a bull; an elephant is an elephant is an elephant. Many signs can also be interpreted as derived hieroglyphics derived from pictorial symbols.

There are, of course, problems in interpreting the orthography of some signs, for exampe:

Does this sign represent a fish or a loop? aya 'fish' Rebus: aya 'iron' ayas 'metal' (Rigveda)

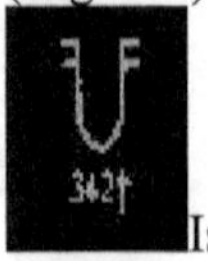

Is this sign depicting a jar or a the face of a bull? *kárṇakā* 'rim of jar' Rebus: *kárṇikā* 'scribe'; *kárṇī* 'supercargo'; *karṇadhāra* m. 'helmsman'

Is this sign depicting a circle, an axle or a wheel with six spokes? eraka 'nave of wheel' Rebus: eraka, arka 'gold, copper, metal infusion, metalcast' *āra* 'spoke' Rebus: *āra* 'brass'.

Hypotheses

Two interlinked hypotheses govern this study for script interpretation and may be elaborated further, as follows:

Hypothesis 1: Indian languages are derived from the lingua franca of the Sarasvati-Sindhu civilization. Selected lexemes of Indian languages provide the morphemes required to attach 'sound-bites' to the pictorials in inscriptions of the Harappan script, thus attesting to the continuity of the civilization in the present-day spoken languages of the sub-continent.

Hypothesis 2: The pictorials in inscriptions of the script represented 'meaningful' messages related to the life-activities of the civilization and, these messages can be read from 'homonyms' of the morphemes attached to the pictorials in inscriptions (cf. Hypothesis 1).

The sounds of the lingua franca of the civilization will be confirmed by identifying homonyms for the pictorials in inscriptions of the inscriptions.

For each morpheme conveyed by a pictorial motif, a similar sounding 'substantive' morpheme (homonym) will be identified. The formula in this rebus methodology is:

Image = Sound = Meaning

All words are semantic indicators. ellāccollum poṟuḷ kuṟittaṉavē எல்லாச்சொல்லும் பொறுள் குறித்தனவே (Tol. Col. Peya. 1) Meluhha/Mleccha: Vākya padīyam artha sampanna (Pali)

Through a number of monographs, superb structural analyses of the inscriptions have been done by both Parpola and Mahadevan. The analyses point to the use of most of the signs as representing 'nouns'.

Use of rebus-metonymy layered method

Rebus (Latin: by means of things) is a graphemic expression of the phonetic shape of a word or syllable. Rebus uses words pronounced alike (homophones) but with different meanings. Sumerian script was phonetized using the rebus principle. So were the Egyptian hieroglyphs based on the rebus principle.

The use of the rebus methodology is justified on the following evidence and analysis: According to the Parpola concordance which contains a corpus of 2942 inscriptions, 300 inscriptions are composed of either one sign or two signs. Many signs occur in predictable pairs; 57 pairwise combinations account for a total frequency of 3154 occurrences (32% of 9798 occurrences of all pairwise combinations). Given the statistical evidence that the average length of a text is 5 signs, it is apparent that one sign or a pair of signs represents a 'substantive category' of information, i.e., a complete message.
In addition to the field symbol, the texts of the inscriptions are composed of an average of five signs. The longest inscription has 26 signs (found on two identical three-sided tablets: M-494 and M-495 of Parpola corpus).

There are over 170 inscriptions with only one sign (in addition to the field symbol); about 30 inscriptions have only two signs (Sepo Koskenniemi et al., 1973, p. x)

A number of signs appear in duplicated pairs: for example, Sign 245 occurs in 70 pairs.

(nine squares in a rectangle or a chequered-rectangle).

These are apparently not duplicated alphabets or syllables.

Rebus: *kāṇḍā* as in ayas *kāṇḍā* 'excellent iron' (Panini); l*okhaṇḍā* 'metalware' (Marathi). *dula* 'pair' rebus; *dul* 'cast metal' Thus, in a pair, the hieroglyph multiplex signifies: *dul kāṇḍā* 'cast iron'.

Hieroglyph: Pk. *kaṁḍa* -- m. ' piece, fragment '; Pk. *kaṁḍārēi* ' scrapes, engraves (CDIAL 2683) KHAṆḌ ' break '. [Of non -- Aryan origin, perh. Mu. EWA i 300: cf. √kaṇḍ and BHSk. gaṇḍa -- m. ' piece, part ']khaṇḍá1 ' broken, crippled ' VarBṛS., ' having gaps or chasms ' Suśr., m.n. ' fragment ' R., °ḍaka -- 1 ' having no nails ' lex., °ḍikā -- f. Pāṇ. [Cf. ' defective ' words listed s.v. baṇḍá -- . -- √khaṇḍ] Pa. khaṇḍa -- ' broken (usu. of teeth) ', m.n. ' piece ', °ḍikā -- f. ' broken bit, stick '; Pk. khaṁḍa -- m.n., °ḍiā -- f. ' piece '; Gy. SEeur. xaịi ' a little ', gr. xandí, xanrík ' a little ', xarno ' humble, low ', rum. boh. xarno ' short ', it. xarnišeró ' judge, magistrate ' (< ' small -- headed, stupid '); Paš. lauṛ. khaṇḍā ' cultivated field ', °ḍī ' small do. ' (→ Par. kheṇ ' field ' IIFL i 265); Gaw. khaṇḍa ' hill pasture ' (see also bel.); Kal. rumb. khōṇḍa ' half '; K. khonḍu ' broken, maimed ', khünḍü f. ' piece '; S. khanu m. ' piece of bread ', °nī f. ' small do. '; L. khannī ' piece, scrap of bread '; P. khannā adj. ' half ', °nī f. ' piece '; Ku. dwī -- khan ' two halves ', khānuṛo ' piece '; N. khā̃ṛeuli ' broken bits of rice '; A. khā̃rā ' cropped, tailless '; B. khān, °nā, °ni ' piece, article (as a determinative) ' with irreg. n ODBL 365; Bi. khaṇḍā, khā̃ṛī ' woman's sāṛī ' (semant. cf. *lugna --); Bhoj. khā̃ṛā ' piece '; H. khaṇḍā m. ' broken rice '; G. khā̃ḍũ ' broken '; M. khā̃ḍ n. ' piece ', f. ' break, fissure ', khā̃ḍoḷẽ n. ' piece '; Si. kaḍa ' broken piece, piece, piece of cloth '. -- Ext. -- ra -- : Kho. (Lor.) kh*lṇḍar ' broken (of dishes), a broken dish, half (of anything) '; K. khạnḍarun ' to break in pieces '; H. khaṇḍar ' broken ', m. ' hole, pit ', khā̃ṛar ' dilapidated ', m. ' broken ground, chasm, hole ' (see also *khaṇḍaghara --).As ' hill, mountain pass ' (< ' *rock ' < ' piece ' or < ' *pass ' < ' gap ' and perh. X skandhá -- : cf. IIFL i 265, iii 3, 104, AO xviii 240): Gaw. khaṇḍa ' hill pasture ' (see ab.); Bshk. khan m. ' hill ', Tor. khān, (Grierson) khaṇḍ, Mai. khān, Chil. Gau. kān, Phal. khā̃ṇ; Sh. koh. khŭṇ m., gur. khonn, pales. khōṇə, jij. khɔ̃ṇ ' mountain ', gil. (Lor.) kh*ln m. ' mountain pass '.(CDIAL 3792)

Many pictorials in inscriptions in field symbols also occur in pairs: two tigers, two bisons, two heads of the unicorn.

These statistics establish the following facts:

- A combination of pictorials without the use of any sign constitute the message.
- One or two signs and/or a pair of signs are adequate to compose the core of the messages.

This leads to the apparent conclusion that the solus sign or each sign in a pairwise combinations (which constitute the core of information conveyed) is not an alphabet or a syllable, but a WORD.

This apparent evidence is echoed in Koskenniemi et al: "... the Indus script is in all likelihood a relatively crude morphemographic writing system. The graphemes would usually stand for he lexical morphemes... This hypothesis is based on the approximate date this writing system was created (circa 26th century B.C.), the parallel presented by the Sumerian writing system of that time (the Fara texts of the 26th century), the brevity of recurring combinations, and the number of different graphemes." (Koskenniemi and Parpola, 1982, pp. 10-11). Another echo is found in the structural analysis of Mahadevan: " G.R. Hunter (1934, p. 126) formulated a set of criteria for segmentation of the texts and found that almost every sign of common occurrence functioned as a single word. The Soviet group (M.A. Probst and A.M. Kondratov in Y.V. Knorozov et al., Proto-Indica, Moscow, 1965) analyzed texts on the computer and concluded that the Indus script is essentially morphemic in character, resembling the Egyptian hieroglyphic system in this respect. I have described the logical word-division procedures developed by me (I. Mahadevan, "Recent advances in the study of the Indus script", Puratattva, Vol. 9, p. 34), which show that most of the signs of the Indus script are word-signs... no one has so far been able to establish by objective analytical procedures the existence of purely phonetic syllabic signs in the Indus script... Phonograms formed by the rebus principle can be recognized only if the underlying language is known or assumed as a working hypothesis. Since the identity of the Harappan language has not yet been established beyond doubt, I cannot be said that any phonogram has been recognized with certainty... It is however very likely that there are rebus-based phonograms in the Indus script, as otherwise, it is very difficult to account for the presence of such unlikely objects such as the fish, birds, animals and insects in what are most probably names and titles on the seal-texts. It is likely that the Indus scrip resembles in this respect the Egyptian scrip in which pictographic signs serve as phonetic signs based on the rebus principle (e.g. the picture of a 'goose' stands for 'son' as the two words are homonymous in the Egyptian language). It is no always possible in the present state of our knowledge to distinguish between ideograms and phonograms..." (I. Mahadevan, "Towards a grammar of the Indus texts: 'intelligible to the eye, if not to the ears', Tamil Civilization, Vol. 4, Nos. 3 and 4, Tanjore, 1966, pp. 18-19).

Orthography and analysis of some sequences of graphemes in the inscriptions

Parpola notes (1994, pp. 84-85), echoing similar observations by Mahadevan:

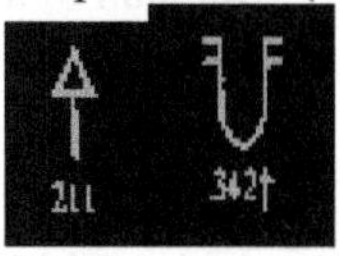

kāṇḍa 'arrow' Rebus: *kāṇḍā* 'excellent (metal)ware' (Panini)
kárṇakā 'rim of jar' Rebus: *kárṇikā* 'scribe'; *kárṇī* 'supercargo'; *karṇadhāra* m. 'helmsman'

"...a few signs are indeed found mostly at the end of inscriptions, notably sign 342 ('jar' grapheme)and sign 211 ('arrow' grapheme) and they are major aids in the segmentation of texts. The sign 342 ('jar' grapheme) is by far the most common sign of the Indus script, representing about 10 percent of all sign occurrences. About one-third of all inscriptions end with this sign...the sign is never found at the beginning of inscriptions...The sequence sign 102 ('three short strokes') followed by sign 192 mainly occurs at the end of inscriptions, and is never followed by the usual 'end' sign 342 ('jar' grapheme)..."

 kolom ‘three’ Rebus: kolami ‘smithy, forge’. *gaṇḍa* 'four' Rebus: *kanda* 'fire-altar' *kolmo* 'rice plant' Rebus: *kolami* 'smithy, forge'
The sign 192 appears to be a four-fold ligaturing of the underlying basic sign:  *gaṇḍa* 'four' Rebus: kanda 'fire-altar' kolmo 'rice plant' Rebus: kolami 'smithy, forge'

maṇḍa ‘ some sort of framework (?) ’. [In *nau -- maṇḍḗ* n. du. ‘ the two sets of poles rising from the thwarts or the two bamboo covers of a boat (?) ’ ŚBr. (as illustrated in BPL p. 42); and in BHSk. and Pa. *bōdhi -- maṇḍa* -- n. perh. ‘ thatched cover ’ rather than ‘ raised platform ’ (BHS ii 402). If so, it may belong tomaṇḍapá -- and maṭha --]
Ku. *mā̃ṛā* m. pl. ‘ shed, resthouse ’(CDIAL 9737)

Hieroglyph: ladder Rebus: guild master: *śrēṣṭrī2 ‘ line, ladder ’. [For mng. ‘ line ’ conn. with √śriṣ2 cf. śrḗṇi -- ~ √śri. -- See śrití -- . -- √śriṣ2] Pk. sēḍhī̆ -- f. ‘ line, row ’ (cf. pasēḍhi -- f. ‘ id. ’. -- < EMIA. *sēṭhī -- sanskritized as śrēḍhī -- , śrēṭī -- , śrēḍī<-> (Col.), śrēdhī -- (W.) f. ‘ a partic. progression of arithmetical figures ’); K. hēr, dat. °ri f. ‘ ladder ’.(CDIAL 12724) Rebus: 12725 śrḗṣṭha ‘ most splendid, best ’ RV. [śrī́ --]Pa. seṭṭha -- ‘ best ’, Aś.shah. man. sreṭha -- , gir. sesṭa -- , kāl. seṭha -- , Dhp. śeṭha -- , Pk. seṭṭha -- , siṭṭha -- ; N. seṭh ‘ great, noble, superior ’; Or. seṭha ‘ chief, principal ’; Si. seṭa, °ṭu ‘ noble, excellent ’.(CDIAL 12725) śrēṣṭhin m. ‘ distinguished man ’ AitBr., ‘ foreman of a guild ’, °nī -- f. ‘ his wife ’ Hariv. [śrḗṣṭha --]Pa. seṭṭhin -- m. ‘ guild -- master ’, Dhp. śeṭhi, Pk. seṭṭhi -- , siṭṭhi -- m., °iṇī -- f.; S. seṭhi m. ‘ wholesale merchant ’; P. seṭh m. ‘ head of a guild, banker ’, seṭhaṇ, °ṇī f.; Ku.gng. śēṭh ‘ rich man ’; N. seṭh ‘ banker ’; B. seṭh ‘ head of a guild, merchant ’; Or. seṭhi ‘ caste of washermen ’; Bhoj. Aw.lakh. sēṭhi ‘ merchant, banker ’, H. seṭh m., °ṭhan f.; G. śeṭh, śeṭhiyɔ m. ‘ wholesale merchant, employer, master ’; M. śeṭh, °ṭhī, śeṭ, °ṭī m. ‘ respectful term for banker or merchant ’; Si. siṭu, hi° ‘ banker, nobleman ’ H. Smith JA 1950, 208 (or < śiṣṭá -- 2?)(CDIAL 12726)

Parpola notes (1994, pp.103-104): "A comparative study of the allographs provides one important means of identifying the iconic meaning of even fairly abstract shapes…the (allograph) continuum)…Taken together, these signs can be understood as pictures of a single object, namely, ‘steps, staircase or ladder’; taken individually, such a conclusion would hardly be possible."

On the use of circumgraphs associated with the 'fish' sign, Parpola notes (1994, pp.69-70): "…the four strokes around the ‘fish’ sign may in fact be understood to be read after it, and that their meaning is close to the sign 'arrow' that is often found in this position." The following sequences are shown as evidence.

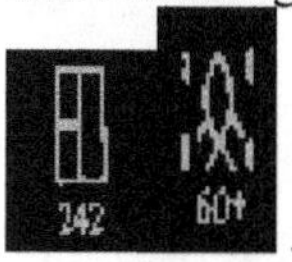

5477 kole.l 'temple' Rebus: kole.l 'smithy' (Kota) aya 'fish' Rebus: aya 'iron' ayas 'metal' PLUS *gaṇḍa* 'four' Rebus: *kanda* 'fire-altar'

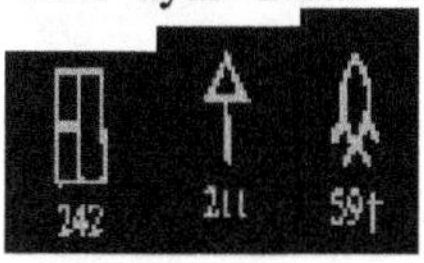

1554 kole.l 'temple' Rebus: kole.l 'smithy' PLUS *kāṇḍa* 'arrow' Rebus: *kāṇḍā* 'excellent (metal)ware' (Panini) aya 'fish' Rebus: aya 'iron' ayas 'metal'

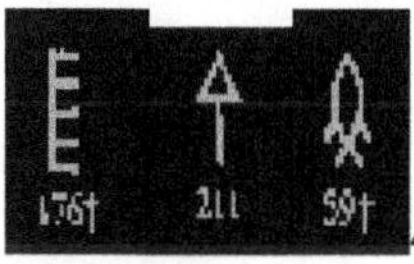

4604 *kharedo* = a currycomb Rebus: *kharādī* ' turner' *kāṇḍa* 'arrow' Rebus: *kāṇḍā* 'excellent (metal)ware' (Panini) aya 'fish' Rebus: aya 'iron' ayas 'metal'

5477 *kharedo* = a currycomb Rebus: *kharādī* ' turner' aya 'fish' Rebus: aya 'iron' ayas 'metal' PLUS *gaṇḍa* 'four' Rebus: *kanda* 'fire-altar'

Twenty signs occur with the circumgraph of four short strokes; many of these 20 signs occur as final motifs of the text, functioning similar to the 'jar' sign

which terminates many texts. The circumgraph may, therefore, be the terminating 'word' of the text, functioning similar to the 'arrow' sign. The 'arrow' sign terminates 184 inscriptions (out of a total of 227 inscriptions in which the 'arrow' occurs).

The frequencies of occurrence of the pictorials in inscriptions (field symbols and signs) are as follows (according to Mahadevan corpus):

dula 'pair' Rebus: dul 'cast metal' kolom 'three' Rebus: kolami 'smithy, forge' Thus, together: dul kolami 'castmetal smithy'; aya 'fish' Rebus: aya 'iron' ayas 'metal' *kāṇḍa* 'arrow' Rebus: *kāṇḍā* 'excellent (metal)ware' (Panini) doḷā, ḍoḷā ' pupil of eye ' (Or.); M. ḍoḷā m. 'eye' Rebus: dul 'cast'. kondh 'corner' Rebus: *kũdār* 'turner'.

śagaḍī (Gujarati) = lathe san:gāḍo a lathe; sãghāḍiyo a worker on a lathe (Gujarati) sãgaḍ part of a turner's apparatus (Marathi); sə̄gāḍī lathe (Tulu)

Jar	1395
Bearer + jar (ligatured)	126
One-horned young bull Standard (occur together)	900+
Standard	19
Two short strokes (superscripted)	649
Arrow	227
Spoked wheel	195
Fish	381
Fish (with four gills)	279
Fish (with inverted 'V' ligatured)	216
Fish (with oblique cross-line)	188
Fish (with circumgraph of 4 short strokes)	29
Harrow	132
Pot	323
Dotted circle	67
Svastika (Mahadevan counts only 3 as signs)	47
Zebu (humped bull)	54
Trough	50+
Bull (bison, short-horned)	95
Elephant	55
Rhinoceros	39
Goat-antelope (markhor, short-tail)	36
Leaf	35
Leaf (ligatured)	
Tree	34
Tiger	21
Gavial (crocodile)	49
Fish-shaped object	14

Ox-antelope (markhor, long tail)	26
Composite (ram, bull, elephant, tiger, tail)	20
Hare	15 kulai 'hare' (Santali) Rebus: kol 'working in iron'
Double-shield or axe	17
Buffalo	14
Camel? + head at both ends (Parpola)	14 karabha Rebus: karba 'iron'
Standing person + horns	13
Horned person seated (7 if counted in combination with other motifs)	9 kamaDha 'penance' Rebus: kampaTTa 'mint, coiner'
Serpent (entwined, in bas relief)	3
Person grappling with two tigers	5
Tiger + person on tree	4
Endless knot	3
Boat	3
Leaf-shaped object	2 loa 'ficus religiosa' Rebus: loh 'copper'
Scorpion	2 bichi Rebus: bica 'sandstone mineral ore'
Bird in flight	2 baṭa 'quail'; bhaṭa 'furnace' (G.); baṭa 'a kind of iron' (G.)
Tortoise	1 kamaṭha Rebus: kampaTTa 'mint, coiner'
Radiating sun	1 arka Rebus: arka, eraka 'gold, copper'
Frog	1 mūxā Rebus: *muha* 'the quantity of iron produced at one time in a native smelting furnace' *mũh* 'metal ingot'

Components of hieroglyphs (pictorials)

Trough motif appears before many animals, even wild animals such as: rhinoceros, tiger, bison etc. This motif should, therefore,be recognized as an important pictorial component of the inscriptions and should be interpreted for its 'meaning' conveyed through the entire message of the seal or tablet.

Ligatures (Combinations of hieroglyph components)

A dominant orthographic principle governs the pictorials in inscriptions of the Harappan script. The principle is: ‘ligaturing’. Ligatures are basic signs and/or pictorials in inscriptions super-imposed on one another to compose a composite representation of components -- realizing hieroglyph multiplexes.

Ligaturing is a procedure for attaching two signs or field symbols or parts of field symbols (e.g. combining heads of unicorn, short-horned bull, antelope, or leaf images) into one composite motif.

Blurred distinctions between 'pictorials' and 'signs'

The distinction between pictorial motifs and signs gets blurred in many compositions presented in the script inscriptions.

Thus, a svastika appears together with an elephant or a tiger

M-488 A

M-488 B

M-488 C

The 'svastika' is a pictorial and also a sign--Sign

148  karibha ‘trunk of elephant’ ibha ‘elephant’ Rebus: karba ‘iron’ sattva ‘svastika hieroglyph’ Rebus: jasta ‘zinc’; sattva ‘zinc’ kola ‘tiger’ Rebus: kol ‘working in iron’; kolhe ‘smelters’ krammara ‘turn back’ Rebus: kamar ‘artisan’ heraka ‘spy’ Rebus: eraka ‘copper, metal infusion, moltencast’.

A fish appears together with a combined field symbol of the head of a unicorn attached to a short-horned bull motif.

m298

Inscriptions are recorded on many ‘tablets’ with upto six sides. Harappan ‘miniature tablets’ are incised flat plates of steatite. Mohenjodaro has yielded engraved copper tablets. Moulded terracotta or faience tablets occur with many repeated texts produced in bas-relief. "On one particular moulded tablet (existing in several identical copies), we see an anthropomorphic deity sitting on a low dais, flanked on either side by a kneeling man and a snake; one of these supplicant men has both his hands raised in worship, while the other is giving what looks like a sacrificial vessel to the deity. Another moulded tablet (again available in several copies) has a similar offering scene, except that here the kneeling worshipper holds out the pot towards a tree. On both tablets the sacrificial vessel looks exactly like the U-formed Indus sign." (Parpola, 1996).

Mohejodaro, tablet in bas relief (M-478)

On m488, the pictorial of a kneeling 'worshipper' is echoed in the script signs, ligatured with the 'pot' sign:

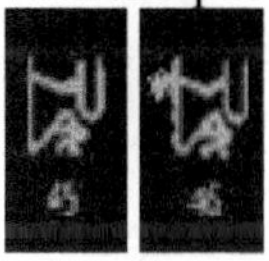

Pictorial ligatures

Human figures are also depicted with bovine features such as hoofed legs.

Triangular terracotta amulet, one side (Md 013), surface find Mohenjodaro; seated horned person on a throne with hoofed legs, surrounded by fishes, gavials and snakes; Ashmolean Museum, Oxford; Parpola, 1994,. p. 186.

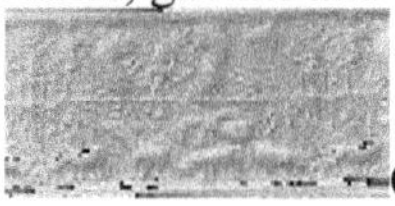

Cylinder seal impression; unknown near eastern origin; Musee du Louvre/AO Collection Du Clercq 1.26; one person wears a crown of water buffalo horns with the leafed branch of a fig and sits on a throne with hoofed legs; surrounded by a pair of horned snakes, a pair of fishes and a pair of water buffaloes. The other person stands, fighting two tigers, and surrounded by trees, a markhor goat and a vulture above a rhinoceros. Parpola, 1994, p. 186.

There are many pictorial ligatures exemplied by such compositions of animals, further exemplified by the composition referred to as the 'fabulous animal'.

m300 (Body of a ram, horns of a bull, trunk of an elephant, hindlegs of a tiger and an upraised serpent-like tail).
This can be viewed as a 'short-hand' crypt of the representation of some of these animals which appear in groups.

m1393A

Sumerian seal from Tell Asmar depicting a rhinoceros, elephant and an alligator. (After Frankfort, 'The Indian Civilization and the near East, *Annual Bibliography of Indian Archaeology*, 1932, p.3, Pl. I and Heras, 1953, p. 219)

Cylinder seal impression; rhinoceros, elephant, gavial (fish-eating alligator); glazed steatite, height 3.4 cm., Frankfort, 1955: no. 642; Collon 1987: no. 610 (IM 14674)

The following occur in groups:

- rhinoceros, elephant, unicorn
- rhinoceros, tiger
- rhinoceros, elephant, tiger, buffalo, markhor (around a horned, seated person)
- rhinoceros, elephant, tiger, two bisons face to face, scorpion
- gharial, fish

The following ligatured motifs contain parts of field symbol motifs:

- three tigers joined into a rhomb: cAli 'entwined animals' Rebus: sal 'workshop' kolom 'three' Rebus: kolami 'smithy, forge' kola 'tiger' Rebus: kol 'kolhe smelters'; kol 'working in iron'; kolle 'blacksmith'; kole.l 'smithy, temple' kolimi 'smithy, forge'.
- bison + one-horned young bull (head)
- markhor + one-horned young bull (copper tablet)
- rhinoceros + elephant + zebu + snake (copper tablet)
- rhinoceros + tiger + zebu (copper tablet)

- tiger + zebu + buffalo (copper tablet)
- tiger (head and front part of the body) + rhinoceros (back part of the body) + zebu (horns)(copper tablet)
- bison (body) + three heads of: one-horned young bull, markhor, bison
- six heads: one-horned young bull, bison, markhor, tiger + 2 other animals
- one-horned young bull (head) + one-horned young bull (head) + leaves + stem?
- One-horned young bull (head) + octopus
- tiger (body) + person + markhor (horns)

Composite, ligatured motifs contain the following field-symbol components:

- zebu (horns) + face of man + tusks and trunk of elephant + neck and front legs of markhor + one-horned young bull body) + hind legs of tiger + snake for a tail
- (This image is also interpreted as: body of a ram, horns of a bison, trunk of elephant, hindlegs of a tiger and an upraised serpent-like tail)
- Standing person has the shoulders of a man with horns and the hind-part of a bovine
- Antelope has the face of a bearded person

Graphemes or 'signs' of the script and ligatures of graphemes

Back to Table of Contents

Parpola (1994) identifies 386 (+12?) signs (or graphemes) and their variant forms. Mahadevan (1977) identifies 419 graphemes; out of these 179 graphemes have variants totalling 641 forms. Parpola observes: "...the grapheme count might be as low as 350...The total range of signs once present in the Indus script is certain to have been greater than is observable now, for new signs have kept turning up in new inscriptions. The rate of discovery has been fairly low, though, and the new signs have more often been ligatures of two or more signs already known as separate graphemes than entirely new signs." (Parpola, 1994, p. 79).

Properties of Graphemes

Many short and long linear strokes on the texts (when read in combination with the external archaeological evidence of the finds of binary chert weights) indicate the underlying practice of some form of 'accounting or measurement' or just 'counting' (?of property items) conveyed through the objects inscribed with messages (messages composed of pictorials and/or clusters of signs constituting texts of inscriptions).

Tablet in bas-relief

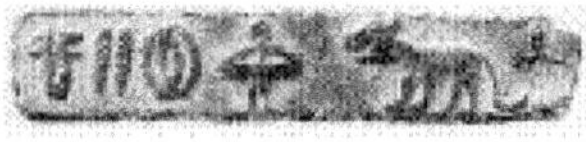

H182

In this tablet the repetition of the 'svastika' sign sequence five times points the possibility of the'svastika' sign denoting an 'object'

Each of the signs (162, 325 and 59) seems to denote an ‘object’, and is frequently preceded by ‘numerical strokes’.

sattu (Tamil), satta, sattva (Kannada), jasth, 'zinc, spelter, pewter', zasath 'zinc, spelter, pewter', jastuvu 'made of zinc or pewter' (Kashmiri) taTTa 'five' (Santali) Rebus: ThaTTha 'brass'; ThaTTar 'an alloy of copper and bell metal' (Nepali); ThaTThAra 'brass worker' (Prakritam); ThaThero id. (Ku.)(CDIAL 5491, 5493).

Thus, on h182, the five svastika hieroglyphs are read together: *taTTa sattva* ‘five svastika hieroglyphs’ Rebus: ‘alloy of zinc, spelter, pewter’.

dhollu 'drummer' (WPahari) Rebus: *dul* 'cast metal' kola ‘tiger’ Rebus: kol ‘working in iron’ kolle ‘blacksmith’ kolhe ‘smelter’.

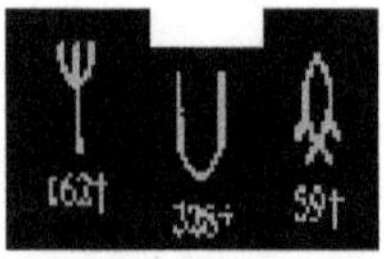

r. to l. aya ‘fish’ Rebus: aya ‘iron’ ayas ‘metal’ baTa ‘rimless pot’ Rebus: baTa ‘furnace’ kolmo ‘rice plant’ Rebus: kolami ‘smithy, forge’Sign 372 (‘oval’ grapheme) ligatures with sign 162, yielding sign 387

It is merely a conjecture that these signs 162, 325, 59 ane 387 denote landing-points in numeration, say, eight, twelve, twenty. These signs may, in combination with numerical strokes, connote a counted number of 'objects' and combinations of 'objects'.

Mirror-reflected pairs of graphemes

Mahadevan notes, "Compounds of mirror-reflected pairs. A rather curious feature of the script is the occurrence of mirror-reflected pairs as bound signs." (Mahadevan, 1977, p. 16) He adds that the mirror-reflected pairs may have the sign doubled on the horizontal or vertical axis.

Hieroglyph: सांडणी [sāṇḍaṇī] f (H) An instrument of goldsmiths. It is hooked or curved at the extremity; and is used to draw things out of the fire. (Marathi) saṁdaṁśá m. ' tongs, pincers ' AV., °śaka -- m., °śikā -- f. ' small tongs ' Daś. 2. *saṁdaṁśī -- . [√daṁś]1. Pk. saṁdaṁsa -- m. ' right hand '; K. śranz, sranz m. ' blacksmith's tongs, pincers '(CDIAL 12897)

Rebus: Sandana2 [cp. Vedic syandana] a chariot Mhvs 21, 25; Dpvs 14, 56; Vv 642; J iv.103; v.264; vi.22. (Pali)

dula 'pair' Rebus: dul 'cast metal' Thus, as a mirrored pair, the hieroglyphs signify: *dul sandana* 'cast metal chariot'.

Hieroglyph: डांग (p. 351) [ḍāṅga] m n (H Peak or summit of a hill. (Marathi) Rebus: Dhangar 'blacksmith' dula 'pair' Rebus: dul 'cast metal' Thus, together, the mirrored pair signify: *dul Dhangar* 'cast metalsmith'

Hieroglyph: N. goṭo ' piece ', goṭi ' chess piece '; A. goṭ ' a fruit, whole piece ', °ṭā ' globular, solid ', guṭi ' small ball, seed, kernel '; B. goṭā ' seed, bean, whole '; Or. goṭā ' whole, undivided ', M. goṭā m. ' roundish stone ' (CDIAL 4271) Rebus: goṭī f. 'lump of silver' (Gujarati) dula 'pair' Rebus: dul 'cast metal' Thus, together, the mirrored hieroglyphs signify: dul goṭī 'cast silver'.

Hieroglyph: aḍar 'harrow' Rebus: aduru 'native metal' dula 'pair' Rebus: dul 'cast metal' Thus, together the mirrored hieroglyphs signify: dul aduru 'native metal castings'.

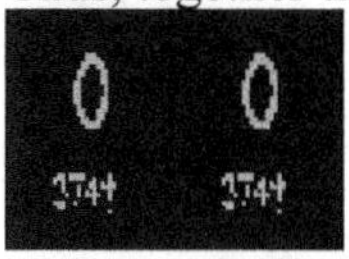

Hieroglyph: aḍar 'harrow' Rebus: aduru 'native metal' dula 'pair' Rebus: dul 'cast metal' Thus, together the mirrored hieroglyphs signify: dul aduru 'native metal castings'.

Hieroglyph: Kol. kor (pl. koḍl) hen, (SR.) cock, fowl. Nk. kor (pl. koḍḷ) hen. Pa. korr (pl. -ul) cock, hen, fowl. Ga. (Oll.) kor, (S.) korru (pl. korgūl) cock. Go. (Tr.) korr fowl; (A. Y. G.) kor, (Mu. Ko.) korr, (Ma.) koṟ id., hen (Voc. 917). Konḍa koṟu (pl. koRku) hen. Pe. kozu (pl. kosku), kuzu (pl. kusku) fowl. Manḍ. kuy id. Kui koju (pl. koska) id. Kuwi (F.) koiyū (pl. kōska), (Su. P.) koyu (pl. koska) id., hen.(DEDR 2160) Rebus: koD 'workshop' dula 'pair' Rebus: dul 'cast metal' Thus, the pair of cocks as hieroglyphs signify: dul koD 'cast metal workshop'

dula 'pair' Rebus: dul 'cast metal' aya 'fish' Rebus: aya 'iron' ayas 'metal'. Thus, together, the pair of hieroglyphs signify: *dul aya* 'cast metal'.

dula 'pair' Rebus: dul 'cast metal' eraka 'nave of wheel' Rebus: eraka 'metal infusion'. Thus, together the pair of spoked wheel hieroglyphs signify: *dul eraka* 'cast metal infusion'

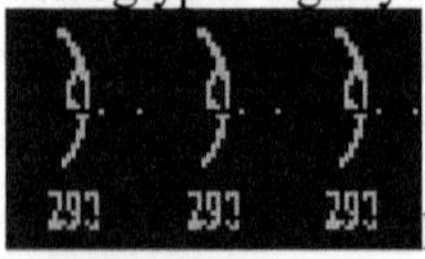

kolom 'three' Rebus: kolami 'smithy, forge' doḷā, ḍoḷā ' pupil of eye ' (Or.); M. ḍoḷā m. 'eye' Rebus: dul 'cast'. Thus, the triplet hieroglyphs signify: 'metalcastings smithy'

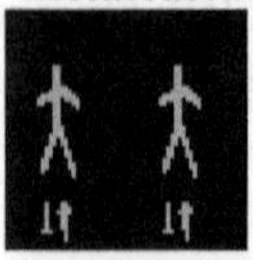

dula 'pair' Rebus: dul 'cast metal' meD 'body' Rebus: meD 'iron' Thus, the pair of hieroglyphs signify: 'cast iron'

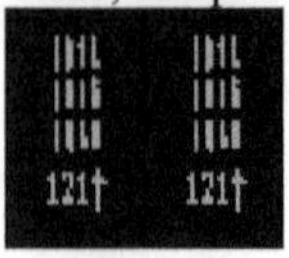

baroṭi 'twelve' *bhārata* 'a factitious alloy of copper, pewter, tin' (Marathi) dula 'pair' Rebus: dul 'cast metal'. The cast metal is pewter signified in Meluhha *baraḍo* = spine; backbone (Tulu) Rebus: *baran, bharat* 'mixed alloys' (5 copper, 4 zinc and 1 tin) (Punjabi).

The 'arch' hieroglyph is repeated as a count on a metal weapon. I suggest that the rebus reading signifies an alloy of copper and bell metal: ThaTTar (Nepalese)

Hieroglyph: *thaṭṭhal ' framework '. [Poss. < taṣṭá -- , but cf. *traṭṭa --]K. ṭhoṭhu m. ' bridge -- pier of logs piled horizontally ', ṭhaṭhur m. ' part of a house -- wall made of logs laid horizontally '; P. ṭhaṭh f. ' bridge -- pier '; N. ṭhā̃ṭi ' inn (lit. shed made of or covered with bamboo matting?) '; B. ṭhāṭ ' framework '; Or. thāṭa ' framework, skeleton ', ṭhāṭa ' bamboo framework for decoration, build of one's body, body '; Mth. ṭhāṭ ' bamboo frame of a thatch or of a mat house '; OAw. ṭhāṭa m. ' frame of a roof on which thatch is laid '; H. ṭhāṭh m. ' frame of a roof ', ṭhāṭar m. ' bamboo frame '; G. ṭhāṭhũ n. ' framework, body ', ṭhā̃ṭhũ n. ' skeleton ', ṭhāṭhṛī f. ' bamboo bier '; M. thāṭ, ṭhāṭ m. ' frame of a roof '.WPah.kc. thaṭo m. ' projecting part of a verandah '. (CDIAL 6089)

Rebus: ThaTTha 'brass'; ThaTTar 'an alloy of copper and bell metal' (Nepali); ThaTThAra 'brass worker' (Prakritam); ThaThero id. (Ku.)(CDIAL 5491, 5493).

There are also paired or re-duplicated occurrences of signs.

 loa 'ficus religiosa' Rebus: loh 'copper' dula 'pair' dul 'cast metal'

baTa 'rimless pot' Rebus: baTa 'furnace' dula 'pair' dul 'cast metal'

 khaNDa 'division' Rebus: khANDA 'metalware' dula 'pair' dul 'cast metal'

gaNDa 'four' Rebus: kanda 'fire-altar' kolmo 'rice plant' Rebus: kolami 'smithy, forge'. Thus the quadruplicated hieroglyphs signify: smithy fire-altar. There are some stable sequences of signs in inscriptions, stability being measured by the frequency of occurrence of two signs within each inscription..

The following seven pairs have between 93 and 291 occurrences in the inscriptions.

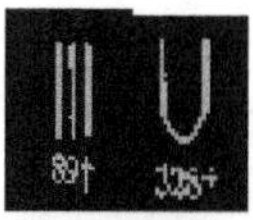 l. to r. kolom 'three' Rebus: kolami 'smithy, forge' baTa 'rimless pot' Rebus: baTa 'furnace'

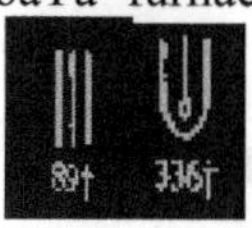 kolom 'three' Rebus: kolami 'smithy, forge' baTa 'rimless pot' Rebus: baTa 'furnace' Hieroglyph: Ta. caṭṭukam, caṭṭuvam ladle, metal spatula with a long handle for turning and removing a cooked cake. Ma. caṭṭukam ladle, metal spoon; ? caṭṭuvam shoulder-bone (or with 2303 Kol. saṭṭa). Ko. caṭy go·l iron ladle with flat, round blade,

for taking rice from pot. Ka. saṭuka, saṭṭu, saṭṭuga, soṭaka ladle, spoon. Koḍ. caṭṭuva wooden spoon used for stirring. Tu. saṭṭi a kind of wooden ladle; saṭṭuga, taṭṭuga a flat kind of trough for serving boiled rice. Te. caṭṭuvamu a sort of spoon with a shallow bowl having holes in it. Ga. (P.) saṭve ladle. Konḍa saṭva ladle made of wood for serving soup or curry. Pe. haṭva ladle; oar. Kuwi (Su.) haṭva ladle. / Cf. Skt. caṭuka- a wooden vessel for taking up fluid; Pkt. (DNM; Norman) caṭṭu- wooden spoon; Turner, CDIAL, no. 4575. (DEDR 2309) Rebus: sattva 'zinc, spelter'; jasta id. (Hindi). Thus, together, the pair of hieroglyh complexes Sign 336 PLUS Sign 89 read: *saṭva baTa kolom* 'zinc furnace smithy'

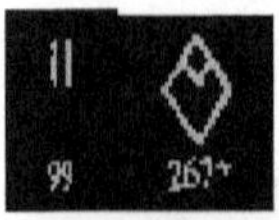
r. to l. kondh 'corner' Rebus: *kũdār* 'turner'. sal 'splinter' Rebus: sal 'workshop' Thus, the pair of hieroglyphs signify: turner's workshop.

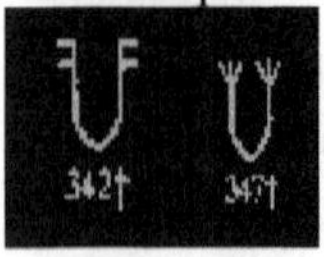
r. to l. dula 'pair' Rebus: dul 'cast metal' kolmo 'rice plant' Rebus: kolami 'smithy, forge' Thus, the hieroglyph multiplex reads: dul kolami 'metalcasting smithy' PLUS karNIka 'scribe, supercargo'

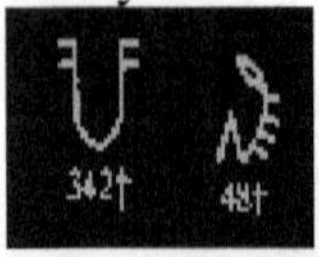
kaNDa 'backbone' Rebus: kANDa 'excellent metal' (Panini) PLUS karNIka 'scribe, supercargo'

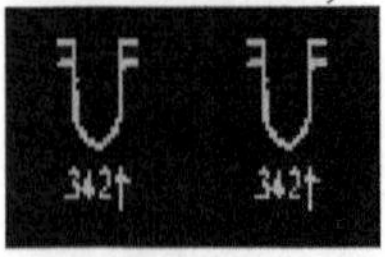
dula 'pair' Rebus: dul 'cast metal' PLUS karNIka 'scribe, supercargo' Thus, together the pair of 'rim of jar' hieroglyhs signify: supercargo of metalcastings.

There are five pairs with between 65 and 87 occurrences in the inscriptions.

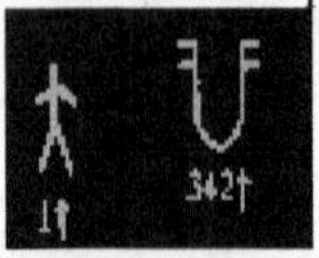
karNIka 'scribe, supercargo' PLUS meD 'body' Rebus: meD 'iron' Thus, ironware supercargo.

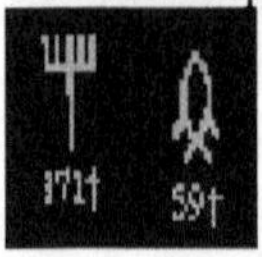
aya 'fish' Rebus: aya 'iron' ayas 'metal, alloy' PLUS Hieroglyph: aḍar 'harrow' Rebus: aduru 'native metal' Thus, native metal alloys.

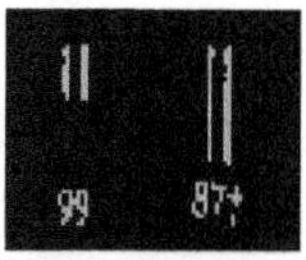 dula 'pair' Rebus; dul 'cast metal' sal 'splinter' Rebus: sal 'workshop' Thus, together, the hieroglyph pair signifies 'workshop for metalcastings'.

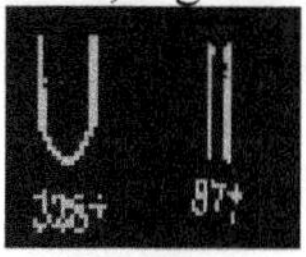 dula 'pair' Rebus: dul 'cast metal' PLUS baTa 'rimless pot' Rebus: baTa 'furnace'. Thus, the hieroglyph pair signifies 'metalcasting furnace'.

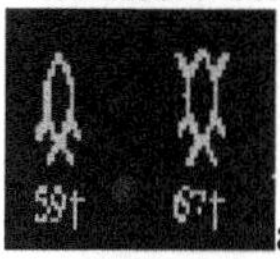aya 'fish' Rebus: aya 'iron' ayas 'metal' gaNDa 'four' Rebus: kanda 'fire-altar' Thus, together, the hieroglyph multiplex reads: ayaskANDa 'excellent iron' PLUS aya 'fish' Rebus: aya 'iron' ayas 'metal'. Together, the reading: ayaskANDa aya 'excellent iron, metal alloy'

Ligatures of graphemes

Two or more signs can be combined into one sign motif. For example, the 'jar' sign is ligatured in four instances:

There are many other ligatured Signs: An inverted 'v' is ligatured on Signs 65, 66, 75 (fishes), Sign 163 (corn sheaf), Sign 138 (cross-road), Sign 334 (pot). This inverted 'v' is also ligatured on a jar pictorial(Fig. 111 field symbol, Mahadevan corpus).

FS 111 Hieroglyph: *erga* = act of clearing jungle (Kui) Rebus: *eraka* 'nave of wheel' (Kannada) eraka 'moltencast copper' (Tulu) Hieroglyph: kola 'tiger' Rebus: kolle 'blacksmith' Hieroglyph: krammara 'turn back' Rebus: kamar 'smith' Hieroglyph: kuTi 'tree' Rebus: kuThi 'smelter' Hieroglyph: heraka 'spy' Rebus: eraka 'moltencast copper'

M-1657 A M-1657 B

Mohenjo-daro Inscribed object: inscription, tree. kuTi 'tree' Rebus: kuThi 'smelter'

The 'jar' sign is also ligatured with short linear strokes.

Ligatured signs appear together with pictorials in inscriptions.

Thus, Fig. 97 Mahadevan.

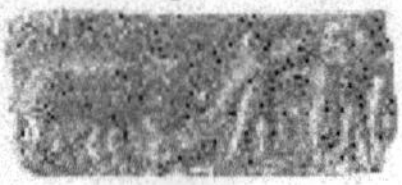 This composition is a combination of three pictorials and the

sign: 

The person standing in the middle seems to point with one hand at this sign and at the 'trough' with the other sign, seemingly conveying both 'trough' and the ligarured sign 15 which is a composition of the 'jar' and 'the water-carrier' represention s.

A characteristic feature of the use of graphemes in the inscriptions is 'ligaturing'.

Hieroglyph multiplex: 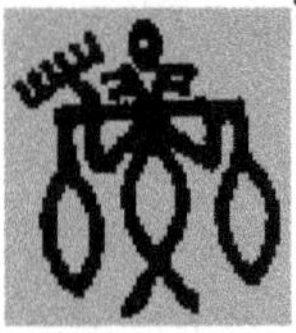 Hieroglyph components: 

Hieroglyph: aya 'fish' Rebus: aya 'iron' ayas 'metal'
Hieroglyph: aḍar 'harrow' Rebus: aduru 'native metal'
Hieroglyph: kuTi 'water-carrier' Rebus: kuThi 'smelter'

Hieroglyph: Kur. goṭā any seed which forms inside a fruit or shell. Malt. goṭa a seed or berry(DEDR 069) N. goṭo ' piece ', goṭi ' chess piece '; A. goṭ ' a fruit, whole piece ', °ṭā ' globular, solid ', guṭi ' small ball, seed, kernel '; B. goṭā ' seed, bean, whole '; Or. goṭā ' whole, undivided ', M. goṭā m. ' roundish stone ' (CDIAL 4271) Rebus: goṭī f. 'lump of silver' (Gujarati)

Hieroglyph: karNIka 'rim of jar' Rebus: karNi 'supercargo'; karNIka 'scribe'.

 Components: 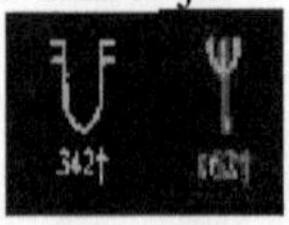 Sign 352, rim-of-jar + corn/maize/riceplant sheaf: kolmo 'rice plant' Rebus: kolami 'smithy, forge'. Hieroglyph: karNIka 'rim of jar' Rebus: karNi 'supercargo'; karNIka 'scribe'.

 Components:  Sign 394, rim-of-jar and oval: Hieroglyph: Kur. goṭā any seed which forms inside a fruit or shell. Malt. goṭa a seed or berry(DEDR 069) N. goṭo ' piece ', goṭi ' chess piece '; A. goṭ ' a fruit, whole piece ', °ṭā ' globular, solid ', guṭi ' small ball, seed, kernel '; B. goṭā ' seed, bean, whole '; Or. goṭā ' whole, undivided ', M. goṭā m. ' roundish stone ' (CDIAL 4271) Rebus: goṭī f. 'lump of silver' (Gujarati)

Hieroglyph: karNIka 'rim of jar' Rebus: karNi 'supercargo'; karNIka 'scribe'.

 Components:  Sign 353, rim-of-jar and pot: baṭa = rimless pot (Kannada) Rebus: baṭa = a kind of iron; bhaṭa 'furnace. Hieroglyph: karNIka 'rim of jar' Rebus: karNi 'supercargo'; karNIka 'scribe'.

 Components: 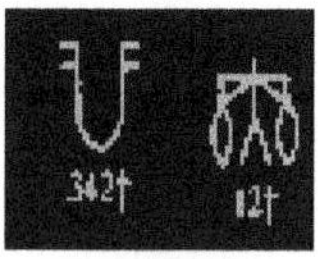 Sign 15 itself seems to be a ligature of signs 12 and 342: Hieroglyph: karNIka 'rim of jar' Rebus: karNi 'supercargo'; karNIka 'scribe'. Hieroglyph: kuTi 'water-carrier' Rebus: kuThi 'smelter'

 Components:  Signs 45/46 (seated person) seem to ligature the pictorial of a kneeling-adorant with sign 328:

Hieroglyph: bichi 'scorpion' Rebus: bichi 'sand stone ore'
Hieroglyph: maṇḍa -- 5 m. ' frog ' (CDIAL 9736) Rebus: mā̃ḍ 'array of instruments'

Hieroglyph: *miṇḍāl* 'markhor' (Tōrwālī) *meḍho* a ram, a sheep (Gujarati)(CDIAL 10120) Rebus: *mē̃ṛhē̃t, meḍ* 'iron' (Mu.Ho.)

Hieroglyph: baṭa = rimless pot (Kannada) Rebus: baṭa = a kind of iron; bhaṭa 'furnace.

Hieroglyph: Ta. maṇṭi kneeling, kneeling on one knee as an archer. Ma. maṇṭuka to be seated on the heels. Ka. maṇḍi what is bent, the knee. Tu. maṇḍi knee. Te. maṇḍī̃ kneeling on one knee. Pa. maḍtel knee; maḍi kuḍtel kneeling position. Go. (L.) meṇḍā, (G. Mu. Ma.) minḍa knee (Voc. 2827). Konḍa (BB) meḍa, meṇḍa id. Pe. menḍa id. Manḍ. menḍe id. Kui menḍa id. Kuwi (F.) menda, (S. Su. P.) menḍa, (Isr.) meṇḍa id. Cf. Skt. maṇḍūkī- part of an elephant's hind leg; Mar. meṭ knee-joint. (DEDR 4677)

Rebus: array of instruments: maṇḍa2 m. ' ornament ' lex. [√maṇḍ] Pk. maṁḍaya -- ' adorning '; Ash. mōṇḍa, mōnda, mūnda NTS ii 266, mōṇə NTS vii 99 ' clothes '; G. mā̃ḍ m. ' arrangement, disposition, vessels or pots for decoration ', māṇ f. ' beautiful array of household vessels '; M. mā̃ḍ m. ' array of instruments &c. '; Si. maḍa -- ya ' adornment, ornament '.(CDIAL 9736)

Components: 

Sign 355 seems to ligature sign 347 and sign 391: Hieroglyph: eraka 'nave of wheel' ara 'spoke' Rebus: eraka 'moltencast' ara 'brass'. dula 'pair' Rebus: dul 'cast metal' PLUS kolmo 'rice plant' Rebus: kolami 'smithy, forge'.

Components: 

Sign 232 seems to be a ligature of sign 230 and sign 326: Hieroglyph: loa 'ficus religiosa' Rebus: loh 'copper' Hieroglyph: WPah.kṭg. (kc.) kaṇḍɔ m. ' thorn, mountain peak ', J. kā̃ḍā m.(CDIAL 2668) Rebus: kaNDa 'metalware'; cf. ayaskANDa 'excellent iron' (Panini) Thus, kANDa has the semantics: 'excellent metal'.

Components: 

Sign 243 seems to ligature sign 242 and sign 328: Hieroglyph: kole.l 'temple' Rebus: kole.l 'smithy' PLUS Hieroglyph: baṭa = rimless pot (Kannada) Rebus: baṭa = a kind of iron; bhaṭa 'furnace. Hieroglyph: *khuṇṭa2 ' corner '. 2. *kuṇṭa -- 2. [Cf. *khōñca --]1. Phal. khun ' corner '; H. khũṭ m. ' corner, direction ' (→ P. khũṭ f. ' corner, side '); G. khũṭrī f. ' angle '. <-> X kōṇa -- : G. khuṇ f., khūˇṇɔ m. ' corner '.2. S. kuṇḍa f. ' corner '; P. kũṭ f. ' corner, side ' (← H.).(CDIAL 3898) Rebus: Firepit: Ta. kuṭṭam depth, pond; kuṭṭai pool, small pond; kuṇṭam deep cavity, pit, pool; kuṇṭu depth, hollow, pond, manure-pit. Ma. kuṇṭam, kuṇṭu what is hollow and deep, hole, pit. Ka. kuṇḍa, koṇḍa, kuṇṭe pit, pool, pond; guṇḍa hollowness and deepness; guṇḍi hole, pit, hollow, pit of the stomach; guṇḍige pit of the stomach; guṇḍitu, guṇḍittu that is deep; guṇpu, gumpu, gumbu depth, profundity, solemnity, secrecy. Koḍ. kuṇḍï pit; kuṇḍitere manure-pit. Tu. kuṇḍa a pit; koṇḍa pit, hole; guṇḍi abyss, gulf, great depth; gumpu secret, concealed. Te. kuṇṭa, guṇṭa pond, pit; kuṇḍu cistern; guṇḍamu fire-pit; (Inscr.) a hollow or pit in the dry bed of a stream; gunta pit, hollow, depression. Kol. (Pat., p. 115) gunḍi deep. Nk. ghuṇḍik id. Pa. guṭṭa pool. Go. (A.) kunṭa id. (Voc. 737). Konḍa guṭa pit, hollow in the ground. Kui kuṭṭ a large pit (Chandrasekhar, Trans. Linguistic Circle Delhi 1958, p. 2). Kuwi (S.) guntomi pit; (Isr.) kuṇḍi pond. Cf. 1818 Ta. kuṟal and 2082 Kur. xoṇḍxā. / Cf.

Skt. kuṇḍa- round hole in ground (for water or sacred fire), pit, well, spring.(DEDR 1669)

 Components:  Sign 286 seems to ligature sign 267 and sign 391: Hieroglyph khuṇṭa 'corner ' Rebus: kuṇḍa 'fire-altar' PLUS Hieroglyph: eraka 'nave of wheel' Rebus: 'metal infusion'.

 Components:  Sign 19 seems to ligature sign 1 and sign 171: Hieroglyph: aḍar 'harrow' Rebus: aduru 'native metal' meD 'body' Rebus: meD 'iron' (Ho.)

 Components:  Sign 218 seems to ligature sign 217 and sign 328: Hieroglyph: ḍato 'claws or pincers of crab' (Santali) rebus: dhatu 'ore' (Santali). Hieroglyph: baṭa = rimless pot (Kannada) Rebus: baṭa = a kind of iron; bhaṭa 'furnace.

 Components: 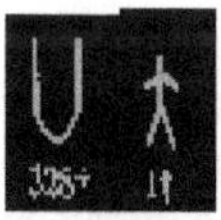 Sign 32 seems to ligature sign 1 and sign 328: Hieroglyph: meD 'body' Rebus: meD 'iron' (Ho.) Hieroglyph: baṭa = rimless pot (Kannada) Rebus: baṭa = a kind of iron; bhaṭa 'furnace.

 Components:  Sign 372 is a three-fold ligature with signs 397 and 162: Hieroglyph: baṭa = rimless pot (Kannada) Rebus: baṭa = a kind of iron; bhaṭa 'furnace Hieroglyph: kandi 'bead' Rebus: kanda 'fire-altar'. kolmo 'rice plant' Rebus: kolami 'smithy, forge'.

 Components:  Sign 387, corn sheaf within an oval

Ligature of sign 162 and sign 373 yields sign 387: Hieroglyph: khuṇṭa 'corner ' Rebus: kuṇḍa 'fire-altar' PLUS kolmo 'rice plant' Rebus: kolami 'smithy, forge'.

 Components:  Signs 63 and 64, bird and fish: Hieroglyph: aya 'fish' Rebus: aya 'iron' ayas 'metal' (Gujarati.Rigveda) Hieroglyph: karaṇḍa2-- m. ' duck '

(Samskritam) S. karaṛa-- ḍhĩgu m. ' a very large aquatic bird '(Sindhi)(CDIAL 2787)

करडा (p. 137) [karaḍā] Hard from alloy--iron, silver &c (Marathi)

Components:  Sign 36, man and pincers: Hieroglyph: ḍato 'claws or pincers of crab' (Santali) rebus: dhatu 'ore' PLUS meD 'body' Rebus: meD 'iron' (Ho.)

 Components: 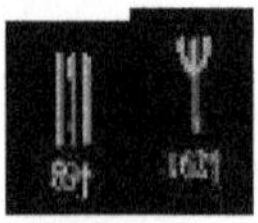 Sign 90, three linear strokes and corn sheaf/maize/riceplant: Hieroglyph: kolmo 'rice plant' Rebus: kolami 'smithy, forge' kolom 'three' Rebus: kolami 'smithy, forge' (Phonetic reinforcement)

 Components:  Sign 362, oval and a pair of combs:Hieroglyph: *khareḍo* = a currycomb Rebus: *kharādī* ' turner' *dula* 'pair' Rebus: *dul* 'cast metal' khuṇṭa 'corner ' Rebus: kuṇḍa 'fire-altar'

Components: Sign 383 ligatures signs 374, 373 and 176: Hieroglyph: *khareḍo* = a currycomb Rebus: *kharādī* ' turner' dula 'pair' Rebus: dul 'cast metal' khuṇṭa 'corner ' Rebus: kuṇḍa 'fire-altar' *khareḍo* = a currycomb Rebus: *kharādī* ' turner' dula 'pair' Rebus: dul 'cast metal' khuṇṭa 'corner ' Rebus: kuṇḍa 'fire-altar' : Hieroglyph: Kur. goṭā any seed which forms inside a fruit or shell. Malt. goṭa a seed or berry(DEDR 069) N. goṭo ' piece ', goṭi ' chess piece '; A. goṭ ' a fruit, whole piece ', °ṭā ' globular, solid ', guṭi ' small ball, seed, kernel '; B. goṭā ' seed, bean, whole '; Or. goṭā ' whole, undivided ', M. goṭā m. ' roundish stone ' (CDIAL 4271) Rebus: goṭī f. 'lump of silver' (Gujarati)

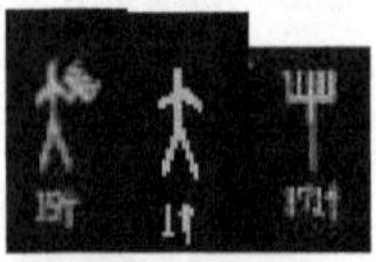 Sign 19, man and harrow Hieroglyph: meD 'body' Rebus: meD 'iron' (Ho.) Hieroglyph: *aḍar* 'harrow' Rebus: aduru 'native metal'

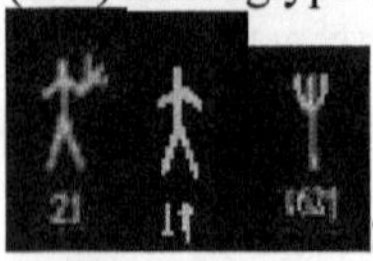Sign 21, man and corn sheaf meD 'body' Rebus: meD 'iron' (Ho.) Hieroglyph: *kolmo* 'rice plant' Rebus: kolami 'smithy, forge'

 Components:  Sign 173 is a ligatured hieroglyph multiplex: representation of a pair of the sign 172: Hieroglyph: *aḍar* 'harrow' Rebus: aduru 'native metal' *dula* 'pair' rebus: *dul* 'cast metal'

 Components:  (See paring in Sign 173)Sign 348 ligatures with sign 162 and a pair of 172: Hieroglyph: *aḍar* 'harrow' Rebus: aduru 'native metal' *dula* 'pair' rebus: *dul* 'cast metal'PLUS kolmo 'rice plant' Rebus: kolami 'smithy, forge' PLUS Hieroglyph: baṭa = rimless pot (Kannada) Rebus: baṭa = a kind of iron; bhaṭa 'furnace.

Types of Objects, find-spots and functions served by the messages conveyed through the objects

Many tablets (both incised and embossed varieties, generally made of faience, terracotta or stone) occur in multiples suggesting some form of distribution of common, identical 'messages' (or underlying material life-support phenomena).

Copper tablets found in Mohenjodaro are incised with pictorials in inscriptions and script signs. The historical periods record the evidence of the use of copper tablets to authenticate title deeds or property transactions. This evidence is an apparent legacy of the Sarasvati-Sindhu Civilization. No other contemporary civilization has produced such definitive evidence of conveying property through copper-plate inscriptions. (Cylinder seals and clay tablets had been used in Mesopotamia to convey movable property items).

Hieroglyph: *eraka* 'upraised arm' (Telugu) Rebus: *eraka* 'copper' 'metal infusion' (Tulu)
bhaTa 'warrior' Rebus: *baṭa* = a kind of iron; *bhaṭa* 'furnace
ayaskANDa 'fish PLUS arrow': 'excellent iron' (Panini)

miṇḍāl 'markhor' (Tōrwālī) *meḍho* a ram, a sheep (Gujarati)(CDIAL 10120)
Rebus: *mẽṛhẽt, meḍ* 'iron' (Mu.Ho.)

kõdā खोंड [khōṇḍa] m A young bull, a bullcalf. (Marathi) Rebus 1: kọṇḍu or konḍu ।

कुण्डम् m. a hole dug in the ground for receiving consecrated fire (Kashmiri) Rebus 2: A. *kundār*, B. *kũdār*, °*ri*, Or. *kundāru*; H. *kũderā* m. ' one who works a lathe, one who scrapes ', °*rī* f., *kũdernā* ' to scrape, plane, round on a lathe '.(CDIAL 3297).

Banawali Seal Impression (B-23); A mighty person stands in front of 'unicorn' and 'markhor' with upturned faces (apparently listening to the person); two signs occur: 'fish' and 'arrow' graphemes. The sealing is on terracotta. The ten steatite seals and one sealing have only come from the lower town, not the citadel…these seals were generally recovered from houses which on the basis of their contents…have been tentatively attributed to a trader or jeweler (Bisht, R.S., 1982, Excavations at Banawali: 1974-77, in: Gregory L. Possehl,*Harappan Civilization*, Delhi, p.118).

Apart the use of copper tablets and in a few cases, the use of silver and copper for seals which indicates that the messages are possibly engraved by metal- and/or fire-workers (cf. the use of fired-in faience for seals), the dramatic clue to the decipherment of the script comes from the characteristic shapes of a few objects.

There are also inscriptions on bronze implements, re-inforcing the deduction that the metal- and/or fire-workers were the major script-writers of the civilization. If the writers of the script were also the owners of or traders in the products made from metal- and fire-work, then the messages conveyed were likely to be related to their life-activities. This is a possibility because at this stage of the evolution of chalcolithic cultures, ca. 3000 B.C., the differentiation in the labour-force might not have reached a stage when a separate group of or the profession of 'script-writers' had been recognized.

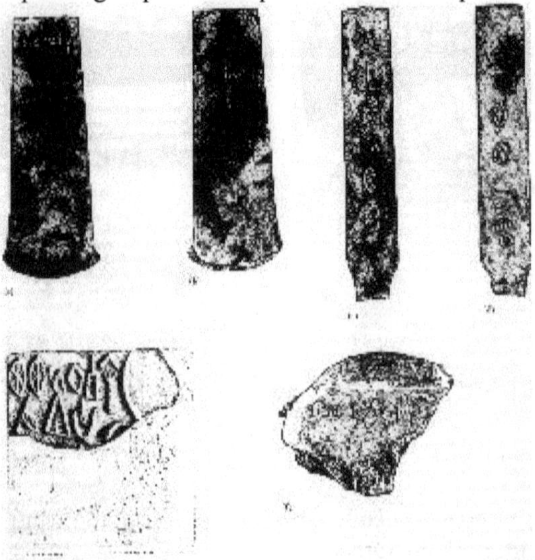

Seven script signs recurring on two inscribed copper axes and on a seal and a seal impression, Mohenjodaro; obverse (a,c)

and reverse (b.d) of two axe blades (2798=DK7856 and 2796=DK7535) in room 15, house I, block 12A,G section, DK area together with a copper hoard; e is a fragmentary seal (2119) from room 5, house I, block 26,G section, DK area; f is an impression of a seal (c. 4.5cm sq.) on a clay tag found in the drain 124, house X, block 8, HR-B area. Drawn after Mackay 1938: II, pl. 126:t and pl. 131:35-6; Photo archive of the ASI, Sind Vol. 17, p. 79: 400 (=a,b); Mackay 1938: II, pl. 126:2; pl. 131:31; Sind vol. 17, p. 80: 403-4 (=c,d); Mackay 1938: II, pl. 85: 119 (=e); CISI 2: 183, M-1384 (=f); cf. Parpola, 1994, p. 108.

Some objects are shaped like a double-axe (FS 133), some like a sickle (?or crescent FS 131), some like a fish (FS 68), some like a tortoise (FS 70), some like a leaf (FS 79).

Fish signs

Fish on miniature tablets, Harappa (a) H-302; (b) 3452; after Vats 1940: II, 452 B. Parpola, 1994, p. 194.

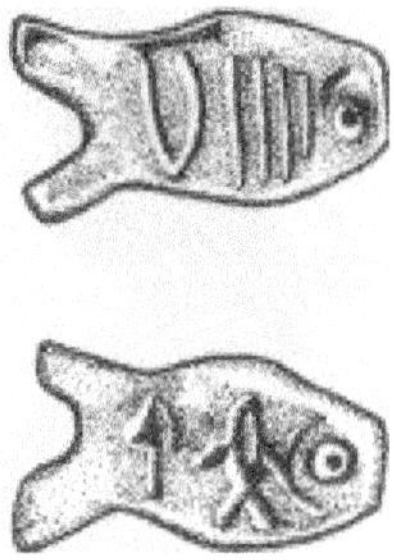

Fish-shaped tablet (3428), Harappa with incised text; eye is a dotted circle; after Vats 1940: II, pl. 95, no.428; Parpola, 1994, p. 194.

A configuration of nine tablets depicts in high relief on one side of nine inscribed tablets, a representation of 'ring-stones (or entwined serpent?)' set on a pillar (FS 73).

[Using the rebus method, it should be possible to interpret the 'fish', 'tortoise', 'leaf', 'pillar' to discern the underlying substantive 'meanings'.]

A remarkable legacy of the civilization occurs in the use of 'fish' sign on a copper anthropomorph found in a copper hoard. This is an apparent link of the 'fish' broadly with the profession of 'metal-work'.

One anthropomorph had fish hieroglyph incised on the chest of the copper object, Sheorajpur, upper Ganges valley, ca. 2nd millennium BCE, 4 kg; 47.7 X 39 X 2.1 cm. State Museum, Lucknow (O.37) Typical find of Gangetic Copper Hoards. miṇḍāl markhor (Tor.wali) meḍho a ram, a sheep (G.)(CDIAL 10120) Rebus: meḍh 'helper of merchant' (Gujarati) meḍ iron (Ho.) meṛed-bica = iron stone ore, in contrast to bali-bica, iron sand ore (Munda) ayo 'fish' Rebus: ayo, ayas 'metal. Thus, together read rebus: *ayo meḍh* 'iron stone ore, metal merchant.'

A remarkable legacy of the civilization occurs in the use of 'fish' sign on a copper anthropomorph found in a copper hoard. This is an apparent link of the 'fish' broadly with the profession of 'metal-work'. The 'fish' sign is apparently related to the copper object which seems to depict a 'fighting ram' symbolized by its in-curving horns. The 'fish' sign may relate to a copper furnace. The underlying imagery defined by the style of the copper casting is the pair of curving horns of a fighting ram ligatured into the outspread legs (of a warrior).

The center-piece of the makara symbolism is that it is a big jhasa, big fish, but with ligatured components (alligator snout, elephant trunk, elephant legs and antelope face). Each of these components can be explained (alligator: manger; elephant trunk: sunda; elephant: ibha; antelope: ranku; rebus: mangar 'smith'; sunda 'furnace'; ib 'iron'; ranku 'tin'); thus the makara jhasa or the big composite fish is a complex of metallurgical repertoire.)

One nidhi was makara (syn. Kohl, antimony); the second was makara (or, jhasa, fish) [bed.a hako (ayo)(syn. bhed.a 'furnace'; med. 'iron'; ayas 'metal')]; the third was kharva (syn. karba, iron).

Title / Object: anthropomorphic sheorajpur
Fund context: Saipai, Dist. Kanpur
Time of admission: 1981
SAI South Asian Archaeology

Pool:

M-898 a

Image ID: 213 101
Copyright: Dr Paul Yule, Heidelberg

Photo credit: Yule, Metalwork of the Bronze in India, Pl 23 348 (dwg)
Saipal, Dist. Etawah, UP. Anthropomorph, type I. 24.1x27.04x0.76 cm., 1270 gm., both sides show a chevron patterning, left arm broken off (Pl. 22, 337). Purana Qila Coll. Delhi (74.12/4) -- Lal, BB, 1972, 285 fig. 2d pl. 43d

Potters' marks/signs used at Harappa and on Iranian borderlands (e.g., Shahdad, Tepe Yahya):

m-898 shows  'numeral' three strokes ligatured to 'rice-plant' hieroglyph, followed by a structure denoting kole.l 'temple, smithy'. *kolom* 'three' phonetic determinant hieroglyph of *kolmo* 'rice-plant'.
Hieroglyphs: *kolom* 'three'; kolmo 'rice plant' Rebus: *kolami* 'smithy, forge'; *kole.l* 'smithy, temple.

Hieroglyphs: *tagaraka* '*tabernae montana*' Rebus: *tagara* 'tin'. *ranku* 'antelope' rebus: *ranku* 'tin'. ranku 'a species of deer' (Samskritam) (CDIAL 10559) kuranga 'a kind of antelope' (Pali)

Note: Three-stroke 'sprout' denotes: *kolmo* 'rice-plant'; five-stroke 'sprout' denotes *tagaraka* '*tabernae montana*' (with five-petals of flower). Both hieroglyphs denote tin/copper (ranku, mleccha) metalwork in: smithy, furnace.

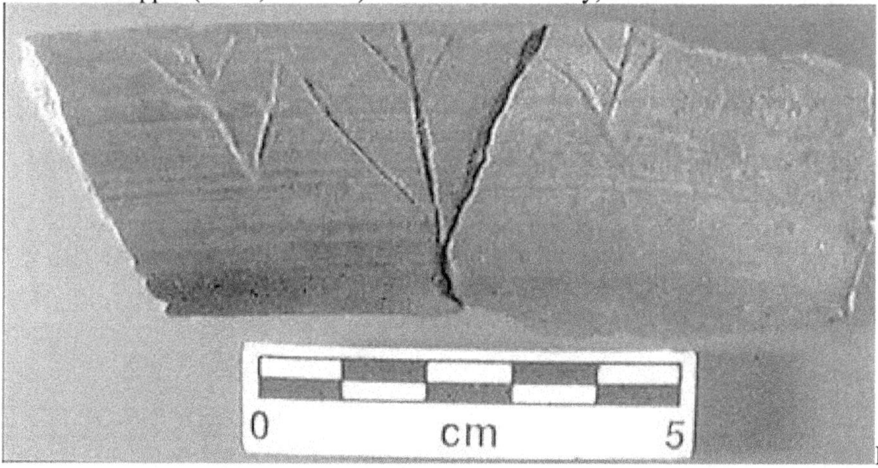

Potsherd discovered by HARP in Harappa dated to c. 3500 BCE Three signs of Indus Writing System.The central sign variant has 5 strokes.

Lal notes: ...Potter's marks tradition "form(s) part and parcel of the signary available on the Harappan seals. " (Lal, B.B., 1975, The Indus Script: Some observations based on archaeology, *Journal of the Royal Asiatic Society*: 173-177.).

Potts raises this question, noting some of the parallels between potter's marks and both Proto-Elamite and Harappan scripts: "...does this represent the conscious selection of certain signs from Proto-Elamite by the peoples of the Indo-Iranian borderlands, and in turn the intentional incorporation of some of the same signs in Harappan because of the symbolic and/or syllabic values of these signs?" (Potts, D., 1981, The Potter's Marks of Tepe Yahya, in: *Paleorient*, Vol. 7, Issue 7-1, pp.107-122, p.119)

Antelope 'tail' is shown with a Sign of three strokes (See Banawali b-12).

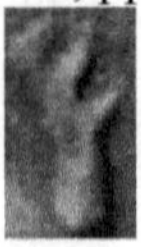

Hieroglyph: *Kur.* xolā tail. *Malt.* qoli id. (DEDR 2135) kulva ' bald ' KātyŚr., *átikūˊlva* -- VS. Pk. *kulla* -- ' having the tail cut off, weak '(CDIAL 3355)

Rebus: 133 *Ta.* kol working in iron, blacksmith; kollaṉ blacksmith.
Ma. kollan blacksmith, artificer. *Ko.* kole·l smithy, temple
in Kota village. *To.* kwala·l Kota smithy.*Ka.* kolime, kolume, kulame, kulime, kulume, k ulme fire-pit, furnace; (Bell.; U.P.U.) konimi blacksmith; (Gowda) kolla id.
Koḍ. kollë blacksmith. *Te.* kolimi furnace. *Go.* (SR.) kollusānā to mend implements; (Ph.) kolstānā, kulsānā to forge; (Tr.) kōlstānā to repair (of ploughshares);
(SR.) kolmi smithy (*Voc.* 948).*Kuwi* (F.) kolhali to forge. (DEDR 2133) Pk. *kullaḍa* -- n. ' small vessel, fireplace '(CDIAL 3354)

Hieroglyph: *miṇḍāl* 'markhor' (Tōrwālī) *meḍho* a ram, a sheep (Gujarati)(CDIAL 10120)
Rebus: *mẽṛhẽt, meḍ* 'iron' (Munda.Ho.) *mṛeka, melh* 'goat' (Telugu. Brahui)
Rebus: *melukkha* '*milakkha*, copper'; *mleccha* 'copper' (Samskritam). If the animal carried on the right hand of the Meluhha seafaring merchant is an antelope, the possible readings could also be: *ranku* 'antelope' Rebus: *ranku* 'tin'.

Hieroglyph: *Ka.* mēke she-goat; mē the bleating of sheep or goats. *Te.* mẽka, mēka goat. *Kol.* me·ke id. *Nk.* mēke id. *Pa.* mēva, (S.) mēya she-goat. *Ga.* (Oll.) mēge, (S.) mēge goat. *Go.* (M) mekā, (Ko.) mēka id. ? *Kur.* mēxnā (mīxyas) to call, call after loudly, hail. *Malt.* méqe to bleat. [*Te.* mṟēka (so correct) is of unknown meaning. *Br.* mēḻẖ is without etymology; see MBE 1980a.] / Cf. Skt. (*lex.*) meka- goat. (DEDR 5087) Rebus: Milakkhu [the Prk. form (A -- Māgadhī, cp. Pischel, *Prk. Gr.* 105, 233) for P. milakkha] As milakkhuka at Vin iii.28, where Bdhgh expls by "Andha -- Damil' ādi.; °rajana "of foreign dye"(Pali)

The rollout of Shu-ilishu's Cylinder seal. Courtesy of the Department des Antiquites Orientales, Musee du Louvre, Paris. Akkadian. Cylinder seal Impression. Inscription records that it belongs to 'S'u-ilis'u, Meluhha interpreter', i.e., translator of the Meluhhan language (EME.BAL.ME.LUH.HA.KI) The Meluhhan being introduced carries an goat on his arm. Musee du Louvre. Ao 22 310, Collection De Clercq 3rd millennium BCE. The Meluhhan is accompanied by a lady carrying a kamaṇḍalu (ranku 'liquid measure' rebus: ranku 'tin').

Since he needed an interpreter, it is reasonably inferred that Meluhhan did not speak Akkadian.

Antelope carried by the Meluhhan is a hieroglyph: mlekh 'goat' (Br.); mṟeka (Te.); mēṭam (Ta.); meṣam (Skt.) Thus, the goat conveys the message that the carrier is a Meluhha speaker. A phonetic determinant.mṟeka, mlekh 'goat'; Rebus: melukkha Br. mē̠ḻ̠h 'goat'. Te. mṟeka (DEDR 5087) meluh.h.a

Shahdad. Cylinder seal.

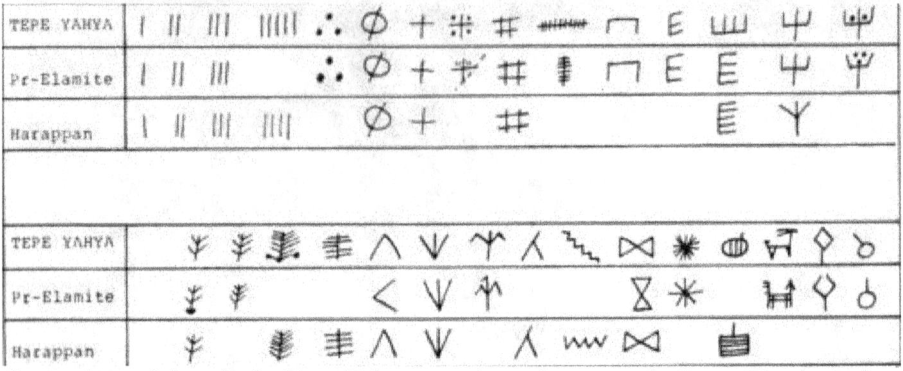

Comparison of signs in the Tepe Yahya potter's mark corpus, the Proto-Elamite script, and the Harappan script (After Fig. 4 in: Potts, D., 1981, The Potter's Marks of Tepe Yahya, in: Paleorient, Vol. 7, Issue 7-1, p.117)

Comparison of potter's marks from sites in the Indo-Iranian borderlands, Central Asia, and the Indian sub-continent (After Fig. 3, Potts, D., ibid., p. 115).

The following six potter's marks of Tepe Yahya can be read rebus on Indus writing, using Meluhha (Mleccha) words of Indian *sprachbund*; it is remarkable that all words relate to Bronze Age metallurgy indicating that Indus Writing was devised by artisans/merchants dealing with metalware and documenting metalware catalogs of Bronze Age:

Hieroglyph: four 'strokes': gaṇḍaka m. ‘ a coin worth four cowries ’ lex., ‘ method of counting by fours ’ W. [← Mu. Przyluski RoczOrj iv 234] S. *gaṇḍho* m. ‘ four in counting ’; P. *gaṇḍā* m. ‘ four cowries ’; B. Or. H. *gaṇḍā* m. ‘ a group of four, four cowries ’; M. *gaṇḍā* m. ‘ aggregate of four cowries or pice ’.(CDIAL 4001)
Rebus: *kanda* 'fire-altar'

Hieroglyph: three 'strokes': *kolom* 'three' Rebus: *kolami* 'smithy, forge'.

tagaraka 'tabernae montana' Rebus: *tagara* 'tin'. The glyph appears on a bronze axe.

aḍi (as in paṭṭaḍi): 'feet' Rebus: anvil

khareḍo = a currycomb Rebus: *kharādī* ' turner'

ranku 'liquid measure' Rebus: ranku 'tin' (casseterite) The glyph occurs on Haifa tin ingots.

kolom'sprout'; kolom = cutting, graft; to graft, engraft, prune; kolma hoṛo = a variety of the paddy plant; kolmo 'rice plant' Rebus: kolami 'furnace,smithy'

ranku 'antelope' Rebus: ranku 'tin' (cassiterite) The glyph occurs on Haifa tin ingots.

http://www.scribd.com/doc/157948731/Potts-D-1981-The-Potter-s-Marks-of-Tepe-Yahya-in-Paleorient-Vol-7-Issue-7-1-pp-107-122

B-12 a

B-10 A

B-9 a

Banawali seals (B-9, B-10, B-12) Banawali is on west bank of River Sarasvati.

A variant Sign with 5 strokes (See m-673).

Sign 162

Sign 163

Sign 164

Sign 165

Sign 166

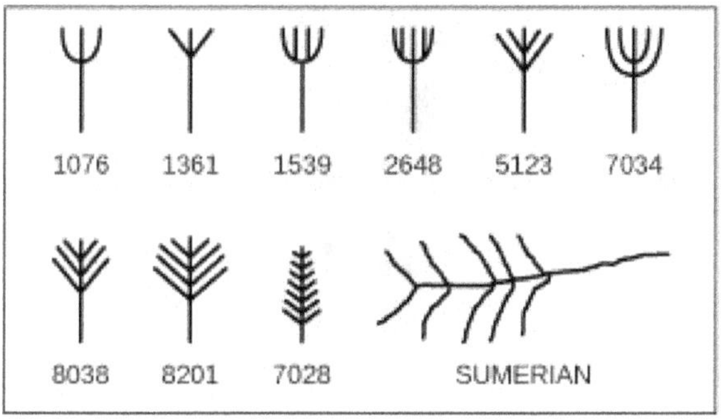

Sign 162, variants Sign 167, 168 compared with Sumerian 'grain' hieroglyph.

M-178 a

M-179 a

M-749 A

M-898 a

m-178, m-179, m-749, m-898

K-19 a

M-673 a

H-38 a

Kalibangan-19, m-673, Harappa-38,

K-65 a

K-50 a

M-178 a

Kalibangan-65, Kalibangan-50, m-838

The potsherd h1522 discovered in Harappa on the banks of River Ravi by archaeologists of HARP (Harvard Archaeology Project) is dated to ca. 3500 BCE. Citing this find, the report quoted one of the excavators, Richard Meadow: "...these primitive inscriptions found on pottery may pre-date all other known writing."

As the hieroglyphic writing system evolved, the impact was also evidenced in Susa, with the foundation of a settlement on the banks of Karkheh and Dez Rivers dated to 5th millennium BCE. The interactions between Elamite, Persian and Parthian empires of Iran and seafaring merchants of Meluhha can be re-evaluated in the context of the evidence provided by Indus writing.

Discussing 3rd millennium BCE cultural relationships of Indus valley with the Helmand and Baluchistan, Cortesi et al refer to artifacts found at Shahr-I Sokhta and nearby sites (Iranian Seistan) presumably imported from Baluchistan, Mundigak (Kandahar, Afghanistan) and the Indus domain and indicating local adaptation of south-eastern manufactures and practices.

tagaraka 'tabernae montana'. Rebus: tagara 'tin'. Mineral tin alloyed with mineral copper yields bronze metal. One variant glyphic is an Indus script glyph (Sign 162) found on a potsherd dated to c. 3500 BCE.

The tabernae montana glyph characteristically depicted with five petals gains currency where Meluhha settlements existed or where Meluhha traders had contacts:

Cylinder seal showing tabernae montana.

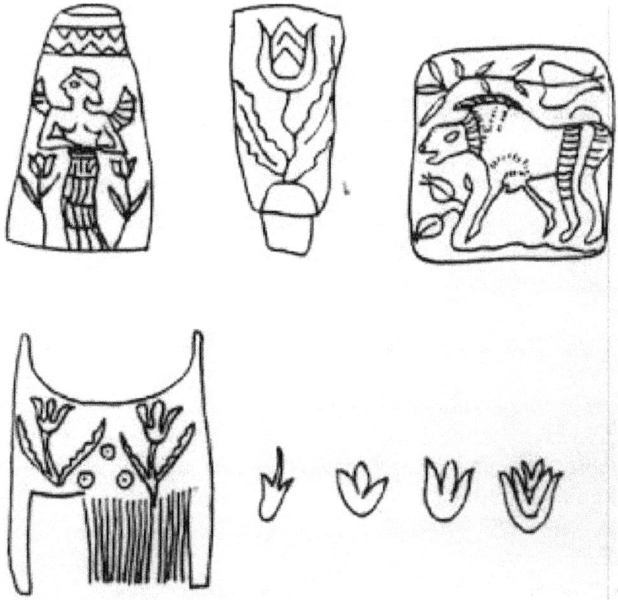

Tabernae montana glyph on Ancient Near East artefacts.

Tabernae montana glyph on a bronze axe-head. Tell Abraq axe with epigraph ('tulip' glyph + a person raising his arm above his shoulder and wielding a tool + dotted circles on body) [After Fig. 7 Holly Pittman, 1984, *Art of the Bronze Age: Southeastern Iran, Western Central Asia, and the Indus Valley*, New York, The Metropolitan Museum of Art, pp. 29-30].

tabar = a broad axe (Punjabi).

Rebus: *tam(b)ra* 'copper' *tagara* '*tabernae montana*',

'tulip'. Rebus: *tagara* 'tin'. Glyph: *eṛaka* 'upraised arm' (Tamil); rebus: *eraka* = copper (Kannada)

A rebus reading of the hieroglyph is: *tagaraka*, *tabernae montana*. Rebus: *tagara* 'tin' (Kannada); tamara id. (Skt.) Allograph: *ṭagara* 'ram'. Since *tagaraka* is used as an aromatic unguent for the hair, fragrance, the glyph gets depicted on a stone flask, an ivory comb and axe of Tell Abraq.

Mlecchita vikalpa is listed by a Hindu philosopher of pre-common era, that is, of over 2 millennia ago -- वात्स्यायन Vātsyāyana as one of the 64 arts to be taught to the youth in a chapter titled: विद्यासमुद्देश *vidyAsamuddeza,*'objectives of education'.

म्लेच्छित [p= 838,1] *mfn.* = म्लिष्ट Paln2. 7-2 , 18 Sch. **म्लिष्ट [p= 837,3]** *mfn.* spoken indistinctly or barbarously Paln2. 7-2 , 18 *n.* indistinct speech (Monier-Williams).

Hemacandra Muni's देशीनाममाला *Dēśīnāmamālā* lists many examples of such indistinct speech which are recognized as *tatsama, tadbhava* Prakritam forms in Samskritam. Hence, mleccha (meluhha) is identifiable as ancient Prakritam form of Indian *sprachbund* (speech union).

A brief overview of the deciphered script is presented with some examples. The word 'mleccha' denotes copper in Samskritam. Hence, the appropriateness of interpreting *mlecchita vikalpa* as metalworkers' speechforms, sprachbund in ancient India of *Bhāratam Janam*.(a phrase by Rishi Visvamitra which identifies the ancestors of Sarasvati's children, i.e. the people who nurtured a civilization on the banks of Rivers Sarasvati and Sindhu from ancient times).

Note: Samskritam gloss Mleccha cognate Pali Milakkha [cp. Ved. Sk. mleccha barbarian, root **mlecch**, onomat. after the strange sounds of a foreign tongue, cp. babbhara & mammana] a barbarian, foreigner, outcaste, hillman S v.466; J vi.207; DA i.176; SnA

236 (°mahātissa -- thera Np.), 397 (°bhāsā foreign dialect). The word occurs also in form **milakkhu** (q. v.).Milakkhu [the Prk. form (A -- Māgadhī, cp. Pischel, *Prk. Gr.* 105, 233) for P. milakkha] a non -- Aryan D iii.264; Th 1, 965 (°rajana "of foreign dye" trsl.; Kern,*Toev.* s. v. translates "vermiljoen kleurig"). As **milakkhuka** at Vin iii.28, where Bdhgh expls by "Andha -- Damil' ādi."Milāca [by -- form to milakkha, viâ *milaccha>*milacca> milāca: Geiger, *P.Gr.* 622; Kern, *Toev.* s. v.] a wild man of the woods, non -- Aryan, barbarian J iv.291 (not with C.=janapadā), cp. luddā m. ibid., and milāca -- puttā J v.165 (where C. also expls by bhojaputta, i. e. son of a villager).

(Pali) **म्लेच्छ [p=837,3]** *m.* a foreigner, barbarian, non-Aryan, man of an outcast race , any person who does not speak Sanskrit and does not conform to the usual Hindu institutions S3Br. &c (*f*(ई).)a person who lives by agriculture or by making weapons L.; copper; vermillion (Monier-Williams)

Subjects of 64 Arts and Sciencies studied (as translated by Richard Burton) including *mlecchita vikalpa*:

- Singing
- Playing on musical instruments
- Dancing
- Union of dancing, singing, and playing instrumental music
- Writing and drawing
- Tattooing
- Arraying and adorning an idol with rice and flowers
- Spreading and arranging beds or couches of flowers, or flowers upon the ground
- Colouring the teeth, garments, hair, nails and bodies, i.e. staining, dyeing, colouring and painting the same
- Fixing stained glass into a floor
- The art of making beds, and spreading out carpets and cushions for reclining
- Playing on musical glasses filled with water
- Storing and accumulating water in aqueducts, cisterns and reservoirs
- Picture making, trimming and decorating
- Stringing of rosaries, necklaces, garlands and wreaths
- Binding of turbans and chaplets, and making crests and top-knots of flowers
- Scenic representations, stage playing Art of making ear ornaments Art of preparing perfumes and odours
- Proper disposition of jewels and decorations, and adornment in dress
- Magic or sorcery
- Quickness of hand or manual skill
- Culinary art, i.e. cooking and cookery
- Making lemonades, sherbets, acidulated drinks, and spirituous extracts with proper flavour and colour
- Tailor's work and sewing
- Making parrots, flowers, tufts, tassels, bunches, bosses, knobs, etc., out of yarn or thread
- Solution of riddles, enigmas, covert speeches, verbal puzzles and enigmatical questions

- A game, which consisted in repeating verses, and as one person finished, another person had to commence at once, repeating another verse, beginning with the same letter with which the last speaker's verse ended, whoever failed to repeat was considered to have lost, and to be subject to pay a forfeit or stake of some kind
- The art of mimicry or imitation
- Reading, including chanting and intoning
- Study of sentences difficult to pronounce. It is played as a game chiefly by women, and children and consists of a difficult sentence being given, and when repeated quickly, the words are often transposed or badly pronounced
- Practice with sword, single stick, quarter staff and bow and arrow
- Drawing inferences, reasoning or inferring
- Carpentry, or the work of a carpenter
- Architecture, or the art of building
- Knowledge about gold and silver coins, and jewels and gems
- Chemistry and mineralogy
- Colouring jewels, gems and beads
- Knowledge of mines and quarries
- Gardening; knowledge of treating the diseases of trees and plants, of nourishing them, and determining their ages
- Art of cock fighting, quail fighting and ram fighting
- Art of teaching parrots and starlings to speak
- Art of applying perfumed ointments to the body, and of dressing the hair with unguents and perfumes and braiding it
- The art of understanding writing in cypher, and the writing of words in a peculiar way
- The art of speaking by changing the forms of words. It is of various kinds. Some speak by changing the beginning and end of words, others by adding unnecessary letters between every syllable of a word, and so on
- Knowledge of language and of the vernacular dialects
- Art of making flower carriages
- Art of framing mystical diagrams, of addressing spells and charms, and binding armlets
- Mental exercises, such as completing stanzas or verses on receiving a part of them; or supplying one, two or three lines when the remaining lines are given indiscriminately from different verses, so as to make the whole an entire verse with regard to its meaning; or arranging the words of a verse written irregularly by separating the vowels from the consonants, or leaving them out altogether; or putting into verse or prose sentences represented by signs or symbols. There are many other such exercises.
- Composing poems
- Knowledge of dictionaries and vocabularies
- Knowledge of ways of changing and disguising the appearance of persons
- Knowledge of the art of changing the appearance of things, such as making cotton to appear as silk, coarse and common things to appear as fine and good
- Various ways of gambling

- Art of obtaining possession of the property of others by means of muntras or incantations
- Skill in youthful sports
- Knowledge of the rules of society, and of how to pay respect and compliments to others
- Knowledge of the art of war, of arms, of armies, etc.
- Knowledge of gymnastics
- Art of knowing the character of a man from his features
- Knowledge of scanning or constructing verses
- Arithmetical recreations
- Making artificial flowers
- Making figures and images in clay

http://www.bharatadesam.com/literature/vatsyayana_kamasutras/vatsyayana_kamasutra_3.php

One-horned young bull. Hieroglyph multiplex: aquatic bird.

Anser indicus, bar-headed goose, Himalayan aquatic bird,"...is a goose that breeds in Central Asia in colonies of thousands near mountain lakes and winters in South Asia, as far south as peninsular India." https://en.wikipedia.org/wiki/Bar-headed_goose कारण्ड [p= 274,3] kAraNDa, *kāraṇḍava m.* a sort of duck R. vii , 31 , 21 (cf. करण्ड.)(Monier-Williams)

Rebus: करडा (p. 137) [karaḍā] Hard from alloy--iron, silver &c.(Marathi)

Rakhigarhi. One-horned young bull, sealing.Hieroglyph: one-horned young bull

kõdā खोंड [khōṇḍa] m A young bull, a bullcalf. (Marathi) Rebus

1: kọ̃ndu or konḍu ।

कुण्डम् m. a hole dug in the ground for receiving consecrated fire (Kashmiri) Rebus
2: A. *kundār*, B. *kũdār*, °*ri*, Or. *kundāru*; H. *kũderā* m. ' one who works a lathe, one who scrapes ', °*rī* f., *kũdernā* ' to scrape, plane, round on a lathe '.(CDIAL 3297).

Hieroglyph: 'rim-of-jar': Phonetic forms: *kan-ka* (Santali) *karṇika* (Sanskrit) Rebus: *karṇī,* supercargo for a boat shipment. *karṇīka* 'account (scribe)'.

Hieroglyph: sprout ligatured to rimless pot: baṭa = rimless pot (Kannada) Rebus: baṭa = a kind of iron; bhaṭa 'furnace; dul 'pair' Rebus: dula 'cast (metal) kolmo 'sprout' Rebus: kolami 'smithy/forge' Thus the composite hieroglyph: furnace, metalcaster smithy-forge

Hieroglyph:मेंढा [mēṇḍhā] A crook or curved end (of a stick) Rebus: meḍ 'iron'.

Nd-1A One-horned young bull, lathe-furnace. 12723 *śrēṣṭrī1 ' clinger '. [√śriṣ1] Phal. *šẽṣṭrī̃* ' flying squirrel '? (CDIAL 12723) Rebus: foreman of a guild: śrḗṣṭha ' most splendid, best ' RV. [śrī́ --]Pa. *seṭṭha* -- ' best ', Aś.shah. man. *sreṭha* -- , gir. *sesṭa* -- , kāl. *seṭha* -- , Dhp. *śeṭha* -- , Pk. *seṭṭha* -- , *siṭṭha* -- ; N. *seṭh* ' great, noble, superior '; Or. *seṭha* ' chief, principal '; Si. *seṭa*, °*ṭu* ' noble, excellent '.(CDIAL 12725) śrēṣṭhin m. ' distinguished man ' AitBr., ' foreman of a guild ', °*nī* -- f. ' his wife ' Hariv. [śrḗṣṭha --]Pa. *seṭṭhin* -- m. ' guild -- master ', Dhp. *śeṭhi*, Pk. *seṭṭhi* -- , *siṭṭhi* -- m., °*iṇī* -- f.; S. *seṭhi* m. ' wholesale merchant '; P. *seṭh* m. ' head of a guild, banker ', *seṭhaṇ*, °*ṇī*f.; Ku.gng. *śēṭh* ' rich man '; N. *seṭh* ' banker '; B. *seṭh* ' head of a guild, merchant '; Or. *seṭhi* ' caste of washermen '; Bhoj. Aw.lakh. *sēṭhi* ' merchant, banker ', H.*seṭh* m., °*ṭhan* f.; G. *śeṭh*, *śeṭhiyɔ* m. ' wholesale merchant, employer, master '; M. *śeṭh*, °*ṭhī*, *śeṭ*, °*ṭī* m. ' respectful term for banker or merchant '; Si. *siṭu*, *hi*° ' banker, nobleman ' H. Smith JA 1950, 208 (or < śiṣṭá -- 2?)(CDIAL 12726)

kondh 'corner' Rebus: *kũdār* 'turner'.sangaDa 'lathe' Rebus: sangAta 'combination'; vajrasamghAta 'adamantine glue'

šẽṣṭrī̃ ' flying squirrel ' (Phal.) Rebus: seṭh ' head of a guild, merchant ' (Bengali)(CDIAL 12726)

kaNDA 'notch' Rebus: kANDA 'excellent metalware'

dula 'pair' Rebus: dul 'cast metal' kolom 'three' Rebus: kolami 'smithy, forge' dula 'pair' Rebus: dul 'cast metal' kolmo 'rice plant' Rebus: kolami 'smithy, forge'

karNaka 'rim of jar' Rebus: karNI 'supercargo'; karNIka 'scribe'

kole.l 'smithy' Rebus: kole.l 'smithy'

koDa 'one' Rebus: koD 'workshop'

aya 'fish' Rebus: aya 'iron' (Gujarati) ayas 'metal' (Rigveda)

kondh 'corner' Rebus: *kũdār* 'turner'

m18 One-horned young bull, lathe-furnace

kondh 'young bull' Rebus: *kũdār* 'turner'.sangaDa 'lathe' Rebus: sangAta 'combination'; vajrasamghAta 'adamantine glue'

Hieroglyph: *baroṭi* 'twelve' *bhārata* 'a factitious alloy of copper, pewter, tin' (Marathi) dula 'pair' Rebus: dul 'cast metal'. The cast metal is pewter called in Meluhha *baraḍo* = spine; backbone (Tulu) Rebus: *baran, bharat* 'mixed alloys' (5 copper, 4 zinc and 1 tin) (Punjabi).

Hieroglyph: karNaka 'rim of jar' Rebus: karNI 'supercargo'; karNIka 'scribe'

Hieroglyph: **kṓṣṭha**2 n. ' pot ' Kauś., ' granary, storeroom ' MBh., ' inner apartment ' lex., °*aka* -- n. ' treasury ', °*ikā* f. ' pan ' Bhpr. [Cf. *kōttha -- , *kōtthala -- : same as prec.?]Pa. *koṭṭha* -- n. ' monk's cell, storeroom ', °*aka*<-> n. ' storeroom '; Pk. *koṭṭha* -- , *kuṭ*°, *koṭṭhaya* -- m. ' granary, storeroom '; Sv. *dāntar* -- *kuṭha* ' fire -- place '; Sh. (Lor.) *kōti* (*ṭh*?) ' wooden vessel for mixing yeast '; K. *kōṭha* m. ' granary ', *kuṭhu* m. ' room ', *kuṭhü* f. ' granary, storehouse '; S. *koṭho* m. ' large room ', °*ṭhī* f. ' storeroom ';

L. *koṭhā* m. ' hut, room, house ', °*ṭhī* f. ' shop, brothel ', awāṇ. *koṭhā* ' house '; P. *koṭṭhā, koṭhā* m. ' house with mud roof and walls, granary ', *koṭṭhī,koṭhī* f. ' big well -- built house, house for married women to prostitute themselves in '; WPah. pāḍ. *kuṭhī* ' house '; Ku. *koṭho* ' large square house ', gng. *kōṭhi* ' room, building '; N. *koṭho* ' chamber ', °*ṭhi* ' shop '; A. *koṭhā, kõṭhā* ' room ', *kuṭhī* ' factory '; B. *koṭhā* ' brick -- built house ', *kuṭhī* ' bank, granary '; Or. *koṭhā* ' brick -- built house ', °*ṭhī* ' factory, granary '; Bi. *koṭhī* ' granary of straw or brushwood in the open '; Mth. *koṭhī* ' grain -- chest '; OAw. *koṭha* ' storeroom '; H. *koṭhā* m. ' granary ', °*ṭhī* f. ' granary, large house ', Marw. *koṭho* m. ' room '; G. *koṭhɔ* m. ' jar in which indigo is stored, warehouse ', °*ṭhī* f. ' large earthen jar, factory '; M.*koṭhā* m. ' large granary ', °*ṭhī* f. ' granary, factory '; Si. *koṭa* ' storehouse '. -- Ext. with -- *ḍa* -- : K. *kūṭhürü* f. ' small room '; L. *koṭhṛī* f. ' small side room '; P. *koṭhṛī*f. ' room, house '; Ku. *koṭheṛī* ' small room '; H. *koṭhrī* f. ' room, granary '; M. *koṭhḍī* f. ' room '; -- with -- *ra* -- : A. *kuṭharī* ' chamber ', B. *kuṭhrī*, Or. *koṭhari;* -- with -- *lla* -- : Sh. (Lor.) *kotul* (*ṭh*?) ' wattle and mud erection for storing grain '; H. *koṭhlā* m., °*lī* f. ' room, granary '; G. *koṭhlɔ* m. ' wooden box '.WPah.kṭg. *kóṭṭhi* f. ' house, quarters, temple treasury, name of a partic. temple ', J. *koṭhā* m. ' granary ', *koṭhī* f. ' granary, bungalow '; Garh.*koṭhu* ' house surrounded by a wall '; Md. *koḍi* ' **frame** ', <-> *koři* ' cage ' (X kōṭṭa --). -- with ext.: OP. *koṭhārī* f. ' crucible ', P. *kuṭhālī* f., H. *kuṭhārī* f.; -- Md. *koṭari*' room '.(CDIAL 3546)

m66 One-horned young bull, lahe-furnace

kondh 'young bull' Rebus: *kũdār* 'turner'.sangaDa 'lathe' Rebus: sangAta 'combination'; vajrasamghAta 'adamantine glue'

goṭo 'kernel' Rebus: : खोट (p. 212) [khōṭa] *f* A mass of metal (unwrought or of old metal melted down); an ingot or wedge. (Marathi) PLUS kolom 'three' Rebus: kolami 'smithy, forge' kamaDha ‘crab’ Rebus: kampaTTa ‘mint, coiner’ PLUS goṭo m. ‘ gold or silver lace ’ (Sindhi) Rebus: : खोट (p. 212) [khōṭa] *f* A mass of metal (unwrought or of old metal melted down); an ingot or wedge. (Marathi) PLUS kolom ‘three’ Rebus: kolami ‘smithy, forge’

Ma. kaṇ, kaṇṇu eye, nipple, star in peacock's tail, bud.(DEDR 1159) Rebus: kan 'copper' PLUS sal ‘splinter’ Rebus: sal ‘workshop’. Thus, together, *sal kan* ‘copper workshop.’

aya ‘fish’ Rebus: aya ‘iron’ ayas ‘metal’ PLUS aDar ‘lid’ Rebus: aduru ‘native metal’

ranku ‘liquid measure’ Rebus: ranku ‘tin’

kolmo ‘rice plant’ Rebus: kolami ‘smithy, forge’

karNaka ‘rim of jar’ Rebus; karNI ‘supercargo’ karNIka ‘scribe’.

m8 One-horned young bull, lathe-furnace

kondh ‘young bull’ Rebus: *kũdār* ‘turner’.sangaDa 'lathe' Rebus: sangAta 'combination'; vajrasamghAta 'adamantine glue' PLUS kandi ‘bead’ Rebus: kanda ‘fire-altar’

kole.l ‘temple’ Rebus: kole.l ‘smithy’
baTa ‘warrior’ Rebus: baTa ‘furnace’

baTa ‘rimless pot’ Rebus: baTa ‘furnace’ Hieroglyph: Ta. caṭṭukam, caṭṭuvam ladle, metal spatula with a long handle for turning and removing a cooked cake. Ma. caṭṭukam ladle, metal spoon; ? caṭṭuvam shoulder-bone (or with 2303 Kol. saṭṭa). Ko. caṭy go·l iron ladle with flat, round blade, for taking rice from pot. Ka. saṭuka, saṭṭu, saṭṭuga, soṭaka ladle, spoon. Koḍ. caṭṭuva wooden spoon used for stirring. Tu. saṭṭi a kind of wooden ladle; saṭṭuga, taṭṭuga a flat kind of trough for serving boiled rice. Te. caṭṭuvamu a sort of spoon with a shallow bowl having holes in it. Ga. (P.) saṭve ladle. Konḍa saṭva ladle made of wood for serving soup or curry. Pe. haṭva ladle; oar. Kuwi (Su.) haṭva ladle. / Cf. Skt. caṭuka- a wooden vessel for taking up fluid; Pkt. (DNM; Norman) caṭṭu- wooden spoon; Turner, CDIAL, no. 4575. (DEDR 2309) Rebus: sattva 'zinc, spelter'; jasta id. (Hindi). Thus, together, the pair of hieroglyh complexes Sign 336 PLUS Sign 89 read: *saṭva baTa kolom* 'zinc furnace smithy'

m6 One-horned young bull, lathe-furnace

This shows the bottom bowl of the 'standard device' superimposed with dotted circles. Since the top portion of the 'device' is a drill-lathe, these dotted circles are orthographic representations of drilled beads which were the hallmark of lapidaries' work of the civilization. Rebus reading of the kandi 'beads' (Pa.) is: kaND, kandu 'fire altar, smelting furnace of a blacksmith' (Santali.Kashmiri)Glyphs of dotted circles on the bottom portion of the 'standard device': kandi (pl. -l) beads, necklace (Pa.); kanti (pl. -l) bead, (pl.) necklace; kandit. bead (Ga.)(DEDR 1215). Rebus: लोहकारकन्दुः f. a blacksmith's smelting furnace (Grierson Kashmiri lex.) (B) {V} ``(pot, etc.) to ^overflow''. See `to be left over'. @B24310. #20851.(B) {V} ``to be ^left over, to be ^saved''. Caus. . @B24300. #20861. Rebus: loa 'iron' (Mu.)Re(B),,(B) {N} ``^iron''. Pl. <-le>

san:ghāḍo, saghaḍī (G.) = firepan; saghaḍī, śaghaḍi = a pot for holding fire (G.)sãghāṛɔ m. 'lathe' (G.) Rebus: san:gatarāśū = stone cutter (S.) jangaḍ iyo 'military guard who accompanies treasure into the treasury'; san:ghāḍiyo, a worker on a lathe (G.)

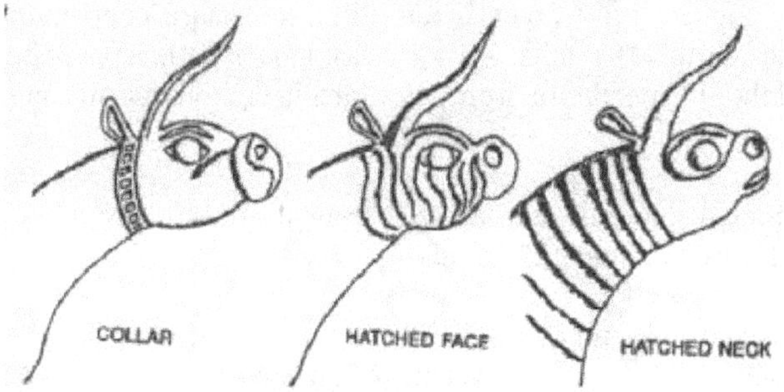

kod. 'one horn'; kot.iyum [kot., kot.i_ neck] a wooden circle put round the neck of an animal (G.)kamarasa_la = waist-zone, waist-band, belt (Te.)kot.iyum [kot., kot.i_ neck] a wooden circle put round the neck of an animal (G.) [cf. the orthography of rings on the neck of one-horned young bull]. ko_d.iya, ko_d.e = young bull; ko_d.elu = plump young bull; ko_d.e = a. male as in: ko_d.e du_d.a = bull calf; young, youthful (Te.lex.) ko_d.iya, ko_d.e young bull; adj. male (e.g., ko_d.e du_d.a bull calf), young, youthful; ko_d.eka~_d.u a young man (Te.); ko_d.e_ bull (Kol.); khor.e male calf (Nk.); ko_d.i cow; ko_r.e young bullock (Kond.a); ko_d.i cow (Pe.); ku_d.i id. (Mand.); ko_d.i id., ox (Kui); ko_di cow (Kuwi); kajja ko_d.i bull; ko_d.i cow (Kuwi)(DEDR 2199). kor.a a boy, a young man (Santali) go_nde bull, ox (Ka.); go_da ox (Te.); konda_ bull (Kol.); ko_nda bullock (Kol.Nk.); bison (Pa.); ko_nde cow (Ga.); ko_nde_ bullock (Ga.); ko_nda_, ko_nda bullock, ox (Go.)(DEDR 2216). Rebus: kot. 'artisan's workshop'.(Kuwi)kod. = place where artisans work (G.lex.)kõda कोंद । कुलालादिकन्दुः f. a kiln; a potter's kiln (Rām. 1446; H. xi, 11); a brick-kiln (Śiv. 133); a lime-kiln. -bal -बल् । कुलालादिकन्दुस्थानम् m. the place where a kiln is erected, a brick or potter's kiln (Gr.Gr. 165)(Kashmiri)

ko_nda bullock (Kol.Nk.); bison (Pa.)(DEDR 2216). Rebus: कोंद kōnda 'engraver, lapidary setting or infixing gems' (Marathi) Grierson takes the word कन्दुः (Skt.) to be a cognate of kaNDa 'pot' rebus: kaNDa 'fire altar' (Santali)

Thus, the bullock or ox glyph seems to be an allograph of 'rim-of-jar' glyph in Indus Script corpora. When two bullocks are juxtaposed, the semantics of pairing point to dol 'likeness, pair'(Kashmiri); rebus: dul 'cast iron'(Santali) Thus, the pair of bullocks or oxen are read rebus: dul kõda 'two bullocks'; rebus: casting furnace or kiln'.

koḍiyum 'heifer' (G.). Rebus: koṭ 'workshop' (Kuwi) koṭe = forge (Santali)kōḍiya, kōḍe = young bull (G.)Rebus: ācāri koṭṭya 'smithy' (Tu.)

Seal m0296. Necks and Faces of a pair of young bulls (with one horn each) flanking a 'standard device' and nine leaves emerging from a stylized tree.

lo 'nine' (Santali); no 'nine' (Bengali); on-patu (Tamil). loa 'species of fig tree, ficus glomerata, the fruit of ficus glomerata (Santali) Rebus: lo 'iron' (Assamese, Bengali); loa 'iron' (Gypsy); lauha 'made of copper or iron', metal, iron (Skt.); lohakaara 'coppersmith, ironsmith' (Pali); lohaara 'blacksmith' (Pt.); lohaLa id. (Oriya); loha 'metal, esp. copper or bronze' (Pali); copper (VS); loho, lo 'metal, ore, iron' (Si.); loha luTi 'iron utensils and implements' (Santali)

dol 'likeness, picture, form' (Santali). Rebus: dul 'cast iron' (Santali) dul 'to cast metal in a mould' (Santali) dul meṛeḍ cast iron (Mundari. Santali)

saṅghāra f. ' chain, string of beads ', (Sindhi): śr̥ṅkhala m.n. ' chain ' MārkP., °*lā* -- f. VarBr̥S., *śr̥ṅkhalaka* -- m. ' chain ' MW., ' chained camel ' Pāṇ. [Similar ending in mḗkhalā --]Pa. *saṅkhalā* -- , °*likā* -- f. ' chain '; Pk. *saṁkala* -- m.n., °*lā* -- , °*lī* -- , °*liā* -- , *saṁkhalā* -- , *siṁkh°*, *siṁkalā* -- f. ' chain ', *siṁkhala* -- n. ' anklet '; Sh. *šăṅāḷi̯* f., (Lor.) *š***lṅāli*, *šiṅ°* ' chain ' (lw .with *š* -- < *śr̥* --), K. *hö̃kal* f.; S. *saṅgharu* m. ' bell round animal's neck ', °*ra* f. ' chain, necklace ', *saṅghāra* f. ' chain, string of beads ', *saṅghirī* f. ' necklace with double row of beads '; L. *saṅglī* f. ' flock of bustard ', awāṇ. *saṅgul* ' chain '; P. *saṅgal* m. ' chain ', ludh. *suṅgal* m.; WPah.bhal. *śaṅgul* m. ' chain with which a soothsayer strikes himself ', *śaṅgli* f. ' chain ', *śiṅkhal* f. ' railing round a cow -- stall ', (Joshi) *śā̃gaḷ* ' door -- chain ', jaun. *śā̃gal*, *śā̃gaḍ* ' chain '; Ku. *sā̃glo* ' doorchain ', gng. *śāṅaw* ' chain '; N. *sāṅlo* ' chain ', °*li* ' small do. ', A. *xikali*, OB. *siṅkala*, B. *sikal*, *sikli*, *chikal*, *chikli*,

(Chittagong) *hĩol* ODBL 454, Or. *sāṅk(h)uḷā, °ḷi, sāṅkoḷi, sikaḷā̆, °ḷi, sikuḷā, °ḷi*; Bi. *sīkaṛ* ' chains for pulling harrow ', Mth. *sī̃kaṛ*; Bhoj. *sī̃kar, sīkarī* ' chain ', OH. *sāṁkaḍa, sīkaḍa* m., . *sā̃kal, sā̃kar, °krī, saṅkal, °klī, sikal, sīkar, °krī* f.; OG. *sāṁkalu* n., G. *sā̃kaḷ, °ḳlī* f. ' chain ', *sā̃kḷũ* n. ' wristlet '; M. *sā̃k(h)aḷ,sāk(h)aḷ, sā̃k(h)ḷī* f. ' chain ', Ko. *sāṁkaḷ*; Si. *säkilla, hä°, ä°* (st. *°ili* --) ' elephant chain '.WPah.kṭg. (kc.) *śáṅgəḷ* f. (obl. -- *i*) ' chain ', J. *śā̃gaḷ* f., Garh. *sā̃gaḷ*. śr̥ṅkhalayati ' enchains ' Daś. [śr̥ṅkhala --]Ku.gng. *śāṅaī* ' intertwining of legs in wrestling ' (< *śr̥ṅkhalita* --); Or. *sāṅkuḷibā* ' to enchain '.(CDIAL 12580, 12581) ***சங்கிலி***[1] *caṅkili, n. < šr̥ṅkhalaā.* [M. *caṅ- kala.*] 1. Chain, link; **தொடர்.** **சங்கிலிபோ லீர்ப்புண்டு (சேதுபு. அகத்.** 12). 2. Land-measuring chain, Gunter's chain 22 yards long; **அளவுச் சங்கிலி.** (C. G.) 3. A superficial measure of dry land=3.64 acres; **ஓர் நிலவளவு.** (G. Tn. D. I, 239). 4. A chain-ornament of gold, inset with diamonds; **வயிரச்சங்கிலி என்னும் அணி. சங்கிலி நுண்டொடர் (சிலப்.** 6, 99).(Tamil) శృంఖలము [śr̥ṅkhalamu] *ṣrinkhalamu.* [Skt.] n. A chain or fetter, especially for an elephant; a chain of silver worn as a man's girdle or zone. సంకెల. ఏనుగుసంకెల, మగవానిమొలనూలు.సంకెల [saṅkela] or సంకిలియ *sankela.* [from Skt. శృంఖలము.] n. A fetter, or iron. సంకెలవాడు *sankela-vāḍu.* n. A convict, a prisoner in irons.(Telugu) शंखळा [śaṅkhaḷā] *f* (Corr. from शृंखला) A chain. शृंखला [śr̥ṅkhalā] *f* S pop. शृंखळा *f* A chain.(Marathi)

saṅgá m. ' battle ' RV., ' contact with ' TS., ' addiction to ' Mn. [√sañj] Pa. *saṅga* -- m. ' attachment, cleaving to ', Dhp. *ṣaǵa*<-> (see sájati: → Khot. *a* -- *ṣaṁga* -- H. W. Bailey BSOAS xi 776), Pk. *saṁga* -- m.; K. *sang* m. ' union '; S. *saṅu* m. ' connexion by marriage ', *saṅgu* m. ' body of pilgrims '; L. *saṅg*, (Ju.) *sãg* m. ' body of pilgrims or travellers ';P. *saṅg* m. ' id., association '; N. *sā̃gi* ' ritual defilement by contact ' (or < **sāṅgiya* -- ?); OB. *sāṅga* ' union, coitus ', B. *sāṅāt* ' companion '; Or. *sāṅga* ' company, companion '; H. *sãgwānā* ' to collect '. -- In an obl. case as an adv. (LM 413 < *sáṁgata* --): Phal. *saṅgī́* ' with, to '; P. *saṅg* ' along with ', Ku.gng.*śaṅ*, N. *saṅa*; Or. *sāṅge, saṅge* ' near, with '; Bhoj. *saṅ* ' with ', H. *saṅg*, G. *sãge*, M. *sãgẽ*. -- In mng. ' company of travellers &c. ', though there is no trace of aspirate, poss. < or at least infl. by saṁghá -- . saṅga -- : WPah.kṭg. (kc.) *sɔ́ṅg* m. ' union, companionship ', kṭg. *sɔ́ṅge* ' together (with), simultaneously, with, by ' prob. ← H. Him.I 212.(CDIAL 13082) 3084 saṅgin ' attached to, fond of ' MBh. [saṅgá --]Pk. *saṁgi* -- , *saṁgilla* -- ' attached to '; S. L. P. *saṅgī* m. ' comrade ' (P. also ' one of a party of pilgrims '), N. *saṅi*, Or. *sāṅga, °gī*, H. *saṅgī* m., M. *sãgyā, sāgyā*m.Addenda: saṅgin -- : WPah.kṭg. (kc.) *sɔ́ṅgi* m. ' friend ', kṭg. *sɔ́ṅgəṇ*, kc. *sɔṅgiṇ* f., J. *saṅgī, saṅgu* m. (prob. ← H. Him.I 212).(CDIAL 13084) *sāṅgaka ' relating to a company '. [saṅgá --]S. *sãgo* m. ' companionship, caravan '.(CDIAL 13328)

सगडी [sagaḍī] *f* (Commonly शेगडी) A pan of live coals or embers.

सांगड (p. 840) [sāṅgaḍa] *m f* (संघट्ट S) A float composed of two canoes or boats bound together: also a link of two pompions &c. to swim or float by. 2 *f* A body formed of two or more (fruits, animals, men) linked or joined together. 3 That member of a turner's apparatus by which the piece to be turned is confined and steadied. सांगडीस धरणें To take into linkedness or close connection with, lit. fig.सांगडणी (p. 840) [sāṅgaḍaṇī] *f* (Verbal of सांगडणें) Linking or joining together.सांगडणें (p. 840) [sāṅgaḍaṇēṃ] *v c* (सांगड) To link, join, or unite together (boats, fruits, animals). 2 Freely. To tie or bind up or unto.

सांगडी (p. 840) [sāṅgaḍī] *f* (Commonly सांगड) A float &c.

सांगड्या (p. 840) [sāṅgaḍyā] *a* sometimes सांगडी *a* That works a सांगड or canoe-float.

सांगाडा (p. 840) [sāṅgāḍā] *m* The skeleton, box, or frame (of a building, boat, the body &c.), the hull, shell, compages. 2 Applied, as *Hulk* is, to any animal or thing huge and unwieldy.

सांगाडी (p. 840) [sāṅgāḍī] *f* The machine within which a turner confines and steadies the piece he has to turn.

संगति [saṅgati] *c* (S) pop. संगती *c* or संगत *c* A companion, associate, comrade, fellow. सांगाती [sāṅgātī] *a* (Better संगती) A companion, associate, fellow.(Marathi. Molesworth)

खोदकाम [khōdakāma] *n* Sculpture; carved work or work for the carver.

खोदगिरी [khōdagirī] *f* Sculpture, carving, engraving: also sculptured or carved work.

खोदणावळ [khōdaṇāvaḷa] *f* (खोदणें) The price or cost of sculpture or carving.

खोदणी [khōdaṇī] *f* (Verbal of खोदणें) Digging, engraving &c. 2 fig. An exacting of money by importunity. *v* लाव, मांड. 3 An instrument to scoop out and cut flowers and figures from paper. 4 A goldsmith's die.

खोदणें [khōdaṇēṃ] *v c & i* (H) To dig. 2 To engrave. खोद खोदून विचारणें or -पुसणें To question minutely and searchingly, *to probe*.

खोंदळणें [khōndaḷaṇēṃ] *v c & i* See खंवदळणें.

खोदाई [khōdāī] *f* (H) Price or cost of digging or of sculpture or carving.

खोदींव [khōdīṃva] *p* of खोदणें Dug. 2 Engraved, carved, sculptured.

Ta. kōṭu (*in cpds.* kōṭṭu-) horn, tusk, branch of tree, cluster, bunch, coil of hair, line, diagram, bank of stream or pool; kuvaṭu branch of a tree; kōṭṭāṉ, kōṭṭuvāṉ rock horned-owl (cf. 1657 Ta. kuṭiñai). *Ko.* ko·ṛ (*obl.* ko·ṭ-) horns (one horn is kob), half of hair on each side of parting, side in game, log, section of bamboo used as fuel, line marked out. *To.* kw&idie;*obl.* kw&idier;ṭ-) horn, branch, path across stream in thicket. *Ka.* kōḍu horn, tusk, branch of a tree; kōṟ horn. *Tu.* kōḍů, kōḍu horn.

Te. kōḍu rivulet, branch of a river. *Pa.* kōḍ (*pl.* kōḍul) horn. *Ga.* (Oll.) kōr (*pl.* kōrgul) id. *Go.* (Tr.) kōr (*obl.* kōt-, *pl.*kōhk) horn of cattle or wild animals, branch of a tree; (W. Ph. A. Ch.) kōr (*pl.* kōhk), (S.) kōr (*pl.* kōhku), (Ma.) kōṟu (*pl.* kōẖku) horn; (M.) kohk branch (*Voc.*980); (LuS.) kogoo a horn. *Kui* kōju (*pl.* kōska) horn, antler.(DEDR 2200)

కోడె [kōḍe] *kōḍe*. [Tel.] n. A bullcalf. కోడెదూడ. A young bull. కాడిమరపదగినదూడ. Plumpness, prime. తరుణము. జోడుకోడయలు a pair of bullocks. కోడె adj. Young. కోడెత్రాచు a young snake, one in its prime. "కోడెనాగముం బలుగుల రేడుతన్ని కొని పోవుతెరంగు" రామా. vi. కోడెకాడు *kōḍe-kāḍu*. n. A young man. పడుచువాడు. A lover విటుడు.

Te. kōḍiya, kōḍe young bull; *adj.* male (e.g. kōḍe dūḍa bull calf), young, youthful; kōḍekā̃ḍu a young man. *Kol.* (Haig) kōḍē bull. *Nk.* khoṛe male calf.*Konḍa* kōḍi cow; kōṛe young bullock. *Pe.* kōḍi cow. *Manḍ.* kūḍi id. *Kui* kōḍi id., ox. *Kuwi* (F.) kōdi cow; (S.) kajja kōḍi bull; (Su. P.) kōḍi cow. DED(S) (DEDR 2199)

कोंडण [kōṇḍaṇa] *f* A fold or pen.कोंडवाड [kōṇḍavāḍa] *n f* C (कोंडणें & वाडा) A pen or fold for cattle.

खोंड [khōṇḍa] *m* A young bull, a bullcalf. 2 A variety of जोंधळा. खोंडरूं [khōṇḍarūṃ] *n* A contemptuous form of खोंडा in the sense of कांबळा-cowl.खोंडा [khōṇḍā] *m* A कांबळा of which one end is formed into a cowl or hood. 2 fig. A hollow amidst hills; a deep or a dark and retiring spot; a dell. 3 (also खोंडी& खोंडें) A variety of जोंधळा.खोंडी [khōṇḍī] *f* An outspread shovelform sack (as formed temporarily out of a कांबळा, to hold or fend off grain, chaff &c.) See under खुंडी. 2 A species or variety of जोंधळा.

G. *godhɔ* m. ' bull ', °*dhũ* n. ' young bull ', OG. *godhalu* m. ' entire bull ', G. *godhliyũ* n. ' young bull '(CDIAL 4315)

*cunda1 ' wood or ivory work '. [Cf. kunda -- 1]Pa. *cunda* -- m. ' ivory worker '; Or. *cundibā* ' to do woodwork '.(CDIAL 4861) *cundakāra m. ' turner '. [Cf. kundakara -- . -- *cunda -- 1, kāra -- 1]Pa. *cundakāra* -- m.; Ku. *cunāro* ' maker of wooden vessels ', N. *cunāro, can°, cũdāro, cãd°*.(CDIAL 4862)

kunda1 m. ' a turner's lathe ' lex. [Cf. *cunda -- 1]N. *kũdnu* ' to shape smoothly, smoothe, carve, hew ', *kũduwā* ' smoothly shaped '; A. *kund* ' lathe ', *kundiba* ' to turn and smooth in a lathe ', *kundowā* ' smoothed and rounded '; B. *kũd* ' lathe ', *kũdā, kõdā* ' to turn in a lathe '; Or. *kū̆nda* ' lathe ', *kũdibā, kũ̄d°* ' to turn ' (→ Drav. Kur. *kũ̄d* ' lathe '); Bi. *kund* ' brassfounder's lathe '; H. *kunnā* ' to shape on a lathe ', *kuniyā* m. ' turner ', *kunwā* m.(CDIAL 3295) kundakara m. ' turner ' W. [Cf. *cundakāra -- : kunda -- 1, kará -- 1]A. *kundār*, B. *kũdār*, °*ri*, Or. *kundāru*; H. *kũderā* m. ' one who works a lathe, one who scrapes ', °*rī* f., *kũdernā* ' to scrape, plane, round on a lathe '.(CDIAL 3297)

m238A Two-horned bison, auroch, trough

balivárda (*balīv*° ŚBr.) m. ' ox, bull ' TBr., *balivanda-* m. Kāṭh., *barivarda* -- m. lex. [Poss. a cmpd. of *balín* -- (cf. *balilla --) and a non -- Aryan word for ' ox ' (cf. esp. Nahālī *baddī* and poss. IA. forms like Sik. *pāḍō* ' bull < *pāḍḍa -- : EWA ii 419 with lit.)]

Pa. *balivadda* -- m. ' ox ', Pk. *balīvadda* -- , *balidda* -- , *baladda* -- m. (cf. *balaya* -- m. < **balaka* -- ?); L. *baledā*, mult. *baled* m. ' herd of bullocks ' (→ S.*b̲aledo* m.);

P. *bald*, *baldh*, *balhd* m. ' ox ', *baled*, *baledā* m. ' herd of oxen ', ludh. *bahld*, *balēd* m. ' ox '; Ku. *balad* m. ' ox ', gng. *bald*, N. (Tarai) *barad*, A.*balad*(*h*), B. *balad*, Or. *baḷada*, Bi. *barad*(*h*), Mth. *barad* (hyper -- hindiism *baṛad*), Bhoj. *baradh*, Aw.lakh. *bardhu*, H. *balad*, *barad*(*h*), *bardhā* m. (whence *baladnā* ' to bull a cow '),

G. *baḷad* m.Addenda: balivárda -- [Cf. Ap. *valivaṇḍa* -- ' mighty ', OP. *balavaṇḍā*]: WPah.kc. *bɔḷəd* m., kṭg. *bɔḷd* m. (LNH 30 *bŏḷd*), J. *bald* m., Garh. *baḷda* ' bullock '.(CDIAL 9176) balivardin m. ' *oxherd ' (nom. prop. Kāś.). [bali- várda --]P. *baledī* m. ' oxherd '; Ku. *baldiyā* ' cattle -- dealer '; H. *baredī* m. ' herdsman '(CDIAL 9177)

m278A elephant karibha 'trunk of elephant' (Pali) ibha 'elephant' Rebus: karba 'iron' ib 'iron'. kole.l 'temple' Rebus: kole.l 'smithy' kolmo 'rice plant' Rebus: kolami 'smithy, forge' gaNDa 'four' Rebus: kanda 'fire-altar' sal 'splinter' Rebus: sal 'workshop' kondh 'corner' Rebus: *kūdār* 'turner'

m276A rhinoceros, trough
kāṇṭā 'rhinoceros (Tamil). Rebus: *kāṇḍa* 'tools, pots and pans and metal-ware' (Gujarati)

பத்தர்[1] pattar, n. 1. See பத்தல், 1, 4, 5. 2. Wooden trough for feeding animals; தொட்டி. பன்றிக் கூழ்ப்பத்தரில் (நாலடி, 257). 3. Cocoanut shell or gourd used as a vessel; குடுக்கை. கொடிக்காய்ப்பத்தர் (கல்லா. 40, 3).

பத்தர்[2] pattar , n. < T. battuḍu. A caste title of goldsmiths; தட்டார் பட்டப்பெயருள் ஒன்று. (Tamil Lexicon, p. 2461)

It is significant that both பட்டறை[1] paṭṭaṟai and பத்தர் pattar refer to a guild (of workmen, goldsmiths), community, factory. பட்டறை[1] paṭṭaṟai , n. < பட்டடை[1]. 1. See பட்டடை, 1, 3, 5, 7, 8, 12, 14. 2. Machine; யந்திரம். 3. Rice-hulling machine; நெல்லுக் குத்தும் யந்திரம். Mod. 4. Factory; தொழிற்சாலை. பட்டறை[2] paṭṭaṟai , n. < K. paṭṭale. 1. Community; சனக்கூட்டம். 2. Guild, as of workmen; தொழிலாளர் சமுதாயம். (Tamil, p. 2422)

Hieroglyph: The ancient Meluhha (Indian sprachbund, speech) form could be Bi. baṛahī, Bhoj. H. baṛhaī m., signified by the hieroglyph: baḍhi 'boar, rhinoceros'; variant: varAha 'boar' (Samskritam) वराह [p= 923,2] *m.* (derivation doubtful) a boar , hog , pig , wild boar RV. &c (ifc. it denotes , " superiority , pre-eminence " ; » g. व्याघ्रा*दि) varāhá -- , *varā́hu* -- m. ‘ wild boar ’ RV Pa. Pk. *varāha* -- m. ‘ boar ’; A. B. *barā* ‘ boar ’ (A. also ‘ sow, pig ’), Or. *barāha*, (Sambhalpur)

Rebus: bar.ea 'merchant' (Santali). vardhaki m. ‘ carpenter ’ MBh. [√vardh] Pa. vaḍḍhaki -- m. ‘ carpenter, building mason ’; Pk. vaḍḍhaï -- m. ‘ carpenter ’, °aïa -- m. ‘ shoemaker ’; WPah. jaun. bāḍhōī ‘ carpenter ’, (Joshi) bāḍhi m., N. baṛhaï, baṛahi, A. bārai, B. bāṛaï, °ṛui, Or. baṛhaï, °ṛhāi, (Gaṛjād) bāṛhoi, Bi. baṛahī, Bhoj. H. baṛhaī m., M. vāḍhāyā m., Si. vaḍu -- vā. WPah.kṭg. báḍḍhi m. ‘ carpenter ’; kṭg. bəṛhe\i, báṛhi, kc. baṛhe ← H. beside genuine báḍḍhi Him.I 135), J. bāḍhi, Garh. baṛhai, A. also bāṛhai AFD 94; Md. vaḍīn, vaḍin pl. (CDIAL 11375)

Text of inscription:

kaNDa 'backbone' Rebus: kANDa 'excellent metal'

baTa ‘rimless pot’ Rebus: baTa ‘furnace’ Hieroglyph: caṭṭuvam 'ladle' Rebus: *saṭva* 'zinc'

kolom 'three' Rebus: kolami 'smithy, forge'

kANda 'arrow' Rebus: kANDa 'excellent metal'

Water-buffalo, bos gaurus

Hieroglyph: rāngo 'water buffalo bull' (Ku.N.)(CDIAL 10559) Rebus: rango 'pewter'. ranga, rang pewter is an alloy of tin, lead, and antimony (anjana) (Santali) Hieroglyphs: dul 'two'; ayo 'fish'; kANDa 'arrow': dula 'cast' ayo 'iron, metal' (Gujarati. Rigveda); kANDa 'metalware, pots and pans, tools' (Marathi) Hieroglyph: Rings on neck: koDiyum (Gujarati) koṭiyum = a wooden circle put round the neck of an animal; koṭ = neck (Gujarati)Rebus: koD 'artisan's workshop'(Kuwi) koD = place where artisans work (Gujarati) koṭe 'forge' (Mu.) koṭe meṛed = forged iron, in contrast to dul meṛed, cast iron (Mundari)

m1103A zebu पोळ [pōḷa] *m* A bull dedicated to the gods, marked with a trident and discus, and set at large. poL 'zebu' Rebus: poLa 'magnetite'. खांडा (p. 202) [khāṇḍā] A

jag, notch, or indentation (as upon the edge of a tool or weapon). (Marathi) Rebus: khaṇḍā 'excellent metalware' as in lokhaṇḍā. eraka 'nave of wheel' Rebus: eraka 'metal infusion, copper'; ranku 'liquid measure' Rebus: ranku 'tin'; kolmo 'rice plant' Rebus: kolami 'smithy, forge' dula 'pair' rebus: dul 'cast metal' Thus, smithy for metalcastings with baTa 'rimless pot' Rebus: baTa 'furnace' .
baTa 'rimless pot' Rebus: baTa 'furnace' Hieroglyph: caṭṭuvam 'ladle' Rebus: *saṭva* 'zinc'

kole.l 'temple' Rebus: kole.l 'smithy, forge.'

m1118 पोळ [pōḷa] *m* A bull dedicated to the gods, marked with a trident and discus, and set at large. poL 'zebu' Rebus: poLa 'magnetite'; gaNDa 'four' Rebus: kanda 'fire-altar' aya 'fish' Rebus: aya 'iron' ayas 'metal' Together: ayaskANDa 'excellent iron' (Panini) A varriant hieroglyph multiplex is presented on Kalibangan 32 seal: fish PLUS arrow: ayas PLUS kANDa 'arrow' Rebus: ayaskANDa 'excellent metal, iron'.

Kalibangan 32 the hieroglyphs presented relate to the lexemes: ayas + kaNDa read rebus: metal smelter (furnace). The Harappa seal presents the hieroglyphs: kodo 'millet' (Mu.) + kolmo 'three (numeral strokes)'(Mu.) read rebus: konda 'casting furnace, kiln' + kolami 'forge, smithy' (Te.)

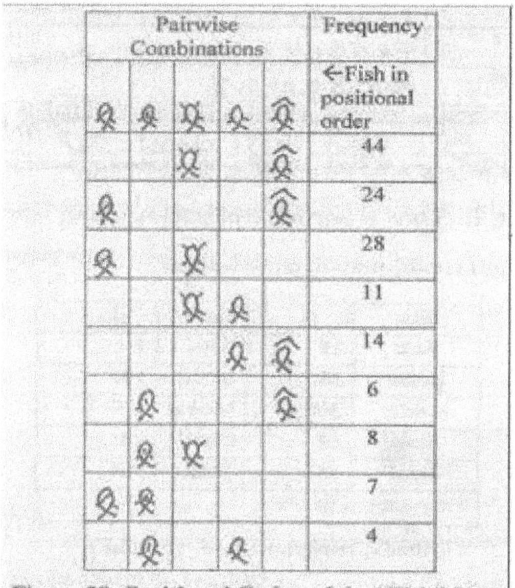
Pairwise Combinations
Frequency
←Fish in positional order
44
24
28
11
14
6
8
7
4
Figure 20: Positional Order of the "Fish" Signs

Fish + corner, *aya koṇḍa*, 'metal turned or forged'
Fish, *aya* 'metal'
Fish + scales, *aya ãs (amśu)* 'metallic stalks of stone ore'. Vikalpa: *badhoṛ* 'a species of fish with many bones' (Santali) Rebus: *baḍhoe* 'a carpenter, worker in wood'; *badhoria* 'expert in working in wood'(Santali)
Fish + splinter, *aya aduru* 'smelted native metal'
Fish + sloping stroke, *aya ḍhāḷ* 'metal ingot'
Fish + arrow or allograph, Fish + circumscribed four short strokes

Santali lexeme, *hako* 'fish' is concordant with a proto-Indic form which can be identified as *ayo* in many glosses, Munda, Sora glosses in particular, of the Indian linguistic area. *beḍa hako (ayo)* 'fish' (Santali); *beḍa* 'either of the sides of a hearth' (G.) Munda: So. *ayo* `fish'. Go. ayu `fish'. Go <ayu> (Z), <ayu?u> (Z),, <ayu?> (A) {N} ``^fish". Kh. kaDOG `fish'. Sa. Hako `fish'. Mu. hai (H) ~ haku(N) ~ haikO(M) `fish'. Ho haku `fish'. Bj. hai `fish'. Bh.haku `fish'. KW haiku ~ hakO |Analyzed hai-kO, ha-kO (RDM). Ku. Kaku`fish'.@(V064,M106) Mu. ha-i, haku `fish' (HJP). @(V341) ayu>(Z), <ayu?u> (Z) <ayu?>(A) {N} ``^fish". #1370. <yO>\\<AyO>(L) {N} ``^fish". #3612. <kukkulEyO>,,<kukkuli-yO>(LMD) {N} ``prawn". !Serango dialect. #32612. <sArjAjyO>,,<sArjAj>(D) {N} ``prawn". #32622. <magur-yO>(ZL) {N} ``a kind of ^fish". *Or.<>. #32632. <ur+GOl-Da-yO>(LL) {N} ``a kind of ^fish". #32642.<bal.bal-yO>(DL) {N} ``smoked fish". #15163. Vikalpa: Munda: <aDara>(L) {N} ``^scales of a fish, sharp bark of a tree".#10171. So<aDara>(L) {N} ``^scales of a fish, sharp bark of a tree".

Indian mackerel Ta. *ayirai, acarai, acalai* loach, sandy colour, *Cobitis thermalis*; *ayilai* a kind of fish. Ma.*ayala* a fish, mackerel, scomber; *aila, ayila* a fish; *ayira* a kind of small fish, loach (DEDR 191) aduru native metal (Ka.); ayil iron (Ta.) ayir, ayiram any ore (Ma.); ajirda karba very hard iron (Tu.)(DEDR 192). Ta. ayil javelin, lance, surgical knife, lancet.Ma. ayil javelin, lance; ayiri surgical knife, lancet. (DEDR 193). aduru = gan.iyinda tegadu karagade iruva aduru = ore taken from the mine and not subjected to melting in a furnace (Ka. Siddhānti Subrahmaṇya' Śastri's new interpretation of the AmarakoŚa, Bangalore, Vicaradarpana Press, 1872, p.330); adar = fine sand (Ta.); ayir – iron dust, any ore (Ma.) Kur. adar the waste of pounded rice, broken grains, etc. Malt. adru broken grain (DEDR 134). Ma. aśu thin, slender;ayir, ayiram iron dust.Ta. ayir subtlety, fineness, fine sand, candied sugar; ? atar fine sand, dust. அய.ர[3] ayir, n. 1. Subtlety, fineness; நணசம. (த_வ_.) 2. [M. ayir.] Fine sand; நணமணல. (மலசலப. 92.) ayiram, n. Candied sugar; ayil, n. cf. ayas. 1. Iron; 2. Surgical knife, lancet; Javelin, lance; ayilavan̲, Skanda, as bearing a javelin (DEDR 341).Tu. gadarů a lump (DEDR 1196)

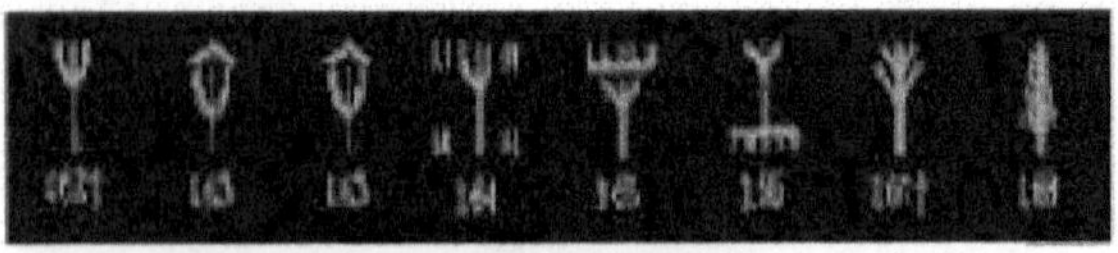

Sign 162 (Mahadevan) and related ligatured signs

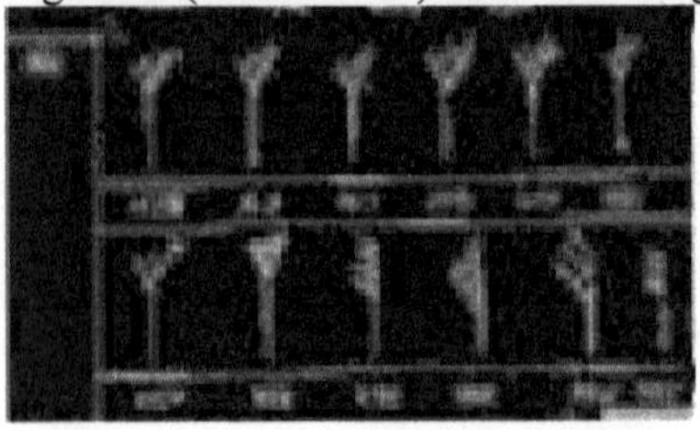

Sign 169 and variants.

One 'plant' glyph shows three prongs (as on the Harappa zebu seal); another shows five. (i.e. Sign 162 - with three prongs and Sign 169 - with five prongs)

kūli-dolu rice plant; (Isr.) dulomi plant. (DEDR 3517) Rebus: dul 'cast (metal)(Santali)

Vikalpa (alternative): Three prongs glyph (Sign 162) of the plant may denote kodo 'millet'. Five prongs glyph (Sign 169) of the plant may denote tagara 'a kind of flowering tree' (Telugu). If this vikalpa holds, the scribe and artisan may have used the two signs distinctly to denote types of casting or smelting furnaces: one for tin (tagaraka) and the other for other metals.

kammarsāla 'pannier' (Telugu)Rebus: karmāraśāla = workshop of blacksmith (Skt.) Synonym: kammāra [Vedic karmāra] a smith, a worker in metals generally D ii.126, A v.263; a silversmith Sn 962= Dh 239; Ji.223; a goldsmith J iii.281; v.282. The smiths in old India do not seem to be divided into black -- , gold -- and silver -- smiths, but seem to have been able to work equally well in iron, gold, and silver, as can be seen e. g. from Jiii.282 and VvA 250, where the smith is the maker of a needle. They were constituted into a guild, and some of them were well -- to -- do as appears from what is said of Cunda at D ii.126; owing to their usefulness they were held in great esteem by the people and king alike J iii.281. (Pali.lex.)

Catalogs of *pola, kuṇṭha, goṭa, bichi* native metalwork in Meluhha Indus script hieroglyphs

Mirror:https://www.academia.edu/8489879/Catalog

Boris Hlebec's research article of 2014, on the origin of 'copper' words in some European languages provides a framework for a philological tracking of of other metalwork terms in Indus writing of Meluhha glosses.

Glosses for three mineral ores in Asuri (Meluhha) speech to distinguish among three types of ferrite (iron) ores are: *pola* (magnetite), *gota* (laterite), *bichi* (hematite). The three ferrous oxide minerals are represented in Meluhha hieroglyphs. Ferrous oxide metalwork is denoted by the Meluhha gloss *aduru*, 'native metal'. It is notable that this gloss is found to be cognate with other metal forms:*ayil* iron (Tamil) *ayir, ayiram* any ore (Malayalam); *ajirda karba* very hard iron (Tulu); aduru 'native metal' (Kannada)(DEDR 192). This etymon cluster gives the early semantics of 'native metal' that it may denote any stone ore (such as *bicu*) which produced hard metal after smelting.

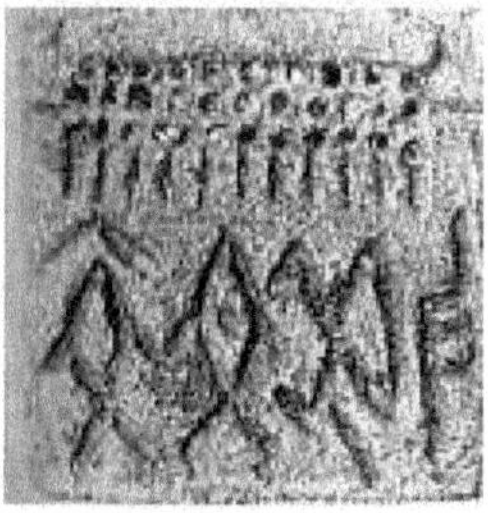

Lothal 51

Zebu, *bos indicus.* Hieroglyphs on the pictorial motif of this seal are: 1. Zebu; 2. Hump; 3. Dewlap.

A type of hard native metal, ferrous oxide – *kuṇṭha munda (loha)* is denoted by *khũṭ* 'zebu'/ *mũ̃ḍhā* 'hump' hieroglyphs.

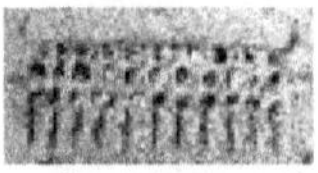

pola, 'magnetite' is denoted by *pōḷī,* 'dewlap, honeycomb' hieroglyphs.

goṭi, 'silver, laterite' are denoted by *goṭa*, 'seed' hieroglyph.

bichi , 'hematite' is denoted by hieroglyph *bicha* 'scorpion' (Assamese)
Rebus: *bica* 'stone ore' (Santali).

A Meluhha gloss for hard stone ore or iron stone is *mẽṛhẽt, meḍ* 'iron' (Mu.Ho.) which is denoted by the hieroglyph, 'markhor'. Meluhha glosses are annexed which indicate association with cire perdue (or lost wax) method of casting metals using beeswax, particularly in the glosses for *miedź, med'* 'copper' in Northern Slavic and Altaic languages and in Meluhha denoting both 'copper' and 'honey', beeswax'. Meluhha trade transactions along the Tin Road may explain the presence of Meluhha glosses in northern Europe.

C-23 a

Chanhudaro 23a *miṇḍāl* 'markhor' (Tōrwālī) *meḍho* a ram, a sheep (Gujarati)(CDIAL 10120) Rebus: *mẽṛhẽt, meḍ* 'iron' (Mu.Ho.)

loa 'ficus religiosa' Rebus: *lo* 'iron, copper' (Sanskrit) PLUS unique ligatures: लोखंड [lōkhaṇḍa] *n* (लोह S) Iron. लोखंडाचे चणे खावविणें or चारणें To oppress grievously.लोखंडकाम [lōkhaṇḍakāma] *n* Iron work; that portion (of a building, machine &c.) which consists of iron. 2 The business of an ironsmith.लोखंडी [lōkhaṇḍī] *a* (लोखंड) Composed of iron; relating to iron. (Marathi)

sal 'splinter' Rebus: sal 'workshop'

1. Zebu

पोळ [pōḷa] *m* A bull dedicated to the gods, marked with a trident and discus, and set at large.

aḍar ḍangra 'zebu' read rebus: *aduru ḍhangar* 'native-unsmelted-metal blacksmith' (Santali); *aduru* denotes 'unsmelted, native metal'. *ḍhangar* 'blacksmith'

(Maithili) aduru ಗಣಿಯಿಂದ ತೆಗದು ಕರಗದೆ ಇರುವ ಅದುರು (Kannada) *gan.iyinda tegadu karagade iruva aduru* = ore taken from the mine and not subjected to melting in a furnace (Ka. Siddhānti Subrahmaṇya Śastri's new interpretation of the Amarakośa, Bangalore, Vicaradarpana Press, 1872, p.330). *adar* = fine sand (Tamil) *aduru* native metal (Kannada); *ayil* iron (Tamil) *ayir, ayiram* any ore (Malayalam); *ajirda karba* very hard iron (Tulu)(DEDR 192). Rebus: *ḍhangar* 'blacksmith' (Maithili)

khũṭ m' Brahmani bull ' (Kathiawar).(CDIAL 3899) (Kathiawar) *khũṭro* m. ' entire bull used for agriculture, not for breeding'(Gujarati). Rebus 1: *khũṭ* 'community' (Guild). Cf. *khũṭ* a community, sect, society, division, clique, schism, stock (Santali) *kuṭhi, kut.i* (Or.; Sad. *koṭhi*) the smelting furnace of the blacksmith.

kuṇṭha munda (loha) 'hard iron (native metal)'

Allograph: कुंठणें [kuṇṭhaṇēṃ] *v i* (कुंठ S) To be stopped, detained, obstructed, arrested in progress (Marathi)

2. Hump

H. *muḍḍhā* m. ' shoulder ', *mũḍhā* m. ' lump, hump, shoulder ' Or. *muṇḍā* ' lump '.(CDIAL 10189) Rebus: *muṇḍa* 'iron' (Sanskrit) mRdu, 'soft', *kuṇṭha*, 'hard', kad*āra* 'brittle' are three varieties of *muṇḍa loha*(Vagbhata, *Rasaratnasamuccaya*, 69-74). *muṇḍitam*, *muṇḍa loham* 'iron'; *muṇḍajam* 'steel' (Sanskrit) Thus, zebu reads rebus: *kuṇṭha munda (loha),* a type of iron native metal. (Vagbhata, *Rasaratnasamuccaya*, 69-74).
S. *gũmbaṭu* m. ' bullock's hump '; L. *gumbaṭ* m.,*gummaṭ* f. ' bullock's hump ', mult. *gummaṭ* m. ' knob on yoke '(CDIAL 4217) Rebus: కుంపటి (p. 0289) [kumpaṭi] *kumpaṭi*. [Tel.] n. A chafing dish, a goldsmith's portable furnace
3. Dewlap

पोळी [pōḷī] dewlap. Rebus: Russian gloss, *bulat* is cognate *pola* 'magnetite' iron in Asuri (Meluhha). Magnetite is the most magnetic of all the naturally occurring igneous and metamorphic rocks with black or brownish-black with a metallic luster. These magnetite ore stones could have been identified as *pola* iron by Meluhha speakers. Kannada gloss *pola* meaning 'point of the compass' may link with the characteristic of magnetite iron used to create a compass.*pŏlāduwu* made of steel; *pŏlād* प्वलाद् or *phōlād* फोलाद् मृदुलोहविशेषः] m. steel (Gr.M.; Rām. 431, 635, *phōlād*). *pŏlödi pōlödi phōlödi* लोहविशेषमयः adj. c.g. of steel, steel (Kashmiri) urukku what is melted, fused metal, steel.(Malayalam); ukk 'steel' (Telugu)(DEDR 661) This is cognate with famed 'wootz'steel. "Polad, Faulad" for steel in late Indian languages is traceable to Pokkhalavat, Polahvad. Pokkhalavat is the name of Pushkalavati, capital of Gandhara famed for iron and steel products.

Allograph: पोळें [pōḷēṃ] 'honeycomb' (shown as a pictorial motif on Lothal Seal 51). Lothal Seal 51

Pictorial motif on Seal Lothal 51 is a honeycomb.

The pictorial motif shows two rows with 12 holes in each row.
Ku. *nak -- poṛ* ' nostril '; N. *poro* ' small hole ' (or < 2); G. *poṛũ* n. ' thin scaly crust ' (semant. cf. *pōppa --); M. *poḷ*, *°ḷẽ* n. ' honeycomb ' (or < 3: semant. cf. *pōka--) L. *polā* ' hollow, porous, loose (of soil) '; M. see 1.4. Pk. *polla* -- , *°aḍa* -- , *pulla* -- ' hollow '; P. *pollā* ' hollow ', *pol* m., *pulāī* f. ' hollowness '; Or. *pola* ' hollow ', sb. ' puffed -- up pastry ', *polā* ' empty '; G. *poli* f. ' cavity ', *polũ*, *polrũ* ' hollow ', *polāṇ* n. ' hollowness '; M. *pol* n. ' empty tube or grain ', *polā* ' hollow '; WPah.kṭg. *pollɔ* ' hollow ', J. *polā*.(CDIAL 8398) *Br.* pōlō hollow, empty; Ta. poḷḷal boring a hole, chiselling, hole, rent, fissure, hollow in a tree; poḷ, poḷḷai hole; Kuwi. porongo hollow; (Isr.) poloṅgã hollow in a tree. (DEDR 4560). Rebus: *pola,* 'magnetite'

baroṭi 'twelve' *bhārata* 'a factitious alloy of copper, pewter, tin' (Marathi) dula 'pair' Rebus: dul 'cast metal'. The cast metal is pewter called in Meluhha *baraḍo* = spine; backbone (Tulu) Rebus: *baran, bharat* 'mixed alloys' (5 copper, 4 zinc and 1 tin) (Punjabi).

The pictorial motif is ligatured with a currycomb.
khareḍo = a currycomb (Gujarati) खरारा [*kharārā*] *m* (H) A currycomb. 2 Currying a horse. (Marathi) Rebus: करडा [*karaḍā*] Hard from alloy--iron, silver &c. (Marathi) *kharādī* ' turner' (Gujarati)
Rebus reading of the hieroglyph: *polā* 'hollow, poli 'honeycomb' Rebus: *pola*, 'magnetite' ore PLUS *kōḍu* horn Rebus: *kōḍu* 'workshop' PLUS *khareḍo* 'currycomb' Rebus: *karaḍā* 'hard alloy'

Text of inscription: *aya aḍaren* (homonym: *aduru*) 'alloy native metal' *aya kāṇḍa* 'alloy metalware'
kamaḍha 'crab' Rebus: *kammaṭa* 'mint, coiner'.*ḍato* = claws of crab (Santali) Rebus: *dhātu* 'mineral ore'
PLUS खांडा [*khāṇḍā*] *m* A jag, notch, or indentation (as upon the edge of a tool or weapon). Rebus: *kāṇḍa* 'tools, pots and pans and metal-ware' Thus, mint metalware, ore.

kolom 'three' Rebus: kolami 'smithy, forge' with circumscript: | *koḍa* 'one' Rebus: *koḍ* 'workshop' dula 'pair' Rebus: dul 'cast metal'. Thus metal smithy castings workshop.
kōḍu horn (Kannada. Tulu. Tamil) Rebus: *kōḍu horn Rebus: 'workshop'*. Also ligatured is a hieroglyph ligature which denotes a hard alloy (perhaps derived from adding magnetite ore):

Allograph: పొల [pola] or పొలసు *pola*. పొలుసు [polusu][Telugu] A scale of a fish. చేపమీది పొలుసు. *Tu.* poḍasů scales of fish. *Te.* pola, polasu, polusu id. *Kui* plōkosi id. (DEDR 4480). పొలుపు [polupu] or పొల్పు *polupu*. [Telugu] Firmness,స్థైర్యము. "పొలుపుమీరిన నెలవంకిబొమలు జూచి, రమణదళుకొత్తు బింబాధరంబుజూచి." Rukmang. i. 158

gota, laterite

The gloss used by Meluhha speakers for laterite iron ores is *gota.*

In rebus readings of some hieroglyphs, the decipherment has been suggested as: dulo 'hole' Rebus: dul 'cast metal'.

An alternative reading could be that the hieroglyph denoted *goṭa*, laterite, deploying small globular shapes to denote *goṭ* ' a fruit, whole piece'. In Munda etyma, the gloss *goṭ* is used as a numeral intensive suffix. Rebus reading of the hieroglyph can thus refer to metal castings achieved using *gota*, 'laterite' mineral ore. This is a possible alternative technical specification reading as alloys with laterite ores -- for hieroglyphs deciphered as dul 'cast metal'.

Thus, when three linear strokes are deployed the rebus reading could be: *kolmo goṭa* 'count of three' Rebus: *kolami got* 'furnace for laterite stone ore'. Almost all hieroglyphs with use of numeral counts can be read with this suffix: *goṭa* 'numerative particle'.

Laterites are rusty soil types with iron oxides rich in iron and aluminium. They are formed in hot and wet tropical areas. Laterites can be easily cut with a spade into regular-sized blocks.

P. *goṭṭā* ' gold or silver lace ', H. *goṭā* m. ' edging of such ' (→ K. *goṭa* m. ' edging of gold braid ', S. *goṭo* m. ' gold or silver lace '); M. *goṭ* ' hem of a garment, metal wristlet '(CDIAL 4271)

Kur. goṭā any seed which forms inside a fruit or shell. *Malt.* goṭa a seed or berry(DEDR 069) N. *goṭo* ' piece ', *goṭi* ' chess piece '; A. *goṭ* ' a fruit, whole piece ', °*ṭā* ' globular, solid ', *guṭi* ' small ball, seed, kernel '; B. *goṭā* ' seed, bean, whole '; Or. *goṭā* ' whole, undivided ', M. *goṭā* m. ' roundish stone ' (CDIAL 4271) <gOTa>(P) {ADJ} ``^whole''. {SX} ``^numeral ^intensive suffix''. *Kh., Sa., Mu., Ho<goTA>,B.<goTa> `undivided'; Kh.<goThaG>(P), Sa.<goTAG>,~<gOTe'j>, Mu.<goTo>; Sad.<goT>, O., Bh.<goTa>; cf.Ju.<goTo> `piece', O.<goTa> `one'. %11811. #11721. <goTa>(BD) {NI} ``the ^whole''. *@. #10971. (Munda etyma)

Rebus: <gota> {N} ``^stone". @3014. #10171. Note: The stone may be gota, laterite mineral ore stone. *khoṭ* m. 'base, alloy' (Punjabi) Rebus: koṭe 'forging (metal)(Mu.) Rebus: goṭī f. 'lump of silver' (G.) goṭi = silver (G.) koḍ 'workshop' (Gujarati).

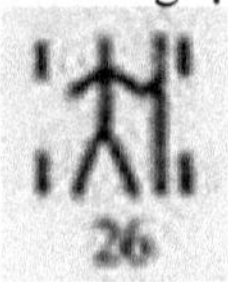

meḍ 'body' Rebus: *meḍ* 'iron' (Ho.) *gaṇḍa* 'four' Rebus: *kaṇḍa* 'furnace, fire-altar' (Santali) *kāṭhī* 'stick' Rebus: 'stature of body' (Marathi) Rebus: fireplace trench (Tamil). காடி&sup6; kāṭi, *n.* < U. *ghāṭī.* 1. Trench of a fort; அகழி. 2. A fireplace in the form of a long ditch; கோட்டையடுப்பு. (Tamil)

Ligature hieroglyph: 'stick' or 'one'

Sign1 Hieroglyph: काठी [kāṭhī] *f* (काष्ट S) (or शरीराची काठी) The frame or structure of the body: also (viewed by some as arising from the preceding sense, Measuring rod) stature (Marathi) B. *kāṭhā* ' measure of length '(CDIAL 3120).

H. *kāṭhī 'wood'* f. G. *kāṭh* n. ' wood ', °*ṭhī* f. ' stick, measure of 5 cubits '(CDIAL 3120). + kāṭi 'body stature; Rebus: fireplace trench.The 'stick' hieroglyph is a phonetic reinforcement of 'body stature' hieroglyph. Alternatively, koḍ 'one' Rebus: koḍ 'workshop'+ kāṭi 'body stature; Rebus: fireplace trench.. Thus, workplace of furnace fire-trench.

Rebus: G. *kāṭɔṛɔ* m. ' dross left in the furnace after smelting iron ore '.(CDIAL 2646)

காடியடுப்பு kāṭi-y-aṭuppu

Rebus: S.kcch. *kāṭhī* f. ' wood 'Pa. Pk. *kaṭṭha* -- n. ' wood '(CDIAL 3120).

muka 'ladle' (Tamil)(DEDR 4887) Rebus: *mū̃h* 'ingot' (Santali) *baṭa* = rimless pot (Kannada) Rebus:) *baṭa* = a kind of iron (G.)) *bhaṭa* furnace (Gujarati) Thus, iron ingot.kolom 'three' Rebus: kolami 'smithy, forge'

ABSTRACT of Boris Hlebec's article: The present research has been stimulated by the recent discovery of the earliest copper treatment in the regions of Bulgaria and eastern Serbia, and its aim is to establish the origin of some copper terms, the relative or approximate dates of their emergence, and at least some directions of their spread. In this article we have focused on three terms, represented by Latin cuprum, Balkan bakar and the root Ö*bar ~ var. [Boris Hlebec, Faculty of Philology, Belgrade University, Beograd, Serbia has presented a fascinating account tracing the roots of copper words in some European languages. Turkish is part of the Ural-Altaic linguistic group.] http://www.science.org.ge/moambe/8-1/Hlebec.pdf (Hlebec, Boris, 2014, The origin of *cuprum, bakar* and *var*, in: Bulletin of the Georgian National Academy of Sciences, Vol. 8, No. 1, 2014).

[quote] In his biography of the charismatic teacher and miracle worker Apollonius of Tyana (first century AD), the Greek biographer Lucius Flavius Philostratus of Lemnos (c. 170-c. 245) gives a detail account of Apollonius's journey to India. In the town of Taxila, the capital of the kingdom Hinduš (or Indus-country) he mentions a shrine, in which were hung pictures on Copper tablets representing the feats of Alexander and Porus. In his own words, "The various figures were portrayed in a mosaic of Orichalcum, Silver, Gold, and oxidised Copper, but the weapons in Iron. The metals were so ingeniously worked into one another that the pictures which they formed were comparable to the productions of the most famous Greek artists…The former name of the Turkish town Diyarbakir ('land of copper', as Kemal Attaturk interpreted it) was Amid (from Assyrian times), so that a semantic equivalence *between (a-) mid* (cf. Slavic *med* 'copper') and *(diyur-) bakir* can be established...The classical term for copper before cuprum was introduced, was aes, genitive aeris. It may be so that the Latin aes for some reason (perhaps owing to the near-homonymy with aer, genitive aeris 'air, mist') became inadequate and had to be replaced by cuprum (<cuprium<Cupra)… Sumerian kubabar (blended with Kubaba) 'silver', Sanskrit kapila 'kind of brass' and Bengali kapa~ra 'copper' also indicate that metal terms connected with the name Kubela had been in use long before the Latin cuprum…Another Sumerian word for 'copper' beside urudu was sibar, with initial si- instead of ku-…In Sanskrit, one of the words for copper was audumbara, and early Persian piring 'copper', birinj 'brass' gave rise to Armenian plinj 'copper', Georgian brinjao and Medieval Latin brundium 'bronze'. Akkadian abaru, Arameic 'abara, Arabic 'abarun and Hebrew 'oparet were names for lead. The same root can be recognized in cinnabar 'red form of mercuric sulphide', originally 'the most important ore of mercury' <L cinnabaris, Greek kinnabaris, tinnabaris <pre-Greek *tindabaris. [unquote] ((Hlebec, Boris, 2014, The origin of *cuprum, bakar* and *var*, in: Bulletin of the Georgian National Academy of Sciences, Vol. 8, No. 1, 2014, pp. 133-134).

http://bharatkalyan97.blogspot.com/2014/09/stature-of-body-meluhha-hieroglyphs-48.html

I suggest an alternative possibility that the gloss '*med*' is an adaptation of the Meluhhan gloss vividly identified in Munda languages. *meḍ* 'body' Rebus: *meḍ* 'iron' (Ho.) Santali glosses:

Mĕṛhĕt́. Iron.
Mĕṛhĕt́ icena. The iron is rusty.
Ispat mĕṛhĕt́. Steel.
Dul mĕṛhĕt́. Cast iron.
Mĕṛhĕt́ khanḍa. Iron implements.

Wilhelm von Hevesy wrote about the Finno-Ugric-Munda kinship, like *"Munda-Magyar-Maori, an Indian link between the antipodes new tracks of Hungarian origins"* and *"Finnisch-Ugrisches aus Indien"*. (DRIEM, George van: Languages of the Himalayas: an ethnolinguistic handbook. 1997. p.161-162.) Sumerian-Ural-Altaic language affinities have been noted. Given the presence of Meluhha settlements in Sumer, some Meluhha glosses might have been adapted in these languages. One etyma cluster refers to 'iron' exemplified by *meD* (Ho.). The alternative suggestion for the origin of the gloss *med* 'copper' in Uralic languages may be explained by the word *meD* (Ho.) of Munda family of Meluhha language stream:

Sa. <i>mE~R~hE~'d</i> `iron'. ! <i>mE~RhE~d</i>(M).
Ma. <i>mErhE'd</i> `iron'.
Mu. <i>mERE'd</i> `iron'.
~ <i>mE~R~E~'d</i> `iron'. ! <i>mENhEd</i>(M).
Ho <i>meD</i> `iron'.
Bj. <i>merhd</i>(Hunter) `iron'.
KW <i>mENhEd</i>
@(V168,M080)
http://www.ling.hawaii.edu/austroasiatic/AA/Munda/ETYM/Pinnow&Munda

— Slavic glosses for 'copper'
Мед [Med]*Bulgarian*
Bakar *Bosnian*
Медзь [medz']*Belarusian*
Měď *Czech*
Bakar *Croatian*
Kòper*Kashubian*
Бакар [Bakar]*Macedonian*
Miedź *Polish*
Медь [Med']*Russian*
Meď *Slovak*
Baker*Slovenian*
Бакар [Bakar]*Serbian*
Мідь [mid'] *Ukrainian*[unquote]
http://www.vanderkrogt.net/elements/element.php?sym=Cu
Miedź, med' (Northern Slavic, Altaic) 'copper'.

One suggestion is that corruptions from the German "Schmied", "Geschmeide" = jewelry. Schmied, a smith (of tin, gold, silver, or other metal)(German) result in *med* 'copper'.

Hieroglyph of a worshipper kneeling: *Konḍa* (BB) meḍa, meṇḍa id. *Pe.* menḍa id. *Manḍ.* menḍe id. *Kui* menḍa id. *Kuwi* (F.) menda, (S. Su. P.) menḍa, (Isr.) meṇḍa id. *Ta.* maṇṭi kneeling, kneeling on one knee as an archer. *Ma.*maṇṭuka to be seated on the heels. *Ka.* maṇḍi what is bent, the knee. *Tu.* maṇḍi knee. *Te.* maṇḍī kneeling on one knee. *Pa.*maḍtel knee; maḍi kuḍtel kneeling position. *Go.* (L.) meṇḍā, (G. Mu. Ma.) Cf. 4645 Ta.maṭaṅku (maṇi-forms). / ? Cf. Skt. maṇḍūkī- (DEDR 4677)

Hieroglyph: Pa. *vēdha* -- m. ' prick, wound '; Pk. *vēha* -- m. ' boring, hole ', P. *veh*, *beh* m., H. *beh* m., G.*veh* m.(CDIAL 12108) vēdha m. ' hitting the mark ' MBh., ' penetration, hole ' VarBr̥S. [√vyadh]

Hieroglyph: *Ta.* vēṟam bamboo; European bamboo reed; kaus; sugar-cane; vēy bamboo;

vēyal short-sized bamboo. *Ma.* vēṟam a reed, esp. *Arundo tibialis* and *Bambusa baccifera.*(DEDR 5541) vētasá m. ' ratan, reed ' RV. [See vēta -- , vētrá -- . - Paš. Gmb. indicate **vētaśa* -- Pa. *vētasa* -- m. ' Calamus rotang ', Pk. *vēdasa* -- , *vēasa* -- m.; Ash. *wiẽs* ' willow ', Paš.shut. *wēš*, Gmb. *wyãdotdot;š*; K. *bisa* m. ' Salix babylonica ', L.haz. *bīs*, N. *baĩs* ' Salix tetrasperma '. -- Dm. *bigyē˜'s* ' willow ' (*big*<-> scarcely < vṛkṣá -- , but cf. Ḍ. *bīk* s.v. vēta--). -- Pk. *vēḍasa* -- , °*ḍisa* -- m. ' ratan cane ' (CDIAL 12099)

Hieroglyph: mēthí m. ' pillar in threshing floor to which oxen are fastened, prop for supporting carriage shafts ' AV., °*thī* -- f. KātyŚr.com., *mēdhī* -- f. Divyāv. 2. mēṭhī -- f. PañcavBr.com., *mēḍhī* -- , *mēṭī* -- f. BhP.1. Pa. *mēdhi* -- f. ' post to tie cattle to, pillar, part of a stūpa '; Pk. *mēhi* -- m. ' post on threshing floor ', N. *meh(e)*, *miho*, *miyo*, B. *mei*, Or. *maï* -- *dāṇḍi*, Bi. *mẽh*, *mẽhā* ' the post ', (SMunger) *mehā* ' the bullock next the post ', Mth. *meh*, *mehā* ' the post ', (SBhagalpur)*mīhā̃* ' the bullock next the post ', (SETirhut) *mẽhi bāṭi* ' vessel with a projecting base '.2. Pk. *mēḍhi* -- m. ' post on threshing floor ', *mēḍhaka*<-> ' small stick '; K. *mīr*, *mīrü* f. ' larger hole in ground which serves as a mark in pitching walnuts ' (for semantic relation of ' post -- hole ' see kūpa -- 2); L. *meṛh* f. ' rope tying oxen to each other and to post on threshing floor '; P. *mehṛ* f., *mehaṛ* m. ' oxen on threshing floor, crowd '; OA *meṛha*, *mehra* ' a circular construction, mound '; Or. *meṛhī*, *meri* ' post on threshing floor '; Bi. *mẽṛ* ' raised bank between irrigated beds ', (Camparam) *mẽṛhā* ' bullock next the post ', Mth. (SETirhut)*mẽṛhā* ' id. '; M. *meḍ(h)*, *meḍhī* f., *meḍhā* m. ' post, forked stake '.(CDIAL 10317)

Hieroglyph: *mēṇḍhī ' lock of hair, curl '. [Cf. **mēṇḍha* -- 1 s.v. *miḍḍa --]S. *mī˜ḍhī* f., °*ḍho* m. ' braid in a woman's hair ', L. *mẽ̄ḍhī* f.; G. *mĩḍlɔ*, *miḍ*° m. ' braid of hair on a girl's forehead '; M. *meḍhā* m. ' curl, snarl, twist or tangle in cord or thread '.(CDIAL 10312)

Hieroglyph: *Ka.* mēḍi glomerous fig tree, *Ficus racemosa*; opposite-leaved fig tree, *F. oppositifolia. Te.* mēḍi *F. glomerata. Kol.* (Kin.) mēṛi id. [*F. glomerata* Roxb. = *F. racemosa* Wall.](DEDR 5090)udumbára -- , *udú*° m. ' the tree Ficus glomerata ' TS., n. ' its fruit ' ŚBr. 2.uḍumbára -- m. AV. 3. *dumbara. 4. *ḍumbara -- . [Prob. ← Austro -- as. EWA i 104 with lit.]1. Pa. *udumbara* -- m. ' Ficus glomerata ', Dhp. *udumara*, Pk. *uduṁbara* -- , *uuṁ*°, *uṁ*° m.; Ku. *umar* ' a partic. kind of tree used for burnt offerings '; H. *ūmar* m., °*rī* f. ' F. glomerata '; OG. *ūṁbara* m., G. *umrɔ*, *ū̃brɔ*, *umarṛɔ* m. ' wild fig tree ', *umarṛũ* n. ' its fruit '; M. *ũbar* m. ' F. glomerata ', n. ' its fruit ', Ko. *umbar*.2. Or. *uṛumara* ' F. glomerata '.3. H. *dũbur* m., Si. *diṁbul*, *duṁ*°.4. N. *ḍumri*, A. *ḍimaru*, B. *ḍumur*, Or. *ḍumara*, *ḍambura*, *ḍimbiri*, Mth. *ḍūmri*, Bhoj. *ḍūmari*, H.*ḍūmar* m.(CDIAL 1942)

Hieroglyph: Bi. *mẽṛhwā* ' a bullock with curved horns like a ram's '; M. *mẽḍhrũ̄* n. ' sheep '.(CDIAL 10311) mēṇḍha2 m. ' ram ', °*aka* -- , *mēṇḍa* -- 4, *miṇḍha* -- 2, °*aka* -- , *mēṭha* -- 2,*mēṇḍhra* -- , *mēḍhra* -- 2, °*aka* -- m. lex. 2. *mēṇṭha- (*mēṭha* -- m. lex.). 3. *mējjha -- . [*r*-- forms (which are not attested in NIA.) are due to further sanskritization of a loan -- word prob. of Austro -- as. origin (EWA ii 682 with lit.) and perh. related to the group s.v. bhēḍra --] Pa. *meṇḍa* -- m. ' ram ', °*aka* -- ' made of a ram's horn (e.g. a

bow) '; Pk. *meḍḍha* -- ,*meṁḍha* -- (°*ḍhī* -- f.), °*ṁḍa* -- , *miṁḍha* -- (°*dhiā* -- f.), °*aga* -- m. ' ram ', Dm. Gaw. *miṇ*Kal.rumb. *amŕn/aŕə* ' sheep ' (*a* -- ?); Bshk. *minā'l* ' ram '; Tor. *miṇḍ* ' ram ', *miṇḍā'l* ' markhor '; Chil. *mindh**l*l* ' ram ' AO xviii 244 (*dh*!), Sv. *yēṛo* -- *miṇ*; Phal. *miṇḍ*, *miṇ* ' ram ',*miṇḍṓl* m. ' yearling lamb, gimmer '; P. *mẽḍhā* m., °*ḍhī* f., ludh. *mī̃ḍḍhā*, *mī̃ḍhā* m.; N. *meṛho*,*meṛo* ' ram for sacrifice '; A. *mersāg* ' ram ' (-- *sāg* < *chāgya -- ?), B. *meṛā* m., °*ṛi* f., Or.*meṇḍhā*, °*ḍā* m., °*ḍhi* f.,H. *meṛh*, *meṛhā*, *mẽḍhā* m., G. *mẽḍhɔ*, M. *mẽḍhā* m., Si. *mäḍayā*.2. Pk. *meṁṭhī* -- f. ' sheep '; H. *meṭhā* m. ' ram '.3. H. *mejhukā* m. ' ram '.(CDIAL 10310) <menDa>(A) {N} ``^sheep''. *Des.<meNDa>(GM) `sheep'. #21810<meD>(:) <arij=meD>(Z),,<ari?=me?n>(A) {N} ``^female ^kid''. ^goat. #3022.<kin=meD>(Z) {N} ``^male ^goat, billy goat''. |<kin> `prefix used in names of male animals'. #17072. <auG kinme?n>(A) {N} ``^nanny ^goat''. |<auG> `mother'. #3729.(Gorum)
maṇḍa2 m. ' ornament ' lex. [√maṇḍ](CDIAL 9736) Pk. *maṁḍaya* -- ' adorning '; Ash. *mōṇḍa*, *mōnda*, *mūnda* NTS ii 266, *mōṇə* NTS vii 99 ' clothes '; G. *mā̃ḍ* m. ' arrangement, disposition, vessels or pots for decoration ', *māṇ* f. ' beautiful array of household vessels '; M. *mā̃ḍ* m. ' array of instruments &c. '; Si. *maḍa* -- *ya* ' adornment, ornament '.

maṇḍa -- 5 m. ' frog ' .<menDaka>(A) {N} ``^frog''. *Hi.<mE~dhak>, Skt.<maNDu:kam>. #21820. <poto menDka>(Z) {N} ``^toad''. |<poto> `?'. ^frog (which lives out of water). *Loan?. #27302. <o~ia mendka>(Z),,<oJa mendka>(Z) {N} ``^bullfrog''. |<o~ia> `id.'. ??RECTE D? #24562 (Gorum)

maṇḍa6 ' some sort of framework (?) '. [In *nau* -- *maṇḍḗ* n. du. ' the two sets of poles rising from the thwarts or the two bamboo covers of a boat (?) ' ŚBr. (as illustrated in BPL p. 42); and in BHSk. and Pa. *bōdhi* -- *maṇḍa* -- n. perh. ' thatched cover ' rather than ' raised platform ' (BHS ii 402). If so, it may belong to maṇḍapá -- and maṭha --]Ku. *mā̃ṛā* m. pl. ' shed, resthouse ' (CDIAL 9737)

Rebus: mḗdha m. ' sacrificial oblation ' RV.Pa. *mēdha* -- m. ' sacrifice '(CDIAL 10327)

Ta. mētaravar, mētavar a class of people who do bamboo work. *Ka.* mēda, mēdăra, mādara man who plaits baskets, mats, etc. of bamboo splits, man of the basket-maker caste. *Koḍ.* me·dë man of caste who make baskets and leaf-umbrellas and play drums at ceremonies; *fem.* me·di. *Te.* mēdara, mēdari the basket-maker caste, a basket-maker; of or pertaining to the basket-maker caste. *Kuwi* (S.) mētri (Isr.) mētreˀesi matmaker. / Cf. Skt. meda- a particular mixed caste; Turner, *CDIAL*, no. 10320.(DEDR 5092)mēda m. ' a mixed caste, any one living by a degrading occupation ' Mn. [→ Bal. *mēd* ' boatman, fisher- man '. -- Cf. Tam. *metavar* ' basket -- maker ' &c. DED 4178]Pk. *mēa* -- m., *mēī* -- f. ' member of a non -- Aryan tribe '; S. *meu* m. ' fisherman ' (whence*miāṇī* f. ' a fishery '), L. *mē* m.; P. *meũ* m., f. *meuṇī* ' boatman '. -- Prob. separate from S. *muhāṇo* m. ' member of a class of Moslem boatmen ', L. *mohāṇā* m., °*ṇī* f.(CDIAL 10320)
Ta. mēṭṭi haughtiness, excellence, chief, head, land granted free of tax to the headman of a village; mēṭṭimai haughtiness;leadership, excellence. *Ka.* mēṭi loftiness, greatness, excellence, a big man, a chief, a head, head servant. *Te.* mēṭari, mēṭi chief, head, leader,

lord(DEDR 5091)

Hieroglyph: *அதர்¹ atar, n.* 1. Way, path, public road; வழி. ஆக்க மதர்வினாய்ச் செல்லும் (குறள், 594). Lengthened excavation for a hedge or foundation; நீளக் கிடங்கு. (Tamil)
Hieroglyph: *aṭar* a splinter (Malayalam) *Tu. aḍaruni* to crack(DEDR 66)
Vikalpa: *sal* 'splinter' Rebus: 'workshop'.

IE med(h)- (Skt. madhu, Engl. mead, etc.) :: western IE **melit, Gr. melit-, Hitt. milit, Lat. mel, mell-, Gothic mili",. **med(h)-/ melit- from Finno-Ugrian and PIE to Chinese and Japanese, Hittite and Latin. Spread of the word for bees and honey and beeswax may have been related to the early copper *cire perdue* (lost-wax) technique of casting.<mOdu>(K) {N} ``^honey"<mOONO>(M) `beeswax'. madana m. ' beeswax ' lex., °*aka* -- n. Bhpr. Pk. *mayaṇa* -- n. ' beeswax ', S. *meṇu* m., L. *meṇ* f., WPah.jaun. *maiṇ*, Ku. *maiṇo*, N. *mayan*, *main*, Or. *maaṇa*, *Ta.* maṭṭu honey, toddy, fermented liquor, sweet juice, drink taken at the time of sexual union, liquor jar, fragrant smell; maṭṭam toddy.
Ma. maṭu sweetness, honey; maṭṭu nectar. *Tu.*miṭṭi sweetness (or < IA; cf. Turner, *CDIAL*, no. 10299); miṭṭè pollen (DEDR 4662) *mahaṇa* (-- *h* -- from *mahu* ' honey ' < mádhu -- ?), H. *main*m., G. *mīṇ* n. (whence *mīṇiyũ* ' oily ', n. ' waxcloth '), M. *meṇ* n., Ko. *meṇa*.(CDIAL 9778) Pk. *madhu* -- , *mahu* -- n. ' honey '; mádhu n. ' honey, mead ' RV.Pa. *madhu* -- n. ' honey, wine made from blossoms of Bassia latifolia'(CDIAL 9784)
moh, *moho* n.m. ' honeycomb, hive '(Marathi)

Magnetite and pyrite from, Piedmont, Italy. Magnetite is one of the three common naturally occurring iron oxides (chemical formula Fe_3O_4).

पोळ [pōḷa] *m* A bull dedicated to the gods, marked with a trident and discus, and set at large. पोळी [pōḷī] dewlap. Rebus: पोळें [pōḷēṃ], पोळी [pōḷī] The cake-form portion of a honeycomb.(Marath.

Laterite, Angadipuram, India.

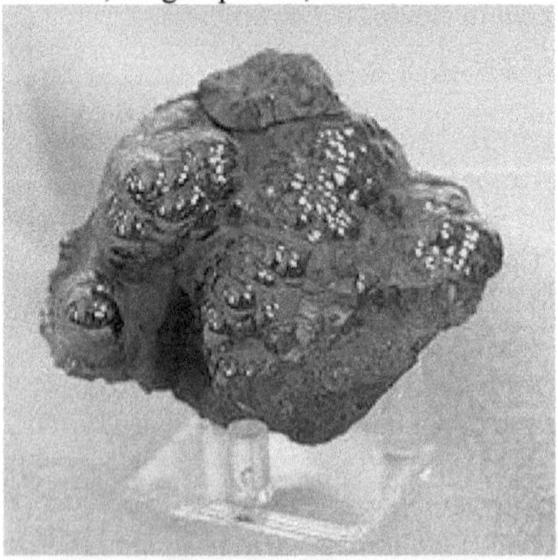

Hematite ore, Michigan.

Louvre 1639. Cypro-Minoan cylinder seal --antelope, eagle -- of hematite, 14th century BCE.

Ku. *nak* -- *poṛ* ' nostril '; N. *poro* ' small hole ' (or < 2); G. *poṛũ* n. ' thin scaly crust ' (semant. cf. *pōppa --); M. *poḷ*, *°ḷẽ* n. ' honeycomb ' (or < 3: semant. cf. *pōka--) L. *polā* ' hollow, porous, loose (of soil) '; M. see 1.4. Pk. *polla* -- , *°aḍa* -- , *pulla* -- ' hollow '; P. *pollā* ' hollow ', *pol* m., *pulāī* f. ' hollowness '; Or. *pola* ' hollow ', sb. ' puffed -- up pastry ', *polā* ' empty '; G. *poli* f. ' cavity ', *polũ*, *polrũ* ' hollow ', *polāṇ* n. ' hollowness '; M. *pol* n. ' empty tube or grain ', *polā* ' hollow '; WPah.kṭg. *pollɔ* ' hollow ', J. *polā*.(CDIAL 8398) *Br.* pōlō hollow, empty; Ta. poḷḷal boring a hole, chiselling, hole, rent, fissure, hollow in a tree; poḷ, poḷḷai hole; Kuwi. porongo hollow; (Isr.) poloṅgã hollow in a tree. (DEDR 4560)

भरत (p. 603) [bharata] *n* A factitious metal compounded of copper, pewter, tin &c.भरताचें भांडें (p. 603) [bharatācē mbhāṇḍēṃ] *n* A vessel made of the metal भरत. 2 See भरिताचें भांडें.भरती (p. 603) [bharatī] *a* Composed of the metal भरत. (Molesworth Marathi Dictionary).

http://www.scribd.com/doc/240843096/Minerals-and-their-exploitation-in-Ancient-and-Pre-modern-India-by-AK-Biswas-2001
http://bharatkalyan97.blogspot.in/2014/09/catalogs-of-pola-kuntha-gota-bichi.html

m1181A Seated person in penance. Hand edges like elephant trunks, twig on hairstyle. *Karabha* the trunk of an elephant; in *karabhoru* (k°+ūru) (a woman) with beautiful thighs Mhbv 29.(Pali) Rebus: *karba*'iron'; *ajirda karba* id. (ayas + karba, metal plus iron) (Tulu)

कूटी [p= 299,3] l. for कूद्/ई.कूदी [p= 300,1]*f.* a bunch of twigs , bunch (v.l. कूट्/ई) AV. v , 19 , 12 Kaus3.accord. to Kaus3. , Sch. = बदरी, "Christ's thorn". Rebus: kuThi 'smelter'.

karál1 ' doing, causing ' AV., m. ' hand ' RV. [√kr̥1]
Pa. Pk. *kara* -- m. ' hand '; S. *karu* m. ' arm '; Mth. *kar* m. ' hand ' (prob. ← Sk.);
Si. *kara* ' hand, shoulder ', inscr. *karā* ' to ' < *karāya.* -- Deriv. S. *karāī* f. ' wrist ';
G. *karā̃* n. pl. ' wristlets, bangles '.(CDIAL 2779) Rebus: khār 1 खार् । लोहकारः m. (sg. abl. khāra 1 खार; the pl. dat. of this word is khāran 1 खारन्, which is to be distinguished from khāran 2, q.v., s.v.), a blacksmith, an iron worker (cf. bandūka-khār, p. 111*b,* l. 46; K.Pr. 46; H. xi, 17); a farrier (El.). This word is often a part of a name, and in such case comes at the end (W. 118) as in Wahab khār, Wahab the smith (H. ii, 12; vi, 17). khāra-basta
khāra-basta खार-बस््त । चर्मप्रसेविका f. the skin bellows of a blacksmith. -büṭhü -ब&above;ठ&below; । लोहकारभित्तिः f. the wall of a blacksmith's furnace or hearth. -bāy -बाय् । लोहकारपत्नी f. a blacksmith's wife (Gr.Gr. 34). -dŏkuru -द्वकुरु&below; । लोहकारायोघनः m. a blacksmith's hammer, a sledge-hammer. -gȧji-ग&above;जि&below; or -güjü -ग&above;जू&below; । लोहकारचुल्लिः f. a blacksmith's furnace or hearth. -hāl -हाल् । लोहकारकन्दुः f. (sg. dat. -höjü -हा&above;जू&below;), a blacksmith's smelting furnace; cf. hāl 5. -kūrü -कूरू&below; । लोहकारकन्या f. a blacksmith's daughter. -koṭu -क&above;टु&below; । लोहकारपुत्रः m. the son of a blacksmith, esp. a skilful son, who can work at the same profession. -küṭü -क&above;टू&below; । लोहकारकन्या f. a blacksmith's daughter, esp. one who has the virtues and qualities properly belonging to her father's profession or caste. -mĕ˘tsü 1 -म्य&above;च&dotbelow;ू&below; । लोहकारमृत्तिका f. (for 2, see [khāra 3]), 'blacksmith's earth,' i.e. iron-ore. -nĕcyuwu -न्यचिवु&below; । लोहकारात्मजः m. a blacksmith's son. -nay -नय् । लोहकारनालिका f. (for khāranay 2, see [khārun]), the trough into which the blacksmith allows melted iron to flow after smelting. -tsañĕ -च्&dotbelow;ञ । लोहकारशान्ताङ्गाराः f.pl. charcoal used by blacksmiths in their furnaces. -wān वान् । लोहकारापणः m. a blacksmith's shop, a forge, smithy (K.Pr. 3). -waṭh -वठ् । आघाताधारशिला m. (sg. dat. -waṭas -वटि), the large stone used by a blacksmith as an anvil.(Kashmiri)

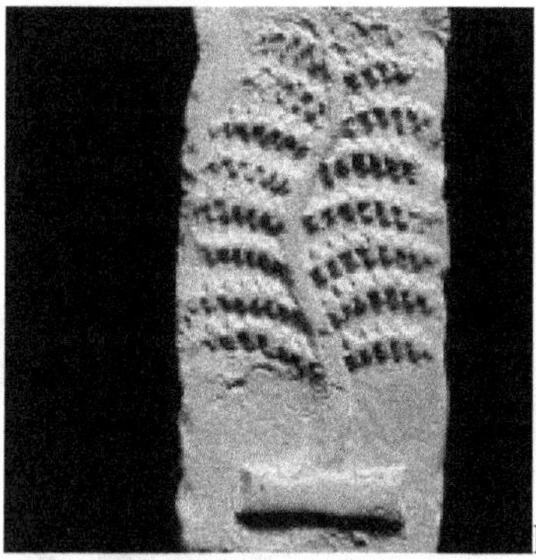
Harappa. Molded terracotta tablet. Tree on 'ingot'. kuTi 'tree' Rebus: kuThi 'smelter'.

m0290

kola 'tiger' (Santali); rebus: kol 'metal' (Tamil); kolle 'blacksmith'; kolhe 'smelters'; kole.l 'smithy, temple'; kolimi 'smithy, forge'; kol 'working in iron' (Tamil)
kaṅghā m. ' large comb (P.) ka_msako, ka_msiyo = a large sized comb (G.)
Rebus: kan:g = brazier, fireplace (K.)(IL 1332) Portable brazier ka~_guru, ka~_gar (Ka.) whence, large brazier = kan:gar (K.) kam.sa = bronze (Te.)
d.hagaraam 'thigh' (Gujarati) Rebus: d.hangar 'smith' (Hindi)
khara1 m. ' donkey ' KātyŚr., °*rī* -- f. Pāṇ. NiDoc. Pk. *khara* -- m., Gy. pal. *ḳăr* m., *kắri* f., arm. *xari*, eur. gr. *kher*, *kfer*, rum. *xerú*, Kt. *kur*, Pr. *korū´*, Dm. *khar* m., °*ri* f., Tir. *kh**l*r*, Paš. lauṛ. *khar* m., *khär*f., Kal. urt. *khār*, Phal. *khār* m., *khári* f., K. *khar* m., *khürü* f., pog. kash. ḍoḍ. *khar*, S. *kharu* m., P. G. M. *khar* m., OM. *khari* f.; -- ext. Ash. *kərəṭék*, Shum.*xareṭá*; <-> L. *kharkā* m., °*kī* f. -- Kho. *khairánu* ' donkey's foal ' (+?).Bshk. Kt. *kur* ' donkey ' (for loss of aspiration Morgenstierne ID 334).(CDIAL 3818) Rebus: *khār* 'blacksmith' (Kashmiri).

Slide 185 harappa tablet.

Slide 90. Tablet with man-in-tree and tiger. Molded terracotta tablet (H2001-5075/2922-01) with a narrative scene of a man in a tree with a tiger looking back over its shoulder. The tablet, found in the Trench 54 area on the west side of Mound E, is broken, but was made with the same mold as ones found on the eastern side of Mound E and also in other parts of the site (see slide 89 for the right hand portion of the same scene). The reverse of the same molded terra cotta tablet shows a deity grappling with two tigers and standing above an elephant (see slide 90 for a clearer example from the same mold). http://www.harappa.com/indus3/185.html

m478 B

Hieroglyph: Or. *dhokaṛa* ' decrepit, hanging down (of breasts) '.(CDIAL 5567). Rebus: *dhokra* 'cire perdue' casting metalsmith.

Kalibangan 49 Tiger looking up. Person seated on tree-branch

Hieroglyph: kolom 'three' Rebus: kolami 'smithy, forge' heraka 'spy' Rebus: eraka 'copper' kuTi 'tree' Rebus: kuThi 'smelter' kola 'tiger' Rebus: kol 'working in iron' krammara 'look back' Rebus: kamar 'artisan'. kuTi 'water-carrier' Rebus: kuThi 'smelter' kolom 'three' Rebus: kolami 'smithy, forge' gaNDa 'four' Rebus: kanda 'fire-altar

m304A Seated person in penance. Hand edges like elephant trunks, twigs on hairstyle, buffalo horns, rhinoceros, elephant, buffalo, tiger, standing person, antelopes

sal = Indian Gaur, Bos Gaurus(or, Gavaeus Gaurus). Rebus : sal = v. open a smithy, work a smithy; open a beer-shop, a sugar-cane press; ale manjhi tolare kamarko sal akata =

the blacksmiths have a smithy in that part of the village where our headman has his house; teken kamarko sal akata = the blacksmiths are working to-day (have started their forge)(Santali.lex.Bodding) tAttAru 'buffalo horn'(Mu.) Rebus: ThaThero ‘brass worker’(Ku.) (L) {N} ``^buffalo horn''. #64001.(S) {N} ``long ^horn, kind of ^conch''. #64010. So(L){N} ``^buffalo horn''.Ta.tu tt&ab revmacr;ri a kind of bugle-horn.Ma. tuttārihorn, trumpet.Ka. tutūri, tuttāri, tuttūri a long trumpet.T u. tuttāri, tuttūri trumpet,horn, pipe.Te.tu tār ā a kind of trumpet. / Cf. Mar.tu tār ī a wind instrument, a sort ofhorn. (DEDR 3316)

Rebus: N. ṭhaṭāunu ‘ to strike, beat ’, ṭhaṭāi ‘ striking ’, ṭhaṭāk -- ṭhuṭuk ‘ noise of beating ’; H. ṭhaṭhānā ‘ to beat ’, ṭhaṭhāī f. ‘ noise of beating ’.(CDIAL 5490). *ṭhaṭṭhakāra ‘ brass worker ’. 2. *ṭhaṭṭhakara -- . [*ṭhaṭṭha -- 1, kāra -- 1]1. Pk. ṭhaṭṭhāra -- m., K. ṭhõṭhur m., S. ṭhã̄ṭhāro m., P. ṭhaṭhiār, °rā m.2. P. ludh. ṭhaṭherā m., Ku. ṭhaṭhero m., N. ṭhaṭero, Bi. ṭhaṭherā, Mth. ṭhaṭheri, H. ṭhaṭherā m.(CDIAL 5493).Ta. taṭṭu (taṭṭi-) to knock, tap, pat, strike against, dash against, strike, beat, hammer, thresh; n. knocking, patting, breaking, striking against, collision; taṭṭam clapping of the hands; taṭṭal knocking, striking, clapping, tapping, beating time; taṭṭāṉ gold or silver smith; fem. taṭṭātti. Ma. taṭṭu a blow, knock; taṭṭuka to tap, dash, hit, strike against, knock; taṭṭān goldsmith; fem. taṭṭātti; taṭṭāran washerman; taṭṭikka to cause to hit; taṭṭippu beating. Ko. taṭ- (tac-) to pat, strike, kill, (curse) affects, sharpen, disregard (words); taṭ a·ṛ- (a·c) to stagger from fatigue. To. toṭ a slap; toṭ- (toṭy-) to strike (with hammer), pat, (sin) strikes; toṛ- (toṭ-) to bump foot; toṭxn, toṭxïn goldsmith; fem. toṭty, toṭxity; toṭk ïn- (ïd̠-) to be tired, exhausted. Ka. taṭṭu to tap, touch, come close, pat, strike, beat, clap, slap, knock, clap on a thing (as cowdung on a wall), drive, beat off or back, remove; n. slap or pat, blow, blow or knock of disease, danger, death, fatigue, exhaustion. Koḍ. taṭṭ- (taṭṭi-) to touch, pat, ward off, strike off, (curse) effects; taṭṭë goldsmith; fem. taṭṭati (Shanmugam). Tu. taṭṭāvuni to cause to hit, strike. Te. taṭṭu to strike, beat, knock, pat, clap, slap; n. stripe, welt; taṭravā̃ḍu goldsmith or silversmith. Kur. taṛnā (taṛcas) to flog, lash, whip. Malt. taṛce to slap.(DEDR 3039).

(B) {V} ``(pot, etc.) to ^overflow''. See `to be left over'. @B24310. #20851.(B) {V} ``to be ^left over, to be ^saved''. Caus. . @B24300. #20861. Rebus: loa 'iron' (Mu.)Re(B),,(B) {N} ``^iron''. Pl. <-le>

kaNDa = a pot of certain shape and size (Santali) Rebus: kaṇḍ = altar, furnace (Santali)लोहकारकन्दु: f. a blacksmith's smelting furnace (Grierson Kashmiri lex.)

Note: कन्दु [Monier-Williams lexicon, p. 250,1]mf. (√स्कन्द् Un2. i , 15), a boiler , saucepan , or other cooking utensil of iron Sus3r. Mallav. Comm. on KaltyS3r.

अयस्--काण्ड [p= 85,1] [L=14772]m. n. " a quantity of iron " or " excellent iron " , (g. कस्का*दि q.v.) If the semantics of kandu 'kiln' (Kashmiri) are applied to the glyph of 'arrow' read as काण्ड, it is possible to surmise that अयस्--काण्ड should have (in the days of artisans who inscribed the Indus script glyphs of 'fish', 'arrow') meant 'iron (smelter or) furnace'.

Ta. maṇṭi kneeling, kneeling on one knee as an archer. Ma. maṇṭuka to be seated on the heels. Ka. maṇḍi what is bent, the knee. Tu. maṇḍi knee. Te. maṇḍī kneeling on one knee.

Pa. maḍtel knee; maḍi kuḍtel kneeling position. Go. (L.) meṇḍā, (G. Mu. Ma.) minḍa knee (Voc. 2827). Konḍa (BB) meḍa, meṇḍa id. Pe. menḍa id. Manḍ. menḍe id. Kui menḍa id. Kuwi (F.) menda, (S. Su. P.) menḍa, (Isr.) meṇḍa id. Cf. 4645 Ta. maṭaṅku (maṇi-forms). / ? Cf. Skt. maṇḍūkī- (DEDR 4677)

maṇḍa = a branch; a twig; a twig with leaves on it (Te.lex.)

Rebus: maṇḍhwa, maṇḍua, maṇḍwa 'a temporary shed or booth erected on the occasion of a marriage' (Santali) maṇḍā = warehouse, workshop (Kon.lex.) maṇḍā = warehouse, workshop (Kon.lex.) maṇḍī. 'large grain market' (Urdu)

.Seal. National Museum: 135. Ox, one-horned young bull, fish

Harappa seal (h350B)

Harappa seal (h330)

The rebus readings of the hieroglyphs are: mẽḍha 'antelope'; rebus: meḍ 'iron' (Ho.) aya 'fish'; rebus: aya 'cast metal' (Gujarati); ayas 'alloy' (Rigveda)

m1429B. Glyphs: crocodile + fish ayakāra 'blacksmith' (Pali)kāru a wild crocodile or alligator (Te.) aya 'fish' (Mu.) The method of ligaturing enables creation of compound messages through Indus writing inscriptions.

Gavialis gangeticus:

The early glosses signifying crocodile: *grābhá* m. seizer. (√grabh).(Rigveda) निग्राभ [nigrābha] [ni-grābhá] m. pressing down , letting sink (Samskritam) In long-a vocalism: grábha- 'action of seizing' vs. grābhá- 'handful, grasp'. ghabh-, 1. ghrebh-, gherbh-, root extension ghrebha- 'to take, grab, seize' (IE) ghreib- 'to grip, grab' (IE) The early forms ghrebha, grābhá have yielded *கரவு² karavu, n.* < கரா 'alligator' (Tamil). The Khmer word is cognate: *krapeh* 'crocodile'. *Phnom Krapeh* means 'Crocodile mountain'. The Vietnamese word is: con sấu. Malay word is: buaya, Javanese 'baya'. Austronesian word for crocodile is: *uaea.*

Pokorny's dictionary provides the form: *grabh* 'to capture' which is cognate with the early Tamil form:*karavu, karā* 'crocodile' and more significantly, the phonetically proximate Khmer form, *krapeh* 'crocodile'.

karabu is probably, early pronunciation of the Meluhha gloss; the hieroglyph signifying this morphme, which connoted the semantics 'crocodile' presents a rhebus-metonymy-layered gloss: *karb* 'iron' which can be consistently deciphered on Indus Script -- as demonstrated in this monograph. karṓti ' does ' BṛĀrUp.
[√kṛ1] Pk. *karēi, karaï*, A. *kariba*, B. *karā*, Or.*karibā*, Mth. *karab*, Bhoj. *karal*, OAw. *karaï*, H. *karnā*, OMarw. *karaï*, G. *karvũ*, M. *karṇẽ*, Ko. *koruka*, Si. *karaṇavā*, inscr. 3 pl. pres. *karat* Pa. *kārēti* ' constructs, builds '; Pk. *kārēi* ' causes to be made ';Or. *karāibā* (CDIAL 2814). This set from Indian sprachbund relates the morpheme *karab* (and variants) to the semantics: 'constructs, builds'. This is as close as possible to the semantics of an artificer,
a vis'vakarman http://bharatkalyan97.blogspot.in/2015/06/meluhha-hieroglyph-on-indus-script.html

m1186 human face ligatured to markhor [Pleiades, scarfed, framework, *ficus religiosa* , scarfed person, worshipper, twigs (on head), horn, markhor, human face ligatured to markhor, stool, ladle, frame of a building]

paṭa 'hood of snake'. *Rebus: padm* 'tempered, sharpness (metal)'. nāga 'serpent' Rebus: nāga 'lead (alloy)'
mũh 'face' Rebus: *mũhe* 'ingot'. *khũ̃ṭ* 'zebu'.khũ̃ṭ 'community, guild' (Munda)
ibha 'elephant' Rebus: ib 'iron'. Ibbo 'merchant' (Gujarati).
ḍhangar 'bull' Rebus: *dhangar* 'blacksmith' (Maithili) *ḍangar* 'blacksmith' (Hindi)
kol 'tiger' Rebus: kol 'working in iron'.
dhaṭu m. (also *dhaṭhu*) m. 'scarf' (WPah.) Rebus: *dhatu* 'mineral (ore)'

Rebus reading of the 'face' glyph: mũhe 'face' (Santali) mũh opening or hole (in a stove for stoking (Bi.); ingot (Santali) mũh metal ingot (Santali) mũhã̄ = the quantity of iron produced at one time in a native smelting furnace of the Kolhes; iron produced by the Kolhes and formed like a four-cornered piece a little pointed at each end; mūhā mẽṛhẽt = iron smelted by the Kolhes and formed into an equilateral lump a little pointed at each of four ends; kolhe tehen mẽṛhẽt ko mūhā akata = the Kolhes have to-day produced pig iron (Santali.lex.) kaula mengro 'blacksmith' (Gypsy) mleccha-mukha

(Skt.) = milakkhu 'copper' (Pali) The Sanskrit loss mleccha-mukha should literally mean: copper-ingot absorbing the Santali gloss, mũh, as a suffix
The animal is a quadruped: pasaramu, pasalamu = an animal, a beast, a brute, quadruped (Te.) Rebus: pasra 'smithy' (Santali) Allograph: panǰắr 'ladder, stairs'(Bshk.)(CDIAL 7760) Thus the composite animal connotes a smithy. Details of the smithy are described orthographically by the glyphic elements of the composition.

The glyphic of the hieroglyph: tail (serpent), face (human), horns (*bos indicus*, zebu or ram), trunk (elephant), front paw (tiger),
moṇḍ the tail of a serpent (Santali) Rebus: Md. moḍenī ' massages, mixes '. Kal.rumb. moṇḍ -- ' to thresh ', urt. maṇḍ -- ' to soften ' (CDIAL 9890) Thus, the ligature of the serpent as a tail of the composite animal glyph is decoded as: polished metal (artifact). Vikalpa: xolā = tail (Kur.); qoli id. (Malt.)(DEDr 2135). Rebus: kol 'pañcalōha' (Ta.)கொல் kol, n. 1. Iron; இரும்பு. மின் வெள்ளி பொன் கொல்லெனச் சொல்லும் (தக்கயாகப். 550). 2. Metal; உலோகம். (நாமதீப. 318.) கொல்லன் kollan̠, n. < T. golla. Custodian of treasure; கஜானாக்காரன். (P. T. L.) கொல்லிச்சி kollicci, n. Fem. of கொல்லன். Woman of the blacksmith caste; கொல்லச் சாதிப் பெண். (யாழ். அக.) The gloss kollicci is notable. It clearly evidences that kol was a blacksmith. kola 'blacksmith' (Ka.); Koḍ. kollë blacksmith (DEDR 2133). Ta. kol working in iron, blacksmith; kollan̠ blacksmith.
Ma. kollan blacksmith, artificer. Ko. kole·l smithy, temple in Kota village. To. kwala·l Kota smithy. Ka. kolime, kolume, kulame, kulime, kulume, kulme fire-pit, furnace; (Bell.; U.P.U.) konimi blacksmith; (Gowda) kolla id. Koḍ. kollë blacksmith. Te. kolimi furnace. Go. (SR.) kollusānā to mend implements; (Ph.) kolstānā, kulsānā to forge; (Tr.) kōlstānā to repair (of ploughshares); (SR.) kolmi smithy (Voc. 948). Kuwi (F.) kolhali to forge (DEDR 2133) கொல்[2] kol Working in iron; கொற்றொழில். Blacksmith; கொல்லன். (Tamil) mũhe 'face' (Santali); Rebus: mũh '(copper) ingot' (Santali);mleccha-mukha (Skt.) = milakkhu 'copper' (Pali) கோடு kōṭu : •நடுநிலை நீங்குகை. கோடிறீக் கூற் றம் (நாலடி, 5). 3. [K. kōḍu.] Tusk; யானை பன்றிகளின் தந்தம். மத்த யானையின் கோடும் (தேவா. 39, 1). 4. Horn; விலங்கின் கொம்பு. கோட்டிடை யாடினை கூத்து (திவ். இயற். திருவிருத். 21). Ko. kṛ (obl. kṭ-) horns (one horn is kob), half of hair on each side of parting, side in game, log, section of bamboo used as fuel, line marked out. To. kwṛ (obl. kwṭ-) horn, branch, path across stream in thicket. Ka. kōḍu horn, tusk, branch of a tree; kōr̤ horn. Tu. kōḍů, kōḍu horn. Te. kōḍu rivulet, branch of a river. Pa. kōḍ (pl. kōḍul) horn (DEDR 2200)Rebus: koḍ = the place where artisans work (G.) kul 'tiger' (Santali); kōlu id. (Te.) kōlupuli = Bengal tiger (Te.)Pk. kolhuya -- , kulha -- m. ' jackal ' < *kōḍhu -- ; H.kolhā, °lā m. ' jackal ', adj. ' crafty '; G. kohlũ, °lũ n. ' jackal ', M. kolhā, °lā m. krōṣṭŕ̥ ' crying ' BhP., m. ' jackal ' RV. = krṓṣṭu -- m. Pāṇ. [√kruś] Pa. koṭṭhu -- , °uka -- and kotthu -- , °uka -- m. ' jackal ', Pk. koṭṭhu -- m.; Si. koṭa ' jackal ', koṭiya ' leopard ' GS 42 (CDIAL 3615). कोल्हा [kōlhā] कोल्हें [kōlhēṃ] A jackal (Marathi)

Rebus: kol 'furnace, forge' (Kuwi) kol 'alloy of five metals, pañcaloha' (Ta.) Allograph: kōla = woman (Nahali) [The ligature of a woman to a tiger is a phonetic determinant; the scribe clearly conveys that the gloss represented is kōla] karba 'iron' (Ka.)(DEDR 1278) as in ajirda karba 'iron' (Ka.) kari, karu 'black' (Ma.)(DEDR 1278) karbura 'gold' (Ka.) karbon 'black gold, iron' (Ka.) kabbiṇa 'iron' (Ka.) karum pon 'iron' (Ta.); kabin 'iron' (Ko.)(DEDR 1278) Ib 'iron' (Santali) [cf. Toda gloss below: ib 'needle'.] Ta. Irumpu iron, instrument, weapon. a. irumpu,irimpu iron. Ko. ibid. To. Ib needle. Koḍ. Irïmbï iron. Te. Inumu id. Kol. (Kin.) inum (pl. inmul)iron, sword. Kui (Friend-Pereira) rumba vaḍi ironstone (for vaḍi, see 5285). (DEDR 486) Allograph: karibha -- m. ' Ficus religiosa (?) [Semantics of ficus religiosa may be relatable to homonyms used to denote both the sacred tree and rebus gloss: *loa*, ficus (Santali); *loh* 'metal' (Skt.)]
miṇḍāl markhor (Tor.wali) meḍho a ram, a sheep (G.)(CDIAL 10120)bhēḍra -- , bhēṇḍa -- m. ' ram ' lex. [← Austro -- as. J. Przyluski BSL xxx 200: perh. Austro -- as. *mēḍra ~ bhēḍra collides with Aryan mḗḍhra -- 1 in mēṇḍhra -- m. ' penis ' BhP., ' ram ' lex. -- See also bhēḍa -- 1, mēṣá -- , ēḍa -- . -- The similarity between bhēḍa -- 1, bhēḍra -- , bhēṇḍa -- ' ram ' and *bhēḍa -- 2 ' defective ' is paralleled by that between mḗḍhra -- 1, mēṇḍha -- 1 ' ram ' and *mēṇḍa -- 1, *mēṇḍha -- 2 (s.v. *miḍḍa --) ' defective '](CDIAL 9606) mēṣá m. ' ram ', °ṣī´ -- f. ' ewe ' RV. 2. mēha -- 2, miha- m. lex. [mēha -- 2 infl. by mḗhati ' emits semen ' as poss. mēḍhra -- 2 ' ram ' (~ mēṇḍha -- 2) by mḗḍhra -- 1 ' penis '?]1. Pk. mēsa -- m. ' sheep ', Ash. mišalá; Kt. məṣe/l ' ram '; Pr. məṣé ' ram, oorial '; Kal. meṣ, meṣalák ' ram ', H. mes m.; -- X bhēḍra -- q.v.2. K. myã̄ -- pūtu m. ' the young of sheep or goats '; WPah.bhal. me\i f. ' wild goat '; H. meh m. ' ram '.mēṣāsya -- ' sheep -- faced ' Suśr. [mēṣá -- , āsyà --](CDIAL 10334) Rebus: meḍ (Ho.); mẽṛhet 'iron' (Mu.Ho.)mẽṛh t iron; ispat m. = steel; dul m. = cast iron (Mu.) Allograph: meḍ 'body ' (Mu.)
Hieroglphs on text of inscription read rebus:
Smithy (temple), Copper (mineral) guild workshop, metal furnace (account)
Sign 216 (Mahadevan). ḍato 'claws or pincers (chelae) of crabs'; ḍaṭom, ḍiṭom to seize with the claws or pincers, as crabs, scorpions; ḍaṭkop = to pinch, nip (only of crabs) (Santali) Rebus: dhatu 'mineral' (Santali) Vikalpa: erā 'claws'; Rebus: era 'copper'. Allograph: kamaṛkom = fig leaf (Santali.lex.) kamarmaṛā (Has.), kamaṛkom (Nag.); the petiole or stalk of a leaf (Mundari.lex.) kamat.ha = fig leaf, religiosa (Skt.)
Sign 342. kaṇḍa kanka 'rim of jar' (Santali): karṇaka rim of jar'(Skt.) Rebus: karṇaka 'scribe, accountant' (Te.); gaṇaka id. (Skt.) (Santali) copper fire-altar scribe (account)(Skt.) Rebus: kaṇḍ 'fire-altar' (Santali) Thus, the 'rim of jar' ligatured glyph is read rebus: fire-altar (furnace) scribe (account)
Sign 229. sannī, sannhī = pincers, smith's vice (P.) śannī f. ' small room in a house to keep sheep in ' (WPah.) Bshk. šan, Phal.šān 'roof' (Bshk.)(CDIAL 12326). seṇi (f.) [Class. Sk. śreṇi in meaning "guild"; Vedic= row] 1. a guild Vin iv.226; J i.267, 314; iv.43; Dāvs ii.124; their number was eighteen J vi.22, 427; VbhA 466. ° -- pamukha the head of a guild J ii.12 (text seni --). -- 2. a division of an army J vi.583; ratha -- ° J vi.81, 49; seṇimokkha the chief of an army J vi.371 (cp. senā and seniya). (Pali)
'body' glyph. mēd 'body' (Kur.)(DEDR 5099); meḍ 'iron' (Ho.)
aya 'fish' (Mu.); rebus: aya 'iron' (G.); ayas 'metal' (Skt.)
sal stake, spike, splinter, thorn, difficulty (H.); Rebus: sal 'workshop' (Santali)
*ஆலை[3] ālai, n. < šālā.

Varint of 'room' glyph with embedded rimless pot glyph (Sign 243 - Mahadevan corpus).

'Room' glyph. Rebus: kole.l = smithy, temple in Kota village (Ko.) kolme smithy' (Ka.) kol 'working in iron, blacksmith (Ta.)(DEDR 2133) The ligature glyphic element within 'room' glyph (Variant Sign 243): baṭi 'broad-mouthed, rimless metal vessel'; rebus: baṭi 'smelting furnace'. Thus, the composite ligatured Sign 243 denotes: furnace smithy.

m1429 Mohenjo-dar tablet showing a boat carrying a pair of metal ingots. bagalo = an Arabian merchant vessel (G.lex.) bagala = an Arab boat of a particular description (Ka.); bagalā (M.); bagarige, bagarage = a kind of vessel (Ka.) bagalo = an Arabian merchant vessel (G.lex.) cf. m1429 seal.

The glyphic of the hieroglyph: tail (serpent), face (human), horns (*bos indicus*, zebu or ram), trunk (elephant), front paw (tiger),

moṇḍ the tail of a serpent (Santali) Rebus: Md. moḍenī ' massages, mixes '. Kal.rumb. moṇḍ -- ' to thresh ', urt. maṇḍ -- ' to soften ' (CDIAL 9890) Thus, the ligature of the serpent as a tail of the composite animal glyph is decoded as: polished metal (artifact). Vikalpa: xolā = tail (Kur.); qoli id. (Malt.)(DEDr 2135). Rebus: kol 'pañcalōha' (Ta.)கொல் kol, n. 1. Iron; இரும்பு. மின் வெள்ளி பொன் கொல்லெனச் சொல்லும் (தக்கயாகப். 550). 2. Metal; உலோகம். (நாமதீப. 318.) கொல்லன் kollan̲, n. < T. golla. Custodian of treasure; கஜானாக்காரன். (P. T. L.) கொல்லிச்சி kollicci, n. Fem. of கொல்லன். Woman of the blacksmith caste; கொல்லச் சாதிப் பெண். (யாழ். அக.) The gloss kollicci is notable. It clearly evidences that kol was a blacksmith. kola 'blacksmith' (Ka.); Koḍ. kollë blacksmith (DEDR 2133).
Ta. kol working in iron, blacksmith; kollan̲ blacksmith. Ma. kollan blacksmith, artificer. Ko. kole·l smithy, temple in Kota village. To. kwala·l Kota smithy. Ka. kolime, kolume, kulame, kulime, kulume, kulme fire-pit, furnace; (Bell.; U.P.U.) konimi blacksmith; (Gowda) kolla id. Koḍ. kollë blacksmith. Te. kolimi furnace. Go. (SR.) kollusānā to mend implements; (Ph.) kolstānā, kulsānā to forge; (Tr.) kōlstānā to repair (of ploughshares); (SR.) kolmi smithy (Voc. 948). Kuwi (F.) kolhali to forge (DEDR 2133) கொல்[2] kol Working in iron; கொற்றொழில். Blacksmith; கொல்லன். (Tamil) mũhe 'face' (Santali);

Rebus: mũh '(copper) ingot' (Santali);mleccha-mukha (Skt.) = milakkhu 'copper' (Pali) கோடு kōṭu : •நடுநிலை நீங்குகை. கோடிறீக் கூற் றம் (நாலடி, 5). 3. [K. kōḍu.]

Tusk; யானை பன்றிகளின் தந்தம். மத்த யானையின் கோடும் (தேவா. 39, 1). 4.

Horn; விலங்கின் கொம்பு. கோட்டிடை யாடினை கூத்து (திவ். இயற். திருவிருத். 21). Ko. kṛ (obl. kṭ-) horns (one horn is kob), half of hair on each side of parting, side in game, log, section of bamboo used as fuel, line marked out. To. kwṛ (obl. kwṭ-) horn, branch, path across stream in thicket. Ka. kōḍu horn, tusk, branch of a tree; kōṟ horn. Tu. kōḍů, kōḍu horn. Te. kōḍu rivulet, branch of a river. Pa. kōḍ (pl. kōḍul) horn (DEDR 2200)Rebus: koḍ = the place where artisans work (G.) kul 'tiger' (Santali); kōlu id. (Te.) kōlupuli = Bengal tiger (Te.)Pk. kolhuya -- , kulha -- m. ' jackal ' < *kōḍhu -- ; H.kolhā, °lā m. ' jackal ', adj. ' crafty '; G. kohlũ, °lũ n. ' jackal ', M. kolhā, °lā m. krōṣṭṛ̊ ' crying ' BhP., m. ' jackal ' RV. = krṓṣṭu -- m. Pāṇ. [√kruś] Pa. koṭṭhu -- , °uka -- and kotthu -- , °uka -- m. ' jackal ', Pk. koṭṭhu -- m.; Si. koṭa ' jackal ', koṭiya ' leopard ' GS 42 (CDIAL 3615). कोल्हा [kōlhā] कोल्हें [kōlhēṃ] A jackal (Marathi)

Rebus: kol 'furnace, forge' (Kuwi) kol 'alloy of five metals, pañcaloha' (Ta.) Allograph: kōla = woman (Nahali) [The ligature of a woman to a tiger is a phonetic determinant; the scribe clearly conveys that the gloss represented is kōla] karba 'iron' (Ka.)(DEDR 1278) as in ajirda karba 'iron' (Ka.) kari, karu 'black' (Ma.)(DEDR 1278) karbura 'gold' (Ka.) karbon 'black gold, iron' (Ka.) kabbiṇa 'iron' (Ka.) karum pon 'iron' (Ta.); kabin 'iron' (Ko.)(DEDR 1278) Ib 'iron' (Santali) [cf. Toda gloss below: ib 'needle'.] Ta. Irumpu iron, instrument, weapon. a. irumpu,irimpu iron. Ko. ibid. To. Ib needle. Koḍ. Irïmbï iron. Te. Inumu id. Kol. (Kin.) inum (pl. inmul)iron, sword. Kui (Friend-Pereira) rumba vaḍi ironstone (for vaḍi, see 5285). (DEDR 486) Allograph: karibha -- m. ' Ficus religiosa (?) [Semantics of ficus religiosa may be relatable to homonyms used to denote both the sacred tree and rebus gloss: *loa*, ficus (Santali); *loh* 'metal' (Skt.)]

miṇḍāl markhor (Tor.wali) meḍho a ram, a sheep (G.)(CDIAL 10120)bhēḍra -- , bhēṇḍa -- m. ' ram ' lex. [← Austro -- as. J. Przyluski BSL xxx 200: perh. Austro -- as. *mēḍra ~ bhēḍra collides with Aryan mḗḍhra -- 1 in mēṇḍhra -- m. ' penis ' BhP., ' ram ' lex. -- See also bhēḍa -- 1, mēṣá -- , ēḍa -- . -- The similarity between bhēḍa -- 1, bhēḍra -- , bhēṇḍa -- ' ram ' and *bhēḍa -- 2 ' defective ' is paralleled by that between mḗḍhra -- 1, mēṇḍha -- 1 ' ram ' and *mēṇḍa -- 1, *mēṇḍha -- 2 (s.v. *miḍḍa --) ' defective '](CDIAL 9606) mēṣá m. ' ram ', °ṣī́ -- f. ' ewe ' RV. 2. mēha -- 2, miha- m. lex. [mēha -- 2 infl. by mḗhati ' emits semen ' as poss. mēḍhra -- 2 ' ram ' (~ mēṇḍha -- 2) by mḗḍhra -- 1 ' penis '?]1. Pk. mēsa -- m. ' sheep ', Ash. mišalá; Kt. məse/l ' ram '; Pr. məṣé ' ram, oorial '; Kal. meṣ, meṣalák ' ram ', H. mes m.; -- X bhēḍra -- q.v.2. K. myā̃ -- pūtu m. ' the young of sheep or goats '; WPah.bhal. me\i f. ' wild goat '; H. meh m. ' ram '.mēṣāsya -- ' sheep -- faced ' Suśr. [mēṣá -- , āsyà --](CDIAL 10334) Rebus: meḍ (Ho.); mẽṛhet 'iron' (Mu.Ho.)mẽṛh t iron; ispat m. = steel; dul m. = cast iron (Mu.) Allograph: meḍ 'body ' (Mu.)

er-agu = a bow, an obeisance; er-aguha = bowing, coming down (Ka.lex.) er-agisu = to bow, to be bent; tomake obeisance to; to crouch; to come down; to alight (Ka.lex.) cf. arghas = respectful reception of a guest (by the offering of rice, du_rva grass, flowers or often only of water)(S'Br.14)(Skt.lex.) erugu = to bow, to salute or make obeisance (Te.) Rebus: eraka 'copper' (Ka.)erka = ekke (Tbh. of arka) aka (Tbh. of arka) copper (metal); crystal (Ka.lex.) eraka, er-aka = any metal infusion (Ka.Tu.) eruvai 'copper' (Ta.); ere dark red (Ka.)(DEDR 446). er-r-a = red; (arka-) agasāle, agasāli, agasālavāḍu = a goldsmith (Telugu)

Hieroglyph: Kur. mūxā frog. Malt. múqe id. / Cf. Skt. mūkaka- id. (DEDR 5023). Hieroglyph: face: Ju<mukhO>(P),,<mukO>(M) {N} ``^face". *Sa.<mukhe> `mouth, face', H.<mUkhA>, O.<mukhO>, Sk.<mUKhA>..<muGka>(L) {N} ``^face". *Or.<>. #47571.>.So<muGka>(L) {N} ``^face". *Oriya.Go<mokom>(ZA) {NB} ``^face(Z)". {ADJ} ``^front(A)". *Skt.?.<mukhO>(P),,<mukO>(M) {N} ``^face". *Sa.<mukhe> `mouth, face', H.<mUkhA>, O.<mukhO>, Sk.<mUKhA>. %22621. #22451.<mu:> {N} ``^nose". @7904. #19931.<muar>,,<muvar> {N} ``^face". @7803. #19941.<sar=mo'>(F) / <mo'>(F) {NB} ``^face". @N27. #22980. <mu=sina=sini=bela>(B) {N} ``^dusk (when people's faces can be recognized with difficulty from a distance)". @B21410. #3673.<A-bO-muGka>(L) {N} ``intimate ^friendship". Lit., one face. #2242.Kh<monkan>(B) {NI} ``^face". (Munda etyma) Ta. mukam face, mouth; mukappu front, forepart, porch, façade; mukari, mukaṉai forepart, front, beginning, headship; mukarimai chieftaincy; mukarai, mōrai face, chin; mukavu façade, porch; mokkaṭṭai, mokkai face. Ma. mukam face, front, mouth, commencement, chief; mukana forepart; mukappu frontispiece; mukaṟu face, forepart; mukaṟuka to go forward; mōr face. To. mïx open ground in front of village, where people sit and buffaloes are milked. Ka. moga face, mouth; mōṟe face. Tu. moga, mugaṇuthe front; mōrè face, visage. Te. moga the front part, beginning, commencement, mouth of a river; mogakonu to face; mogadala the front part, front; mogamu face, mouth, the front; mōmu the face, countenance; mōra face or head, generally of the lower animals; (B.) mokkaṭṭu features, face, likeness. Kol. mokam face. Nk. mokam id. Pa. mokom id.Go. (G. Ma.) mukam, (M.) mukum id. (Voc. 2861); (A. S. Ko.) mokom id. (Voc. 2972). Konḍa mokom id.;mōṟo protruding face of animal. Pe. mūm face. Manḍ. mūmb id.Kui (K.) mrūmbu id. Kuwi (Su. P. Isr. F.) mūmbu, (S.) mūmbū, (Mah.) mūkā id. (DEDR 4889). Ta. mūkku nose, nostril, beak, nose-shaped part of anything; mūkkaṉ man with a large or prominent nose; mukarai, mukari bottom of the nose. Ma. mūkku nose, nozzle, beak; mūkkan long-nosed. Ko. mu·k nose, funnel of bellows; mu·kn man with long nose; fem. mu·ky. To. mu·k nose (in songs); mu·ku·ṛ- (mu·ku·ṛy-) to meet (of persons, rivers); mu·ku·ṭ- (mu·ku·ṭy-) to cause to meet; ? mu·kuṟ- (mu·kuṟy-) (person, ceremony) approaches. Ka. mūgu, mū nose, forepart, snout, beak, nozzle; mūga, mūgi man with a nose. Koḍ. mu·kï nose. Tu. mūku, mūgu, mūṅku nose, beak; mūke man who snuffles or speaks through the nose; fem. mūki. Te. mukku nose, beak, end, point, tip. Kol.muŋgaḍ, (Kin.) mukk, (SR.) mukku nose. Nk. muŋgaṛ id. Nk. (Ch.) muŋgan id. Pa. muvāḍ (pl. muvācil) id. Ga. (Oll.) muŋan,S.) muŋān (P.) muŋgan id. Pe. muŋgel id. Manḍ. muŋgel id. Kui mungeli, (K.) muŋgi id. Kuwi (F.) mūngelli, (S.) mungeli, (Isr.) muṅgeli, (Su. P.) muŋgeli (pl. muŋgelka) id. Kur. muī̃ id. Malt. muṉyu id. (DEDR 5024).Ga. (S.2) mūti snout of pig. Go. (Tr.) massōr, (M.) mosoṛ, (SR.) mosor, (L.) mosor, mosok, (Mu.) mosor (obl. mosoṭ-), (Ma.) mosoṟ(i) (obl. mosoṭ-) nose (Voc. 2996); (G.) mundur beak; (G.) mundori, (Ma.) mundoṟi snout (Voc. 2890); (L.) mohāface (Voc. 2997). Konḍa mūnzi nose; (BB) mūtu beak. Pe. mutla snout of pig. Manḍ. mutli id. Kui munduri snout; muḍra id., upper lip. Kuwi mūti (F.) beak, (Su. Isr.) id., snout of pig. Kur. moccā mouth (not said of men unless in joke or abuse). Malt. mudra face. (DEDR 5031). múkha n. ' mouth, face ' RV., ' entrance ' MBh.Pa. mukha -- m.; Aś.shah. man. gir. mukhato, kāl. dh. jau. °te ' by word of mouth '; Pk. muha -- n. ' mouth, face ', Gy. gr. hung. muy m., boh. muy, span. muí, wel. mūī f., arm.muç, pal. mu', mi', pers. mu; Tir. mū ' face '; Woṭ. mū m. ' face, sight '; Kho. mux ' face '; Tor. mū ' mouth ', Mai. mũ; K. in cmpds. mu -- ganḍ m. ' cheek, upper jaw ', mū -- kāla' having one's face blackened ', rām. mūĩ, pog. mūī, ḍoḍ. mũh ' mouth '; S. mũhũ m. ' face, mouth, opening '; L. mũh m. ' face ', awāṇ. mũ with descending tone, mult. mũhã m. ' head of a canal '; P. mũh m. ' face, mouth ', mũhã m. ' head of a canal '; WPah.śeu. mùtilde; ' mouth, ' cur. mũh; A. muh ' face ', in cmpds. -- muwā ' facing '; B. mu ' face '; Or.muhã ' face, mouth, head, person '; Bi. mũh ' opening or hole (in a stove for stoking, in a handmill for filling, in a grainstore for withdrawing) '; Mth. Bhoj. mũh ' mouth, face ', Aw.lakh. muh, H. muh, mũh m.; OG. muha, G. mɔ̃h n. ' mouth ', Si. muya, muva. -- Ext. -- l<-> or -- ll -- : Pk. muhala -- , muhulla -- n. ' mouth, face '; S. muhuro m. ' face ' (or <mukhará --); Ku. do -- maulo ' confluence of two streams '; Si. muhul, muhuna, mūṇa ' face ' H. Smith JA 1950, 179.; -- -- ḍ -- : S. muhaṛo m. ' front, van '; Bi. (Shahabad)mohṛā ' feeding channel of handmill ' WPah.kṭg. (kc.) mũ (with high level tone) m. (obl. -- a) ' mouth, face '; OMarw. muhaṛaü ' face '. (CDIAL 10158).*mukhakāṣṭha ' doorframe '. [múkha -- , kāṣṭhá --]L. P. muhāṭh f. ' upright of doorframe ', awāṇ. muhāṭh ' threshold '.*mukhaghāṭā ' entrance frame '. [múkha -- , *ghāṭa --]S. muhāṛī f. ' top of a doorway outside a stockade '; L. muhāṛ f. ' upright of doorframe ', °ṛī f. ' wall on each side of a door '.(CDIAL 10159, 10160). मुख [mukha] n (S) The mouth. S adage. मुखमस्तीति वक्तव्यं Used in reproof of one who speaks because he has a mouth. 2 The face. 3 fig. The entrance into a building; the beginning of a work &c. For other figurative senses see तोंड. 4 A means, measure, expedient. 5 S In comp. The fore, prime, or initial thing or part: also the chief, principal, or leading person. 6 In arithmetic &c. The first term of a series. 7 The opposite side to the base of any quadrilateral figure.मुखवटा or मुखोटा [mukhavaṭā or mukhōṭā] m sometimes मुखवट n f (मुख) A face (of silver, brass &c.) made to cover, as a mask, the face of an idol. 2 A mask. 3 A bust. 4 A face drawn upon paper &c. 5 Fashion or cast of countenance, facial lineaments, features, visage.(Marathi, Molesworth lex., p.653) Rebus: *muha* 'the quantity of iron produced at one time in a native smelting furnace' (Santali. Campbell, p. 420)

There are many examples, in Indus Script Corpora, of the depiction of 'human face' ligatured to an animal hieroglyph multiplex:

A common ligaturing element is a human face which is a hieroglyph read rebus in mleccha (meluhha): *mũhe* 'face' (Santali) ; rebus:*mũh* metal ingot (Santali).

m0301 Mohenjodaro seal Hieroglyph components: Human face, horns of zebu, trunk of elephant, scarves on neck, body of bovid, back of tiger, serpent (tail)

m1179. Mohenjo-daro seal.

 Human face, horns of a markhor, or ram (with goatee), scarves on neck, bovid, tail with three forks, body of bovid

m1177 Mohenjo-daro seal.

 Human face, horns of a zebu, trunk of elephant, hand of a person seated in penance, scarves on neck, tail as serpent, body of bovid, hind-part of tiger.

This image is also interpreted in corpora (e.g. Mahadevan's Corpus of Indus script) describing a simpler model of hypertext that the hieroglyph multiplex has: body of a ram, horns of a bison, trunk of elephant, hindlegs of a tiger and an upraised serpent-like tail.

An interpretation by John C. Huntington presents a re-configured composite animal (bovid) on seal m0299:

m0299. Mohenjo-daro seal.

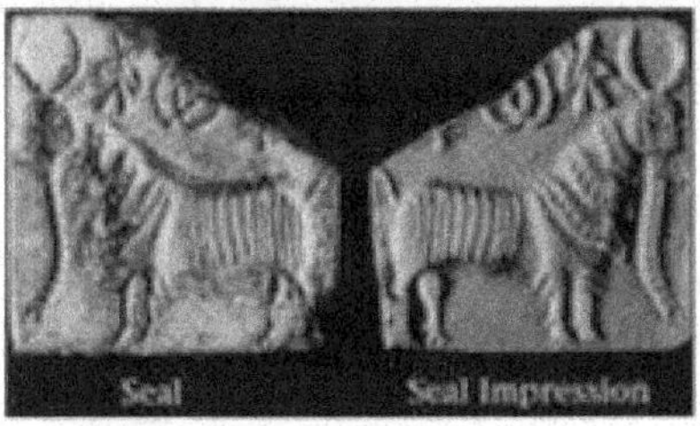

Human face, horns of a zebu, trunk of elephant, scarves on neck, body of

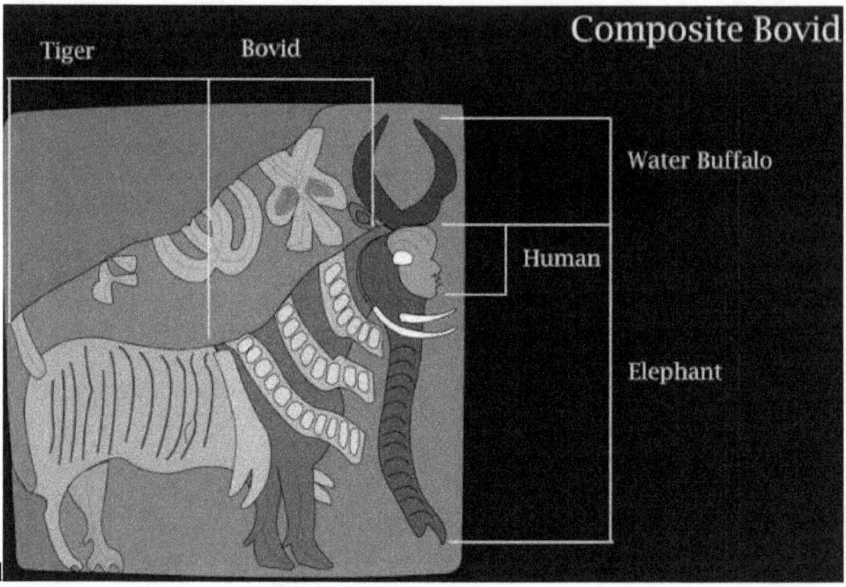

bovid http://huntington.wmc.ohio-state.edu/public/index.cfm

On m0300 seal, Dennys Frenez and Massimo Vidale, identify a number of hieroglyph components: serpent (tail), scorpion, tiger, one-horned young bull, markhor, elephant, zebu, standing man (human face), man seated in penance (yogi).

The yogi seated in penance and other hieroglyphs are read rebus in archaeometallurgical terms: kamaDha 'penance' (Prakritam) rebus: kampaTTa 'mint'. Hieroglyph: kola 'tiger', xolA 'tail' rebus: kol 'working in iron'; kolle 'blacksmith'; kolhe 'smelter'; kole.l 'smithy'; kolimi 'smithy, forge'. खोड [khōṇḍa] m A young bull, a bullcalf (Marathi) rebus: khond 'turner'. dhatu 'scarf' rebus: dhatu 'minerals'. bichi 'scorpion' rebus: bica 'sandstone mineral ore'.miṇḍāl markhor (Tor.wali) meḍho a ram, a sheep (Gujarati) Rebus: meḍ (Ho.); mẽṛhet 'iron' (Mu.Ho.)mẽṛh t iron; ispat m. = steel; dul m. = cast iron (Munda) kara 'elephant's trunk' Rebus: khar 'blacksmith'; ibha 'elephant' rebus: ib 'iron'. Together: karaiba 'maker, builder'.

Dennys Frenez and Massimo Vidale identify a standing man. Two orthographic interpretations are possible for the hieroglyph component of 'human face' joined together with animal hieroglyphs: 1. as human; 2. as human face.

As human

meD 'body' rebus: meḍ (Ho.); mẽṛhet 'iron' (Mu.Ho.)

It is notable that the prefix *kol-* described many ancient people of Bharatam: Koli Dhor, Tokre Koli, Kolcha, Kolgha and listed with Gond, Arakh, Arrakh, Agaria, Asur: Koliabhuta, Koliabhuti are listed as Bharatam Janam in scheduled tribe

enumerations: http://bakulaji.typepad.com/blog/racial-integration/ The kole language is also called Ho, an Austro-asiatic family of languages. kōla1 m. ‘ name of a degraded tribe ’ Hariv. Pk. *kōla* -- m.; B. *kol* ‘ name of a Muṇḍā tribe (CDIAL 3532) kaula ‘ relating to a family ’ R., ‘ of noble family ’ lex. [kúla --]
OSi. -- *kol* ‘ sprung from a noble family ’?(CDIAL 3565) kōlika m. ‘ weaver ’ Yaśast., *kaulika* -- Pañcat. [EWA i 273 ← **kōḍika* -- (in Tam. *kōṭikar* ‘ weaver ’) ~ Mu. word for ‘ spider ’ in Pk. *mak* -- *kōḍā* -- s.v. markaṭa --] Pk. *kōlia* -- m. ‘ weaver, spider ’; S. *korī* m. ‘ weaver ’, *koriaṛo* m. ‘ spider ’; Ku. *koli* ‘ weaver ’, Or. (Sambhalpur) *kuli*, H. *kolī*, *kolhī* m. ‘ Hindu weaver ’; G. *koḷī* m. ‘ a partic. Śūdra caste ’; M. *koḷī* m. ‘ a caste of watercarriers, a sort of spider ’; -G. *karoḷiyɔ*, *karāliyɔ* m. ‘ spider ’ is in form the same as *karoḷiyɔ* ‘ potter ’ < kaulālá -- . WPah.kṭg. *koḷi* m. ‘ low -- caste man ’, *koḷəṇ*, kc. *koḷiṇ* f. ‘ his wife ’ (→ Eng. *cooly* HJ 249).(CDIAL 3535) Thus, the hieroglyh of 'man' may be a synonym of kola 'tiger' with related rebus renderings related to metalwork.
As human face

Hieroglyph: 'human face': *mũhe* ‘face’ (Santali)

Rebus: *mũh* opening or hole (in a stove for stoking (Bi.); ingot (Santali) *mũh* metal ingot (Santali) *mũhã̄* = the quantity of iron produced at one time in a native smelting furnace of the Kolhes; iron produced by the Kolhes and formed like a four-cornered piece a little pointed at each end; *mūhā mẽṛhẽt* = iron smelted by the Kolhes and formed into an equilateral lump a little pointed at each of four ends; *kolhe tehen mẽṛhẽt ko mūhā akata* = the Kolhes have to-day produced pig iron (Santali) *kaula mengro* ‘blacksmith’ (Gypsy) *mleccha-mukha* (Skt.) = *milakkhu* ‘copper’ (Pali)
The Samskritam gloss *mleccha-mukha* should literally mean: copper-ingot absorbing the Santali gloss, *mũh*, as a suffix.

m0300. Mohenjo-daro seal.

Above: Harappan chimaera and its hypertextual components.
Harappan chimera and its hypertextual components. The 'expression' summarizes the syntax of Harappan chimeras within round brackets, creatures with body parts used in their correct anatomic position (tiger, unicorn, markhor goat, elephant, zebu, and human); within square brackets, creatures with body parts used to symbolize other anatomic elements (cobra snake for tail and human arm for elephant proboscis); the elephant icon as exonent out of the square brackets symbolizes the overall elephantine contour of the chimeras; out of brackes, scorpion indicates the animal automatically perceived joining the lineate horns, the human face, and the arm-like trunk of Harappan chimeras. (After Fig. 6 in: Harappan chimaeras as 'symbolic hypertexts'. Some thoughts on Plato, Chimaera and the Indus Civilization (Dennys Frenez & Massimo Vidale, 2012) *A paper by Dennys Frenez and Massimo Vidale on composite Indus creatures and their meaning: Harappa Chimaeras as 'Symbolic Hypertexts'. Some Thoughts on Plato, Chimaera and the Indus Civilization at* *http://a.harappa.com/content/harappan-chimaeras*
Mirror: https://www.scribd.com/doc/270086643/Harappan-chimaeras-as-symbolic-hypertexts-Some-thoughts-on-Plato-Chimaera-and-the-Indus-Civilization-Dennys-Frenez-Massimo-Vidale-2012

Ligatured faces: some close-up images.

Hieroglyph: 'human face': *mũhe* 'face' (Santali)

Rebus: *mũh* opening or hole (in a stove for stoking (Bi.); ingot (Santali) *mũh* metal ingot (Santali) *mũhā̃* = the quantity of iron produced at one time in a native smelting furnace of the Kolhes; iron produced by the Kolhes and formed like a four-cornered piece a little pointed at each end; *mūhā mẽṛhẽt* = iron smelted by the Kolhes and formed into an equilateral lump a little pointed at each of four ends; *kolhe tehen mẽṛhẽt ko mūhā akata* = the Kolhes have to-day produced pig iron (Santali) *kaula mengro* 'blacksmith' (Gypsy) *mleccha-mukha* (Skt.) = *milakkhu* 'copper' (Pali)
The Samskritam gloss *mleccha-mukha* should literally mean: copper-ingot absorbing the Santali gloss, *mũh*, as a suffix.

A remarkable phrase in Sanskrit indicates the link between mleccha and use of camels as trade caravans. This is explained in the lexicon of Apte for the lexeme: auṣṭrika 'belonging to a camel'. The lexicon entry cited *Mahābhārata*: औष्ट्रिक a. Coming from a camel (as milk); Mb.8. 44.28; -कः An oil-miller; मानुषाणां मलं म्लेच्छा म्लेच्छाना-मौष्ट्रिका मलम् । औष्ट्रिकाणां मलं षण्ढाः षण्ढानां राजयाजकाः ॥ Mb.8.45.25. From the perspective of a person devoted to śāstra and rigid disciplined life, Baudhāyana thus defines the word म्लेच्छः mlēcchḥ : -- गोमांसखादको यस्तु विरुद्धं बहु भाषते । सर्वाचारविहीनश्च म्लेच्छ इत्यभिधीयते ॥ 'A person who ears meat, deviates from traditional practices.'

The 'face' glyph is thus read rebus: *mleccha mũh* 'copper ingot'.

It is significant that Vatsyayana refers to cryptography in his lists of 64 arts and calls it mlecchita-vikalpa, lit. 'an alternative representation -- in cryptography or cipher -- of mleccha words.'

The composite animal glyph is one example to show that rebus method has to be applied to every glyphic element in the writing system.

Explaining chimaera as expanded 'hypertext', Frenez and Vidale note: "In the course of time, more dynamic approaches stressed semantic interactions, rather than the presence of links, eventually suggesting that 'interaction with information build associations, and association builds knowledge'. The surprising notion that the same complex form of communication was invented 4500 years ago in the Bronze Age cities of the Indus valley requires a detailed analysis of each example of this animal icon, with the final goal of understanding the diachronic change of its basic model, together with its rules of composition."

Unraveling semantic interactions of the particular hieroglyph multiplex and the underlying spoken words is successful decipherment -- proving the cipher -- with only one unique -- falsifiable -- solution which represents the reality of the building of knowledge in Sarasvati-Sindhu Civilization through the hieroglyph multiplexes of about 7000 inscriptions presented as Indus Script Corpora which has been substantively deciphered as *catalogum catalogorum* of metalwork.

See: http://bharatkalyan97.blogspot.in/2015/05/composite-animal-meluhha-hieroglyph.html

Indus script hieroglyphs: composite animal, smithy

Composite animal on Indus script is a composite hieroglyph composed of many glyphic elements. All glyphic elements are read rebus to complete the technical details of the bill of lading of artifacts created by artisans.

Mohenjodaro seal (m0302).

The composite animal glyph is one example to show that rebus method has to be applied to every glyphic element in the writing system.

This image is also interpreted in corpora (e.g. Mahadevan's Corpus of Indus script) as: body of a ram, horns of a bison, trunk of elephant, hindlegs of a tiger and an upraised serpent-like tail.

The glyphic elements of the composite animal shown together with the glyphs of fish, fish ligatured with lid, arrow (on Seal m0302) are:

--ram or sheep (forelegs denote a bovine)
--neck-band, ring
--*bos indicus* (zebu)(the high horns denote a *bos indicus*)
--elephant (the elephant's trunk ligatured to human face)
--tiger (hind legs denote a tiger)
--serpent (tail denotes a serpent)
--human face

All these glyphic elements are decoded rebus:

meḍho a ram, a sheep (G.)(CDIAL 10120) rebus: meD 'iron' (Ho.Munda)
adar ḍangra, poL 'zebu', 'bull dedicated to the gods' rebus: aduru 'native metal'; pola 'magnetite'
ibha 'elephant' (Skt.); rebus: ib 'iron' (Ko.); karabha 'elephant' (i.e. khar PLUS ibha: khar 'blacksmith'; ib 'iron', thus reconstructed as: kariba 'iron smith')
kolo 'jackal' (Kon.) rebus: kole.l 'smithy'; kolle 'blacksmith'; kol 'working in iron'; kolimi 'smithy'

dhatu 'scarf' (WPah.): *dhaṭa2, dhaṭī -- f. ' old cloth, loincloth ' lex. [Drav., Kan. daṭṭi ' waistband ' etc., DED 2465]Ku. dhaṛo ' piece of cloth ', N. dharo, B. dhaṛā; Or. dhaṛā ' rag, loincloth ', dhaṛi ' rag '; Mth. dhariā ' child's narrow loincloth '. †*dhaṭṭa -- : WPah.kṭg. dhàṭṭu m. ' woman's headgear, kerchief ', kc. dhaṭu m. (also dhaṭhu m. ' scarf ', J. dhāṭ(h)u m. Him.I 105).(CDIAL 6707) Ta. taṭṭi drawers. Ka. daṭṭi waist-band, sash, zone. Tu. daṭṭi waist-band. Te. daṭṭi waist-band or girdle of cloth, sash. Kui ḍaṭa a long cloth. / ? Cf. Skt. dhaṭī- piece of cloth worn over the privities; (Vaijayantī) dhaṭinī- string round the loins; Mar. dhaḍī dhotee (DEDR 3038)

Rebus: dhā́tu n. ' substance ' RV., m. ' element ' MBh., ' metal, mineral, ore (esp. of a red colour) ' Mn., ' ashes of the dead ' lex., ' *strand of rope ' (cf. tridhā́tu -- ' threefold ' RV., ayugdhātu -- ' having an uneven number of strands ' KātyŚr.). [√dhā]Pa. dhātu -- m. ' element, ashes of the dead, relic '; KharI. dhatu ' relic '; Pk. dhāu -- m. ' metal, red chalk '; N. dhāu ' ore (esp. of copper) '; Or. ḍhāu ' red chalk, red ochre ' (whence ḍhāuā ' reddish '; M. dhāū, dhāv m.f. ' a partic. soft red stone ' (whence dhā̆vaḍ m. ' a caste of iron -- smelters ', dhāvḍī ' composed of or relating to iron '); -- Si. dā ' relic '; -- S. dhāī f. ' wisp of fibres added from time to time to a rope that is being twisted ', L. dhāī̃ f.(CDIAL 6773) هژدات hajz̤-dāt, s.m. (6th) (corrup. of S اژدهات) The name of a mixed metal, bell-metal, brass. Sing. and Pl. د و هژداټ غر da hajz̤-dāto g̠har, A mountain of brass, a brazen mountain.

karabhá m. ' camel ' MBh., ' young camel ' Pañcat., ' young elephant ' BhP. 2. kalabhá -- ' young elephant or camel ' Pañcat. [Poss. a non -- aryan *kar* -- ' elephant ' also in karḗṇu -- , karin -- EWA i 165]1. Pk. *karabha* -- m., °*bhī* -- f., *karaha* -- m. ' camel ', S. *karahu*, °*ho* m., P. H. *karhā* m., Marw. *karhau* JRAS 1937, 116, OG. *karahu* m., OM. *karahā* m.; Si.*karaba* ' young elephant or camel '.2. Pa. *kalabha* -- m. ' young elephant ', Pk. *kalabha* -- m., °*bhiā* -- f., *kalaha* -- m.; Ku. *kalṛo* ' young calf '; Or. *kālhuṛi* ' young bullock, heifer '; Si. *kalam̆bayā* ' young elephant '.OMarw. *karaha* ' camel '.(CDIAL 2797)

moṇḍ the tail of a serpent (Santali) Rebus: Md. moḍenī ' massages, mixes '. Kal.rumb. moṇḍ -- ' to thresh ', urt. maṇḍ -- ' to soften ' (CDIAL 9890) Thus, the ligature of the serpent as a tail of the composite animal glyph is decoded as: polished metal (artifact).

mũhe 'face' (Santali); mleccha-mukha (Skt.) = milakkhu 'copper' (Pali)
கோடு kōṭu : •நடுநிலை நீங்குகை. கோடிறீக் கூற் றம் (நாலடி, 5). 3. [K. kōḍu.] Tusk; யானை பன்றிகளின் தந்தம். மத்த யானையின் கோடும் (தேவா. 39, 1). 4. Horn; விலங்கின் கொம்பு. கோட்டிடை யாடினை கூத்து (திவ். இயற். திருவிருத். 21).
Ta. kōṭu (in cpds. kōṭṭu-) horn, tusk, branch of tree, cluster, bunch, coil of hair, line, diagram, bank of stream or pool; kuvaṭu branch of a tree; kōṭṭāṉ, kōṭṭuvāṉ rock horned-owl (cf. 1657 Ta. kuṭiñai). Ko. kṛ (obl. kṭ-) horns (one horn is kob), half of hair on each side of parting, side in game, log, section of bamboo used as fuel, line marked out. To. kwṛ (obl. kwṭ-) horn, branch, path across stream in thicket. Ka. kōḍu horn, tusk, branch of a tree; kōṟ horn. Tu. kōḍů, kōḍu horn. Te. kōḍu rivulet, branch of a river. Pa. kōḍ (pl. kōḍul) horn (DEDR 2200)

meḍ 'iron' (Ho.)
khāḍ 'trench, firepit'
aduru 'native metal' (Ka.) *ḍhangar* 'blacksmith' (H.)
kol 'furnace, forge' (Kuwi) *kol* 'alloy of five metals, pancaloha' (Ta.)
mẽṛhẽt, meḍ 'iron' (Mu.Ho.)

mūhā mẽṛhẽt = iron smelted by the Kolhes and formed into an equilateral lump a little pointed at each of four ends (Santali)
koḍ = the place where artisans work (G.)

Orthographically, the glytic compositions add on the characteristic short tail as a hieroglyph (on both ligatured signs and on pictorial motifs)

xolā = tail (Kur.); qoli id. (Malt.)(DEDr 2135). Rebus: *kol* 'pañcalōha' (Ta.)கொல் kol, n. 1. Iron; இரும்பு. மின் வெள்ளி பொன் கொல்லெனச் சொல்லும் (தக்கயாகப். 550). 2. Metal; உலோகம். (நாமதீப. 318.) கொல்லன் kollaṉ, n. < T. golla. Custodian of treasure; கஜானாக்காரன். (P. T. L.) கொல்லிச்சி kollicci, n. Fem. of கொல்லன். Woman of the blacksmith caste; கொல்லச் சாதிப் பெண். (யாழ். அக.) The gloss kollicci is notable. It clearly evidences that kol was a blacksmith. *kola* 'blacksmith' (Ka.); Koḍ. *kollë* blacksmith (DEDR 2133).
Vikalpa: *dumba*दुम्ब or (El.) *duma* दुम । पशुपुच्छः m. the tail of an animal. (Kashmiri)
Rebus: *ḍōmba* ?Gypsy (CDIAL 5570).

m1180 Mohenjo-daro seal. Human-faced markhor.

m0301 Mohenjo-daro seal.

m0303 Mohenjo-daro seal.

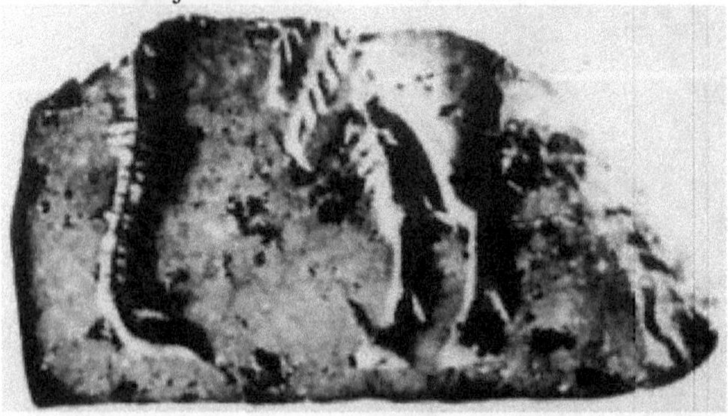

h594. Harappa seal. Composite animal (with elephant trunk and rings (scarves) on shoulder visible).koṭiyum = a wooden circle put round the neck of an animal; koṭ = neck (G.) Vikalpa: kaḍum 'neck-band, ring'; rebus: khāḍ 'trench, firepit' (G.) Vikalpa: khaḍḍā f. hole, mine, cave (CDIAL 3790). kanduka, kandaka ditch, trench (Tu.); kandakamu id. (Te.); kanda trench made as a fireplace during weddings (Konda); kanda small trench for fireplace (Kui); kandri a pit (Malt)(DEDR 1214) khaḍḍa— 'hole, pit'. [Cf. *gaḍḍa— and list s.v. kartá—1] Pk. khaḍḍā— f. 'hole, mine, cave', ḍaga— m. 'one who digs a hole', ḍōlaya— m. 'hole'; Bshk. (Biddulph) "kād" (= khaḍ?) 'valley'; K. khŏḍ m. 'pit', khŏḍü f. 'small pit', khoḍu m. 'vulva'; S. khaḍa f. 'pit'; L. khaḍḍ f. 'pit, cavern, ravine'; P. khaḍḍ f. 'pit, ravine', ḍī f. 'hole for a weaver's feet' (→ Ku. khaḍḍ, N. khaḍ; H. khaḍ, khaḍḍā m. 'pit, low ground, notch'; Or. khā̃ḍi 'edge of a deep pit'; M. khaḍḍā m. 'rough hole, pit'); WPah. khaś. khaḍḍā 'stream'; N. khāṛo 'pit, bog', khāṛi 'creek', khāṛal 'hole (in ground or stone)'. — Altern. < *khāḍa—: Gy. gr. xar f. 'hole'; Ku. khāṛ 'pit'; B. khāṛī 'creek, inlet', khāṛal 'pit, ditch'; H. khāṛī f. 'creek, inlet', khaṛ—har, al m. 'hole'; Marw. khāṛo

m. 'hole'; M. khāḍ f. 'hole, creek', ḍā m. 'hole', ḍī f. 'creek, inlet'. 3863 khā́tra— n. 'hole' HPariś., 'pond, spade' Uṇ. [√khan] Pk. khatta— n. 'hole, manure', aya— m. 'one who digs in a field'; S. khāṭru m. 'mine made by burglars', ṭro m. 'fissure, pit, gutter made by rain'; P. khāt m. 'pit, manure', khāttā m. 'grain pit', ludh. khattā m. (→ H. khattā m., khatiyā f.); N. khāt 'heap (of stones, wood or corn)'; B. khāt, khāṭrū 'pit, pond'; Or. khāta 'pit', tā 'artificial pond'; Bi. khātā 'hole, gutter, grain pit, notch (on beam and yoke of plough)', khattā 'grain pit, boundary ditch'; Mth. khātā, khattā 'hole, ditch'; H. khāt m. 'ditch, well', f. 'manure', khātā m. 'grain pit'; G. khātar n. 'housebreaking, house sweeping, manure', khātriyũ n. 'tool used in housebreaking' (→ M. khātar f. 'hole in a wall', khātrā m. 'hole, manure', khātryā m. 'housebreaker'); M. khāt n.m. 'manure' (deriv. khatāviṇẽ 'to manure', khāterẽ n. 'muck pit'). — Un- expl. ṭ in L. khāṭvā̃ m. 'excavated pond', khāṭī f. 'digging to clear or excavate a canal' (~ S. khātī f. 'id.', but khāṭyāro m. 'one employed to measure canal work') and khaṭṭaṇ 'to dig'. (CDIAL 3790) •gaḍa— 1 m. 'ditch' lex. [Cf. *gaḍḍa—1 and list s.v. kartá—1] Pk. gaḍa— n. 'hole'; Paš. gaṛu 'dike'; Kho. (Lor.) gōḷ 'hole, small dry ravine'; A. garā 'high bank'; B. gaṛ 'ditch, hole in a husking machine'; Or. gaṛa 'ditch, moat'; M. gaḷ f. 'hole in the game of marbles'. 3981 *gaḍḍa— 1 'hole, pit'. [G. < *garda—? — Cf. *gaḍḍ—1 and list s.v. kartá—1] Pk. gaḍḍa— m. 'hole'; WPah. bhal. cur. gaḍḍ f., paṅ. gaḍḍṛī, pāḍ. gaḍōṛ 'river, stream'; N. gaṛ—tir 'bank of a river'; A. gārā 'deep hole'; B. gāṛ, ṛā 'hollow, pit'; Or. gāṛa 'hole, cave', gāṛiā 'pond'; Mth. gāṛi 'piercing'; H. gāṛā m. 'hole'; G. garāḍ, ḍɔ m. 'pit, ditch' (< *graḍḍa— < *garda—?); Si. gaḍaya 'ditch'. — Cf. S. giḍi f. 'hole in the ground for fire during Muharram'. — X khānī̆—: K. gān m. 'underground room'; S. (LM 323) gāṇ f. 'mine, hole for keeping water'; L. gāṇ m. 'small embanked field within a field to keep water in'; G. gāṇ f. 'mine, cellar'; M. gāṇ f. 'cavity containing water on a raised piece of land' WPah.kṭg. gāṛ 'hole (e.g. after a knot in wood)'. (CDIAL 3947) 3860 *khāḍa— 'a hollow'. [Cf. *khaḍḍa— and list s.v. kartá—1] S. khāṛī f. 'gulf, creek'; P. khāṛ 'level country at the foot of a mountain', ṛī f. 'deep watercourse, creek'; Bi. khārī 'creek, inlet'; G. khāṛi , ṛī f., ṛɔ m. 'hole'. — Altern. < *khaḍḍa—: Gy. gr. xar f. 'hole'; Ku. khāṛ 'pit'; B. khāṛī 'creek, inlet', khāṛal 'pit, ditch'; H. khāṛī 'creek, inlet', khaṛ—har, al m. 'hole'; Marw. khāṛo m. 'hole'; M. khāḍ f. 'hole, creek', ḍā m. 'hole', ḍī f. 'creek, inlet'. The neck-bands hung above the shoulder of the composite animal may thus read rebus: trench or fire-pit (i.e. furnace) for the minerals/metals described by the glyphic elements connoting animals: elephant, ram (or zebu, bos indicus).

m1169A joined animals: ox, young bull, antelope
Ancient Near East Bronze Age -- heralded by Meluhha writing

Three artefacts with Indus writing are remarkable for their definitive intent to broadcast the metallurgical message: 1. Dholavira signboard on a gateway; 2. Shahdad standard; and 3. Tablets showing processions of three standards: scarf hieroglyph, one-horned young bull hieroglyph and standard-device hieroglyph. Rebus readings of the inscriptions relate to and document the metallurgical competence of Meluhhan lapidaries-artisans. Some other select set of inscriptions from the wide, expansive area stretching from Haifa to Rakhigarhi, from Altyn Depe (Caucus) to Daimabad (Maharashtra) are presented to show the area which had evidenced the use of Meluhha (Mleccha) language of Indian *sprachbund.*

Hieroglyphs deployed on Indus inscriptions have had a lasting effect on the glyptic motifs used on hundreds of cylinder seals of the Meluhha contact regions. The glyptic motifs continued to be used as a logo-semantic writing system, together with cuneiform texts which used a logo-syllabic writing system, even after the use of complex tokens and bullae were discontinued to account for commodities. The Indus writing system of hieroglyphs read rebus matched the Bronze Age revolutionary imperative of minerals, metals and alloys produced as surplus to the requirements of the artisan communities and as available for the creation and sustenance of trade-networks to meet the demand for alloyed metal tools, weapons, pots and pans, apart from the supply of copper, tin metal ingots for use in the smithy of nations,*harosheth hagoyim* mentioned in the Old

Testament (Judges). This term also explains the continuum of Aramaic script into the cognate *kharoṣṭhī* 'blacksmith-lip' *goya* 'communities'.

Indus-Sarasvatī Signboard Text. Read rebus as Meluhha (Mleccha) announcement of metals repertoire of a smithy complex in the citadel. The 'spoked wheel' is the semantic divider of three segments of the broadcast message. Details of readings, from r. to l.:

Segment 1: Working in ore, molten cast copper, lathe (work)

ḍato 'claws or pincers of crab' (Santali) rebus: *dhatu* 'ore' (Santali)

eraka 'knave of wheel' Rebus: *eraka* 'copper' (Kannada) *eraka* 'molten cast (metal)(Tulu). *sangaḍa* 'pair' Rebus: *sangaḍa*'lathe' (Gujarati)

Segment 2: Native metal tools, pots and pans, metalware, engraving (molten cast copper)

खांडा [khāṇḍā] *m* A jag, notch, or indentation (as upon the edge of a tool or weapon). (Marathi) Rebus: *khāṇḍā* 'tools, pots and pans, metal-ware'.

aḍaren, ḍaren lid, cover (Santali) Rebus: *aduru* 'native metal' (Ka.) *aduru* = gan.iyinda tegadu karagade iruva aduru = ore taken from the mine and not subjected to melting in a furnace (Kannada) (Siddhānti *Subrahmaṇya' śāstri's new interpretation of the Amarakośa*, Bangalore, Vicaradarpana Press, 1872, p. 330)

koṇḍa bend (Ko.); Tu. Kōḍi corner; kōṇṭu angle, corner, crook. Nk. kōnṭa corner (DEDR 2054b) G. khū̃ṭrī f. 'angle' Rebus: *kõdā*'to turn in a lathe'(B.) कोंद kōnda 'engraver, lapidary setting or infixing gems' (Marathi) koḍ 'artisan's workshop' (Kuwi) koḍ = place where artisans work (G.) ācāri koṭṭya 'smithy' (Tu.) कोंडण [kōṇḍaṇa] f A fold or pen. (Marathi) B. kõdā 'to turn in a lathe'; Or.kŭnda 'lathe', kũdibā, kũd 'to turn' (→ Drav. Kur. Kũd ' lathe') (CDIAL 3295) A. kundār, B. kũdār, ri, Or.Kundāru; H. kũderā m. 'one who works a lathe, one who scrapes', rī f., kũdernā 'to scrape, plane, round on a lathe'; kundakara—m. 'turner' (Skt.)(CDIAL 3297). कोंदण [kōndaṇa] n (कोंदणें) Setting or infixing of gems.(Marathi) খোদকার [khōdakāra] n an engraver; a carver. খোদকারি n. engraving; carving; interference in other's work. খোদাই [khōdāi] n engraving; carving. খোদাই করা v. to engrave; to carve. খোদানো v. & n. en graving; carving. খোদিত [khōdita] a engraved. (Bengali) खोदकाम [khōdakāma] n Sculpture; carved work or work for the carver. खोदगिरी [khōdagirī] f Sculpture, carving, engraving: also sculptured or carved work. खोदणावळ [khōdaṇāvaḷa] f (खोदणें) The price or cost of sculpture or carving. खोदणी [khōdaṇī] f (Verbal of खोदणें) Digging, engraving &c. 2 fig. An exacting of money by importunity. V लाव, मांड. 3 An instrument to scoop out and cut flowers and figures from paper. 4 A goldsmith's die. खोदणें [khōdaṇēṃ] v c & i (H) To dig. 2 To engrave. खोद खोदून विचारणें or –पुसणें To question minutely and searchingly, to probe. खोदाई [khōdāī] f (H.) Price or cost of digging or of sculpture or carving. खोदींव [khōdīṃva] p of खोदणें Dug. 2 Engraved, carved, sculptured. (Marathi)

eraka 'knave of wheel' Rebus: *eraka* 'copper' (Kannada) *eraka* 'molten cast (metal)(Tulu).

Segment 3:  Coppersmith mint, furnace, workshop (molten cast copper)

loa 'fig leaf; Rebus: loh '(copper) metal' *kamaḍha* 'ficus religiosa' (Skt.); *kamaṭa* = portable furnace for melting precious metals (Te.); *kampaṭṭam* = mint (Ta.) The unique ligatures on the 'leaf' hieroglyph may be explained as a professional designation: *loha-kāra* 'metalsmith'; *kāruvu* [Skt.] n. 'An artist, artificer. An agent'.(Telugu).
khuṇṭa 'peg'; khũṭi = pin (M.) rebus: kuṭi= furnace (Santali) kūṭa 'workshop' kuṇḍamu 'a pit for receiving and preserving consecrated fire' (Te.) kundār turner (A.); kũdār, kũdāri (B.)

eraka 'knave of wheel' Rebus: *eraka* 'copper' (Kannada) *eraka* 'molten cast (metal)(Tulu).

Size matters. Archaeological context matters. How could one interpret the utility for the people of Dholavira, of 10 large glyphs (35 to 37 cm. high and 25 to 27 cm.wide) carefully laid out, in sequence, using gypsum pieces on an inscription which was a Signboard mounted on a gateway? Maybe, the Signboard text was visible from a distance for seafaring merchants and artisans from Dilmun or Magan or Elam. How can one assume it to be oral literature, for the guidance of tourists or merchants entering the citadel or even for the people of Dholavira (Kotda)? Why should any pundit conceive of the text, arbitrarily, to be non-linguistic? The glyphs are not randomly drawn but are repetitions from several tablets and seals which carry one or more of nearly 500 such distinct glyphs on nearly 7000 inscriptions of Indus writing. Why can't the glyphs be read rebus as hieroglyphs as a cypher code for the underlying sounds & semantics of words in Meluhha (Mleccha) language -- comparable to the rebus reading of N'r-M'r palette which used N'r 'cuttle-fish' and M'r 'awl' hieroglyphs to be read together as Narmer, the name of an Egyptian emperor?

Dholavira Gateway as seen from the citadel. "The first quake hit the township around 2800 BC, the second around 2500 BC, and the third around 2000 BC," said Bisht.

One gateway had a signboard. "It is believed that the stone signboard was hung on a wooden plank in front of the gate. This could be the oldest signboard known to us," said Bisht. http://tinyurl.com/l3cszrr

Dholavira Signboard on GatewayThe citadel had two gateways: one on the northern and the other on the eastern side. Each gateway had an elaborate staircase. The landing of the staircase was at a depth of 2.3 m. After ten steps and a further descent of 2 m., the staircase led to a passage way which was 7 m. long On either side of the passage, there was a chamber which had a roof resting on stone pillars. In one of the chambers, a unique inscription was discovered. The ten letters of the inscription had a height of about 35 to 37 cm. and a width of 25 to 27 cm. The letters wee made of sliced pieces of some 'crystalline material, maybe rock, mineral or paste'. Perhaps mounted on a wooden board, the inscription might have constituted a sign-board. Ring-stones were used to support the pillars.

[quote] RS Bisht opined that the Harappans were a literate people. The commanding height at which the 10-sign board had been erected showed that it was meant to be read by all people.Besides, seals with Indus signs were found everywhere in the city – in the

citadel, middle town, lower town, annexe, and so on. It meant a large majority of the people knew how to read and write. The Indus script had been found on pottery as well. Even children wrote on potsherds. Bisht said: “The argument that literacy was confined to a few people is not correct. You find inscriptions on pottery, bangles and even copper tools. This is not graffiti, which is child’s play. The finest things were available even to the lowest sections of society. The same seals, beads and pottery were found everywhere in the castle, bailey, the middle town and the lower town of the settlement at Dholavira, as if the entire population had wealth.
[unquote] http://varnam.nationalinterest.in/2010/06/the-sign-board-at-dholavira/

The Dholavira Gateway Signboard text is perhaps the world's first advertisement hoarding by any artisan or merchant.

Similar is the function served by the Shahdad standard, as a Meluhha (mleccha) metalware catalog describing the repertoire of a smithy in Shahdad, Marhashi. So, it was that Chanhu-daro was ranked as Sheffied of the Ancient Near East serving a vast contact region with metalware tools, weapons, pots and pans. This regional/archaeological context matters while interpreting Meluhha writing (also called Indus writing) for the sounds of underlying words which became the lingua france of Indian *sprachbund.* That Meluhha is a language is recognized on a cylinder seal of Shu-Ilishu, Akkadian interpreter. That cognate Mleccha is a language is attested in the Great Epic, Mahabharata, in the episode of conversations between Yudhishthira had with Vidura and Khanaka, on the metallic weapons planted in a jatugriha (lac house) to destroy the Pandavas in exile. That Mleccha was a language is attested in an earlier text, Manusamhita as*mleccha vācas*. That Meluhha was a region in proximity to and that there were mleccha settlements in Mesopotamia, Dilmun, Magan, Elam, Marhashi, Susa are evidences well-attested in cuneiform texts. Lexemes '*mlecchamukha*' in Sanskrit and '*milakkhu*' in Pali means 'copper'. A Mleccha dynasty (c. 650 - 900) ruled Kamarupa from their capital at Hadapeshvar in the present-day Tezpur, Assam, after the fall of the Varman dynasty. It is also significant that assur who are smelters par excellence live close to Lohardiva, Malhar, Raja-nal-ki-tila on the Ganga basin, where iron smelters were discovered dated to ca. 18th century BCE.
See: http://bharatkalyan97.blogspot.in/2013/06/asur-metallurgists.html Ancient Near East: Traditions of smelters, metallurgists validate the Bronze Age Linguistic Doctrine.

Vātsyāyana used the term *mlecchitavikalpa* to denote cypher writing as one of the 64 arts to be learnt by the youth, including two other language-related arts: *akṣaramuṣṭika kathanam* 'narration using finger-wrist gestures' and*deśabhāṣājñānam* 'knowledge of vernacular languages'.

See for details:
1. http://bharatkalyan97.blogspot.in/2013/07/shahdad-standard-meluhha-smithy-catalog.html Shahdad standard: Meluhha smithy catalog of Shahdad, Marhashi
2. http://bharatkalyan97.blogspot.in/2013/07/ancient-near-east-shahdad-bronze-age.html Ancient Near East: Shahdad bronze-age inscriptional evidence, a tribute to Ali Hakemi

3. http://bharatkalyan97.blogspot.in/2013/07/location-of-marhashi-and-cheetah-from.html Location of Marhashi and cheetah from Meluhha: Shahdad & Tepe Yahya are in Marhashi
Ancient Near East: Shahdad bronze-age inscriptional evidence, a tribute to Ali Hakemi

http://www.iranicaonline.org/articles/cylinder-seals Shahdad (Šāhdād) cylinder seal. tagaraka 'tabernae montana' rebus: tagaram 'tin'; kola 'woman' rebus: kol 'alloy' (Meluhha, Mleccha) See other rebus readings of hieroglyphs on the seal. Nine plants (tabernae montana tulips) emanate from the woman' s body. lo, no 'nine' rebus: lo 'copper'. Copper alloyed with tin creates bronze. It is possible that the cylinder seal is a commemoration of this breakthrough in the Bronze Age of creating metal alloys.

Shahdad standard is a Meluhha (mleccha) metalware catalog describing the repertoire of a smithy in Shahdad, Marhashi:

pajhaṛ 'kite'. Rebus: pasra 'smithy' (Santali)

Three pots are shown of three sizes in the context of kneeling adorants seated in front of the person seated on a stool. meṇḍā 'kneeling position' (Gondi) Rebus: meḍ 'iron' (Munda)

kōla = woman (Nahali) Rebus: kol 'furnace, forge' (Kuwi) kol 'alloy of five metals, pañcaloha' (Tamil) kol 'working in iron' (Tamil)

kaṇḍō a stool. Malt. Kanḍo stool, seat. (DEDR 1179) Rebus: kaṇḍ = a furnace, altar (Santali)

If the date palm denotes tamar (Hebrew language), 'palm tree, date palm' the rebus reading would be: tam(b)ra, 'copper' (Pkt.)

kaṇḍ kan-ka 'rim of jar' (Santali). kanka 'rim (of jar, kaṇḍ)' (Santali) kárṇa— m. 'ear, handle of a vessel' RV., 'end, tip (?)' RV. ii 34, 3. [Cf. *kāra—6] Pa. kaṇṇa— m. 'ear, angle, tip' (CDIAL 2830). Rebus: 'scribe'. Pk. *kaṁḍa* -- m. ' piece, fragment '; -- Deriv. Pk. *kaṁḍārēi* ' scrapes, engraves ';M. *kā̃ḍārṇẽ*, *karā̃ḍṇẽ* ' to gnaw ', *kā̃ḍārṇẽ* n. ' jeweller's hammer, barber's nail -- parer '. (CDIAL 2683) कंडारणें [kaṇḍāraṇēṃ] *n* An instrument of goldsmiths,--the iron spike which is hammered upon plates in reducing them to shape (Marathi) khanaka m. one who digs , digger , excavator MBh. iii , 640 R. ; a miner L. ; a house-breaker , thief L. ; a rat L. ; N. of a friend of Vidura MBh. i , 5798 f. ; (%{I}) f. a female digger or excavator Pāṇ. 3-1 , 145 Pat. ; iv , 1 , 41 Ka1s3.

kaṇḍ 'jar' (Santali) Rebus: kāḍ 'stone'. Ga. (Oll.) kanḍ, (S.) kanḍu (pl. kanḍkil) stone (DEDR 1298). mayponḍi kanḍ whetstone; (Ga.)(DEDR 4628). (खडा) Pebbles or small stones: also stones broken up (as for a road), metal. खडा [khaḍā] *m* A small stone, a pebble. Rebus: kaṇḍ = a furnace, altar (Santali)

kul 'tiger' (Santali); kōlu id. (Te.) kōlupuli = Bengal tiger (Te.)Pk. Kolhuya -- , kulha — m. ' jackal ' < *kōḍhu -- ; H.kolhā, °lā m. ' jackal ', adj. ' crafty '; G. kohlũ, °lũ n. ' jackal ', M. kolhā, °lā m. krōṣṭŕ̥ ' crying ' BhP., m. ' jackal ' RV. = krṓṣṭu — m. Pāṇ. [√kruś] Pa. koṭṭhu -- , °uka — and kotthu -- , °uka — m. ' jackal ', Pk. Koṭṭhu — m.; Si. Koṭa ' jackal ', koṭiya ' leopard ' GS 42 (CDIAL 3615). कोल्हा [kōlhā] कोल्हें [kōlhēṃ] A jackal (Marathi) Rebus: kol 'furnace, forge' (Kuwi) kol 'alloy of five metals, pañcaloha' (Ta.)

adar ḍangra 'zebu or humped bull'; ḍangar 'bull' Rebus: adar ḍhangar 'native metalsmith'.

Rebus: ḍangar 'blacksmith'; aduru native metal (Kannada). Tu. ajirda karba very hard iron (DEDR 192). aduru = *gaṇiyinda tegadu karagade iruva aduru* = ore taken from the mine and not subjected to melting in a furnace (Ka. Siddhānti Subrahmaṇya śastri's *New interpretation of the Amarakośa,* Bangalore, Vicaradarpana Press, 1872, p. 330) aduru 'native metal' (Kannada); ḍhangar 'blacksmith' (Hindi)

kuṭi 'tree'. Rebus: kuṭhi 'smelter' (Santali). The two trees are shown ligatured to a rectangle with ten square divisions and a dot in each square. The dot may denote an ingot in a furnace mould.

Glyph of rectangle with divisions: *baṭai* = to divide, share (Santali) [Note the glyphs of nine rectangles divided.] Rebus: *bhaṭa* = an oven, kiln, furnace (Santali)
ḍāḷ= a branch of a tree (G.) Rebus: *ḍhāḷuko* = a large ingot (G.) ḍhāḷakī = a metal heated and poured into a mould; a solid piece of metal; an ingot (G.)
Three sets of entwined 'glyphs (like twisted ropes) are shown around the entire narrative of the Shahdad standard.

meṛhao = v.a.m. entwine itself; wind round, wrap round roll up (Santali); maṛhnā cover, encase (Hindi) (Santali.lex.Bodding) Rebus: *meḍ* 'iron' (Mu.Ho.) mẽṛh t iron; ispat m. = steel; dul m. = cast iron (Mu.) meṛed-bica = iron stone ore, in contrast to bali-bica, iron sand ore (Munda) *mẽṛhẽt*'iron'; *mẽṛhẽt icena*'the iron is rusty';*ispat mẽṛhẽt*'steel', *dul mẽṛhẽt*'cast iron'; *mẽṛhẽt khaṇḍa*'iron implements'
(Santali) *meḍ.* (Ho.)(Santali.lex.Bodding) *meṛed, mṛed, mṛd* iron; enga meṛed soft iron; *sanḍi meṛed* hard iron;*ispāt meṛed* steel; *dul meṛed* cast iron; *i meṛed* rusty iron, also the iron of which weights are cast; *bica meṛed* iron extracted from stone ore; *bali meṛed* iron extracted from sand ore (Mu.lex.)

měď (copper)(Czech) mid′ (copper, cuprum, orichalc)(Ukrainian) med′ (copper, cuprum, Cu), mednyy (copper, cupreous, brassy, brazen, brass), omednyat′ (copper, coppering), sul′fatmedi (Copper), politseyskiy (policeman, constable, peeler, policemen, redcap), pokryvat′ med′yu (copper), payal′nik (soldering iron, copper, soldering pen, soldering-iron), mednyy kotel (copper), medno-krasnyy (copper), mednaya moneta (copper). медь (copper, cuprum, Cu), медный (copper, cupreous, brassy, brazen, brass), омеднять (copper, coppering), Сульфатмеди (Copper), полицейский (policeman, constable, peeler, policemen, redcap), покрывать медью (copper), паяльник (soldering iron, copper, soldering pen, soldering-iron), медный котел (copper), медно-красный (copper), медная монета (copper).(Russian)   Mohenjo-daro seal m297a: Harappa h1018a: copper plate The hieroglyphs are explained as fortified enclosures of mleccha smithy guild workshops. veṛhā 'octopus, said to be found in the Indus' (Jaṭki lexicon of A. Jukes, 1900) Rebus: *beṛɔ* m. 'palace', *beṛā* m. id. *beṛā* 'building with a courtyard' (Western Pahari) *vāṛo* m. ' cattle enclosure ' (Sindhi) மேடை mēṭai, *n.* [T. *mēḍa.*] 1. Platform, raised floor; தளமுயர்ந்த இடப்பகுதி. 2. Artificial mound; செய்குன்று. (W.)

Allographs:

meḍ 'body ' (Munda)

mēḍha मेढ 'polar star' (Marathi) mēṭaṉ, *n.* < மேடம்[1]. The planet Mars, as the lord of the sign Aries; [மேஷ ராசிக்கு உடையவன்] செவ்வாய் (நாமதீப. 98.)

मेटींव [mēṭīṃva] *p* of मेटणें A verb not in use. Roughly hewn or chiseled--a stone. (Marathi)

meḍh 'helper of merchant' (Pkt.) meṛha, meḍhi 'merchant's clerk; (Gujarati) मेढ'merchant's helper' (Pkt.); *m.* an elephant-keeper Gal. (cf. मेठ). *Ta.* mēṭṭi haughtiness, excellence, chief, head, land granted free of tax to the headman of a village; mēṭṭimai haughtiness; leadership, excellence. *Ka.* mēṭi loftiness, greatness, excellence, a big man, a chief, a head, head servant. *Te.* mēṭari, mēṭi chief, head, leader, lord; (prob. mēṭi < *mēl-ti [cf. 5086]; Ka. Ta. < Te.; Burrow 1969, p. 277) (DEDR 5091).மேட்டி mēṭṭi, *n.* Assistant house-servant; waiting-boy. மேட்டி +. Headman of the Toṭṭiya caste; தொட்டியர்தலைவன். (E. T. vii, 185.) మేటి [mēṭi] *mēti.* n. Lit: a helper. A servant, a cook, a menial who cleans plates, dishes, lamps and shoes, &c. (Eng. 'mate') మేటి [mēṭi] or మేటరి *mēṭi* [Tel.] n. A chief, leader, head man, lord, శ్రేష్ఠుడు, అధిపుడు. adj. Chief, excellent, noble. శ్రేష్ఠమైన. మేటిదొర a noble man, lord.

Bilh. ii.
50. మెరయుచునుండెడి మేటీరంబులుమేటీరంబులు, అనగామేటి, గొప్పలైన, ఈరంబులు, పొదలు large bushes. "తేటైనపన్నీటతీర్థంబులాడి, మేటికస్తూరిమేనెల్లబూసి." Misc. iii.
22. మేటిగా = మెండుగా. మేటిల్లు *mētillu*. v. n. To excel. అతిశయించు. Medinī (f.)
[Vedic medin an associate or companion fr. mid in meaning to be friendly.]
மேதி[1] mēti, *n*. perh. *mēdas*. 1. Buffalo; எருமை. மேதி யன்ன கல்பிறங் கியவின் (மலைபடு. 111)

meḷh 'goat' (Br.) mē̃ḍha 'antelope' meḍho a ram, a sheep (Gujarati)(CDIAL 10120)

Glyph 'mountain': మెట్ట [meṭṭa] or మిట్ట *meṭṭa*. [Tel.] n. Rising ground, high lying land, uplands. A hill, a rock. ఉన్నతభూమి, మెరక, పర్వతము, దిబ్బ. மேடு mēṭu , *n*. [T. *meṭṭa*, M. K. *mēḍu*.] 1. Height; உயரம். (பிங்.) 2. Eminence, little hill, hillock, ridge, rising ground; சிறுதிடர்.(பிங்.) *Ka.* mede heap. *Te. (VPK*, intro. p.
128) meda id. (DEDR 5065)

Glyph 'fig, ficus racemosa': మేడి [mēḍi] *mēḍi*. [Tel.] అత్తి, ఉదుంబరము. మేడిపండు the fruit of this tree. 5090 *Ka.* mēḍi glomerous fig tree, *Ficus racemosa*; opposite-leaved fig tree, *F. oppositifolia. Te.* mēḍi *F. glomerata. Kol.* (Kin.) mēṛi id. [*F. glomerata* Roxb. = *F. racemosa* Wall.](DEDR 5090).

Glyph 'curved end of stick': मेंढा [mēṇḍhā] *m* A crook or curved end (of a stick, horn &c.) and *attrib*. such a stick, horn, bullock.
mēṭu, mēṭa, mēṭi stack of hay; (Inscr.) (Telugu)
meḍ 'dance' (Santali) మెట్ట [meṭṭa] or మిట్ట *meṭṭa*. மெட்டு[1]-தல் meṭṭu-, v. tr. cf. நெட்டு-. [K. meṭṭu.] To spurn or push with the foot; காலால்தாக்குதல்.நிகளத்தைமெட்டிமெட்டிப்பொடிபடுத்தி (பழனிப்பிள்ளைத். 12). (Tamil) meṭṭu 'to put or place down the foot or feet; to step, to pace, to walk (Ka.)

meḍ 'dance' (Santali)

Glyph 'kneeling (adorant)': మండి [maṇḍi] or మండీ *manḍi*. [Tel.] n. Kneeling down with one leg, an attitude in archery, ఒకకాలితోనేలమీదమోకరించుట, ఆలీఢపాదము. मेट [mēṭa] *n* (मिटणें) The knee-joint or the bend of the knee. मेटेंखुंटीसबसणें To kneel down. *Ta.* maṇṭi kneeling, kneeling on one knee as an archer. *Ma.* maṇṭuka to be seated on the heels. *Ka.* maṇḍi what is bent, the knee. *Tu.* maṇḍi knee. *Te.* maṇḍī kneeling on

one knee. *Pa.* maḍtel knee; maḍi kuḍtel kneeling position. *Go.* (L.) meṇḍā, (G. Mu. Ma.) minḍa knee (*Voc.* 2827).*Konḍa* (BB) meḍa,
meṇḍa id. *Pe.* menḍa id. *Manḍ.* menḍe id. *Kui* menḍa id. *Kuwi* (F.) menda, (S. Su. P.) menḍa, (Isr.) meṇḍa id. Cf. 4645 Ta. maṭaṅku (maṇi-forms). / ? Cf. Skt. maṇḍūkī- part of an elephant's hind leg; Mar. meṭ knee-joint. (DEDR 4677)
Glyph 'oblation, offering': mḗdha m. ' sacrificial oblation ' RV. Pa. *mēdha* -- m. ' sacrifice '; Si. *mehe, mē* sb. ' eating ' ES 69.(CDIAL 10327).
meṛha, mehra ' a circular construction, mound '(Old Assamese)
meṛā m. (Bihari) *meṇḍa* -m. ' ram ' (Pali) *miṇḍā'l* ' markhor ' (Tōrwālī) Glyph 'crookedness of horns': Meṇḍa [dial., cp. Prk. mĕṇṭha & miṇṭha: Pischel, *Prk. Gr.* § 293. The Dhtm (156) gives a root meṇḍ (meḍ) in meaning of "koṭilla," i. e. crookedness. (Pali) M. *mẽḍhā* m. ' crook or curved end (of a horn, stick, &c.) '. Glyph: 'ram with curling horns': H. *mẽṛā, mẽḍā* m. ' ram with curling horns ', °*ḍī* f. ' she -- goat do. ' (CDIAL 10120) Bi. *mẽṛhwā* ' a bullock with curved horns like a ram's '; M. *mẽḍhrū̃* n. ' sheep '.(CDIAL 10311).

beṭhan m. 'pack -- cloth(Hindi)

veṭh, vẽṭh, veṭ, vẽṭ m.f. 'roll, turn of a rope' (Marathi) *bẽḍhnā, bẽdhnā* 'to plait, braid, fold (Hindi) *baṭṇī* ' twisting, twist (of a cord) ' (Kumaoni) *vaṭaṇu*, srk. °*ṭiṇu* ' to twist, plait, wring '(Sindhi) *baṭnā* ' to be twisted ' (Hindi) *meḍhā* m. ' curl, snarl, twist or tangle in cord or thread ' (Marathi)(CDIAL 10312) meḍhi, miḍhī, meṇḍhī = a plait in a woman's hair; a plaited or twisted strand of hair (Punjabi) [dial., cp. Prk. mĕṇṭha & miṇṭha: Pischel, Prk. Gr. § 293. The Dhtm (156) gives a root meṇḍ (meḍ) in meaning of "koṭilla," i. e. crookedness. (Pali)

Glyph 'spear': మేడెము [mēḍemu] or మేడియము *mēḍemu*. [Tel.] n. A spear

or dagger. ఈటె,బాకు. The rim of a bell-shaped earring, set with

ems.రాళ్లుచెక్కిన□మికీఅంచుయొక్క పనితరము. "కటడితినన్నన్వారకమేడెముపొడుతురె." BD.

vi. 116.
meḍ 'body' (Munda)

veḍh n.f. 'ring', m. 'circumference'(Marathi)

mēḍhi -- m. ' post on threshing floor (Prakrit) *meḍhā* m. ' post, forked stake '(Marathi) *mẽhi bāṭi* ' vessel with a projecting base '(Maithili) *meṭṭa*'projecting' (Telugu)

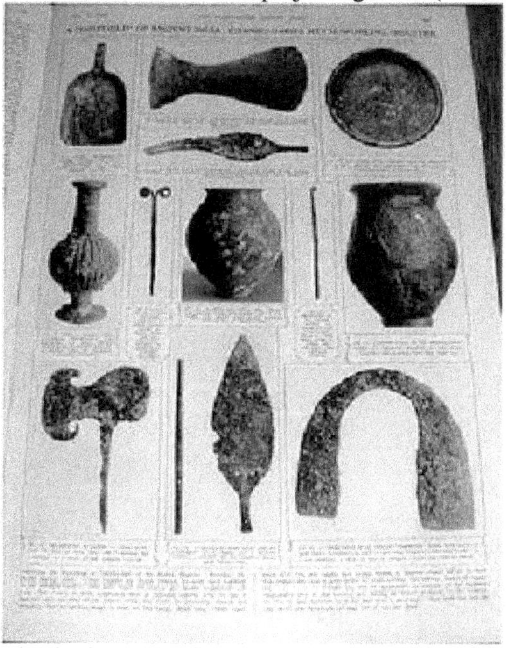

Chanhudaro. Sheffield of Ancient Near East. Metalware catalog in London News Illustrated, November 21,

1936. A 'Sheffield of Ancient India: Chanhu-Daro's metal working industry 10 X photos of copper knives, spears, razors, axes and dishes. The words used in the *lingua franca* of such tin-processing families constitute the words invented to denote the Bronze Age products and artifacts such as tin or zinc or the array of metalware discovered in the Sheffied of the Ancient East, Chanhu-daro as reported in the London News Illustrated by Ernest Mackay.

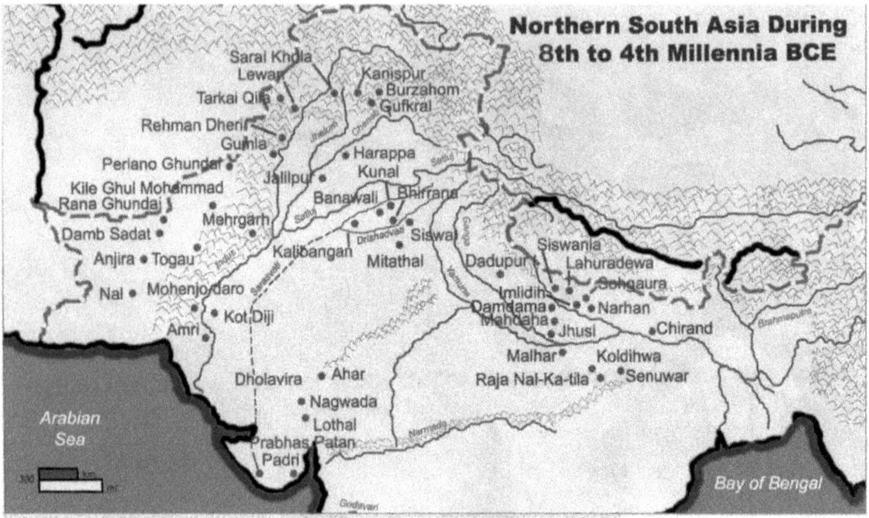

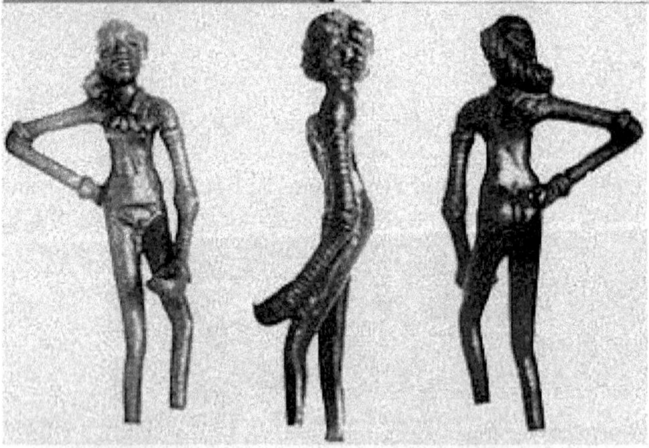

m0493Bt Pict-93: Three dancing figures in a row. Text 2843 Glyph: Three dancers. Kolmo 'three'; meD 'to dance'

Rebus: kolami 'furnace, smithy'; meD 'iron'

Sign 44 (this glyph could be compared with the orthography of three dancers in a row; the glyph is a ligature showing a 'dance step' and a rimless pot). Glyphs: meD 'dance' (Remo); rebus: meD 'iron'; bat.a 'pot'; bat.hi 'furnace'.
So, why a dancing girl? Because, depiction of a dance pose is a hieroglyph to represent what was contained in the pot. The glyph encodes the mleccha word for 'iron': med.
Glyph: meD 'to dance' (F.)[reduplicated from me-]; me id. (M.) in Remo (Munda)(Source: D. Stampe's Munda etyma)me??u to tread, trample, crush under foot, tread or place the foot upon (Te.); me??u step (Ga.); mettunga steps (Ga.). ma?ye to trample, tread (Malt.)(DEDR 5057)
Rebus: meD 'iron' (Mundari. Remo.)

http://asi.nic.in/asi_exca_2007_bhirrana.asp Excavation site: Bhirrana
http://asi.nic.in/asi_exca_2007_bhirrana_images.asp Images of site and artefacts discovered.

A bronze sculpture showing a dance-step becomes a hieroglyph of Indus writing on a Bhirrana potsherd, dance-step. meṭ sole of foot, footstep, footprint (Ko.); meṭṭu step, stair, treading, slipper (Te.)(DEDR 1557). Rebus: meḍ 'iron' (Munda)
Vikalpa: 1. N. *ḍag* ' step, stride ', H. *ḍag* f., OMarw. *ḍaga* f., G. *ḍag*, *ḍaglũ* n.; M. *ḍag* f. ' pace ', *ḍagṇẽ* ' to step over '; -- Or. *ḍagara* ' footstep, road '; Mth. *ḍagar* ' road ', H. *ḍagar* f., *ḍagrā* m., G. *ḍagar* f. 2. P. *ḍĩgh* f. ' foot, step '; N. *ḍeg*, *ḍek* ' pace '; Mth. *ḍeg* ' footstep '; H. *ḍig*, *ḍeg* f. ' pace '. 3. L. *dagg* m. ' road ', *daggaṛ rāh* m. ' wide road ' (mult. *ḍaggar rāh* < *daggaṛ*?); P. *dagaṛ* m. ' road ', H. *dagṛā* m.(CDIAL 5523).
Rebus: damgar 'merchant' (Akkadian)

Glyph: Pk. ḍhaṁkhara -- m.n. ' branch without leaves or fruit '. Rebus: N. ḍāṅro ' term of contempt for a blacksmith '(CDIAL 5524) Vikalpa: Glyph: Ta. kōṭu branch of tree, cluster, bunch, coil of hair, line, diagram kuvaṭu branch of a tree; Go. (Tr.) kōr (obl. kōt-, pl. kōhk) horn of cattle or wild animals, branch of a tree; Ka. kōḍu horn, tusk, branch of a tree (DEDR 2200). Rebus: kōṭ 'workshop'. P. *khoṭ* m.
'base, alloy' M.*khoṭā* 'alloyed' (CDIAL 3931)

[quote] Sept. 12, 2007

The ageless tale a potsherd from Bhirrana tells

T.S. Subramanian

CHENNAI: In a rare discovery, the Archaeological Survey of India has found at Bhirrana, a Harappan site in Fatehabad district in Haryana, a red potsherd with an engraving that resembles the 'Dancing Girl,' the iconic bronze figurine of Mohenjodaro. While the bronze was discovered in the early 1920s, the potsherd with the engraving was discovered during excavations by the ASI in 2004-05.

A few hundred kilometres separate Mohenjodaro, now in Pakistan, and Bhirrana. The potsherd, discovered by a team led by L.S. Rao, Superintending Archaeologist, Excavation Branch, ASI, Nagpur, belonged to the Mature Harappan period. Mr. Rao called it the "only one of its kind" because "no parallel to the Dancing Girl, in bronze or any other medium, was known" until the latest find.

In an article in the latest issue of *Man and Environment* (Volume XXXII, No.1, 2007), published by the Indian Society for Prehistoric and Quaternary Studies, Pune, Mr. Rao says, "... the delineation [of the lines in the potsherd] is so true to the stance, including the disposition of the hands, of the bronze that it appears that the craftsman of Bhirrana had first-hand knowledge of the former."

In his article, Mr. Rao has said the bronze was justly known for its stance and workmanship. "With its tilted head, flexed legs, right hand resting on the hip and the left suspended by its side, the bronze sculpture, although nude, enjoys a modest ornamentation with a necklace, wristlets and armlets. A statuette of 11 cm in height, it occupies a unique position in the sculptural art of the Mature Harappan period."
Mr. Rao called the engraving on the potsherd "a highly stylised figure whose torso resembles that of an hour-glass or two triangles meeting at their apex." Upon the horizontal shoulder line, a partly damaged round head was visible. In consonance with the bronze, "here too, the right hand is akimbo, and the left is suspended by its side. Slight oblique strokes on the right upper arm are suggestive of the presence of armlets. The lower portion of the body is missing owing to damage on the sherd. The clothing is indicated by horizontal hatchings on the chest and abdomen, and vertical hatchings on the thighs."

Mr. Rao called Bhirrana an "exemplary" and "paradigmatic" site that stood out on two more grounds. For the first time in the post-Independence period, artefacts called Hakra ware, belonging to the pre-early Harappan period, were found as independent, stratified deposits at Bhirrana. This and other discoveries established the presence of an unbroken cultural sequence at Bhirrana: from the Hakra ware culture and its evolution into early Harappan, early Mature Harappan and Mature Harappan until the site was abandoned. The discoveries of these periods include underground dwelling pits; house-complexes on streets; a fortification wall; bichrome pottery; terracotta cups; arrowheads, fish-hooks and bangles, all in copper; incised copper celts; terracotta toy-carts and animal figurines; and beads of semi-precious stones.

Seals made of steatite of the Mature Harappan period were found. They have animal figures such as a unicorn, a deer with wavy antlers, a bull with outsized horns, and an animal with three heads — of a deer, a unicorn and a bull. The seals also have typical Harappan legends on them. All these were found during excavations in 2003-04, 2004-05 and 2005-06.

Mr. Rao and colleagues have written on their work in *Puratattva* (Nos. 34, 35 and 36), a bulletin of the Indian Archaeological Society.

[unquote]

http://www.thehindu.com/todays-paper/the-ageless-tale-a-potsherd-from-bhirrana-tells/article1909703.ece

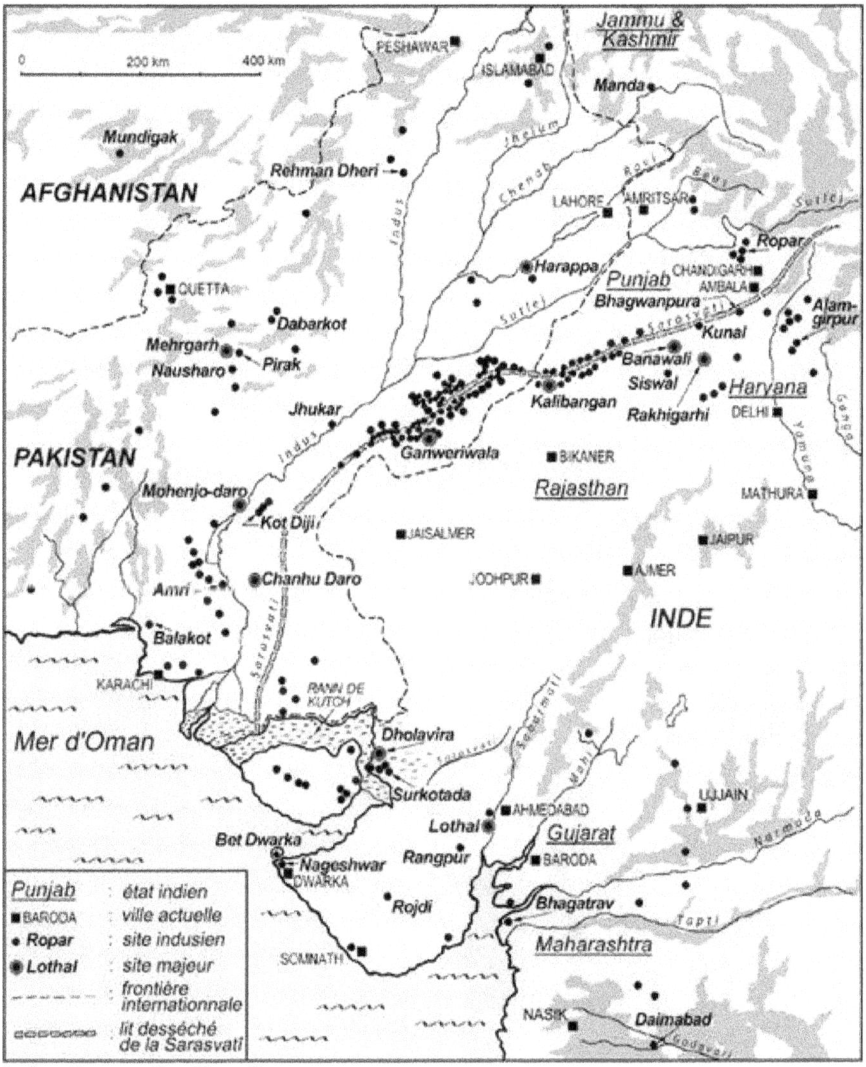

Indus-Sarasvati valley sites

Bronze cart with canopy. 36.2237 Museum of Fine Arts, Boston

4th millennium Indus writing pre-dates all known writing.

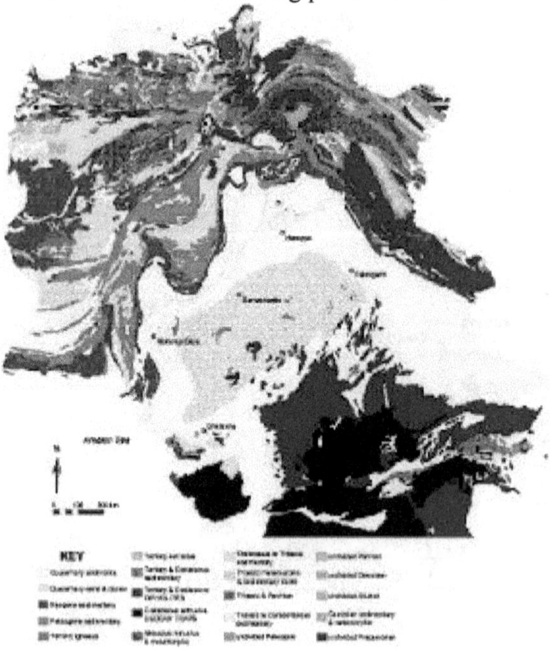

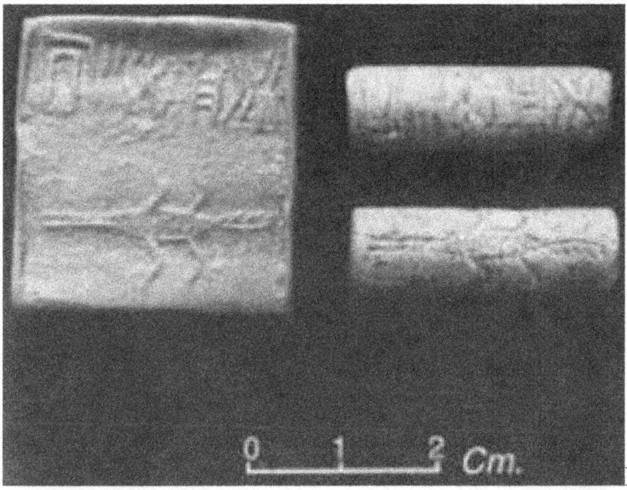

Rakhigarhi

Wādī Salūt, Oman

Tell Asmar

Ur. Seal impression.

m1429C

m417 Standing armed person (hero), joined animals: tiger, young bull, ox, zebu? Hieroglyph: 'ladder': H. sainī, senī f. ' ladder ' Rebus: Pa. sēṇi -- f. ' guild, division of army '; Pk. sēṇi -- f. ' row, collection '; śrēṇi (metr. often śrayaṇi --) f. ' line, row, troop ' RV. The lexeme in Tamil means: Limit, boundary; எல்லை. நளியிரு முந்நீரேணி யாக (புறநா. 35, 1). Country, territory. barad, barat 'ox' Rebus: bharat 'copper, pewter, tin alloy'; poL 'zebu' Rebus: pola 'maganetite'; kola 'tiger' Rebus; kol 'working in iron'; khond 'young bull' Rebus: khondar 'turner'.bhaTa 'warrior' Rebus: baTa 'furnace'.

The glyphics are:
Semantics: 'group of animals/quadrupeds': paśu 'animal' (RV), pasaramu, pasalamu = an animal, a beast, a brute, quadruped (Te.) Rebus: pasra 'smithy' (Santali)

Glyph: 'six': bhaṭa 'six'. Rebus: bhaṭa 'furnace'.
Glyph (the only inscription on the Mohenjo-daro seal m417): 'warrior': bhaṭa.
Rebus: bhaṭa 'furnace'. Thus, this glyph is a semantic determinant of the message: 'furnace'. It appears that the six heads of 'animal' glyphs are related to 'furnace' work.

There are other seals/tablets which depict 5 or 6 animals surrounding a crocodile glyph. [The examples are nine inscribed objects: m02015 A,B, m2016, m1393, m1394, m1395, m0295, m0439, m440, m0441 A,B]. On some tablets, such a glyphic composition is also accompanied (on obverse side, for example, cf. m2015A and m0295) with a glyphic of two joined tiger heads to a single body. In one inscription (m0295), the text inscriptions are also read. The animals shown are: composite animal of three tigers, crocodile, heifer, tiger-looking-back, elephant, rhinoceros, zebu (bos indicus), a pair of bulls, monkey(?).

It is a reasonable inference that these glyphics are related to the community, or guild of artisans. This gets confirmed and unraveled as decipherment provides for rebus readings of all the clearly identifiable glyphic elements.

The identifiable joined animals on m0417 may relate to the lexeme sangaḍa 'joined animals' (Marathi). Rebus: sangāta 'association, guild'.
1. Glyph: 'one-horned heifer': kondh 'heifer'. kũdār 'turner, brass-worker'.
2. Glyph: 'bull': ḍhangra 'bull'. Rebus: ḍhangar 'blacksmith'. Pair of bulls: dula 'pair'. Rebus: dul 'casting (metal)'.
3. Glyph: 'ram': meḍh 'ram'. Rebus: meḍ 'iron'
4. Glyph: 'antelope': mr̤eka 'goat'. Rebus: milakkhu 'copper'. Vikalpa 1: meluhha 'mleccha' 'copper worker'. Vikalpa 2: meṛh 'helper of merchant'.
5. Glyph: 'zebu': khũṭ 'zebu'. Rebus: khũṭ 'guild, community' (Semantic determinant of the 'jointed animals' glyphic composition). kūṭa joining, connexion, assembly, crowd, fellowship (DEDR 1882) Pa. gotta 'clan'; Pk. gotta, gōya id. (CDIAL 4279) Semantics of Pkt. lexeme gōya is concordant with Hebrew 'goy' in ha-goy-im (lit. the-nation-s).
6. The sixth animal can only be guessed. Perhaps, a monkey, a tiger, or a rhinoceros

Glyph: 'monkey': kuṭhāru = a monkey (Skt.lex.) Ta. kōṭaram monkey. Ir. kōḍa (small) monkey; kūḍag monkey. Ko. koṛṇ small monkey. To. kwṛṇ monkey. Ka. kōḍaga monkey, ape. Koḍ. koḍë monkey. Tu. koḍañji, koḍañja, koḍaṅ baboon (DEDR 2196) Konḍa (BB) kōnza red-faced monkey. Kui kōnja black-faced monkey. Kuwi (F.) kōnja monkey (small); (S.) konja ape; konzu monkey; (P.) kōnja black-faced monkey. (DEDR 2194) Rebus: kuṭhāru 'armourer or weapons maker'(metal-worker), also an inscriber or writer.

Glyph: 'tiger?': kol 'tiger'. Rebus: kol 'worker in iron'. Vikalpa (alternative): perhaps, rhinoceros. Glyph: baḍhi 'castrated boar'. Rebus: baḍhoe 'worker in wood and iron'.

Thus, the entire glyphic composition of six animals on the Mohenjo-daro seal m417 is semantically a representation of a śrēṇi, 'guild', a khũṭ, 'community' of smiths and masons.

Pa. gotta -- n. ' clan ', Pk. gotta -- , gutta -- , amg. gōya -- n.; Gau. gū ' house ' (in Kaf. and Dard. several other words for ' cowpen ' > ' house ': gōṣṭhá -- , Pr. gū´ṭu ' cow '; S. goṭru m. ' parentage ', L. got f. ' clan ', P. gotar, got f.; Ku. N. got ' family '; A. got -- nāti ' relatives '; B. got ' clan '; Or. gota ' family, relative '; Bhoj. H. got m. ' family, clan ', G. got n.; M. got ' clan, relatives '; -- Si. gota ' clan, family ' ← Pa. (CDIAL 4279).

This guild, community of smiths and masons evolves into Harosheth Hagoyim, 'a smithy of nations'.
It appears that the Meluhhans were in contact with many interaction areas, Dilmun and Susa (elam) in particular. There is evidence for Meluhhan settlements outside of Meluhha. It is a reasonable inference that the Meluhhans with bronze-age expertise of creating arsenical and bronze alloys and working with other metals constituted the 'smithy of nations', Harosheth Hagoyim.

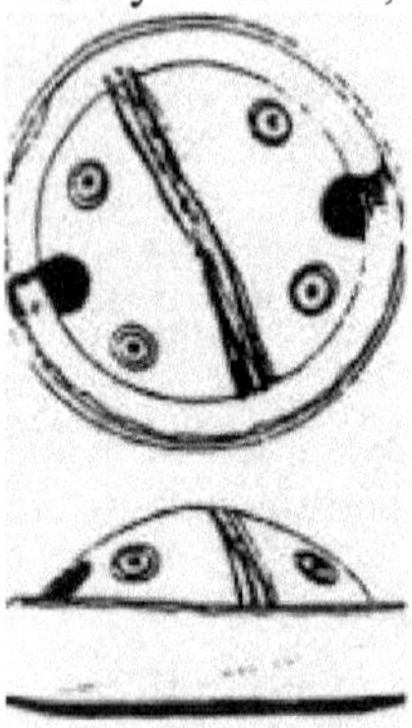

Dilmun seal from Barbar; six heads of antelope radiating from a circle; similar to animal protomes in Failaka, Anatolia and Indus. Obverse of the seal shows four dotted circles. [Poul Kjaerum, The Dilmun Seals as evidence of long distance relations in the early second millennium BC, pp. 269-277.] A tree is shown on this Dilmun seal.

Glyph: 'tree': kuṭi 'tree'. Rebus: kuṭhi 'smelter furnace' (Santali).

Izzat Allah Nigahban, 1991, Excavations at Haft Tepe, Iran, The University Museum, UPenn, p. 97. furnace' Fig.96a.

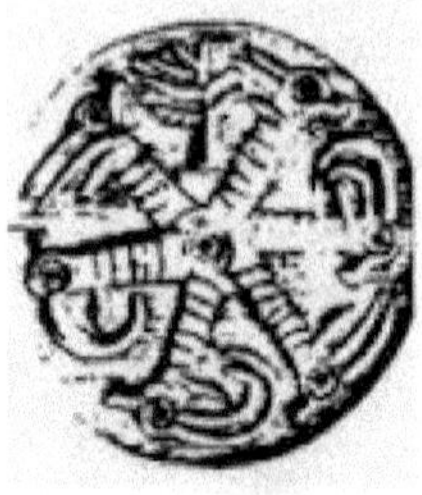

There is a possibility that this seal impression from Haft Tepe had some connections with Indian hieroglyphs. This requires further investigation. "From Haft Tepe (Middle Elamite period, ca. 13th century) in Ḵūzestān an unusual pyrotechnological installation was associated with a craft workroom containing such materials as mosaics of colored stones framed in bronze, a dismembered elephant skeleton used in manufacture of bone tools, and several hundred bronze arrowpoints and small tools. "Situated in a courtyard directly in front of this workroom is a most unusual kiln. This kiln is very large, about 8 m long and 2 and one half m wide, and contains two long compartments with chimneys at each end, separated by a fuel chamber in the middle. Although the roof of the kiln had collapsed, it is evident from the slight inturning of the walls which remain in situ that it was barrel vaulted like the roofs of the tombs. Each of the two long heating chambers is divided into eight sections by partition walls. The southern heating chamber contained metallic slag, and was apparently used for making bronze objects. The northern heating chamber contained pieces of broken pottery and other material, and thus was apparently used for baking clay objects including tablets . . ." (loc.cit. Bronze in pre-Islamic Iran, Encyclopaedia Iranica,http://www.iranicaonline.org/articles/bronze-i Negahban, 1977; and forthcoming).

Many of the bronze-age manufactured or industrial goods were surplus to the needs of the producing community and had to be traded, together with a record of types of goods and types of processes such as native metal or minerals, smelting of minerals, alloying of metals using two or more minerals, casting ingots, forging and turning metal into shapes such as plates or vessels, using anvils, cire perdue technique for creating bronze statues – in addition to the production of artifacts such as bangles and ornaments made of śankha or shell (turbinella pyrum), semi-precious stones, gold or silver beads. Thus writing was invented to maintain production-cum-trade accounts, to cope with the economic imperative of bronze age technological advances to take the artisans of guilds into the stage of an industrial production-cum-trading community.

Tablets and seals inscribed with hieroglyphs, together with the process of creating seal impressions took inventory lists to the next stage of trading property items using bills of lading of trade loads of industrial goods. Such bills of lading describing trade loads were created using tablets and seals with the invention of writing based on phonetics and semantics of language – the hallmark of Indian hieroglyphs.

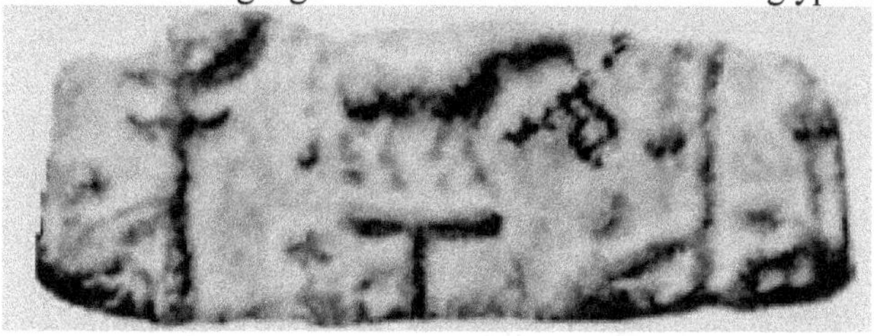

m0491 Tablet. Line drawing (right)

Dawn of the bronze age is best exemplified by a Mohenjo-daro tablet which shows a procession of three hieroglyphs carried on the shoulders of three persons. The hieroglyphs are: 1. Scarf carried on a pole; 2. A heifer carried on a stand; 3. Portable standard device (lathe-gimlet).

Three professions are described by the three hieroglyphs: dhatu kõdā sãgāḍī ‘Associates (guild): mineral worker; metals turner-joiner (forge); worker on a lathe’.

The rebus readings are:

1. WPah.kṭg. dhàṭṭu m. ‘ woman's headgear, kerchief ’, kc. dhaṭu m. (also dhaṭhu m. ‘ scarf ’, J. dhāṭ(h)u m. Him.I 105). dhaṭu m. (also dhaṭhu) m. ‘scarf’ (WPah.) (CDIAL 6707) Rebus: dhatu = mineral (Santali) dhātu ‘mineral (Pali) dhātu ‘mineral’ (Vedic); a mineral, metal (Santali); dhāta id. (G.) H. dhāṛnā ‘to send out, pour out, cast (metal)’ (CDIAL 6771).

2. koḍiyum ‘heifer’ (G.) [kōḍiya] kōḍe, kōḍiya. [Tel.] n. A bullcalf. . k* దూడA young bull. Plumpness, prime. తరుణము. జోడుకోడయలు a pair of bullocks. kōḍe adj. Young. kōḍe-kāḍu. n. A young man.పడుచువాడు. [kārukōḍe] kāru-kōḍe. [Tel.] n. A bull in its prime. खोंड [khōṇḍa] m A young bull, a bullcalf. (Marathi) గోద [gōda] gōda. [Tel.] n. An ox. A beast. kine, cattle.(Telugu) koḍiyum (G.) Rebus: koḍ artisan’s workshop (Kuwi); B. kõdā ‘to turn in a lathe’; Or. kŭnda ‘lathe’, kũdibā, kũd ‘to turn’ (→ Drav. Kur. kũd ‘lathe’) (CDIAL 3295)

3. Drawing. Reconstruction of the glyphic elements in ‘standard device’ shown in front of a heifer on many Indus inscriptions.

san:gaḍa, ‘lathe, portable furnace’; śagaḍī (G.) = lathe san:gāḍo a lathe; sãghāḍiyo a worker on a lathe (G.lex.) sãgaḍ part of a turner's apparatus (M.); s̄gāḍī lathe (Tu.)(CDIAL 12859). sāṅgaḍa That member of a turner's apparatus by which the piece to be turned is confined and steadied. सांगडीस धरणें To take into linkedness or close connection with, lit. fig. (Marathi) सांगाडी [sāṅgāḍī] f The machine within which a turner confines and steadies the piece he has to turn. (Marathi) सगडी [sagaḍī] f

(Commonly शेगडी) A pan of live coals or embers. (Marathi) san:ghāḍo, saghaḍī (G.) = firepan; saghaḍī, śaghaḍi = a pot for holding fire (G.)[culā sagaḍī portable hearth (G.)] Rebus 1: Guild. सांगडणी [sāṅgaḍaṇī] f (Verbal of सांगडणें) Linking or joining together (Marathi). संगति [saṅgati] f (S) pop. संगत f Union, junction, connection, association. संगति [saṅgati] c (S) pop. संगती c or संगत c A companion, associate, comrade, fellow. संगतीसोबती [saṅgatīsōbatī] m (संगती & सोबती) A comprehensive or general term for Companions or associates. संग [saṅga] m (S) Union, junction, connection, association, companionship, society. संगें [saṅgēṃ] prep (संग S) With, together with, in company or connection with. संघात [saṅghāta] m S Assembly or assemblage; multitude or heap; a collection together (of things animate or inanimate). संघट्टणें [saṅghaṭṭaṇēṃ] v i (Poetry. संघट्टन) To come into contact or meeting; to meet or encounter. (Marathi) G. sãghāṛɔ m. ' lathe '; M. sãgaḍ f. part of a turner's apparatus ' (CDIAL 12859) Rebus 2: stone-cutting. sanghāḍo (G.) cutting stone, gilding (G.); san:gatarāśū = stone cutter; san:gatarāśi = stone-cutting; san:gsāru karan.u = to stone (S.) san:ghāḍiyo, a worker on a lathe (G.) Rebus 3: saṁghaṭayati ' strikes (a musical instrument) ' R., ' joins together ' Kathās. [√ghaṭ]Pa. saṅghaṭita -- ' pegged together '; Pk. saṁghaḍia<-> ' joined ', caus. saṁghaḍāvēi; M. sā̃gaḍṇẽ ' to link together '. (CDIAL 12855). Rebus 3: battle. jangaḍiyo 'military guard who accompanies treasure into the treasury' (G.)
Glyph: 'dotted circles': kaṇḍ 'eye'. Rebus: kaṇḍ 'stone (ore) metal'.

A cult object in the Temple of Inanna?

This trough was found at Uruk, the largest city so far known in southern Mesopotamia in the late prehistoric period (3300-3000 BC). The carving on the side shows a procession of sheep (a goat and a ram) approaching a reed hut (of a type still found in southern Iraq) and two lambs emerging. The decoration is only visible if the trough is raised above the level at which it could be conveniently used, suggesting that it was probably a cult object, rather than of practical use. It may have been a cult object in the Temple of Inana (Ishtar), the Sumerian goddess of love and fertility; a bundle of reeds (Inanna's symbol) can be seen projecting from the hut and at the edges of the scene. Later documents make it clear that Inanna was the supreme goddess of Uruk. Many finely-modelled representations of animals and humans made of clay and stone have been found in what were once enormous buildings in the center of Uruk, which were probably temples. Cylinder seals of the period also depict sheep, cattle, processions of people and possibly rituals. Part of the right-hand scene is cast from the original fragment now in the Vorderasiatisches Museum, Berlin

melh, mṟeka 'goat'; rebus: milakkhu 'copper' (Pali). pasara 'domestic animals'. pasra 'smithy, forge'.
Tabernae Montana, a flowering plant of the family Apocynaceae.
Glyphs on the bottom register of Uruk vase.

On the top register right corner, two animal glyphs are shown;: goat and tiger. mṟeka 'goat'. Rebus: milakkhu 'copper. kola 'tiger'. Rebus: kol 'pañcaloha, alloy of five metals', 'working in iron'. The pots are shown to contain stone ore ingots. below these animals two fire-altars with metal ingots (sometimes called 'bun ingots') are shown: kaṇḍ 'fire-altar'. These glyphs recur on Indus script inscriptions.

Another line drawing of top register of the Uruk vase. The head of a bull is shown between two pots containing copper ingots. This is a semantic determinant of the contents of the pots. The bull, glyphic: adar ḍangra. Rebus: aduru ḍhangar 'native metalsmith'. That is, the pots contain aduru 'unsmelted native metal'.

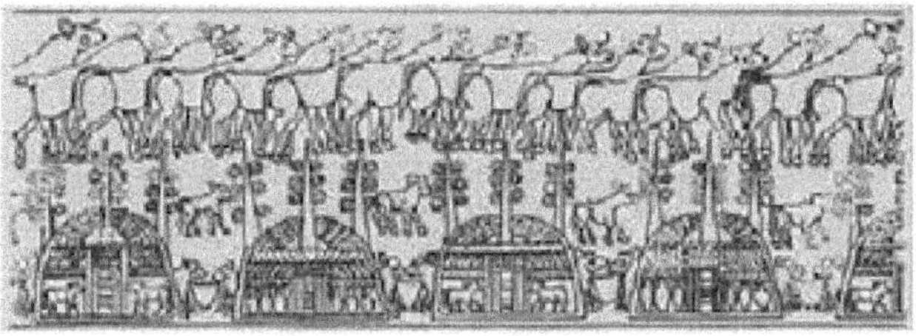

A cow and a stable of reeds with sculpted columns in the background. Fragment of another vase of alabaster (era of Djemet-Nasr) from Uruk, Mesopotamia. Limestone 16 X 22.5 cm. AO 8842, Louvre, Departement des Antiquites Orientales, Paris, France. Six circles decorated on the reed post are semantic determinants of Glyph: bhaṭa 'six'. Rebus: bhaṭa 'furnace'.

The following glyphics of m1431 prism tablet show the association between the tiger + person on tree glyphic set and crocile + 3 animal glyphic set.

m0489A One side of a prism tablet shows: crocodile + fish glyphic above: elephant, rhinoceros, tiger, tiger looking back and up.
m1431A m1431B Crocodile+ three animal glyphs: rhinoceros, elephant, tiger
It is possible that the broken portions of set 2 (h1973B and h1974B) showed three animals in procession: tiger looking back and up + rhinoceros + tiger.
Reverse side glyphs:
eraka 'nave of wheel'. Rebus: era 'copper'.
Animal glyph: elephant 'ibha'. Rebus ibbo, 'merchant'.
Composition of glyphics: Woman with six locks of hair + one eye + thwarting + two pouncing tigers + nave with six spokes. Rebus: kola 'woman' + kaṇga 'eye' (Pego.), bhaṭa 'six'+ dul 'casting (metal)' + kūdā kol (tiger jumping) + era āra (nave of wheel, six spokes), ibha (elephant). Rebus: era 'copper'; kūdār dul kol 'turner, casting, working in iron'; kan 'brazier, bell-metal worker';
The glyphic composition read rebus: copper, iron merchant with taṭu kanḍ kol bhaṭa 'iron stone (ore) mineral 'furnace'.
Glypg: 'woman': kola 'woman' (Nahali). Rebus kol 'working in iron' (Tamil)
Glyph: 'impeding, hindering': taṭu (Ta.) Rebus: dhatu 'mineral' (Santali) Ta. taṭu (-pp-, -tt) to hinder, stop, obstruct, forbid, prohibit, resist, dam, block up, partition off, curb, check, restrain, control, ward off, avert; n. hindering, checking, resisting; taṭuppu hindering, obstructing, resisting, restraint; Kur. ṭaṇḍnā to prevent, hinder, impede. Br. taḍ power to resist. (DEDR 3031)

Altyn depe seals

Haifa, pure tin ingots with Indus Script

Haifa tin ingots

Tin-copper alloy called tin-bronze or zinc-copper alloy called brass, were innovations that allowed for the much more complex shapes cast in closed moulds of the Bronze Age. Arsenical bronze objects appear first in the Near East where arsenic is commonly found in association with copper ore, but the health risks were quickly realized and the quest for sources of the much less hazardous tin ores began early in the Bronze Age. (Charles, J.A. (1979). "The development of the usage of tin and tin-bronze: some problems". In Franklin, A.D.; Olin, J.S.; Wertime, T.A. The Search for Ancient Tin. Washington D.C.: A seminar organized by Theodore A. Wertime and held at the Smithsonian Institution and the National Bureau of Standards, Washington D.C. March 14–15, 1977. pp. 25–32.)

Thus was created the demand for tin metal. This demand led to a trade network which linked distant sources of tin to the markets of Bronze Age.

Zinc added to copper produces a bright gold-like appearance to the alloy called brass. Brass has been used from prehistoric times. (Thornton, C. P. (2007) "Of brass and bronze in prehistoric southwest Asia" in La Niece, S. Hook, D. and Craddock, P.T. (eds.) Metals and mines: Studies in archaeometallurgy London: Archetype Publications) The earliest brasses may have been natural alloys made by smelting zinc-rich copper ores. (Craddock, P.T. and Eckstein, K (2003) "Production of Brass in Antiquity by Direct Reduction" in Craddock, P.T. and Lang, J. (eds) Mining and Metal Production Through the Ages London: British Museum pp. 226–7.)

Zinc is a metallic chemical element; the most common zinc ore is sphalerite (zinc blende), a zinc sulfide mineral. Brass, which is an alloy of copper and zinc has been used for vessels. The mines of Rajasthan have given definite evidence of zinc production going back to 6th Century BCE.
http://www.infinityfoundation.com/mandala/t_es/t_es_agraw_zinc_frameset.htm Ornaments made of alloys that contain 80–90% zinc with lead, iron, antimony, and other metals making up the remainder, have been found that are 2500 years old. (Lehto, R. S. (1968). "Zinc". In Clifford A. Hampel. The Encyclopedia of the Chemical Elements. New York: Reinhold Book Corporation. pp. 822–830.) An estimated million tonnes of metallic zinc and zinc oxide from the 12th to 16th centuries were produced from Zawar mines. (Emsley, John (2001). "Zinc". Nature's Building Blocks: An A-Z Guide to the Elements. Oxford, England, UK: Oxford University Press. pp. 499–505.)

The addition of a second metal to copper increases its hardness, lowers the melting temperature, and improves the casting process by producing a more fluid melt that cools to a denser, less spongy metal. (Penhallurick, R.D. (1986). Tin in Antiquity: its Mining and Trade Throughout the Ancient World with Particular Reference to Cornwall. London: The Institute of Metals.)

Tin extraction and use can be dated to the beginnings of the Bronze Age around 3000 BC, when it was observed that copper objects formed of polymetallic ores with different metal contents had different physical properties. (Cierny, J.; Weisgerber, G. (2003). "The "Bronze Age tin mines in Central Asia". In Giumlia-Mair, A.; Lo Schiavo, F. The Problem of Early Tin. Oxford: Archaeopress. pp. 23–31.)
Tin is obtained chiefly from the mineral cassiterite, where it occurs as tin dioxide, $SnO2$.The first alloy, used in large scale since 3000 BC, was bronze, an alloy of tin and copper. Cassiterite often accumulates in alluvial channels as placer deposits due to the fact that it is harder, heavier, and more chemically resistant than the granite in which it typically forms. Early Bronze Age prospectors could easily identify the purple or dark stones of cassiterite from alluvial sources and could be obtained the same way gold was obtained by panning in placer deposits.

Pewter, which is an alloy of 85–90% tin with the remainder commonly consisting of copper, antimony and lead, was used for flatware.

Here is a pictorial gallery:

Panning for cassiterite using bamboo pans in a pond in Orissa. The ore is carried to the water pond or stream for washing in bamboo baskets.

People panning for cassiterite mineral in the remote jungles of central India.

The ore is washed to concentrate the cassiterite mineral using bamboo pans. Base of small brick and mud furnace for smelting tin.

Hieroglyph: *kuṛi* woman: *kuḍa1 ' boy, son ', °*ḍī* ' girl, daughter '. [Prob. ← Mu. (Sant. Muṇḍari *koṛa* ' boy ', *kuṛi* ' girl ', Ho *koa, kui*, Kūrkū *kōn, kōnjē*); or ← Drav. (Tam. *kuṟa* ' young ', Kan. *koḍa* ' youth ') T. Burrow BSOAS xii 373. Prob. separate from RV. *kŕ̥tā* -- ' girl ' H. W. Bailey TPS 1955, 65. -- Cf. *kuḍáti* ' acts like a child ' Dhātup.]NiDoc. *kuḍ'aǵa* ' boy ', *kuḍ'i* ' girl '; Ash. *kū´ṛə* ' child, foetus ', *istrimalī* -- *kuṛä´* ' girl '; Kt. *kŕū, kuŕuk* ' young of animals '; Pr. *kyúdotdot;ru* ' young of animals, child ', *kyurú* ' boy ', *kurī´* ' colt, calf '; Dm. *kúŕa* ' child ', Shum. *kuṛ*; Kal. *kūŕ**1*k* ' young of animals '; Phal. *kuṛī̃* ' woman, wife '; K. *kūrü* f. ' young girl ', kash.*kōṛī*, ram. *kuṛhī*; L. *kuṛā* m. ' bridegroom ', *kuṛī* f. ' girl, virgin, bride ', awāṇ. *kuṛī* f. ' woman '; P. *kuṛī* f. ' girl, daughter ', P. bhaṭ.WPah. khaś. *kuṛi*, cur. *kuḷī*, cam. *kŏḷā* ' boy ', *kuṛī* ' girl '; -- B. *ā̃ṭ* -- *kuṛā* ' childless ' (*ā̃ṭa* ' tight ')? -- X pṓta -- 1: WPah. bhad. *kō* ' son ', *kūī* ' daughter ', bhal.*ko* m., *koi* f., pāḍ. *kuā, kōī*, paṅ. *koā, kūī*.(CDIAL 3245)

Rebus: *kolā* charcoal: kōkila2 m. ' lighted coal, charcoal ' lex. [PMWS 47 sanskritized from MIA. *kōila* -- ← Proto -- muṇḍa **ko(y)ila* = Sant. *kuilạ* ' black ': all NIA. forms must or may rest on **kōilla* --]Pk. *kōilā* -- f., *kolla* -- m.n. ' burning charcoal '; S. *koilo* m. ' dead coal ', pl. ' charcoal ', L. *koilā* f. (?), *kolā* m., P. *koilā, kolā* m., Ku. *kwelo*, N. *koilā*, B. *kayalā*, Or. *koilā*, Bi. *koelā*, Mth. H. *koilā* m., Marw. *koilo* m., G. *kɔyalɔ* m.S.kcch. *koylo* m. ' coal '; WPah.kc. *koilo* m.(CDIAL 3484)

The tin is refined by remelting the pieces recovered from the furnace in an iron pan. The molten tin is poured into stone-carved moulds to make square- or rectangular-ingots.

As the pictorial gallery demonstrates, the entire tin processing industry is a family-based or extended-family-based industry. The historical traditions point to the formation of artisan guilds to exchange surplus cassiterite in trade transactions of the type evidenced by the seals and tablets, tokens and bullae found in the civilization-interaction area of the Bronze Age.

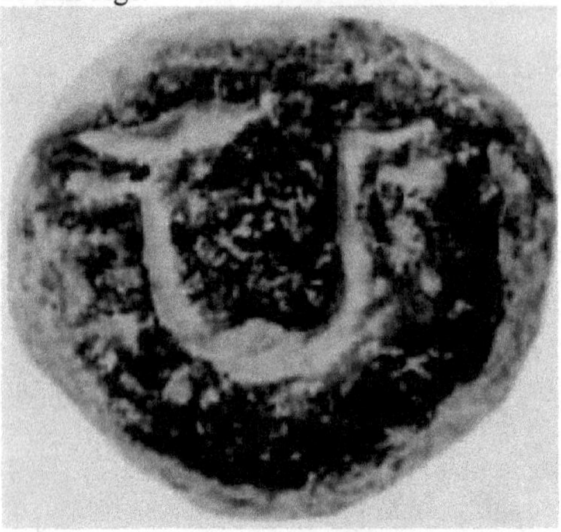

Daimabad seal. Glyph is decoded: *kaṇḍ karṇaka, kaṇḍ kan-ka* 'rim of jar'. Rebus: 'furnace scribe'.

m1656 The glyphics of 'water-overflow' from the 'rim' of the 'short-necked jar' completes the semantic rendering by the *lo* 'overflow'. Rebus readings: (B) {V} ``(pot, etc.) to ^overflow''. See `to be left over'. @B24310. #20851. Re(B) {V} ``(pot, etc.) to ^overflow''. See `to be left over'. (Munda) Rebus: loh 'copper' (Hindi) Glyph of flowing water in the second register: காண்டம் kāṇṭam , *n.* < *kāṇḍa.* 1. Water; sacred water; நீர்; kāṇṭam 'ewer, pot'கமண்டலம். (Tamil) Thus the combined rebus reading: Ku. *lokhaṛ* 'iron tools '; H. *lokhaṇḍ* m. ' iron tools, pots and pans '; G. *lokhā̃ḍ* n. 'tools, iron, ironware'; M. *lokhā̃ḍ* n. ' iron '(CDIAL 11171).

Image of overflowing pot is an abiding metonymy in Mesopotamia.

Clay relief stamped with the figure of the Babylonian hero Gilgamesh, holding a vase from which two streams of water flow. (British Museum No. 21204)
Fragment of limestone sculptured in relief with vases from which streams of water flow. (British Museum No. 95477) [Leonard W. King, 1916, *A History of Sumer and Akkad*, London, Chatto and Windus, p.73) Hieroglyph: *lo* 'pot to overflow' *kāṇḍa* 'water'.
Rebus: *lokhaṇḍ* (overflowing pot) 'metal tools, pots and pans, metalware' (Marathi).

khaṇṭi 'buffalo bull' (Tamil) Rebus: *khãḍ* '(metal) tools, pots and pans' (Gujarati)
Cylinder seal impression of Ibni-sharrum, a scribe of Shar-kalisharri ca. 2183–2159 BCE The inscription reads "O divine Shar-kali-sharri, Ibni-sharrum the scribe is your servant." Cylinder seal. Chlorite. AO 22303 H. 3.9 cm. Dia. 2.6 cm.[i] *khaṇṭi* 'buffalo bull' (Tamil) kaṭā, kaṭamā 'bison' (Tamil)(DEDR 1114) (glyph). Rebus: *khaṇḍ* 'tools, pots and pans, metal-ware'; kaḍiyo [Hem. Des. kaḍa-i-o = (Skt. Sthapati, a mason) a bricklayer, mason (G.)] (B) {V} ``(pot, etc.) to ^overflow''. See `to be left over'. @B24310. #20851. Re(B) {V} ``(pot, etc.) to ^overflow''. See `to be left over'. (Munda) Rebus: loh 'copper' (Hindi) Glyph of flowing water in the second register: காண்டம் kāṇṭam , *n*. < *kāṇḍa*. 1. Water; sacred water; நீர்; kāṇṭam 'ewer, pot' கமண்டலம். (Tamil) Thus the combined rebus reading: Ku. *lokhaṛ* 'iron tools '; H. *lokhaṇḍ* m. ' iron tools, pots and pans '; G. *lokhãḍ* n. 'tools, iron, ironware'; M. *lokhãḍ* n. ' iron '(CDIAL 11171). The kneeling person's hairstyle has six curls. *bhaṭa* 'six'; rebus: *bhaṭa* 'furnace'. मेढा mēḍhā A twist or tangle arising in thread or cord, a curl or snarl. (Marathi) Rebus: meḍ 'iron' (Ho.) Thus, the orthography denotes *meḍ bhaṭa* 'iron furnace'.

[i] http://www.louvre.fr/en/oeuvre-notices/cylinder-seal-ibni-sharrum

http://bharatkalyan97.blogspot.in/2013/08/ancient-near-east-bronze-age-heralded.html

Ancient near East Gudea statue hieroglyph (Indus writing): lokhãḍ, 'copper tools, pots and pans' Rebus: lo 'overflow', kāṇḍa 'sacred water'.

Workers from Elam, Susa, Magan and Meluhha were deployed by Gudea, the ruler of Lagaṣ, to build The Eninnu, the main temple of Girsu, c. 2125 BCE. We are dealing with Indian *sprachbund* when we refer to Meluhha. This *sprachbund* has a remarkable lexeme which is used to signify a smithy, as also a temple: *Kota.* kole·l smithy, temple in Kota village. *Toda.* kwala·l Kota smithy *Ta.* kol working in iron, blacksmith; kollaṉ blacksmith. *Ma.* kollan blacksmith, artificer; *Ka.*kolime, kolume, kulame, kulime, kulume, kulme fire-pit, furnace; (Bell.; U.P.U.) konimi blacksmith; (Gowda) kolla id. *Koḍ.* kollë blacksmith. *Te.* kolimi furnace. *Go.*(SR.) kollusānā to mend implements; (Ph.) kolstānā, kulsānā to forge; (Tr.) kōlstānā to repair (of ploughshares); (SR.) kolmi smithy (*Voc.* 948). *Kuwi* (F.) kolhali to forge. (DEDR 2133).

http://en.wikipedia.org/wiki/File:Gudea.jpg Timber and exotic stones to decorate the temples were brought from the distant lands of Magan and Meluhha (possibly to be identified as Oman and the Indus Valley).
http://www.britishmuseum.org/explore/highlights/article_index/g/gudea,_king_of_lagash_around.aspx

Fig. 8: Gudea Basin SV.7.

Gudea Basin. Water overflowing from vases. : The Representation of an Early Mesopotamian Ruler ... By Claudia E. Suter "The standing statue N (Fig. 5) holds a vase from which four streams of water flow down on each side of the dress into identical vases depicted on the pedestal, which are equally overflowing with water. Little fish swim up the streams to the vase held by Gudea. This statue evidently shows the ruler in possession of prosperity symbolized by the overflowing vase." (p.58) *ayo*'fish' (Munda)
Rebus: *ayo* 'iron' (Gujarati); *ayas* 'metal' (Skt.) Together with *lo*, 'overflow', the compound word can be read as loh+ayas. The compound *lohāyas* is attested in ancient Indian texts, contrasted with *kṛṣṇāyas,* distinguishing red alloy metal (bronze) from black alloy metal (iron alloy). *ayaskāṇḍa* is a compound attested in Pāṇini; the word may be semantically explained as 'metal tools, pots and pans' or as alloyed metal.

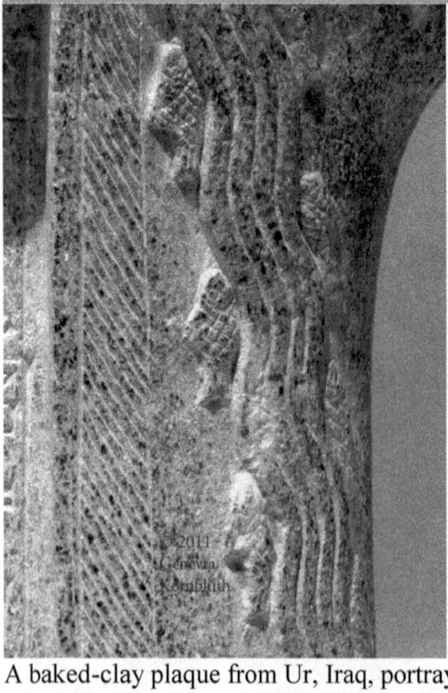

Fig. 5: Gudea Statue N at scale 1:10.

A baked-clay plaque from Ur, Iraq, portraying a goddess; she holds a vase overflowing with water ('hé-gál' or 'hegallu') is a symbol of abundance and prosperity. (Beijing World Art Museum) Fish in water on statue, on viewer's right. Gudea's Temple Building "The goddesses wit overflowing vases. (Fig.8). The large limestone basin (SV.7) restored by Unger from twenty-six fragments is carved in relief on its outside. It shows a row of goddesses walking on a stream of water. Between them they are holding vases from which water flows down into the stream. These, in turn, are fed with water poured from vases which are held by smaller-scale goddesses hovering above. All goddesses wear long pleated dresses, and crowns with a single horn pair. There are remains of at least six standing and four hovering goddesses. Considering the importance the number seven plays in Gudea's inscriptions, Unger's reconstruction of seven goddesses of each type is credible. The inscription on the basin, which relates its fashioning, designates it as a large S'IM, a relatively rare and only vagueely understood term, perhaps to be read agarinX. The fashioning of one or more S'IM is also related in the Cylinder inscriptions, and the finished artifact is mentioned again in the description of the temple...Since the metaphor paraphrasing the basin refers to th ceaseless flow of water, it is possible that the basin(s) mentioned in the account of Eninnu's construction is (are) identical with the fragmentary remains of the one (perhaps two?) actually found within the area of Gudea's Eninnu, as Unger presumed. Several similar and somewhat intuitive identifications of the goddesses with the overflowing vases have been proposed: Heuzey saw personifications of the Euphrates and Tigris; Unger saw personifications of sources and rain clouds that form the Tigris and identified them with Ningirsu and Baba's seven daughters; van Buren saw personifications of higher white clouds and lower rain clouds whom she assigned to Ea's circle. Neither are the seven (not fourteen!) daughters of Ningirsu and Baba ever associated with water, nor can fourteen personified clouds be made out in Ea's circle...The clue must be the overflowing vase which van Buren correctly interpreted as a symbol of abundance and prosperity. This interpretation is corroborated by the Gottertsypentext which states that the images of Kulullu is blessing with one hand (ikarrab) and holding abundance (HE.GAL) in the other. The protective spirit Kulullu is usually associated with abundance and divine benevolence, and may be reminiscent of the god bestowing the overflowing vase upon a human petititioner in much earlier presentation scenes. The narrative context in which the goddess with the overflowing vase occurs is confined to presentations of a human petititioner to a deity. The Akkadian seal fo the scribe Ili-Es'tar shows her accompanying the petitioner, not unlike a Lamma.

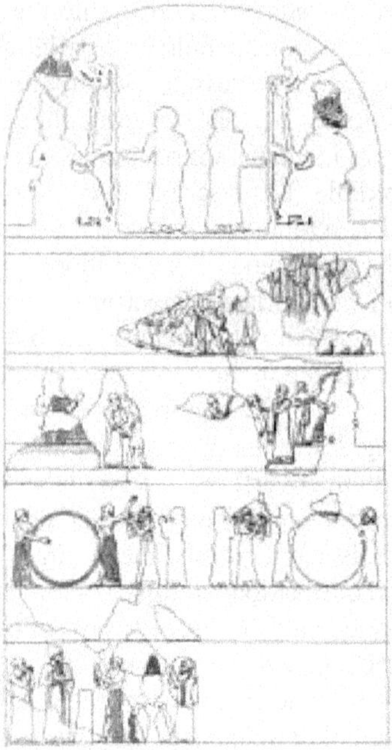

Fig. 33 Urnamma stela. Borker-Klahn's reconstruction.

On the Urmamma Stela, she is hovering over the offering of flowing water to the ruler by the enthroned deity. In this scene the goddess underlines the gift bestowed on the ruler, and figures as a personification of it, while on the seal she may have implied and guaranteed that the petitioner who offers an antelope (?) is pleading for and will receive blessings of abundance in return. The basin of Gudea is dedicated to Ningirsu, and may be understood as a plea for prosperity as well as a boast of its successful outcome."(Claudia E. Suter, 2000, Gudea's Temple Building: the representation of an early Mesopotamian Ruler in text and image, BRILL., II.c.i.d, pp. 62-63).

Location.Current Repository

Musee du Louvre. Inventory No. AO 22126 ca. 2120 BCE Neo-Sumerian from the city-state of Lagash. http://contentdm.unl.edu/ah_copyright.html

gud. ' ea guda ' ea warrior ' emphasis/the best "The best warrior". http://evans-experientialism.freewebspace.com/ling_sumerian.htm

Inscription on base of skirt- God commands him to build house. Gudea is holding plans. Gudea depicted as strong, peaceful ruler. Vessel flowing with life-giving water

w/ fish. Text on garment dedicates himself, the statue, and its temple to the goddess Geshtinanna.
According to the inscription this statue was made by Gudea, ruler of Lagash (c. 2100 BCE) for the temple of the goddess Geshtinanna. Gudea refurbished the temples of Girsu and 11 statues of him have been found in excavations at the site. Nine others including this one were sold on the art market. It has been suggested that this statue is a forgery. Unlike the hard diorite of the excavated statues, it is made of soft calcite, and shows a ruler with a flowing vase which elsewhere in Mesopotamian art is only held by gods. It also differs stylistically from the excavated statues. On the other hand, the Sumerian inscription appears to be genuine and would be very difficult to fake. Statues of Gudea show him standing or sitting. Ine one, he rests on his knee a plan of the temple he is building. On some statues Gudea has a shaven head, while on others like this one he wears a headdress covered with spirals, probably indicating that it was made out of fur. Height 61 cm. The overflowing water from the vase is a hieroglyph comparable to the pectoral of Mohenjo-daro showing an overflowing pot together with a one-horned young bull and standard device in
front. The diorite from Magan (Oman), and timber from Dilmun (Bahrain) obtained by Gudea could have come from Meluhha.

"The goddess Geshtinanna was known as “chief scribe” (Lambert 1990, 298– 299) and probably was a patron of scribes, as was Nidaba/Nisaba (Micha-lowski 2002). " http://www.academia.edu/2360254/Temple_Sacred_Prostitution_in_Ancient_Mesopotamia_Revisited

That the hieroglyph of pot/vase overflowing with water is a recurring theme can be seen from other cylinder seals, including Ibni-Sharrum cylinder seal. Such an imagery also occurs on a fragment of a stele, showing part of a lion and vases.

A person with a vase with overflowing water; sun sign. C. 18th cent. BCE. [E. Porada,1971, Remarks on seals found in the Gulf states, Artibus Asiae, 33, 31-7]. *meḍha* ‘polar star’

(Marathi). *meḍ* ‘iron’ (Ho.Mu.)
The seal of Gudea: Gudea, with shaven head, is accompanied by a minor female diety. He is led by his personal god, Ningishzida, into the

presence of Enlil, the chief Sumerian god. Wind pours forth from of the jars held by Enlil, signifying that he is the god of the winds. The winged leopard (griffin) is a mythological creature associated with Ningishzida, The horned helmets, worn even by the griffins, indicates divine status (the more horns the higher the rank). The writing in the background translates as: "Gudea, *Ensi* [ruler], of Lagash". *lōī* f., *lo* m.2. Pr. *ẓūwī* 'fox' (Western Pahari)(CDIAL 11140-2). Rebus: *loh* 'copper' (Hindi). *Te.* eṟaka, ṟekka, rekka, neṟaka, neṟi id. (DEDR 2591). Rebus: eraka, eṟaka = any metal infusion (Ka.Tu.); urukku (Ta.); urukka melting; urukku what is melted; fused metal (Ma.); urukku (Ta.Ma.); eragu = to melt; molten state, fusion; erakaddu = any cast thng; erake hoyi = to pour meltted metal into a mould, to cast (Kannada)

Now that the Indus Script Corpora has been substantively demonstrated as *catalogum catalogorum* of metalwork of Bronze Age, it is reasonable to hypothesise that the Indus Script 'writing' tradition using rebus-metonymy-layered-Meluhha-cipher continued even upto ca. 2nd century BCE in the area of Indian*sprachbund.* The evidence of the Indus Script continuum is more pronounced in the array of symbols used by mints from Taxila to Karur.
See: https://www.academia.edu/8776901/Indus_script_hieroglyphs_continued_use_in_ancient_Indian_mints_evidenced_by_punch-marked_coins

1890/1901 monographs of Theobald list 342 symbols deployed on punch-marked coins. These symbols also survive on later coinages of Ujjain or Eran or of many janapadas. One view is that early punch-marked coinage in Bharatam is datable to 10th century BCE, predating Lydia's electrum coin of 7th cent. BCE. "The coins to which these notes refer, though presenting neither king's names, dates of inscription of any sort, are nevertheless very interesting not only from their being the earliest money coined in India, and of a purely indigenous character, but from their being stamped with a number of symbols, some of which we can, with the utmost confidence, declare to have originated in distant lands and inthe remotest antiquity…The coins to which I shall confine my remarks are those to which the term 'punch -marked' properly applies. The 'punch' used to produce these coins differed from the ordinary dies which subsequently came into use, in that they covered only a portion of the surface of the coin or 'blank',

and impressed only one, of the many symbols usually seen on their pieces…One thing which is specially striking about most of the symbols representing animals is, the fidelity and spirit with which certain portions of it may be of an animal, or certain attitudes are represented…Man, Woman, the Elephant, Bull, Dog, Rhinoceros,Goat, Hare, Peacock, Turtle, Snake, Fish, Frog, are all recognizable
at a glance…First, there is the historical record of Quintus Curtius, who describes the Raja of Taxila (the modern Shahdheri, 20miles north-west from Rawal Pindi) as offering Alexander 80 talents of coined silver ('signati argenti'). Now what other, except these punch-marked coins could these pieces of coined silver have been? Again, the name by which these coins are spoken of in the Buddhist sutras, about 200 BCE was 'purana', which simply signies 'old', whence the General argunes that the word 'old as applied to the indigenous 'karsha',was used to distinguish it from the new and more recent issues of the Greeks. Then again a mere comparison of the two classes of coins almost itself suffices to refute the idea of the Indian coins being derived from the Greek. The Greek coins present us with a portrait of the king, with his name and titles in two languages together with a great number and variety of monograms indicating, in many instances where they have been deciphered by the ingenuity and perseverance of General Cunningham and others, the names of the mint cities where the coins were struck, and it is our ignorance of the geographical names of the period that probably has prevented the whole of them receiving their proper attribution; but with the indigenous coins it is far otherwise, as they display neither king's head, neame, titles or mongrams of any description…It is true that General Cunningham considers that many of these symbols, though not monograms in a strict sense, are nevertheless marks which indicate the mints where the coins were struck or the tribes among whom they were current, and this contention in no wise invalidates the supposition contended for by me either that the majority of them possess an esoteric meaning or have originated in other lands at a period anterior to their adoption for the purpose they fulfil on the coins in Hindustan."

(W. Theobald, 1890, Notes on some of the symbols found on the punch-marked coins of Hindustan, and on their relationship to the archaic symbolism of other races and distant lands, *Journal of the Asiatic Society of Bengal, Bombay Branch (JASB)*, Part 1. History , Literature etc., Nos. III & IV, 1890, pp. 181 to 184) W. Theobald, Symbols on punch-marked coins of Hindustan (1890,1901).

The artisans of Bharhut were literate people. There are many inscriptions in the known Brāhmī script. This script and Kharoṣṭhī syllabic script were used to explain some images for example citing references to Jataka stories on
many Bauddham monuments extending all over Central Asia and Bharatam -- from Taxila to Amaravati. 82 inscriptions of Bharhut serve as labels for panels depicting the Jatakas, the life of the Buddha, former Manushi Buddhas, other stories and Yakshas and Yakshinis. (Luders, H.; Waldschmidt, E.; Mehendale, M. A., eds. (1963).
"Bharhut Inscriptions". *Corpus Inscriptionum Indicarum* II. Ootacamund: Archaeological Survey of India.)

Still, the literate artisans used images, hieroglyphs because they continued the Indus Script writing tradition with the ability to convey precise comprehensive messages about life-activities.

Not all artifacts or sculptural representations are Bauddham or Jaina or Hindu related; many relate to depiction of and signify life-activities creating wealth through lapidary-metalwork activities, trading activities and working with stones, minerals, metals, alloys and creating cire perdue metal castings which had exchange value across civilization contact areas.

One typical explanation offered by some Art historians is that a tree was an aniconic representation of the Bodhi tree and hence the Buddha. I suggest that this is a flight of fancy and it is possible to explain many sculptural artifacts as hieroglyphic representations of life-activities of the people of the times, for example, the work of metalsmiths, lapidaries, producing wealth. A good start is with the representation of Kubera, the divinity of wealth, the possessor of nava-nidhi, nine treasures. This monograph seeks to demonstrate that the navanidhi are represented as hieroglyphs on sculptures and friezes in the continuum of Indus Script Corpora tradition of rebus-metonymy-layered Meluhha cipher, that is, the hieroglyphs denote glosses from Meluhha (mleccha) speech of Indian sprachbund. The Indus Writing traditions continue into the historical periods and get used together with Brahmī or Kharoṣṭhī syllabic scripts used for titles or names of donors or pilgrims who visit the temples. In Indian sprachbund tradition a smithy is a temple; both semantics are signified by one gloss: kole.l. This gloss is engraves as a number of hieroglyphs in rebus-metonymy-layered cipher rendering by engravers, scribes, sculptors, s'ilpi -- architects who created the magnificence of Bharhut or Sanchi or ivory-bone carverss who created the artistic brilliance of Begram ivories. They were also scribes who communicated messages in writing.

Ta. eruvai European bamboo reed; a species of Cyperus; straight sedge tuber. *Ma.* eruva a kind of grass.(DEDR 819)

Ta. eruvai blood, (?) copper.(DEDR 818)*Ka.* e̱re to pour any liquids, cast (as metal); *n.* pouring; e̱racu, ercu to scoop, sprinkle, scatter, strew, sow; e̱raka, eraka any metal infusion; molten state, fusion. *Tu.* eraka molten, cast (as metal); eraguni to melt.(DEDR 866) *Kur. elkhnā* to pour liquid out (by tilting a vessel standing on the ground); elkhrnā to be poured out. (DEDR 840) dhatu 'scarf' Rebus: dhatu 'mineral; eruvai 'reed' Rebus: 'copper' eraka 'molten cast (as metal)'.

Alternative: *dalī* 'bundle of lighted sticks of pine' (WPah.) Rebus: *ḍhāḷako* 'a large metal ingot' (G.)

Focus is on the'scarf' hieroglyph ligatured to the reed posts on Warka vase.

The narrative of the vase is that ingots of tin and iron are conveyed into the treasury (of minerals and metal ingots) from smithy/forge.

Susa. Ritual basin with goat-fish hieroglyphs flanking palm-tree hieroglyph. Jacques de Morgan excavations, 1904-05 Sb 19 Loure Museum. http://www.louvre.fr/en/oeuvre-notices/ritual-basin-decorated-goatfish-figures *tamar*, 'palm tree, date palm' the rebus reading would be: t*am(b)ra*, 'copper' (Pkt.)

The centre-piece shows a pair of twigs with ingots? on the base, flanked by srivatsa hieroglyph multiplex. nIla? Blue steel ingots? The displayed flowers (lotuses? tAmara 'lotus' rebus: tAmra 'copper'), tree branch with badarI berries (kUTI 'badarI twigs, rebus: kuThi 'smelter').

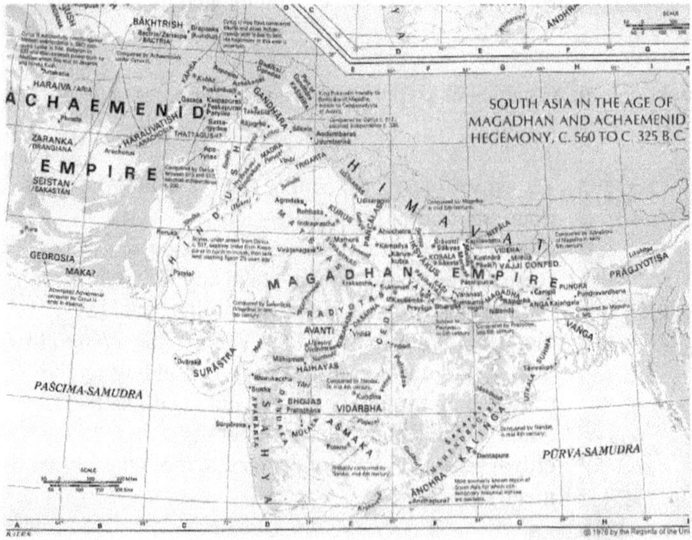

Map of South Asia in the Magadhan and Achaemenid periods. From J. Schwartzberg, *A historical atlas of south Asia*, 1978

Griffins supporting a sacred tree Phoenician, ca. 8th century B.C.E ivory, H 10.6 cm Curved reeds: eruvai 'European reed' eraka 'wing' Rebus: eraka

No. 14. Triśula from Amrávati.

'moltencast' garuDa 'eagle' karaD 'hard alloy'
Srivatsa PLUS lotus on Amaravati railing. xolA 'tail' aya 'fish' rebus: aya kole.l 'metal smithy'; tAmara 'lotus' rebus: tAmra 'copper'. Square coins on base signifying nidhi. tAmra aya kole.l 'copper, metal smithy'

Musee Guimet, Paris. Garland bearing dwarfs.

Amaravathi railing reliefs.

Jaina stupa railing. Kankali Tila. Govt. Museum. Lucknow. eraka 'wing' tAmara 'lotus' rebus: eraka 'moltencast' tAmra 'copper'

Kankali. Mathura. Railing reliefs.
See: http://www.akshardhool.com/2013_03_01_archive.html dAma 'garland' rebus: dhamma 'virtuous conduct, dharma'; dhAma 'furnace'; kharva 'dwarf' karba 'iron'; tAmara 'lotus' rebus: tAmra 'copper'.

Bharhut. A face is shown on a sculptural relief, in a venerated temple arch flanked by two ox-hide ingots and close to a tree (rebus: kuThi 'smelter')
Pillar of light flanked by two 'faces, heads', topped by tree kuTi 'tree' rebus: kuThi 'smelter'. *mēḍha* 'stake' rebus: *meḍ* 'iron, metal' (Ho. Munda). dula 'pair' rebus: dul 'cast metal'. *mũh* 'face' (Hindi) rebus: *mũhe* 'ingot' (Santali) *mũhã̄* = the quantity of iron produced at one time in a native smelting furnace of the Kolhes; iron produced by the Kolhes and formed like a four-cornered piece a little pointed at each end; mūhā mẽṛhẽt = iron smelted by the Kolhes and formed into an equilateral lump a little pointed at each of four ends; *kolhe tehen mẽṛhẽt ko mūhā akata* = the Kolhes have

to-day produced pig iron (Santali);

muṇḍa 'head' rebus: *muḍadāra* 'litharge'.

Woman's Shringhar, Kushana period, scene on a pillar railing (Government Museum, Mathura). The grace and delicacy of the human form is sensitively expressed in this scene, which meets the worshipper's eye as he goes around the stupa. The centre-piece of the doorway of the stupa is the hieroglyph 'ingot': *mukha lo* Rebus: *muh loh* 'ingot copper'. This divinity is venerated by the worshippers wearing large anklets (perhaps of metal).

Tin and iron ingots delivered to the temple with ligatured 'reed-scarf' standard: tagara 'antelope' Rebus: tagara 'tin' + kola 'tiger' Rebus: kol 'iron'.

Scarf is a ligature hieroglyph on Ishtar's (aka Inanna's?) pair of reeds (gi[reed]) of Warka vase. Warka was known as Uruk to the ancient Sumerians. The reeds are also described as two looped temple poles or "asherah," symbolising entrance to a temple.

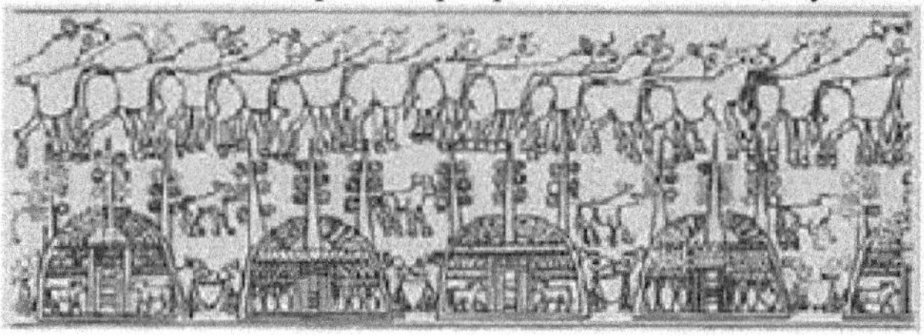

Six circles decorated on the reed post are semantic determinants of hieroglyph: *bhaṭa* 'six'. Rebus: *bhaṭa* 'furnace'.

http://bharatkalyan97.blogspot.in/2013/06/ancient-near-east-scarf-hieroglyph-on.html

How was kharva as one of the nine treasures, navanidhi represented as a hieroglyph on Bharhut sculptural artifacts and what did the hieroglyph signify?

Proso millet
(Panicum miliaceum) spike

Hieroglyph 1: H. *kaṛbī, karbī* f. ' tubular stalk or culm of a plant, esp. of millet ' (→ P. *karb* m.); M. *kaḍbā* m. ' the culm of millet '. (CDIAL 2653) Mar. karvā a bit of sugarcane.(DEDR 1288) Culm, in botanical context, originally referred to a stem of any type of plant. It is derived from the Latin word for 'stalk' (culmus) and now specifically refers to the above-ground or aerial stems of grasses and sedges. Proso millet, common millet, broomtail millet, hog millet, white millet, broomcorn millet *Panicum miliaceum* L. [Poaceae]*Leptoloma miliacea* (L.) Smyth ; *Milium esculentum* Moench; *Milium paniceum* Mill.; *Panicum asperrimum* Fischer ex Jacq.;*Panicum densepilosum* Steud.; *Panicum miliaceum* Blanco, nom. illeg., non *Panicum miliaceum* L.; *Panicum miliaceum*Walter, nom. illeg., non Panicum miliaceum L.; *Panicum miliaceum* var. *miliaceum*; *Panicum milium* Pers. (Quattrocchi, 2006) Proso millet is an erect annual grass up to 1.2-1.5 m tall, usually free-tillering and tufted, with a rather shallow root system. Its stems are cylindrical, simple or sparingly branched, with simple alternate and hairy leaves. The inflorescence is a slender panicle with solitary spikelets. The fruit is a small caryopsis (grain), broadly ovoid, up to 3×2 mm, smooth, variously coloured but often white, shedding easily (Kaume, 2006).*Panicum miliaceum* has been cultivated in eastern and central Asia for more than 5000 years. It later spread into Europe and has been found in agricultural settlements dating back about 3000 years. http://www.feedipedia.org/node/722 *Ta.* varaku common millet, *Paspalum scrobiculatum*; poor man's millet, *P. crusgalli. Ma.* varaku *P. frumentaceum*; a grass *Panicum. Ka.* baraga, baragu *P. frumentaceum*; Indian millet; a kind of hill grass of which writing pens are made. *Te.* varaga, (Inscr.) varuvu *Panicum miliaceum.* / Cf. Mar. barag millet, *P. miliaceum*; Skt. varuka- a kind of inferior grain. [*Paspalum scrobiculatum* Linn. = *P. frumentaceum* Rottb. *P. crusgalli* is not identified in Hooker.] (DEDR 5260)

Tubular stalk: *karb* (Punjabi) kaḍambá, *kalamba* -- 1, m. ' end, point, stalk of a pot- herb ' lex. [See kadambá --] B. *kaṛamba* ' stalk of greens '; Or. *kaṛamba*, °*ma* stalks and plants among stubble of a reaped field '; H. *kaṛbī*, *karbī* f. ' tubular stalk or culm of a plant, esp. of millet ' (→ P. *karb* m.); M. *kaḍbā* m. ' the culm of millet '. -- Or. *kaḷama* ' a kind of firm -- stemmed reed from which pens are made ' infl. by H. *kalam* ' pen ' ← Ar.?(CDIAL 2653) kaḍambī f. ' the potherb Convolvulus repens ', °*ba*- m. Car., *kalambī* -- , °*bikā* -- , °*bū* -- , °*bukā* -- f. lex. [See kadambá --] Pa. *kalamba* -- m., °*bukā* -- f. ' a potherb, prob. Convolvulus repens '; Pk. *kalaṁbu* -- , °*buā* -- f. ' a kind of creeper ', °*bugā* -- f. ' a kind of water plant '; A. *kalmau* ' C. repens '; B. *kalmi* ' a rapidly growing aquatic creeper, C. repens '; Or. *kaṛambī* ' an edible aquatic creeper ', *kaḷama* ' do., Ipomoea aquatica '; H. *kalmī* f. ' C. repens ', *karemū* m. ' an aquatic grass used as an antidote to opium '.(CDIAL 2654) *Ta.* kāmpu flower-stalk, flowering branch, handle, shaft, haft. *Ma.* kāmpu stem, stalk, stick of umbrella. *Ko.* ka·v handle. *To.* ko·f hollow stem, handle of tool. *Ka.* kāmu, kāvu stalk, culm, stem, handle. *Te.* kāma stem, stalk, stick, handle (of axe, hoe, umbrella, etc.), shaft. *Ga.* (S.3) kāŋ butt of axe. *Go.* (Tr.) kāmē stalk of a spoon; (Mu.) kāme handle of ladle (*Voc.* 640). *Kuwi* (F.) kamba, (S.)kāmba handle.(DEDR 1454) Ta. karumpu (in cpds. karuppu-) sugar-cane; karupp-aṭṭi jaggery made from palmyra juice, jaggery. Ma. karimpu sugar-cane; karipp-aṭṭi coarse palmyra-sugar. Ko. kab sugar-cane. To. kab id.;kapoṭy jaggery. Ka. karvu, karbu, kabbu sugar-cane. Koḍ. kaybï id. Tu. karmbu id. / Cf. Mar. karvā a bit of sugarcane.(DEDR 1288) கரும்பு karumpu, *n.* [K. *kabbu*, M. *karimpu*, Tu. *karumbu.*] 1. Sugar-cane, a saccharine grass, *Saccharum officinarum.* கரும்புபோற் கொல்லப் பயன்படுங் கீழ் (குறள், 1078). 2. The Seventh *nakṣatra*; புனர்பூசம். (திவா.)

Hieroglyph 2:खर्व (-र्ब) *a.* [खर्व्-अच्] 1 Mutilated, crippled, imperfect; Yv. Ts.2.5.1.7. -2 Dwarfish, low, short in stature. (Apte. Skt. Lex.)

Rebus 1: karvata [karva*t*a] n. market-place. (Skt.lex.) கர்வம்² karvam , n. < kharva. 1. A billion; இலட்சங்கோடி 2. One of the nine treasures of Kubēra (Tamil lex.) खार्वा khārvāखार्वा The Tretā age or second Yuga of the world. (Apte Skt. lex.) खर्व , -र्वम् A large number (1,,,)(Samskritam) கர்வடம் karvaṭam , *n.* < *kharvaṭa.* Town surrounded by mountains and rivers; மலையும் யாறுஞ் சூழ்ந்த ஊர். (திவா.)

கரும்பொன் karu-m-poṉ , *n.* < id. +. Iron; இரும்பு. கரும்பொ னியல்பன்றி (சீவக. 104)

ಕಬ್ಬಿಣ kabbiṇa. = ಕಬ್ಬ, ಕಬ್ಬುಣ, ಕಬ್ಬುನ, ಕಬ್ಬೂನ, ಕಬೊನ್, ಕಾಬೊನ್. (The dark-coloured, black metal): iron (ಲೋಹ, ಕಾಲಾಯಸ, etc. Si. 332; C.; Tĕ. ಇನುಮು, T. ಇರುಮ್ಬು, ಕರುಮ್ಪೊನ್, iron; Tu. ಕರ್ಬ, iron; see ಕಬ್ 1). ಕಬ್ಬಿಣದ ಕಿಟ್ಟ (ಮಣ್ಡೂರ Si. 332). ಕಬ್ಬಿಣದ ಪ್ರತಿಮೆ (346). ಕಬ್ಬಿಣದ ಕೊಪ್ಪರಿಗೆ (B. 3, 46). ಕಬ್ಬಿಣದ ಅಂಗಡಿಯಲ್ಲಿ ನೊಣಕ್ಕೆ ಏನು ಅಗ್ಗ?—ಕಬ್ಬಿಣದ ಅಂಗಡಿಯಲ್ಲಿ ಕಡ್ಲೆ ಹುಡುಕಿದ ಹಾಗೆ (Prvs.). See ಮುದ್ದೆ. — ಕಬ್ಬಿಣಕಿಟ್ಟ. Rust of iron, scoriae, dross (ಮಣ್ಡೂರ, ಸಿಂಘಾಣ G.). — ಕಬ್ಬಿಣಗೊಮ್ಬೆ. An iron image (ಸ್ಥೂಣೆ Si. 420; G.). — ಕಬ್ಬಿಣಂಚು. -ಅಂಚು. = ಕಬ್ಬುಣಂಚು. An iron plate for baking cakes, etc. (B. 4, 158). — ಕಬ್ಬಿಣದ ಪಾರ. A bar of iron (My.). — ಕಬ್ಬಿಣಸಲಾಕೆ. An iron spike, etc. (ದಸಿ G.).

Rebus 2: *Tu. ajirda karba* very hard iron; *Ta.* ayil iron. *Ma.* ayir, ayiram any ore. *Ka.* aduru native metal (DEDR 192) *Tu.* kari soot, charcoal; kariya black; karṅka state of being burnt or singed; karṅkāḍuni to burn (*tr.*); karñcuni to be burned to cinders;karñcāvuni to cause to burn to cinders; kardů black; karba iron; karvāvuni to burn the down of a fowl by holding it over the fire (DEDR 1278). खर्व (-र्ब) *a.* [खर्व्-अच्] N. of one of the treasures of Kubera (Samskritam)

In the cultural context of Hindu civilization continuum, kharva chauth celebrated on the chaturdashi of Kartika month (9 days before Deepavali) is relatable to the celebration through vrata including fasting, of wealth creating artisan-husband: karuvā 'artist'. kārú -- , °*uka* -- m. ' artisan ' Mn. [√kr̥1] Pa. *kāru* -- , °*uka* -- m., Pk. *kāru* -- m.; A. B. *kāru* ' artist '; Or. *kāru* ' artisan, servant ', *kāruā* ' expert, deft '; G. *kāru* m. ' artisan '; Si. *karuvā* ' artist ' (ES 22 <*kāraka* --).(CDIAL 3066)

The hypothesis is that *karvā* 'a bit of sugarcane' was denoted by tubular stalks shown on toraNa or artistic representations on architraves. The rebus readin was: *karba* 'iron'.

Peacock on a lotus. Afghanistan. National Museum, Kabul. marakaka loha 'copper alloy, calcining metal'; maraka 'peacock'. Is the peacock intended to signify blue colour?

Kubera on Naravahana in Tala, Chattisgarh

Greek scroll supported by Indian yaksha, Amaravati, 3rd century CE, Tokyo National Museum

tAramara 'lotus' Rebus: tAmra 'copper'. dAma 'garland'
Rebus: dhamma, dharma 'righteous conduct'; Rebus: dhAma 'blast furnace'; dhamaka 'blacksmith'
Peacock on a lotus. Afghanistan. National Museum, Kabul. marakaka loha 'copper alloy, calcining metal'; maraka 'peacock'. Is the peacock intended to signify blue colour?

An object lesson for Art historians: learn Meluhha lingua franca of Indus Script Corpora, of Bharatam Janam.

Molluscs, reeds, lotuses, garlands, Yaksha Kubera's navanidhi as wings, as hieroglyphs in art & wealth-creation traditions

A specialist discipline has evolved in some western academia creating a set of 'Art historians' attempting to unravel history, itihAsa. Some Art historians wax eloquent on and conjecture aniconic representations of Gautama the Buddha on early sculptures on Stupas and in architectural monuments of sites such as Kankali-Tila, Bharhut or Sanchi.

Such conjectures may not always be the truth or reality and hence, misrepresentations of messages conveyed by artifacts.

This unfortunate situation has arisen because some art historians have failed to recognize the spoken languages of the artisans who created the artifacts and glosses from the languages which had signified the messages conveyed by hieroglyphs such as a lotus, a rhizome, soles of feet, ox-hide ingot graphics or a dwarf.

The key question that any art historian should ask before interpreting images, say on an ancient sculptural frieze, is this: how did the artisan 'name' a hieroglyph, what did the artisan 'say' about the images in his or her spoken mother tongue, *lingua franca* or speech forms of the guild or community of artisans? If an art historian calls an image, say, a 'vase' or a 'topf' instead of calling it a 'ghaTa' or 'kanda', he or she is likely to end up conveying pot and thus, misrepresent the true import intended to be conveyed by the artisan who created the artifact.

The moral of the story in art appreciation or art history is this: Step 1: name the artifact in the *lingua franca* of the artisan.

Now that the Indus Script Corpora has been substantively demonstrated as *catalogum catalogorum* of metalwork of Bronze Age, it is reasonable to hypothesise that the Indus Script 'writing' tradition using rebus-metonymy-layered-Meluhha-cipher continued even upto ca. 2nd century BCE in the area of Indian*sprachbund*. The evidence of the Indus Script continuum is more pronounced in the array of symbols used by mints from Taxila to Karur.
See: https://www.academia.edu/8776901/Indus_script_hieroglyphs_continued_use_in_ancient_Indian_mints_evidenced_by_punch-marked_coins

This note which presents 1890/1901 monographs of Theobald listing 342 symbols deployed on punch-marked coins. These symbols also survive on later coinages of Ujjain or Eran or of many janapadas. One view is that early punch-marked coinage in Bharatam is datable to 10th century BCE, predating Lydia's electrum coin of 7th cent. BCE. “The coins to which these notes refer, though presenting neither king’s names, dates of inscription of any sort, are nevertheless very interesting not only from their being the earliest money coined in India, and of a purely indigenous character, but from their being stamped with a number of symbols, some of which we can, with the utmost confidence, declare to have originated in distant lands and inthe remotest antiquity…The coins to which I shall confine my remarks are those to which the term ‘punch -marked’ properly applies. The ‘punch’ used to produce these coins differed from the ordinary dies which subsequently came into use, in that they covered only a portion of the surface of the coin or ‘blank’, and impressed only one, of the many symbols usually seen on their pieces…One thing which is specially striking about most of the symbols representing animals is, the fidelity and spirit with which certain portions of it may be of an animal, or certain attitudes are represented…Man, Woman, the Elephant, Bull, Dog, Rhinoceros,Goat, Hare, Peacock, Turtle, Snake, Fish, Frog, are all recognizable at a glance…First, there is the historical record of Quintus Curtius, who describes the Raja of Taxila (the modern Shahdheri, 20miles north-west from Rawal Pindi) as offering Alexander 80 talents of coined silver (‘signati argenti’). Now what other, except these punch-marked coins could these pieces of coined silver have been? Again, the name by which these coins are spoken of in the Buddhist sutras, about 200 BCE was ‘purana’,

which simply signies 'old', whence the General argunes that the word 'old as applied to the indigenous 'karsha',was used to distinguish it from the new and more recent issues of the Greeks. Then again a mere comparison of the two classes of coins almost itself suffices to refute the idea of the Indian coins being derived from the Greek. The Greek coins present us with a portrait of the king, with his name and titles in two languages together with a great number and variety of monograms indicating, in many instances where they have been deciphered by the ingenuity and perseverance of General Cunningham and others, the names of the mint cities where the coins were struck, and it is our ignorance of the geographical names of the period that probably has prevented the whole of them receiving their proper attribution; but with the indigenous coins it is far otherwise, as they display neither king's head, neame, titles or mongrams of any description…It is true that General Cunningham considers that many of these symbols, though not monograms in a strict sense, are nevertheless marks which indicate the mints where the coins were struck or the tribes among whom they were current, and this contention in no wise invalidates the supposition contended for by me either that the majority of them possess an esoteric meaning or have originated in other lands at a period anterior to the
ir adoption for the purpose they fulfil on the coins in Hindustan."
(W. Theobald, 1890, Notes on some of the symbols found on the punch-marked coins of Hindustan, and on their relationship to the archaic symbolism of other races and distant lands, *Journal of the Asiatic Society of Bengal, Bombay Branch (JASB)*, Part 1. History , Literature etc., Nos. III & IV, 1890, pp. 181 to 184) W. Theobald, Symbols on punch-marked coins of Hindustan (1890,1901)

The artisans of Bharhut were literate people. There are many inscriptions in the known Brahmi script. This script and Kharoṣṭhī syllabic script were used to explain some images for example citing references to Jataka stories on many Bauddham monuments extending all over Central Asia and Bharatam -- from Taxila to Amaravati. 82 inscriptions of Bharhut serve as labels for panels depicting the Jatakas, the life of the Buddha, former Manushi Buddhas, other stories and Yakshas and Yakshinis. (Luders, H.; Waldschmidt, E.; Mehendale, M. A., eds. (1963).
"Bharhut Inscriptions". *Corpus Inscriptionum Indicarum* II. Ootacamund: Archaeological Survey of India.)

Still, the literate artisans used images, hieroglyphs because they continued the Indus Script writing tradition with the ability to convey precise comprehensive messages about life-activities.

Not all artifacts or sculptural representations are Bauddham or Jaina or Hindu related; many relate to depiction of and signify life-activities creating wealth through lapidary-metalwork activities, trading activities and working with stones, minerals, metals, alloys and creating cire perdue metal castings which had exchange value across civilization contact areas.

One typical explanation offered by some Art historians is that a tree was an aniconic representation of the Bodhi tree and hence the Buddha. I suggest that this is a flight of fancy and it is possible to explain many sculptural artifacts as hieroglyphic representations of life-activities of the people of the times, for example, the work of metalsmiths, lapidaries, producing wealth. A good start is with the representation of Kubera, the divinity of wealth, the possessor of nava-nidhi, nine treasures. This monograph seeks to demonstrate that the navanidhi are represented as hieroglyphs on sculptures and friezes in the continuum of Indus Script Corpora tradition of rebus-metonymy-layered Meluhha cipher, that is, the hieroglyphs denote glosses from Meluhha (mleccha) speech of Indian sprachbund. The Indus Writing traditions continue into the historical periods and get used together with Kharoṣṭhī and/or Brāhmī syllabic scripts used for titles or names of donors or pilgrims who visit the temples. In Indian sprachbund tradition a smithy is a temple; both semantics are signified by one gloss: kole.l. This gloss is engraves as a number of hieroglyphs in rebus-metonymy-layered cipher rendering by engravers, scribes, sculptors, s'ilpi -- architects who created the magnificence of Bharhut or Sanchi or ivory-bone carverss who created the artistic brilliance of Begram ivories. They were also scribes who communicated messages in writing.

Ta. eruvai European bamboo reed; a species of Cyperus; straight sedge tuber. *Ma.* eruva a kind of grass.(DEDR 819)

Ta. eruvai blood, (?) copper.(DEDR 818)*Ka.* eṟe to pour any liquids, cast (as metal); *n.* pouring; eṟacu, ercu to scoop, sprinkle, scatter, strew, sow; eṟaka, eraka any metal infusion; molten state, fusion. *Tu.* eraka molten, cast (as metal); eraguni to melt.(DEDR 866) *Kur. elkhnā* to pour liquid out (by tilting a vessel standing on the ground); elkhrnā to be poured out. (DEDR 840)

http://www.harappa.com/script/gif/parpola8.gif Impression of an Indus-style cylinder seal of unknown Near Eastern origin.

Two bos gaurus flank a circle (right-bottom-corner). The circle may be read as: doḷā, ḍoḷā ' pupil of eye ' (Or.); M. ḍoḷā m. ' eye ' (CDIAL 6582); rebus: dul 'cast'.

Property Items made by fire-workers: weapons, impements,ornaments, weights, bangles, and beads

Bronze weapons

Metal crafts

Almost identical bronze carts discovered at Chanhu-daro and Harappa, seem to indicate a common manufacturing origin.

Gold was almost certainly imported from the group of settlements that sprang up in the vicinity of the goldfields of northern Karnataka, because the composition indicates electrum (gold-silver compound, called soma) and copper could have come principally from Rajasthan. Lead may have come from Rajasthan.

Quarters of the lower city in Mohenjodaro seem to have housed artisans specializing in different crafts indicating the possibility of occupational specialization among the fire- and metal-workers. Copper and bronze were used for making tools and implements. These included flat oblong axes, chisels, knives, spears, arrowheads , small saws, and razors. All these could be made by simple casting, chiseling, and hammering.Four main varieties of metal have been found: crude copper lumps in the state in which they left the smelting furnace; refined copper, containing trace elements of arsenic and antimony; an alloy of copper with 2 to 5 percent of arsenic; and bronze with a tin alloy, often of as much as 11 to 13 percent. The copper and bronze vessels of the Harappans are among their finest products, formed by hammering sheets of metal. Casting of copper and bronze was understood, and figurines of men and animals were made by the cire-perdue (lost-wax) technique.

Other metals used were gold, silver, and lead. Lead was employed occasionally for making small vases and such objects as plumb bobs. Silver is relatively more common than gold, and more than a few vessels are known, generally in forms similar to copper and bronze examples. Two examples of silver seals have been found. Gold was generally reserved for such small objects as beads, pendants, and brooches.

Other crafts

Lapis lazuli was probably imported from Iran rather than directly from the mines at Badakhshan. Turquoise probably came from Iran; fuchsite from Karnataka; alabaster from Iran; amethyst from Maharashtra; and jade from Central Asia.

Other special crafts include the manufacture of faience (earthenware decorated with coloured glazes)--for making beads, amulets, sealings, and small vessels--and the working of stone for bead manufacture and for seals. The seals were generally cut from steatite and were carved in intaglio or incised with a copper burin (cutting tool). Beads were made from a variety of substances, but the carnelians are particularly noteworthy. They include several varieties of etched carnelian and long barrel beads made with extraordinary skill and accuracy. Shell and ivory were also worked and were used for beads, inlays, combs, bracelets, and the like.

Ffragments of cotton textiles recovered at Mohenjodaro provide the earliest evidence of a crop and industry for which India has long been famous. Perhaps, raw cotton was brought in bales to the cities to be spun, woven, and perhaps dyed, as the presence of dyers' vats would seem to indicate.

Neighbours

In the Metropolitan Museum of Art is the bronze sword of King Adad-nirari I, a unique example from the palace of one of the early kings of the period (14th-13th century BC) during which Assyria first began to play a prominent part in Mesopotamian history.

The Persian bronze industry was also influenced by Mesopotamia. Luristan, near the western border of Persia (Iran), is the source of many bronzes that have been dated from 1500 to 500 BC and include chariot or harness fittings, rein rings, elaborate horse bits, and various decorative rings, as well as weapons, personal ornaments, different types of cult objects, and a number of household vessels.

A sword, found in the palace of Mallia and dated to the Middle Minoan period (2000-1600 BC), is an example of the extraordinary skill of the Cretan metalworker in casting bronze. The hilt of the sword is of gold-plated ivory and crystal. A dagger blade found in the Lasithi plain, dating about 1800 BC (Metropolitan Museum of Art), is the earliest known predecessor of ornamented dagger blades from Mycenae. It is engraved with two spirited scenes: a fight between two bulls and a man spearing a boar. Somewhat later (c. 1400 BC) are a series of splendid blades from mainland Greece, which must be attributed to Cretan craftsmen, with ornament in relief, incised, or inlaid with varicoloured metals, gold, silver, and niello. The most elaborate inlays--pictures of men hunting lions and of cats hunting birds--are on daggers from the shaft graves of Mycenae, Nilotic scenes showing Egyptian influence. The bronze was oxidized to a blackish-brown tint; the gold inlays were hammered in and polished and the details then engraved on them. The gold was in two colours, a deeper red being obtained by an admixture of copper; and there was a sparing use of neillo.

Weapons and implements

1. Spear and lance heads and arrow heads. These weapons occurred at all levels at Harappa, Lothal, Kalibangan and Chanhudaro. Chanhudaro arrowheads are made from sheets of .02 to .05 in. thickness and have backward projecting barbs. The Lothal arrowheads are thin and without a barb.
2. Knives. Knives occur in a variety of shapes: triangular with leaf-shaped blades with curved ends, plain, narrow, straight; some have curved edges and some have rectangular sections.
3. Swords and Dirks. These have a pronounced mid-rib and thick tang with holes located at the base of blade or on the tang itself.
4. Blade axes and celts. Long, short, narrow, broad. Some are flat copper celts with a lenticular cross-section, broken butt, slightly concave sides and sometimes concentric working edge. A shouldered celt and a sleeved copper which is perhaps a precursor to the anthropomorphic copper hoard were also found.
5. Socketed axes. Mohenjodaro and Chanhudaro. The axe from Chanhudaro is made of bronze and perhaps belongs to the Zhukar period.
6. Maces. Pear-shaped copper maces.
7. Razors. Of several shapes.
8. Chisels. Of several shapes and in relatively large numbers. Sizes vary from short to long, sections vary from rectangular, round to square. The edges are doubly sloped, abrupt and occasionally displayed. Typical ones are with broad, rectacular sectioned tangs and narrow blades.
9. Saws. Bronze. With very regular, small teeth. Was proably fixed with a wooden handle with 2 or 3 rivets placed wide apart. Circular saw was found at Lothal and was perhaps used to cut grooves in cylindrical objects.
10. Sickle blade. Infrequent occurrence.
11. Tubular drills. Coghlan refers to these as the earliest examples in the world. The drills are the tapered tubes of thin copper and bronze. The groove left between the core and the

wall varies in width indicating variance in the circumferences of the tools. A twisted drill, the fore-runner of the modern drill was found at Lothal.
12. Fish hooks. Made of sheet copper with an eye on the top and a barb at the pointed end. A few unbarbed fish hooks have also been found. Metallic fish-hooks are the earliest examples found anywhere in the world.
13. Others: awls and reamers, mid-ribbed swords, mirror, gouges, net sinker, needles, crapers, daggers and shovel.
Techniques. Annealing entails heating of cold worked brittle metal to regain its malleability. The Harappans seem to be acquainted with this technique (See Chanhudaro wire TF-C48; ASI, No. 49 and Chanhudaro Celt TF-C4-3; ASI No. 252 252988).
Smelting (See furnace at Pl. VI, Figs. 33-35). Smelting oxide and carbonate ores involved placing the ore in wood or charcoal fire over a clay-lined pit. The metal regulus was kept and the slag portion thrown away. Melting of native copper was done by putting the regulus over furnace or fire in a crucible and then casting it. Smelting of sulphide ores to obtain refined copper involved the following stages (Agrawala, op. cit., p. 157):
a. the ore was roasted to remove the bulk of sulphur.
b. the roasted ore was smelted which removed slag from copper matte (copper and iron).
c. the copper matte was roasted. This process yielded blue material rich in copper and slag rich in copper and iron.
d. further roasting of blue material.
e. the roasted blue material was smelted with charcoal which resulted in 3 gradients: 1. black copper; 2. rich copper matte; 3. slag rich in copper.
f. the black copper was melted which separated refined copper from slag rich in copper.
g. the pure copper thus obtained was cast and used in making a variety of vessels, tools, implements and jewellery.
The native and oxide ores were in common use as shown in Mohenjodaro and Rangpur artefacts. Use of sulphide ores is suggested by Chanhudaro adze (TF-C4-1, ASI N.2593 P; M 43, Pl. LXIV, 10).
Casting. Open cast method used for flat axes. Closed moulds were used for the heads of staves.
Cire Perdue or Lost Wax process (See Pl. VI, Fig. 31). The toy cart, the figure of a dancing girl and fine toy animals and birds found at Lothal and other sites indicate use of this method. Wax model is made on a clay core. The thickness of the wax depends upon the thickness of the required metal. Then a single outer mould of clay is bilt up with a sprue-cup. The whole unit is then heated up so that wax melts and runs out. Core chaplets are inserted to prevent shift of clay. Molten metal is poured into the cavity. Then the outer clay mould is broken. The object which comes out with a rough surface is smoothed by polishing and rubbing down with horn.
Furnaces. Sixteen furnaces of three shapes were found at Harappa. One of them was a pottery jar embedded into earth. The technique is used even today by gold- and silver-smiths in India. Two other furnaces, one 3ft. 4 in. dia and cylindrical and the other 3ft. 5 in.dia. and pear-shaped are lined with bricks with their walls having mud-plastered vitrified slags. A window allows the placement of crucible with metal. The find of molten metal and thick terracotta bowl-like crucible near a circular furnace at Lothal confirms that copper ingots were melted in it. Another rectangular furnace was found in copper-smith's workshop at the same site. A few furnaces were also found at Kalibangan.

Running on method of joining. The parts to be joined are cleaned and molten bronze is poured over the parts to be joned. A tanged sword was joined to its hilt by this method. Soldering method involved the use of an alloy which has a lower melting point. The soft solder is applied by a heated metal rod. Sanahullah notes that Harappans could perform gold and silver soldering.
Rivetting method involved the hammering down of simple metal rods at both ends to constitute a rivet. Rivet holes have been noticed in knives, bracelets and lances.
Lapping was the method used to join tubular handles to the vessel. Teal welding was also known to the Harappans.
Alloying. Ten, lead and arsenic were alloyed with copper. The criteron of determining whether the alloying is deliberate is accidental is the presence of more than one percent of tin. Out of 100 artefacts examined, 30 had tin content ranging from 8 to 12 percent. Arsenic alloying was used in 8 percent of the artefacts. Nickle alloying was used in 4 percent of the artefacts and lead alloying in six percent of the artefacts.
Higher percentage tin was used in alloys used for bangles and pins.
Spear 2.27%; engraver 3.96%; mirror 5.47%; chisel 9.62%; bangle 11.82%; pin 13.83%.
The Harappans were metal forgers, smiths and craftspersons capable of producing weapons, tools, instruments, pots, toys, jewellery and decorative pieces of metal.
Electrum
Arthas'a_stra states: pure and impure silver may be heated four times with copper sulphate, mixed with powdered bone (asthituttha) again four times with an equal quantity of lead and again four times with dry copper sulphate (sushkatuttha), again three times in skull and lastly twice in cow dung. (Stanza 88). The use of the skull which is calcium phosphate is a cupellation process for purification of silver. Galena was first smelted to crude lead and silver concentrated by a process called Pattinson Process. The proess is based on the fact that i fused argentiferous lead is cooled, a point is reached when nearly pure lead separates in crystals. If crystals of lead were withdrawn by perforated ladles the remaining liquid alloy would become increasingly rich in silver. About 7/8ths of the original lead is removed by this process and the rest of the lead is reoved by cupellation process. Separation of silver and other impurities from gold (electrum) was invented before Amarna age, possibly during or shortly after Ur III period (ca. 2200-2000 B.C.)
Sources:
D.P. Agrawal, The copper and bronze age in India, pp. 191,239;
Marshall, MIC, Pl. CXXXV and CXXXVI; Vol. II-III, 501-2, Pl. CXXXVI, Pl. CXXXV; Pl. CXXXVIII, 6-7; Pl. CXXXVIII, 4,8; Pl. CXLIII, 24-25; Pl. CXLII, No.14; CXLIII, 31,33,37; Pl. CXLII, 20-21, 36
M.S.Vats, Excavations at Harappa, VOl. I-II, 387-88, Pl. CXXV, 15-18 and 22-64; Pl. CXXV, 52, 62-64; Pl. CXXXIV, No.29; Pl. CXXV, 38 and 58.
E.Mackay, FEM, Vol. 1-2, Pl. XXI, 105; Pl. CXIX; Pl. CXIII,3; Pl. CXIII,2; Pl. CXXI, 25 to 32 aqnd 36, Pl. CXVIII, No.7; Pl. CXXV, No.39, CXIX, No.1; Pl. CXIV, No. 235; Pl. CXIV, 6; Pl. CXIII, No.3
E.Mackay, 'Arts and Crafts of Mohenjodaro', Art and Letters, No. XIII, p. 18.
S.R.Rao, Lothal and the Indus Civilization, 1972, p. 28; fig. 20, no. 21; p. 84
E.Mackay, Chanhudaro Excavations, Pls. LXXII, 11; LXIII,16; LXXX, 21-25; LXXVI, 8, 25-27; Pl. LXXII, 25 and LXXVI, 137; Pl. LXXIII, No.32; Pl. XXXIII, No.31; Pl. LXII, 7; LXXX,9; lXXXI, 15; Pl. LXXX; Pls. LXVIII, 13,15; LXXV, 9; LXXVI, 38; Pl. LXXIV, 13.

S.R.Rao, Ancient India, Nos. 18-19, No. 663, p. 30, fig.417, Pl. XXXVa, 3 and 4; fig. 442, p. 150;
Coghlan in C.Singer, History of Technology, Vol. I
IAR, 1956-57, Pl. XVI.

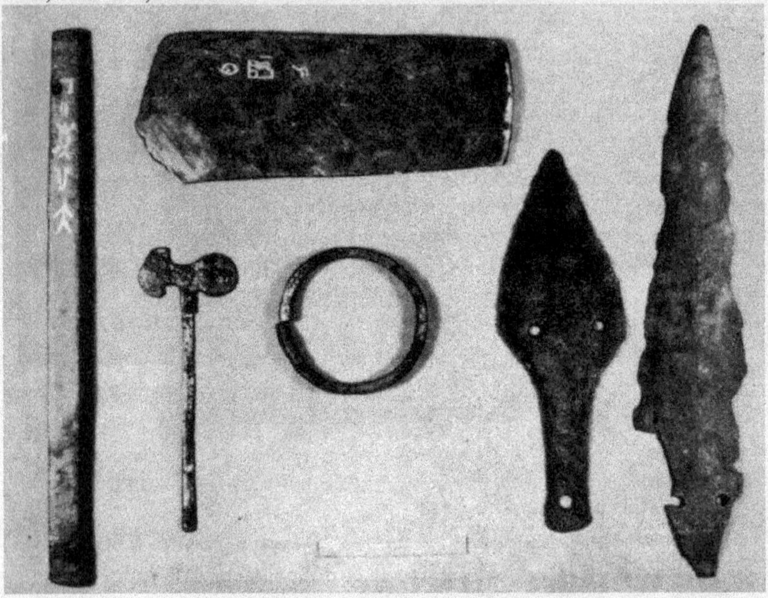

Kalibangan; copper implements; Agrawala, R.C. and Vijay Kumar, 1982, Pl. 11.12

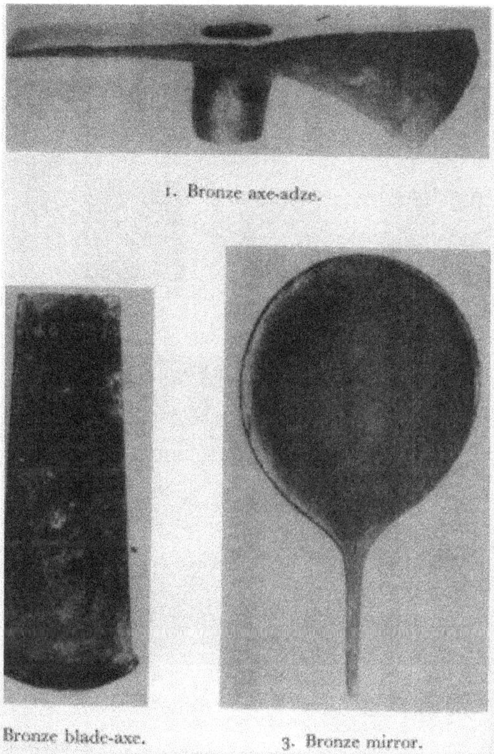

Bronze axe-adze, blade-axe and mirror (After Mackay, *Indus Civilization*,1935, Pl. N.)

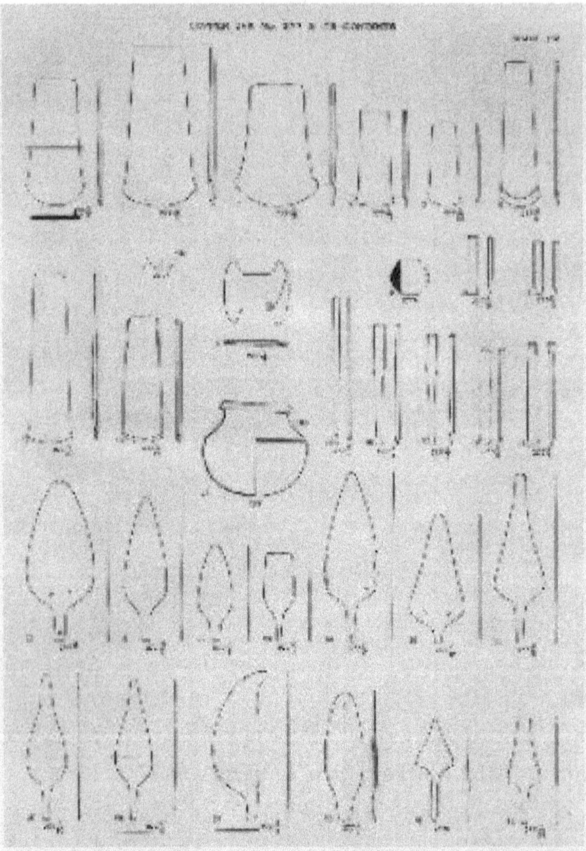

Jar No. 277 and contents of the jar, Harappa (After Vats, Pl. CXXI). cf. Pl. CXXIV, 27 and 28 showing the copper jar No. 277 which contained a hundred objects.

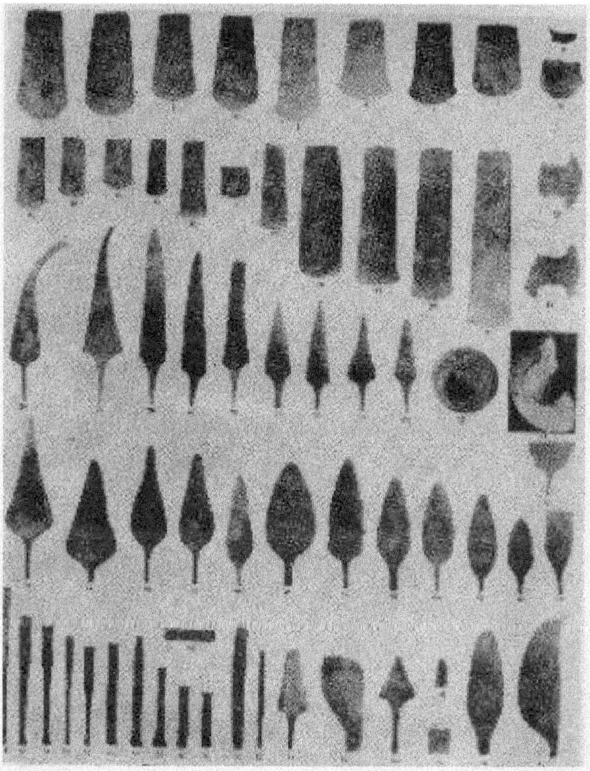

Copper jar No. 277 contained these objects; the figure also shows a marble macehead no. 573 (After Vats, Pl. CXXIII) Thirteen blade-axes with or without shoulders (Nos. 1-13), eight long and narrow axes (Nos. 14-21), two double-axes (Nos. 22 and 23), eleven daggers with tapering sides (Nos. 24-32 and 64-64), one mace-head (No.33), thirteen spear-heads and flaying knives (Nos. 35-47), one lance-head (No.66), one arrow-head (No.63), one chopper (No.67), two saws (Nos. 61 and 62), ten chisels with or without shanks (Nos. 49-58)J, two cast bars for making chisels (Nos. 59 and 60), and a flat strip (No.48).

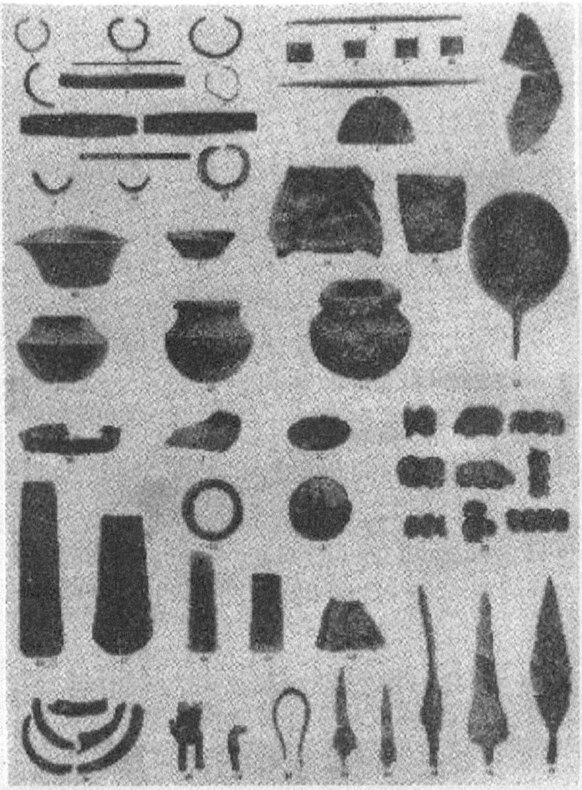

Copper and bronze weapons, implements and utensils (After Vats, Pl. CXXII). No. 24 carinated copper jar; No.32 shallow inverted dish; No. 26 round copper vase 6 in. dia; No.30 deep cup with flared mouth; No. 31 saucer with slightly incurved rim; No.29 ring-stand for jar. No.13 adze; No.19 adze inscribed with three faint pictograms; 5.15 in. long, 2.15 in. broad at the cutting edge; No.18 lower part of a broken axe. No. 17 razor.

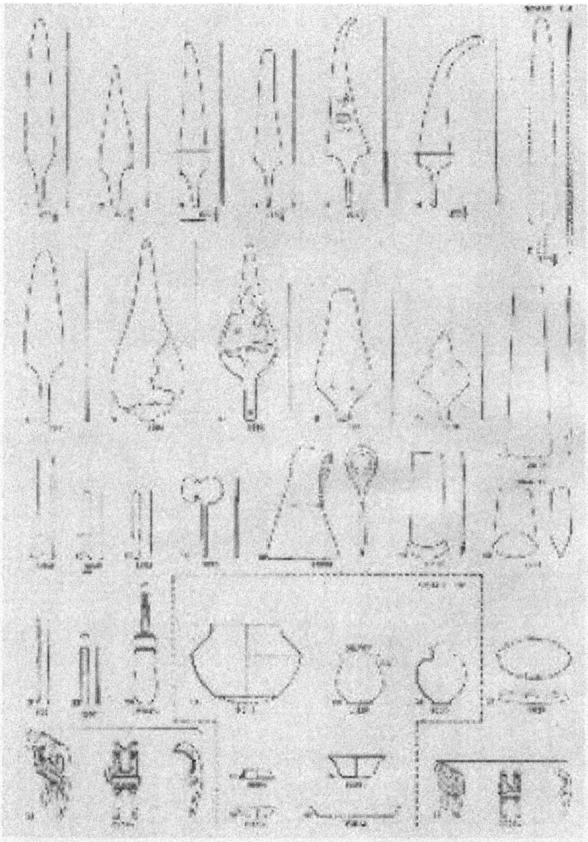

Copper, bronze, silver and gold objects, Harappa (After Vats, Pl. CXXV). Nos. 65-77 spear-heads. Nos. 15-18 and 22-24 chisels. Nos. 28-31, 52 and 62-64 knives and sickles; Nos. 38 and 58 scrapers; Nos. 46 and 47 razors. Nos. 40-42 and 44 bronze gouges (to hollow out, groove or rib wood, bone, ivory and stone) No.39 nail-parer; No.1 a bunch of three bronze instruments held together by their looped or interlaced ends; the right hand tool is a double-edged knife (4.4 in.) and the left hand one a piercing rod (5.3in.); the middle one is a pincers (5.2 in.) all three are a surgical or toilet set. No.32 cobbler's awl(?) Nos. 37 and 45 needles; Nos. 25-27 pins; Nos. 33,34 and 36 antimony rods. No.8 a fish-hook. Nos. 13 and 14 arrow-heads. No.53 silver vase. No.57 a hasp (typical Indian kund.i) made of round copper bar.

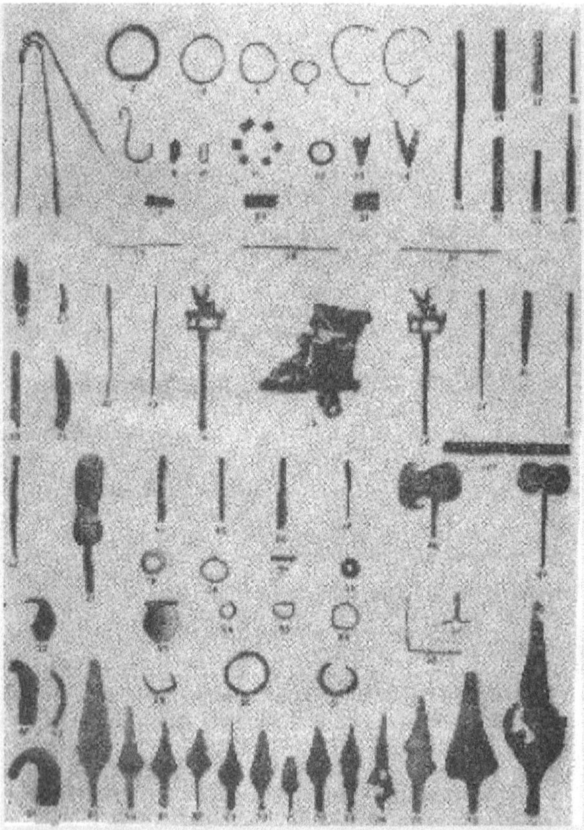

Copper and bronze ornaments, utensils, implements, weapons, Harappa (After Vats, Pl. CXXIV). A stilus (No.19), a beam of a weighing scale (No.14), a semi-oval, hollow terminal (No.20), five solid bangles (Nos. 1,2,3,5 and 7), a rod intended to be fashioned into a solid bangle (No.4), three hollow bangles (Nos.11-13), two flattened leaves to be made into hollow bangles (Nos. 8 and 9; Nos. 6 and 10), four thick rectangular copper pieces (Nos. 15-18), a thin bowl with tapering sides (No.23), two large folded sheets of copper (Nos. 24 and 25), two thick broken pieces bearing prominent hammer marks (Nos. 21), a lump of lollingite (used to extract arsenic used for hardening the cutting edges of tools instead of the tin alloy). No.29 is an oval copper mirror. No.44 a copper hook. Nos. 42 and 43 caste bronze latches (?)

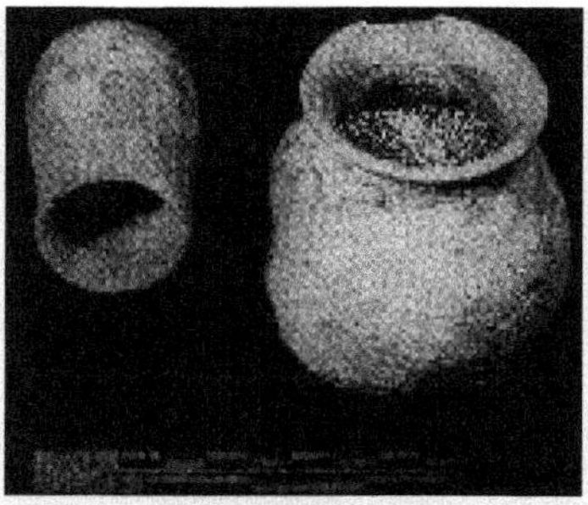

Miniature jar fitted with a cork-like, hollow, baked clay stopper; containing microbeads mixed with fine ash; the jar was buried under a house floor at Zekda (23.53N and 71.26E), Banaskanta District, Gujarat (Hegde, K.T.M. et al, 1982, Pl. 21.2.

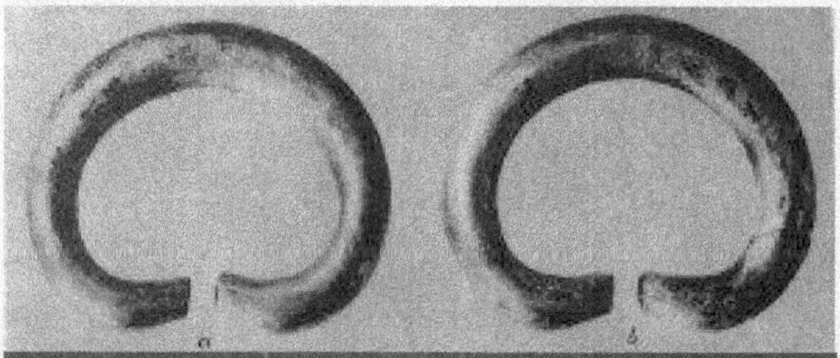

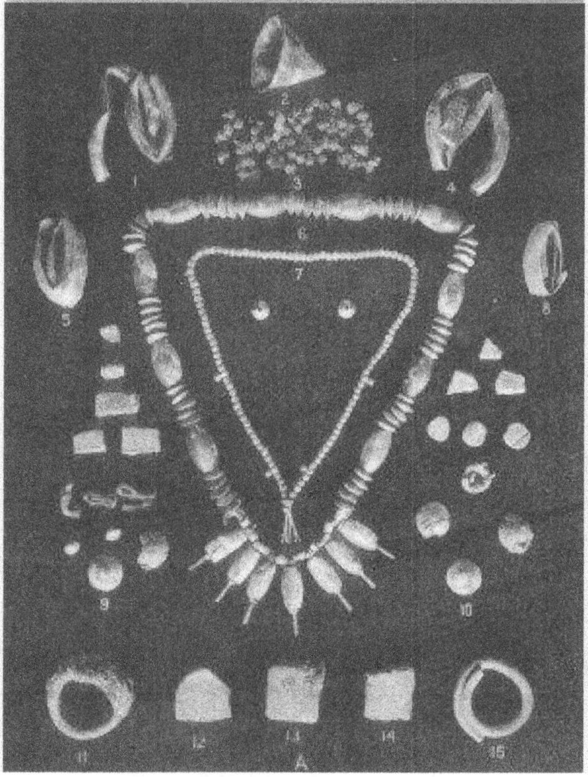

Gold jewellery, Mohenjodaro (After Marshall, Pl. CXLVIII).

The jewellery was found in a silver vase. The large necklace is made up of barrel-shaped beads of a translucent, light-green jade. Each jade bead is separated from its neighbours on either side by five disc-shaped gold beads, 0.4 in. dia made by soldering two cap-like pieces together. Seven pendants of agate-jasper are suspended by means of a thick gold wire. The pendants are separated one from another by a small cylindrical bead of steatite capped at each end with gold. The smaller necklace (No. 7) inside the large one is made up of small globular gold beads, all of which are cast. The spacers were made by soldering two of these beads together, and it is probable that the beads were originally strung into a bracelet of two rows. The two bangles (Nos. 1 and 4) were each made of thin sheet gold wrapped over a core (dia. 3 in.) No.2 is a conical gold cap (1.3 in. high) beaten out from a plate of gold; it is perhaps a hair ornament.

Two silver bracelets were also found with this hoard. (Marshall, Pl. CLXIV)

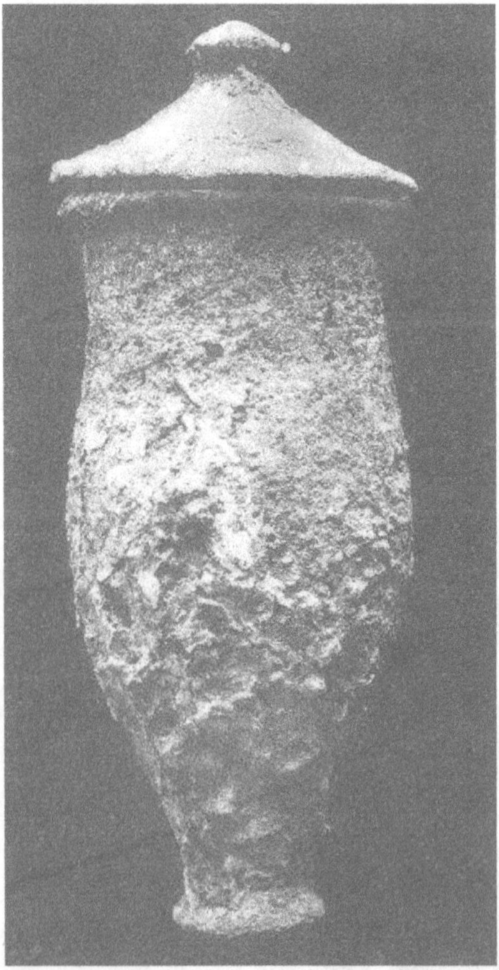

Silver vase, Mohenjodaro (After Marshall, Pl. CXLVIII). The silver vase contained gold jewellery.

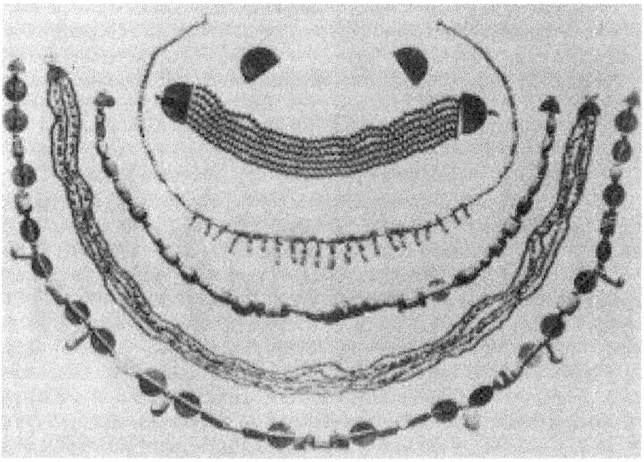

Jewellery, Mohenjodaro (After Marshall, Pl. CXLIX). No.3 is a gold bracelet. (Other bracelets are made of blue glazed faience or a vitrified clay, dark brown or black on the surface, sometimes with very minute inscriptions). The gold spacers found with these beads show that they were originally threaded in six rows with semi-circular terminals of gold. The small beads were cast and the spacers cut out of sheet metal. No.4 below this bracelet is made of minute gold beads, globular and cylindrical in shape, interspaced with tiny globular beads of steatite, perhaps of original blue glaze. The small cylindrical pendants on the necklace are made of gold and glaze; the loops of thin gold ribbon wire. No.5 is of beads of various coloured stones, such as riband-jasper and carnelian, alternating with small gold beads; some beads are capped with gold. No. 6 is a string made of gold and glazed steatite cylindrical beads in five rows held by eight five-holed spacers. No. 7 is of flat gold beads, beads of onyx, green felspar and turquoise matrix and small globular beads. Nos. 1 and 2 are dome-shaped caps of the pendants with small gold loops inside. (After Marshall, Pl. CXLIX).

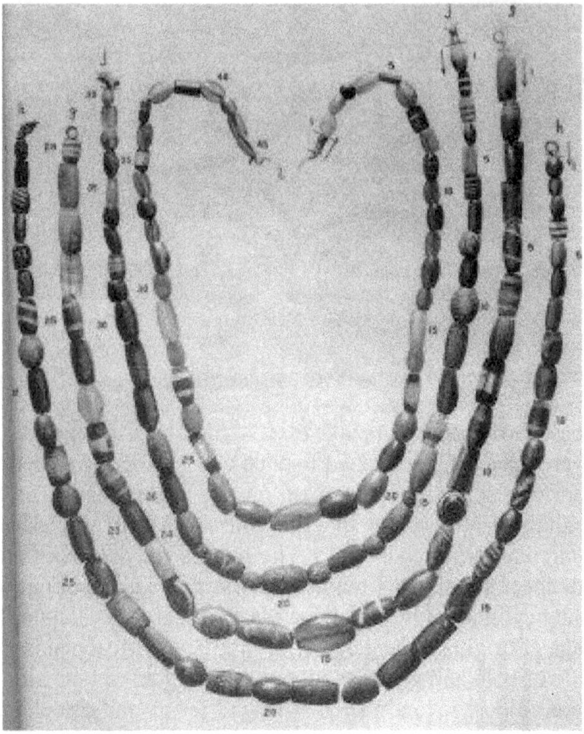

From inside out: No.1: A necklace of very fine beads of jade, jasper, carnelian, chalcedony and agate. The first bead is of gold; No. 2: beads of jasper, carnelian, agate, lapis-lazuli and six of silver; No.3: stones of diverse materials, colours and shapes including two cleverly cut onyx eye-beads; No.4: extraordinary variety in shape, markings and colour. A long flat bead, oval in section was a favourite shape. This necklace also includes several skilfully cut 'cat's eye' onyx beads. (After Marshall, Pl. CL). Silver was used more freely than gold at Mohenjodaro. Maybe, silver was extracted from sulphide or chloride form, mixed with metals such as lead or copper. Gold used in Mohenjodaro, resembles electrum.

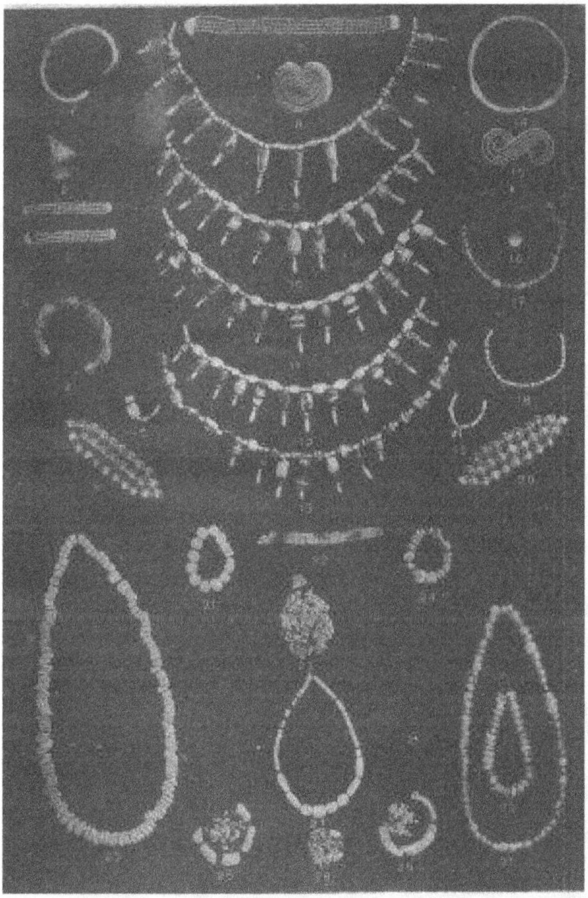

At *a* are specimens of fillets consisting of thin bands of beaten gold with holes for cords at their endsThe long carnelian beads of the necklace or girdle are 4.85 in. in length by 0.4 in. dia. The shorter beads are 3.25 in. in length. These beads are of a bright translucent red colour. They were bored from both ends, the holes averaging 0.17 in. dia. At each of the necklace or girdle there is a semi-circular terminal of hollow bronze like a flattened cup. The globular beads at each end of the stone ones are of bronze. Nos. 7, 8 and 11 are gold studs, 1.2 in. dia. apparently intended for the ears. Nos. 3-5 and 12-14 are gold needles. A number of bead-caps made of gold, coppery-red to pale yellow in colour are above No.9 which is a turquoise bead capped with gold. (After Marshall, Pl. CLI).

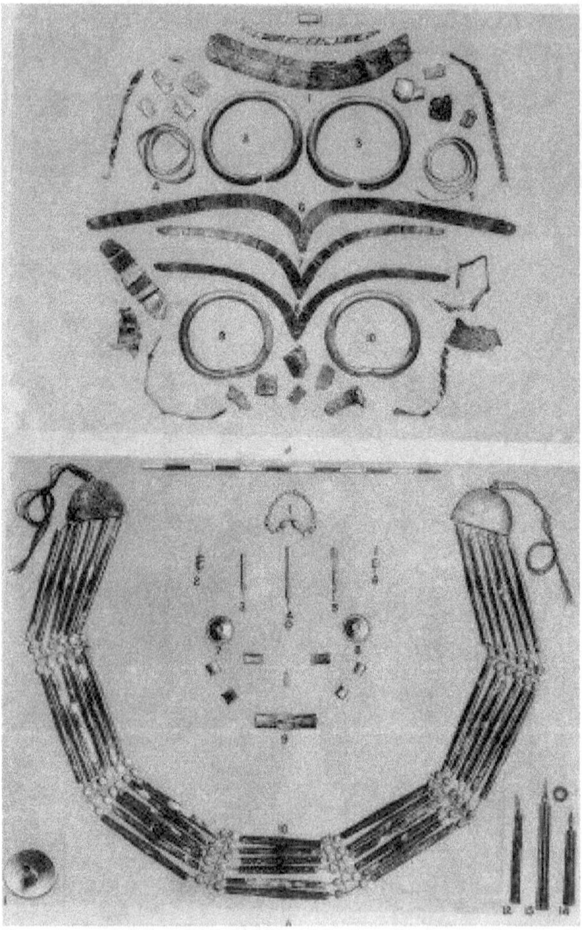

Jewellery, Mohenjodaro. No. 13 shows waste pieces of metal, probably the hoard of a goldsmith. (After Marshall, Pl. CLII).

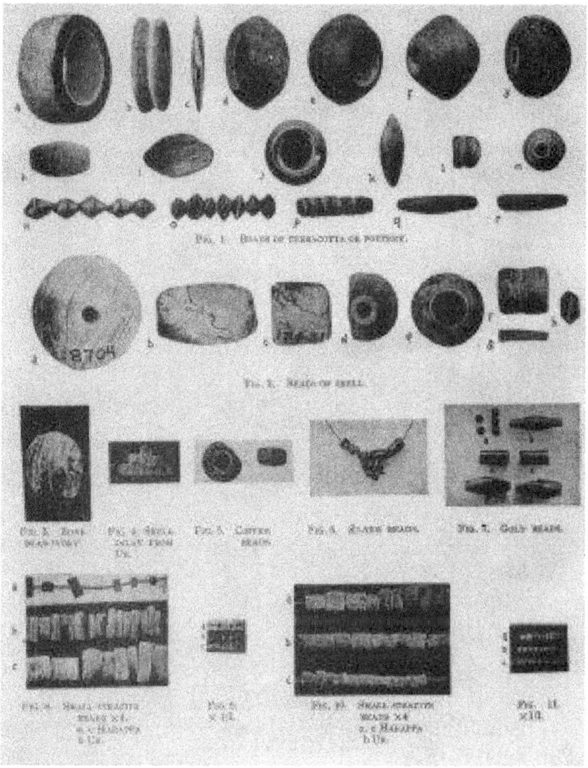

Beads: terracotta, shell, ivory, copper, silver, gold, steatite, Harappa and Ur (After Vats, Pl. CXXXIV).

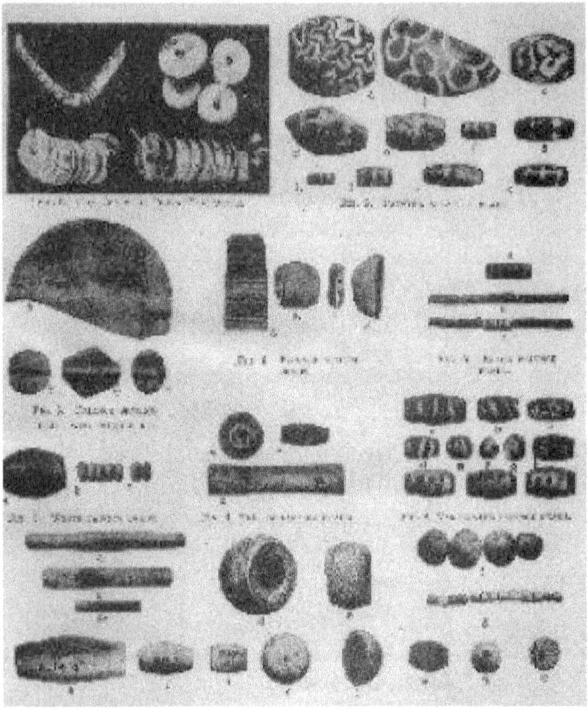

Beads: steatite disc, painted steatite, faience: black, yellow, white, variegated, blue or green (After Vats, Pl. CXXXIII).

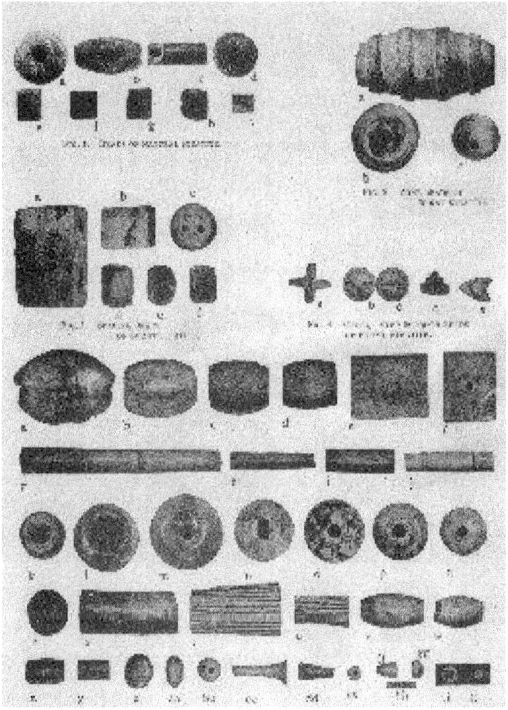

Beads: natural steatite, burnt steatite (After Vats, Pl. CXXXII).

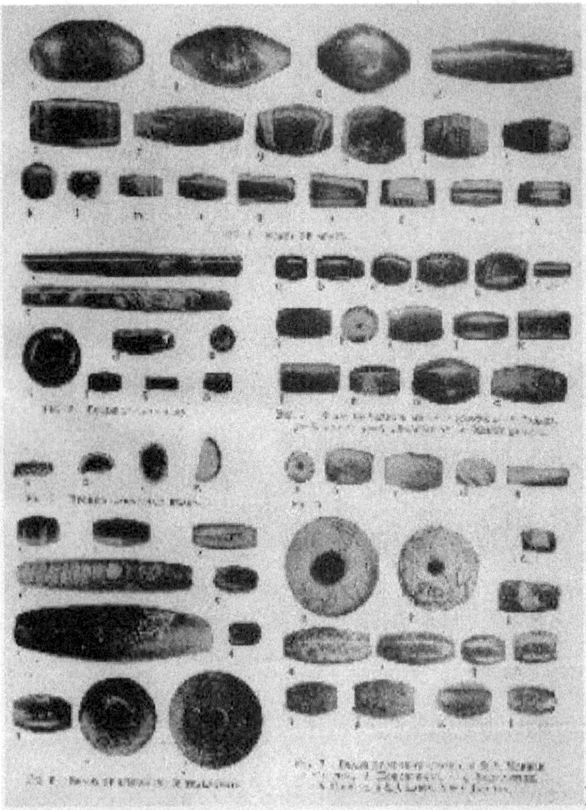

Beads: agate, carnelian, jasper, chert, chalcedony, milky quartz, etched carnelian, limestone, stalagmite, marble, calcite, hornblende, serpentine, deorite, lapis and jadeite (After Vats, Pl.

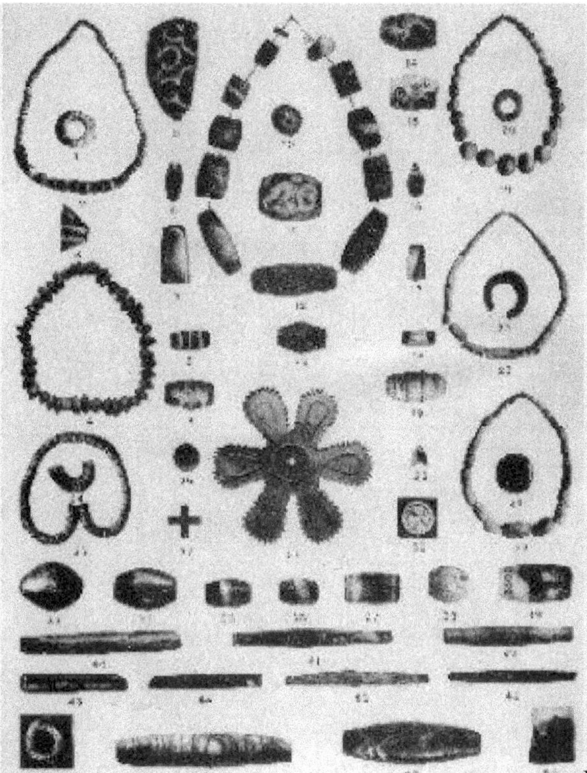

Miscellaneous beads, Harappa (After Vats, Pl. CXXXI).

CXXVIII). 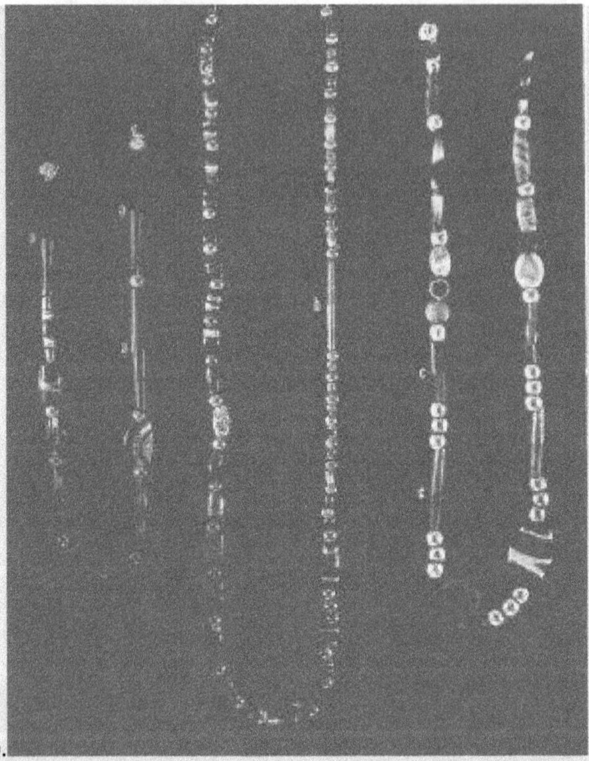 Long barrel-cylinder beads from the Royal Graves of Ur; Akkadian Period (ca. 2250-1894 B.C.); 'a' is of dark green stone; bead 'b' is carnelian and 6.4 cm. long; bead 'c' is carnelian; Chakrabarti, D.K. 1982, Pl. 24.2. (UPenn Museum: 30-12-566 and 567; 32-40-

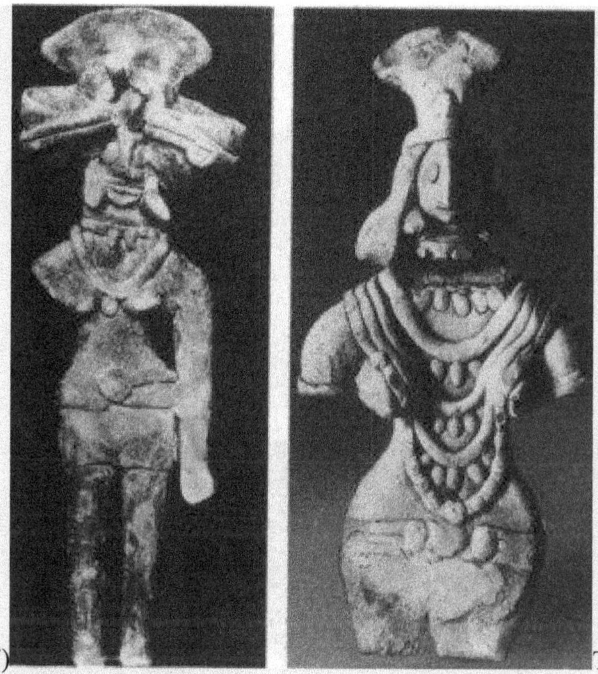

227) Terracotta figurines, Mohenjodaro, wearing jewellery (cf. Allchin, 1982, Fig.

8.14) 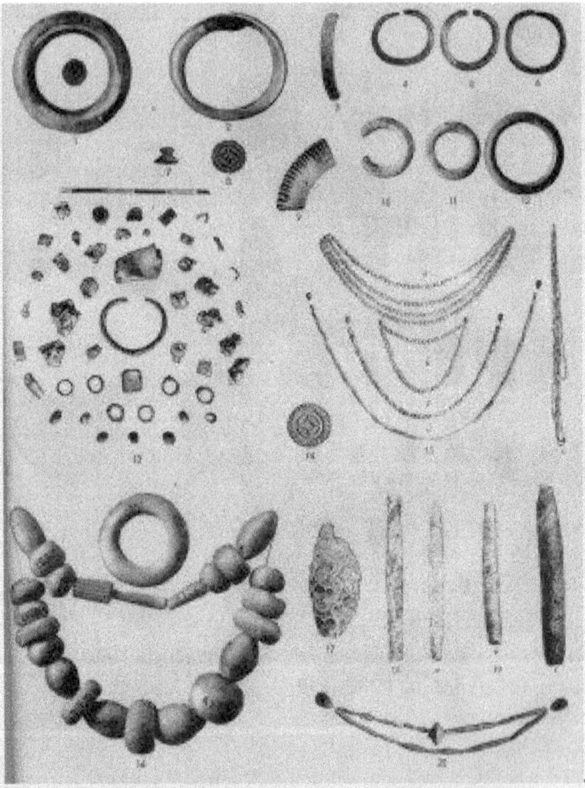 Jewellery from House 2, Trench IV, Mound F, Harappa (After Vats, Pl. CXXXVII)

Harappa: reconstructed platform close-up (white colouring is caused by salt seepage)

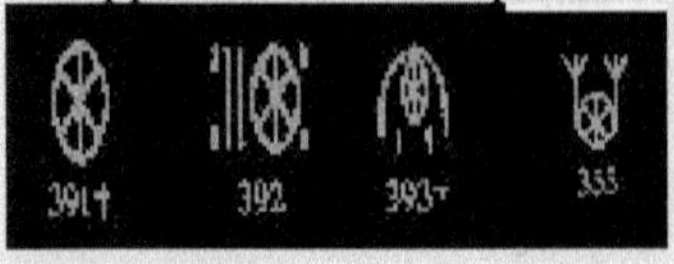

Signs 391-393 and 355 of the script are reminiscent of this circle-shaped platform

Workshop Platforms at Harappa (inside houses and courtyards):

Harappa, platforms in perspective Harappa, platform: one view

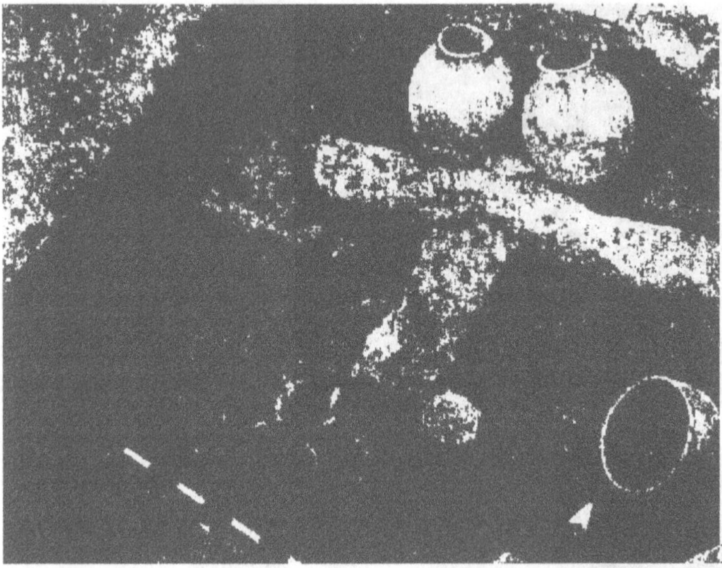

Excavations at Sibri (ca. 2000 B.C.)(Jarrige)

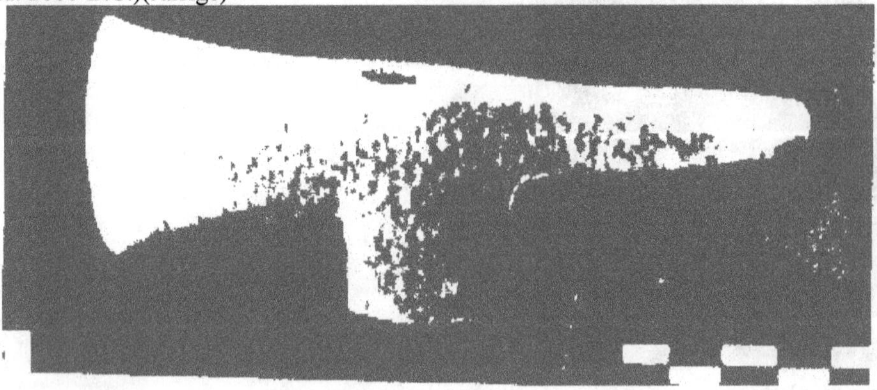

Bronze shaft-hole axe-adze, Sibri (Jarrige)

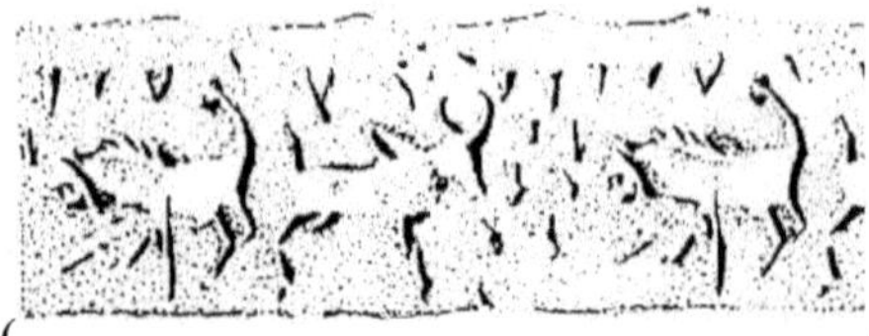

(A cylinder seal with zebu and lion, Sibri {Jarrige)

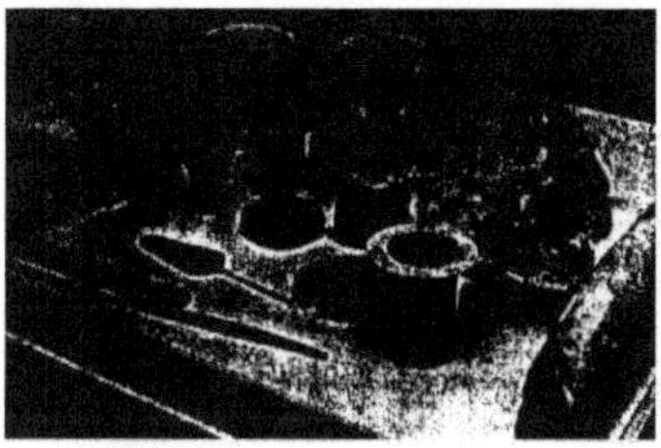

Quetta treasure with alabaster vases, gold goblet, gold bulls, bronze implements and terracotta vase

Dagger, battle double-axe, battle-axe, Ur.

Note the dagger on the image of the fox (Mesopotamian imagery)

Bactria; cosmetic flacon, fig. 1.2 and fig. 1.6 (V.Sarianidi, p. 646); there is an exact replica of the flacon with a chequered body and distinctive base, fig. 1.6 at Chanhudaro (Mackay 1943: pl. LXXIII 39). Similar falcons have been found in Luristan

Bactria: tablet depicting an animal with its head looking back; similar pictorials are seen in seals at Chanhudaro (Mackay 1943: pl. L1).

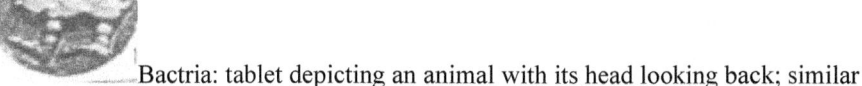

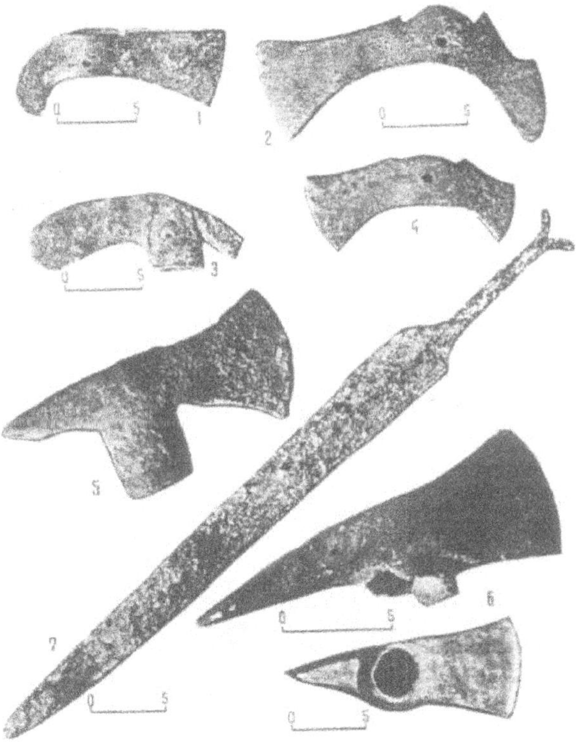

Bactria; axes [(i)utilitarian: figs. 4.5,6; with analogies in the Indus valley, southern regions of central Asia and in late bronze age Iran). Unique are the spur-head axes in Bactria (fig. 4.1-4); (ii) cultic: so-called because of their characteristic heads, cast in the form of a 'cock tail' which have parallels in Luristan axes (Schaeffer 1948: fig. 265.8)] Fig. 4.2 is perhaps the head of a mace, cast as a massive cylinder with spikes and thickenings at ends resembling similar spiked Luristan heads (Amiet 1976: nos. 5,6).

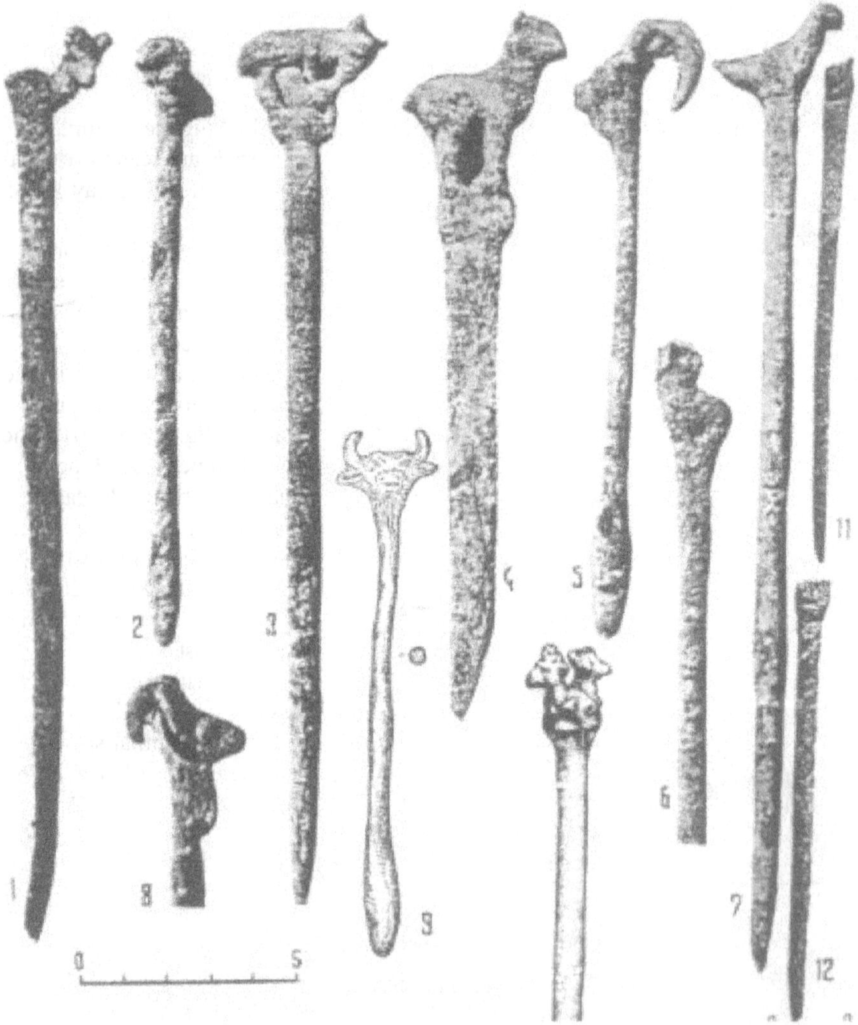

Bactria; metal pins; fig 2.10 is a pin with a head in the shape of two sitting rams; this resembles a pin was found in Mohenjodaro with a head in the form of seated goats with helically bent horns (Mackay 1937: pl. C3). Pins with zoomorphic heads is typically noticed in southwest Iran and the Near East. Fig. 2.11-12 show pins with heads in the shape of clenched fist with parallels of similar pins in Mesopotamian royal tombs of Ur (Maxwell-Hyslop 1971: 13, fig.11). Good examples of Iranian-Afghan-Indian ties.

"It transpired that in the 2nd millennium BC there existed in the territory of ancient Bactria a highly-developed, largely original culture of the ancient-oriental type. A close, or rather identical culture spread at that time through the southern regions of central Asia, particularly in Margiana, which gave grounds for singlign out a special Bactrian-Margian Archaeological Complex (BMAC). The basic features of this complex are: the coexistence of non-fortified settlements and of rectangular fortresses with round corner turrets. The latter belonged to individual families or clans... Occurring in sufficient quantities, along with stone and flint tools and wapons, are copper and bronze ones. These are sickles, knives, adzes, awls, razors, daggers, massive spearheads, battle axes; of the ornaments there are mirrors, toilet pins, cosmetic falcons, bracelets, ear-rings, rings... At present we may regard as an established fact the existence of an Iranian-Turkmenian metallurgical province where, beginning from the turn of the 5th and 4th millennia BC, uni-typical wares take shape and exist for a long time.There is every ground to assume the dissemination from it of metal-works (celts, daggers, pins) and specific forms of earthenware (stemmed vases, saucers, etc.) in the eastern direction down to the vally of the Indus, by way of exchange, trade and cultural contacts. This period embraces the existence of the Harappan civilization and does not presuppose the arrival of any new tribes. This is strikingly proved by the Harappa culture itself, which demonstrates a continuous line of development without any invasions from outside... We shall merely remark that southwestern Iran and possibly Caucasus emerge as a zone where numerous metal articles come to be produced (mid- 2nd millennium BC), while Iranian Khorassan is doubtlessly the main venue for their penetration into the souther areas of central Asia, Bactria and possibly the valley of the Indus river."(Viktor I. Sarianidi, 1979, New Finds in Bactria and Indo-Iranian Connections, pp. 643-659, in:*South Asian Archaeology 1977*, Naples).

Horse in Sarasvati Sindhu Civilization

MEL Mallowan (1965, *Early Mesopotamia and Iran,* London, Thames and Hudson, p. 123) notes:

"...dating Tepe Hissar IIIB a little before 2000 B.C... in Hissar IIIB the skull of a horse was found and furthermore the horse is alleged to have been domesticated at Shah Tepe much earlier still, thus long anticipating the first appearance of it at Boghazkoy in Central Asia Minor in the early Hittite period...."

Tepe Hissar is a key archaeological site with vivid links to the Sarasvati Sindhu civilization with many seals, motifs, artefacts...

A.K.Sharma, The Harappan horse was buried under the dunes of..., in *Puratattva, Bulletin of the Indian Archaeological Society*, No. 23, 1992-93, pp. 30-34]: "At Surkotada the bones of the true horse (equus caballus Linn.) identified are from Period IA, IB and IC. (radiocarbon dates: 2315 B.C., 1940 B.C. and 1790 B.C respectively). With the correction factors, the dates fall between 2400 B.C. and 1700 B.C... In 1938 Mackay (FEM, Vol. I, p. 289) had remarked on the discovery of a clay model of horse from Mohenjodaro. 'I personally take it to represent horse. I do not think we need be particularly surprised if it should be proved that the horse existed thus early at Mohenjo-daro'. About this terracotta figurine Wheeler wrote: (Indus Civilization, Cambridge, 1968, p. 92): 'One terracotta from a late level of Mohenjodaro seems to represent a horse, reminding us that the jaw bone of a horse is also recorded from the same time, and that the horse was known at considerably early period in northern Baluchistan... It is likely enough that camel, horse and ass were in fact all familiar feature of the Indus caravans.'... appearance of true horse from the neolithic sites of Koldihwa and Mahagara in Uttar Pradesh..." (Note: camel is also not depicted on Harappan inscriptions) The identification by Sharma has been endorsed by Prof. Sandor Bokonyi, Director of the Archaeological Institute, Budapest, Hungary (an archaeozoologist); he wrote in a letter dated 13 Dec. 1993 to the Director General of the Archaeological Survey of India: 'Through a thorough study of the equid remains of the prehistoric settlement of Surkotada, Kachchha, excavated under the direction of Dr. J.P. Joshi, I can state the following: The occurrence of true horse (equus caballus L.) was evidenced by the enamel pattern of the upper and lower cheek and teeth and by the size and form of incisors and phalanges (toe bones). Since no wild horses lived in India in post-Pleistocene times, the domestic nature of the Surkotada horses is undoutbtful. This is also supported by an intermaxilla fragment whose incisor tooth shows clear signs of crib biting, a bad habit only existing among domestic horses which are not extensively used for war."

"Perhaps the most interesting of the model animals is one that I personally take to represent a horse.' (Mackay 1938, vol. I, p. 289; vol. II, pl. LXXVIII). Lothal has yielded a terracotta figure of a horse. It has an elongated body and a thick stumpy tail, mane is marked out over the neck with a low ridge. Faunal remains at Lothal yielded a second upper molar. Bhola Nath of the Zoological Survey of India and GV Sreenivasa Rao of the Archaeological Survey of India note (S.R.Rao, 1985, p. 641): 'The single tooth of the horse referred to above indicates the presence of the horse at Lothal during the Harappan period. The tooth from Lothal resembles closely with that of the modern horse and has pli-caballian (a minute fold near the base of the spur or protocone) which is well distinguishable character of the cheek teeth of the horse.' "However, the most startling discovery comes from the recent excavation at Nausharo, conducted by Jarrige et al. (in press). In the Harappan levels over here have been found clearly identifiable terracotta figurines of this animal." (Lal, 1998, opcit., p. 112).

Central Asia: Altyn-depe and Parkhai

Harappan contacts with Central Asia are now beyond doubt especially after the discovery of; (1) a few Harappan pottey types in Namazga V sites, (2) a Harappan inscribed seal at Altin Depe, (3) comparable ivory objects at Altin Depe, and (4) a close similarity in a few copper artefacts (Gupta 1979: Vol. 2)...

"The discovery in Altyn-Depe of a proto-Indian seal with two signs deserves special mention. V.M. Masson pointed out, that what the seal depicted was a pictogram and not just a representation of animals. In his opinion this means that some of the ancient residents of Altyn-Depe were able to read this text.(G. Bongard-Levin, 1989, Archaeological Finds in Central Asia throw light on Ancient India, Jagdish Vibhakar and Usha Gard (Eds.), *Glimpses of Ancient India through Soviet Eyes*, Delhi, Sundeep Prakashan)

Finds at Atlyn-depe: ivory sticks and gaming pieces (?) obtained from Sarasvati Sindhu civilization; similar objects with dotted circles found in Mohenjodaro and Harappa.

Two seals found at Altyn-depe (Excavation 9 and 7) found in the shrine and in the 'elite quarter'. Hieroglypoh: *aḍar* 'harrow'; rebus: *aduru* 'native metal' (Kannada) Hieroglyph: *kolmo* 'rice plant' Rebus: *kolami* 'smithy, forge'. Hieroglyph: *satthia* 'svastika glyph' Rebus: *jasta* 'zinc' (Hindi); *sattva* id. (Kannada)

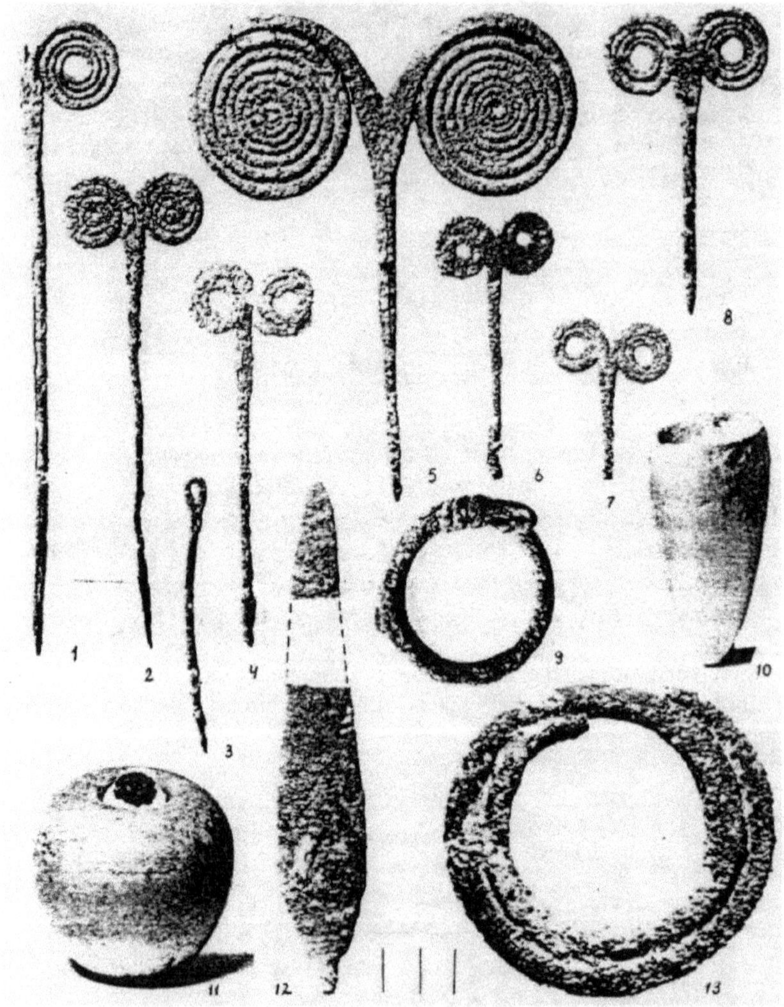

Bronze artefacts found in Parkhai cemetery II: double-edged knives, small fragments and spiral-headed pins; the pins of different sizes had spirals no fewer than four lops; six spiral-headed pins are known from the northern foothills of Kopet Dagh; one came from Kysyl Arvant and dated to Namazga IV period; all identical to the Parkhai examples and considered an import from the Sumbar Valley; the remainder---two from the southern mound at Anau, two from Namazga-depe and one from Shor-depe -- had small loops twisted only 1.5-2 times. They were found in Namazga V levels from cemeteries in northern Afghanistan and Tajikistan. Slightly twisted spiral-head pins from Mundigat (periods IV, I-IV, 3) and multi-looped spiral-headed pins from Tepe Hissar (period IIB), which are identical to those from Parkhai II, are also related to this period; the dates of Parkhai finds are ca. middle of the third millennium B.C.

V.M. Masson, Seals of a Proto-Indian Type from Altyn-depe, pp. 149-162; V.M. Masson, Urban Centers of Early Class Society, pp. 135-148; I.N. Khlopin, The Early bronze age cemetery in Parkhai II: The first two seasons of excavations, 1977-78, pp. 3-34 in: Philip L. Kohl (ed.), 1981, The Bronze Age Civilization in Central Asia, Armonk, NY, ME Sharpe, Inc.

Bronze in Mohenjodaro

Copper-bronze artefacts from Mohenjodaro exhibited at the Mohenjodaro museum (Dr. Abdul Jabbar Junejo and Mohammad Qasim Bughio, 1988, Cultural Heritage of Sind, International Arabi Conference, University of Sind, Hyderabad, Sindhi Adabi Board); out of 13 artefacts analysed. 6 were found to contain between 4.51% to 13.21% tin; the artefacts were: bronze rod, bronze button, bronze chisel, bronze slab, bronze chisel and bronze lump.

Evidence of contact between Sarasvati Sindhu and Mesopotamian civilizations:

Cylinder seal showing running goats turning their heads, appearing in perpetual motion; ca. 2800 B.C. (Uruk IV) (M.E.L.Mallowan, 1965, *Early Metopotamia and Iran*, London, Thames and Hudson); the antelope with its head turned backward is a typical motif on the seals of the Sarasvati Sindhu civilization.

Dark grey steatite bowl carved in relief. Zebu or brahmani bull is shown with its hump back; a male figure with long hair and wearing akilt grasps two sinuous objects, representing running water, which flows in a continuous stream. Around the bowl, another similar male figure stands between two lionesses with their head turned back towards him; he grasps a serpent in each hand. A further scene (not shown) represents a prostrate bull which is being attacked by a vulture and a lion.

The zebu is reminiscent of Sarasvati Sindhu seals. The stone used, steatite, is familiar in Baluchistan and a number of vessels at the Royal Cemetery at Ur were made out of this material.

The bowl dates from c. 2700-2500 B.C. and the motif shown on it resembles that on a fragment of a green stone vase from one of the Sin Temples at Tell Asmar of almost the same date.
By the Early Dynasty III period, the Mesopotamian craftsmen had mastered the techniques for working copper, lead, silver, gold and tin. The Royal Cemetery at Ur has yielded a corpus of metal work where true tin bronze is found, apart from the common arsenical bronze and precious metals: gold, silver and electrum. Metal blades were produced in many sizes to serve as arrows, spears, daggers. Also found are sickles and hoes. Axes come in many shapes and sizes, some cast and some hammered with the tang beaten round a haft (See the drawing of a Sumerian soldier carrying spear and axe.) (Crawford, H., p. 133). Muhly (1983) quotes a passage from the late third millennium Laws of Eshnunna that a workman issued with tools for the harvest must return the same weight of metal at the end of the season, even if some of it is scrap. This is an indication that temples had metalsmithies where metal could be melted down and recast. Simug was the metalsmith.

In the Ur III period, the royal mausoleum of Shulgi at Ur yielded scraps of gold leaf which seem to have been part of architectural decoration, as was the case in the Jemdat Nasr period where the altar of the Eye temple at Tell Brak was decorated with gold leaf. The texts state that large numbers of metal-workers were employed by both the temple and the palace to produce a whole range of goods from tools to jewellery. These workers at Ur worked in groups under a foreman who reported to a general overseer. An assay office issued the metals to the foreman and weighed the finished article before counter-signing the receipts issued by the general overseer. In provincial towns, the governor himself issued metal from the treasury. Private metal merchants handled the supply of raw materials. (Mallowan 1947; Crawford, op.cit., p. 134).

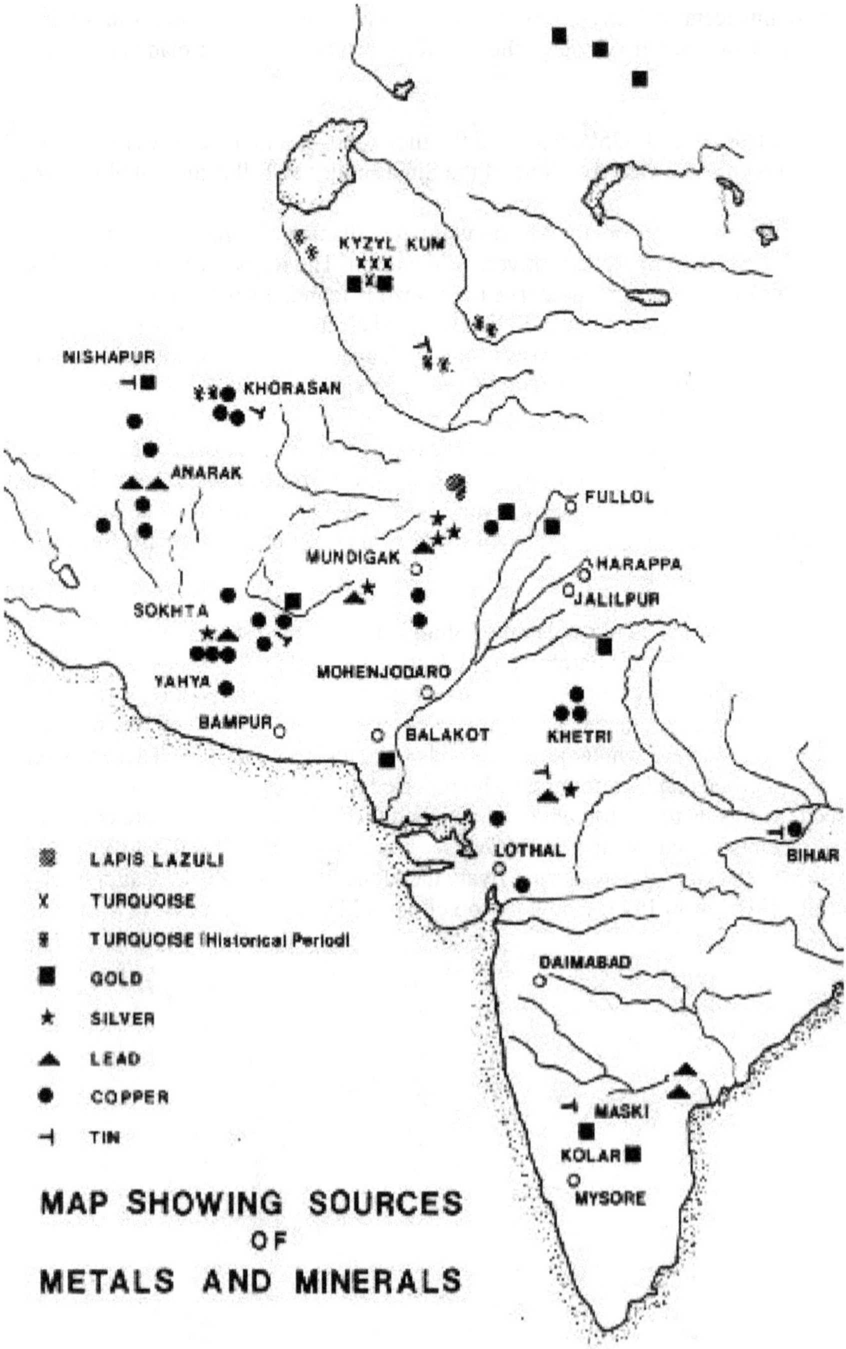

MAP SHOWING SOURCES OF METALS AND MINERALS

The sources for the minerals and metals and semi-precious stones were: Baluchistan, Afghanistan, Iran, Central Asia, the lands bordering the Persian Gulf as well as interior, peninsular India (Map based on Shashi Asthana, Harappan Trade in Metals and Minerals: A Regional Approach, in: Frontiers of Indus Civilization.)

Sources of gold: Coimbatore (Hadabanatta, Kavudahalli and near Porsegaundanpalayam), Wynaad and Kolar (Marshall 1931: 674). "South of the Caucasus, in Armenia, the famous metal workers, the Chalybes, are credited with rich mines. This probably means the deposits near the Taldjen River, close to Artwin... The Muruntau mountains in the Kyzyl Kum desert has the largest deposit of gold (Forbes 1971: 166; Kalesnik and Pavlenko 1976: 202)... The discovery of the famous Fullol Hoard in the Hindu Kush of northern Afghanistan (Tosi and Waradak 1972: 9-17) contained a number of gold objects with Mesopotamian and South Turkmenian motifs. This proves that the region (the Oxus basin--northern Hindu Kush) was as important to the Middle East for gold as it was for lapis lazuli. Incidentally, the Harappan trading posts at Shortugai are also in the same region (Francfort and Potter 1978:29).
Cupellation was used ca. 3000 B.C. to refine gold and also silver. Silver was a product of the district associated with the Hittites, the name of whose capital was written with the ideograph for silver. Silver and lead were found in the mineral called galena (lead sulphide). This mineral could be converted into a lead-silver alloy by roasting it. The roasting oxidizes some of the sulphur. The next step of heating it to a higher temperature further reduced the sulphur content, yielding the alloy at the bottom of the furnace where the charcoal fuel prevented reoxidation. Sometimes, seams of galena contained metallic silver. The silver-lead alloy was melted in a porous clay crucible (the cupel), blowing a blast of air upon it. This oxidized the lead and removed it. The process if completed when a shining button of silver appears suddenly. (T.K.Derry and Trevor I. Williams, 1961, *A short history of Technology*, New York, Oxford University Press, p. 116).

Lead is plentiful in Mohenjodaro (Marshall 1931: 524)... Rajasthan (Rao 1973: 116), Bihar and Orissa (Marshall 1931: 675) contain several silver-bearing lead deposits; but these are small... the Ajmer and Jawar mines in Rajasthan are likely sources for these metals... Gold mines at Kolar and Anantapur also yield silver with gold, but not in quantity enough for commercial purposes... Lead mines, which could have been a source for silver as well, are situated in Faranjal in the Ghorband Valleyof Afghanistan and are common in southern Afghanistan, especially at Hazara Jat. Well-known silver mines are also known to have existed near the head of the Panjsher Valley in the southeastern Hindu Kush and in the vicinity of Herat... Lead was added to copper to increase the feasibility of molding and has been extensively reported in Harappan artefacts (Agrawal 1971: 156)... Lead might have been used mainly as a smelting flux. This is evident because of the discovery of copper ore together with a small piece of lead in a bricklined pit in a house at Mohenjodaro (Mackay 1938: 41)...

Rajasthan copper mines are at Khetri, Singhana, Kho-Dariba (Alwar), Delwara Kirovli (Udaipur) and Debari (Udaipur) (Seth 1956)... spectroscopic analysis of the Harappan artefacts and various ores shows that there is a close correspondence with the Khetri mines (Agrawal 1971: 175)... there are copper celts, Indus arrowheads and pottery of the third millennium B.C. (Agrawala 1978, 1979) from Ganeshwar (Sikar District)... Khetri is only 60 kilometres from Ganeshwar... There are copper deposits in Zhob district (Mughal 1970: 194), Robat (Hunting Survey Corporation 1961) and Shah Bellaul (Forbes 1972) area of Baluchistan... Huan Tsang mentions copper mines in Afghanistan and ancient workings have been located near the Safed-Kuh between Kabul and Kurram (Forbes 1972: 13). Shah Maqsud also contains rich veins of copper ore and it is said that Nadir Shah exploited them (Forbes 1972: 13). Rich ores are also said to occur at Nesh, 100 kilometers from Kandahar. Other localities are Tezin, east of Kabul, Musai in the Shadkani Pass and the Silwatu Pass (Forbes 1972:13). Iran is rich in copper, and metallurgy has a long tradition going back to the fifth millennium B.C. at Tal-i Iblis in Kirman (Caldwell 1967). The best mines are in Kirman as well as Kal-seb Zarre, Sabzwar and Cahr Daud near Meshad, Kaleh near Astrabad and in Elburz mountain districts of Kashan Kohund and Isfahan and Anarak (Wertime 1968)... Kyzyl Kum desert has a copper industry at Temba Bulach but this is of uncertain antiquity (Kalesnik and Pavlenko 1976). The eastern Iranian border also has a long belt of copper deposits... The ore cassiterite yielded tin. Antimony was another alloy with copper to make bronze; antimony was derived from Caucasian ores. Arsenic was also used as an alloy to yield brass.

Stein collected a few bronzes from Shahi Tump, Mehi, Siah Damb and Segak Mound, all of which have a high tin percentage... tinwas a precious commodity as is evident from the findings of bronze scraps, stored along with other valuables in copper vessels at both Harappa and Mohenjodaro (Vats 1940: 381; Marshall 1931: 488). According to Agrawal (1971: 168) only 14 percent of Harappan tools were alloyed in the optimum range of 8 to 12 percent tin. Furthermore tin bronze is more abundant (23 percent of the tools) in the upper levels of Mohenjodaro than in the lower levels (6 percent)... Tin deposits known in India are located in Palampur region of Maharashtra, Dharwar district in Karnataka and Hazari Bagh District of Bihar (Marshall 1931: 682). Bhilwara in Rajasthan and Hosainpura in Gujarat are also known to have a limited quantity of tin (Chakrabarti 1979: 70). Outside India, on the western frontier, tin is known to occur in Kuh Banan, Karadagh and Khorasan (Marshall 1931: 483-484; Vats 1940: 378-82) between Astrabad and Shah Rud in Iran (Gowland 1912) and between Bukhara and Samarkand in Soviet Central Asia (Crawford 1974; Masson and Sarianidi 1972: 128)... The main supply of tin may... have come from the western regions: Khorasan and the area between Bukhara and Samarkand (Chakrabarti 1979: 70) through sites like Shortugai... Tin was one of the commodities which the Sumerians got from Meluhha (Leemans 1970; Muhly 1976: 306-307)... it is possible that tin was basically a trading item which the Harappans were obtaining from Khorasan and Central Asia for export to Mesopotamia, just as they obtained lapis lazuli from Badakshan for export there...

Based on the presence of arsenic, nickel and lead in artefacts from Mohenjodaro and Harappa, Ullah (1940) determined the sources of their copper to have been Khetri, Alwar, Singhbhum and Afghanistan mines where nickel and arsenic both are supposed to be present in the copper ores. He held that the Sumerian ores could be distinguished from Indian ores since the former are virtually free from arsenic (Ullah 1940)... Agrawal's Table 11 (1971) shows that at Khafaje and Ur, 88 percent of the artefacts contain arsenic.

...literary sources... sources of silver, including Dilmun, Aratta, Elam, Marhashi and Meluhha, all of which are to theast or south of Mesopotamia, Sargon of Akkad referred to a locale in Anatolia as the 'Silver Mountain'...

Archaeology and Language

"As the archaeologist armed with pick and shovel, descends into the depths of the earth, in order to trace the footsteps of the past in bone and stone-remains, so the student of language-- washed on the shore of history from ages immeasurably remote-- to reconstruct the picture of the primeval age... (Evolving a new method called the 'Comparative Antiquities')... It is on this triple basis that the present work is founded, being designed as a comprehensive account of what we know at present about the pre-historic period of the Indo-European race."Schrader, O., *Pre-historic Antiquities of the Aryan Peoples*, 1890, Translation by Jevons, F.B.,from German *Sprachvergleichung und Urgeschichte*, 1890 (From the Author's Preface to the English Translation, p. iii-iv).

Finds of svastika on seals and finds of weapons

"A copper blade (Marshall 1931: pl. 136, f.3) found in one of the upper levels, though termed a spear-blade, may conceivably have been a knife (Plate IX, no.1). An exactly similar blade, but with a slightly longer tang, was found in the A mound at Kish (Mackay 1929a: pl. 39, gp. 3, f.4)... attention should be called to a steatite seal from Kish, now in Baghdad Museum, which bears thesvastika symbol. This seal, both in shape and design upon it, exactly resembles the little square seals of steatite and glazed paste that are so frequently found at Mohenjodaro (Marshall 1931: pl. 144, f. 507-15). I do not think that I err in regarding the Kish example, which was found by Watelin, as either of Indian workmanship or made locally for an Indian resident in Sumer... The curious perforated vessels shown (Marshall 1931: pl. 84, f. 3-18) are very closely allied to perforated vessels found at Kish (Mackay 1929a: pl. 54, f. 36), especially in the fact that besides the numerous holes in the sides there is also a large hole in the base, which suggests that by this means they were supported on a rod or something similar... I have suggested, from evidence obtained by Sir Aurel Stein in southern Baluchistan, that these perforated vessels were used as heaters..."(E.J.H.Mackay, Further links between ancient Sind, Sumer and elsewhere, *Antiquity*, Vol. 5, 1931, pp. 459-473).

Substrate language of Sumer and Indian lexemes

'One of the most significant and impressive archaeological achievements of the twentieth century centers around the discovery of the ancient Indus civilization which probably flourished from about 2500 to 1500 B.C., and extended over a vast territory from the present Pakistan-Iran border to the foot of the Himalayas and to the Gulf of Cambay... That there was considerable commercial trade between Sumer and Indus land is proved beyond reasonable doubt by some thirty Indus seals which have actually been excavated in Sumer-- and no doubt hundreds more are still lying buried in the Sumerian ruins-- and which must have been brought there in one way or another from their land of origin. There is, therefore, good reason to conclude that the Sumerians had known the name of the Indus land as well as some of its more imortant featues and characteristics, and that some of the innumerable Sumerian texts might turn out to be highly informative in this respect... According to a long-known Sumerian 'Flood'-story, Dilmun, the land to which Ziusudra, the Sumerian Noah, was transported to live as an immortal among the gods, is 'the place where the sun rises', and was therefore located somewhere to the east of Sumer. In another Sumerian text, Dilmun is described as a blessed, prosperous land dotted with 'great dwellings', to which the countries of the entire civilized world known to the Sumerians, brought their goods and wares... The only rich, important land east of Sumer which could be the source of ivory, was that of the ancient Indus civilization, hence it seems not unreasonable to infer that the latter must be identical with Dilmun... there are two faces of the Indus civilization which are especially significant for its identification with Dilmun: the cult of a water deity and sea-plowing ships... the god most intimately related to Dilmun is Enki, the Sumerian Poseidon, the great Sumerian water god in charge of seas and rivers. Thus we find a Sumerian Dilmun-myth which tells the following story: Dilmun, a land described as 'pure', 'clean', and 'bright', a land which knows neither sickness nor death, had been lacking originally in fresh, life-giving water. The tutelary goddess of Dilmun, Ninsikilla by name, therefore pleaded with Enki, who is both her husband and father, and the latter orders the sun-god Utu to fill Dilmun with sweet water brought up from the earth's water-sources; Dilmun is thus turned into a divine garden green with grain-yielding fields and acres. In this paradise of the gods eight plants are made to sprout by Ninhursag, the great mother goddess of the Sumerians, perhaps more originally Mother Earth... because Enki wanted to taste them, his messenger, the two-faced god Isimud, plucks these plants one by one and gives them to his master who proceeds to eat them each in turn. Whereupon the angered Ninhursag pronounces the curse of death against Enki and vanishes from among the gods. Enki's health at once begins to fail and eight of his organs become sick. As Enki sinks fast, the great gods sit in the dust, seemingly unable to cope with the situation. Whereupon the fox comes to the rescue and after being promised a reward, he succeeds by some ruse in having the mother goddess return to the gods and heal the dying water god. She seats him by her vulva and after inquiring which eight organs of his body ache, she brings into existence eight corresponding deities-- one of these is Enshag, the Lord of Dilmun-- and Enki is brought back to life and health...

'The land Dilmun is holy, Holy Sumer--present it to him, The land Dilmun is holy, The land Dilmun is holy, the land Dilmun is pure, The land Dilmun is clean, the land Dilmun is holy... In Dilmun the raven utters no cry, The wild hen utters not the cry of the wild hen, The lion kills not... He (the god Enki) cleaned and purified the land Dilmun, Placed the goddess Ninsikilla in charge of it. '

In fact the very name of the goddess whom Enki placed in charge of Dilmun is a Sumerian compound word whose literal meaning is 'the pure queen'... the Indus civilization depended largely on water-borne trade, coastal and riverine... one of the Sumerian rulers by the name of Ur-Nanshe, who lived as early as about 2400 B.C., speaks of timber-carrying Dilmun boats arriving at his city, Lagash... In the myth 'Enki and the World Order' mentioned earlier, Enki boasts of the moored Dilmun boats. Ivory-bearing boats from Dilmun to Ur have already been mentioned; according to the texts these also carried timber, gold, copper, and lapis lazuli. No wonder that in the 'Paradise' myth cited above, Dilmun is described as 'dockyard-house of the (inhabited) land.'...the pre-Indus settlements excavated at Harappa, Kot Diji, or Amri, which could be regarded as the forerunner of the Indus cities and towns with their carefully planned buildings and streets, their water cult and purification rites, their well-developed pictographic script, and their bustling water-borne trade...

The names of the two great Mesopotamian rivers, the Tigris and Euphrates, or idiglat and buranun as they read in the cuneiform texts, are Ubaidian-- not Sumerian-- words. So, too, are the names of the most important centers of 'Sumer': Eridu, Ur, Larsa, Isin, Adab, Kullab, Lagash, Nippur, and Kish. In fact the word Dilmun itself may, like the word buranun for the Euphrates, be Ubaidian. More important still, such culturally significant words as engar (farmer), udul (herdsman), shupeshdak (fisherman), api_n (plow),apsin (furrow), nimbar (palm), sulumb (date), tibira (metalworker), simug (s mith), nangar (carpenter), addub (basket maker),ishbar (weaver), ashgab (leather worker), pahar (potter), shidim (mason), and perhaps even damgar (merchant), are probably all Ubaidian rathern than Sumerian, as has been usually assumed... Another crucial word which may turn out to be Ubaidian, is Ea, one of the two names by which the Mesopotamian water god is known in the cuneiform texts, the other being Enki... while the latter is a typical Sumerian compound with the meaning 'Lord of the Earth', Ea is a word whose linguistic affiliations are still uncertain... The Assyrian king Tukulti-Ninurta uses in his titles the expression 'king of Dilmun and Meluhha' ... There is another king by the name of Hundaru in whose days booty taken from Dilmun consisted of objects made of copper and bronze, sticks of precious wood, and large quantities of kohl, used as an eye-paint. A crew of soldiers is sent from Dilmun to Babylon to help King Sennacherib raze that city to the ground, and they bring with them bronze spades and spikes which are described as characteristic products of
Dilmun...

from the myth 'Enki and the World Order', the god Enki boasts of the moored Dilmun boats.

The lands of Magan and Dilmun
Looked up at me, Enki,
Moored (?) the Dilmun-boat to the ground (?),
Loaded the Magan-boat sky high.

(Samuel N. Kramer, The Indus Civilization and Dilmun: The Sumerian Paradise Land, *Expedition*, Vol. 6, No. 3, 1964, pp. 44-52).

"(1) Some inscriptions (Luckenbill 1926: Vol. 2, sect. 41, 70, 92 and 185; Cornwall 1944: Vol. 2, sect. 81 and 99) of Sargon of Assyria state that Uperi, King of Dilmun, 'lives a fish 30 beru away in the midst of the sea of the rising sun.'.. (2) 30 beru may refer to the number of hours required to reach Dilmun by sea from the starting point... at a speed of 5 miles an hour a bark would have to travel 600 miles... "(Peter B. Cornwall, On the location of Dilmun, Bulletin of the American School of Oriental Research, No. 103, 1946, pp. 3-11).

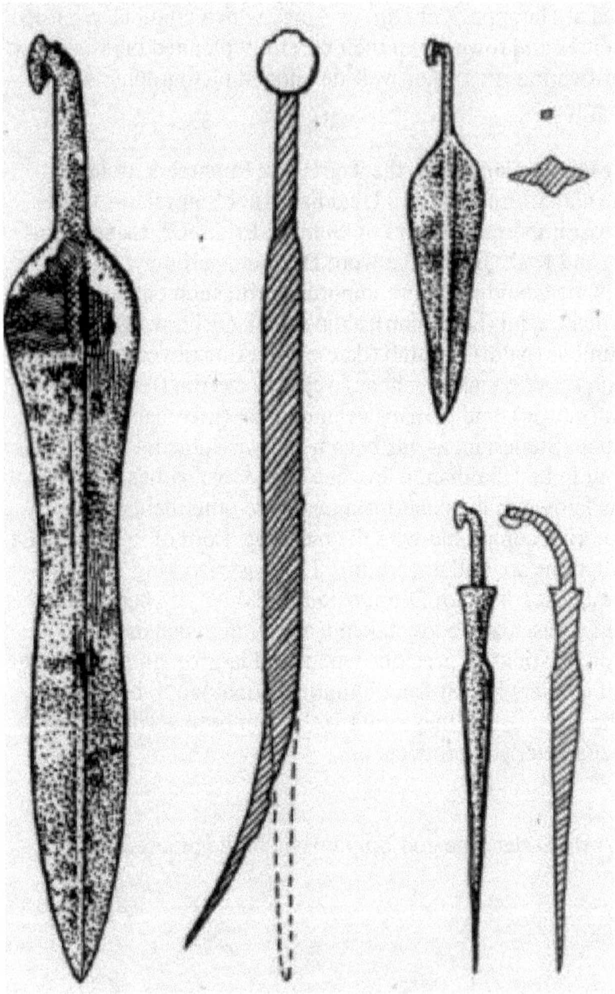

Tepe Hissar, ca. 2000 B.C.: spears with medial ribs and ridge-stopped tangs (Mallowan, Ill. 133) Tepe Hissar yielded gold, variegated jewellery, copper and silver vessels, many varieties of beads, among them much lapis lazuli; perhaps, Hissar was an entrepot in trade with taking the stone from the mines of Badakhshan.

Spears with medial ribs have parallels from Carchemish and Ugarit in north Syria dated a century before 2000 B.C. Such spears do not appear to occur in Mohenjodaro or other Harappan sites.

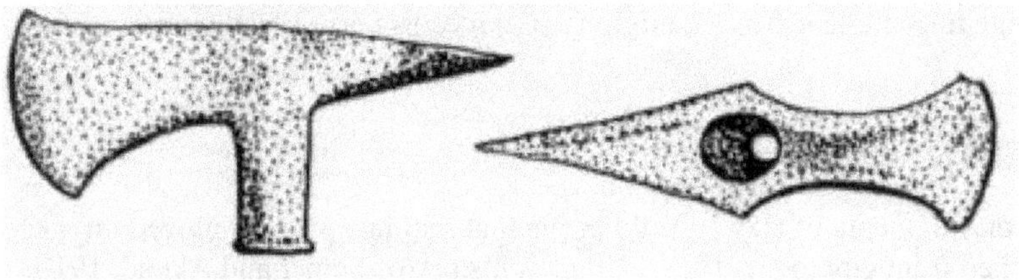

Tepe Hissar; from the 'Burnt Building' in level IIIB, ca. 2000 B.C. after Schmidt; combination of the basic forms of an axe and adze produced the axe-adze. Similar instrument was found in the reign of Shalmaneser III, ca. 850 B.C. Typical trough-sprouted vessels found at Tepe Hissar are similar to the types used in the karum at Kultepe in Cappadocia. Use of lead vessels is also paralleled in Kultepe, ca. 1900 B.C. [Kultepe is the place in Anatolia, with tin mines, see Yener's notes.]

Hissar III B dated a little before 2000 B.C. yielded the skull of a horse; the horse was domesticated at Shah Tepe much earlier, thus long anticipating the first appearance of it at Boghazkoy in Central Asia Minor in the early Hittite period. (Mallowan, p. 123). Smiths (Sum. simug, Akk. nappa_hum), responsible for (s)melting and casting, were distinguished from metalworkers (Sum.tibira, Akk. gurgurrum) who worked metal and created objects. These, on the other hand, were distinctly different from jewellers (Sum. zadim) and goldsmiths (Sum. ku-dim/dim, Akk. kutimmum)... Given the large number of metal tools, weapons and vessels recovered from sites in southern Mesopotamia, there is, as with ceramics, a frustrating lack of excavated workshop facilities.(D.T.Potts, Mesopotamian Civilization: The Material Foundations, 1997, Ithaca, Cornell University Press).

"The Avesta kows the beginning or source of the Aryans as Airyana Vaejo (Pahlavi Iran-Vej). The Avestan Vaejo corresponds to the Sanskrit bi_j meaning 'beginning or source'. The Avesta describes it as a place of extreme cold that became over-crowded (Vend. I. 3-4; II. 8-18). ... Whether the Mitannian kings (1475-1280 B.C.) on the upper Euphrates were a direct offshoot of the Aryans or not there names are certainly Aryan, for example Saussatar, Artatama, Sutarna, Tusratta and Mattiuaza (H. Oldenburg: in Journal of the Royal Asiatic Society, 1909, p. 1094-1109)... Mattiuaza, in his treaty with the Hittite king Aubbiluliuma signed in 1380 B.C. at Boghazkoy, invokes not only Babylonian gods to witness the treaties, but Mitra, Varun.a, Indra, and Na_satya in the form in which they appear in the Rigveda (S. Konow: Aryan gods of the Mitani people, 1921, pp. 4-5). They occur in the treaty as ila_ni Mi-it-ra-as-si-il ila_ni A-ru-na-as-si-il In-da-ra ila_ni Na-sa-at-ti-ya-an-na. Since the form for Na_satya is quite different in the Avestan language (Naonhaithya) it is argued that the Mitannian did not speak Iranian but Indo-Aryan (E.Meyer: Sitzungsberichte der K. Preuss. Akad. der Wissen, 1908, I, p. 14f.)... The name for 'fire' in the Persian Avesta is quite different, being atar, and this does not occur in the Indian Veda except in the Vedic proper name Atharvan, which corresponds to the Avestan name of the fire priest. Agni, as a messenger between gods and man, was known to the Vedas as Nara_-s'amsa. This corresponds with the Avestan messenger of Ahura, Nairyo_-sangha. (R.A. Jairazbhoy, 1995, Foreign Influence in Ancient Indo-Pakistan, Karachi, Sind Book House). [Note the use of the word san:ga in the Sumerian substrate language to connote a priest. san:ghvi_ (G.) means a priest leading the pilgrims.]

Some inscriptions were used as bills of lading

"The addresses on fragments of clay at Tello prove that sealings were employed on bundles despatched from city to city (L.W. King: A history of Sumer and Akkad, 1910, pp. 236-7)...

Tilmun, Telmun, Dilmun, the land of the famous red stone

Documents of the Larsa period in Ur were on tablets. Volume UET V includes texts which deal with Ur as the port of entry for copper into Mesopotamia during the time of the Dynasty of Larsa. The copper was imported by boat from Telmun. (Tilmun is associated with the famous red stone, of which Gudea speaks repeatedly as being imported from Meluhha.) "This 'Telmun-trade' was in the hands of seafaring merchants-- called alik Telmun-- who worked hand in hand with enterprising capitalists in Ur to take garments to the island in order to buy large quantities of copper there... In our period-- that of the fifth to seventh king of the Dynasty of Larsa-- the island exported not only copper in ingots but also copper objects, beads of precious stones, and-- most of all-- ivory... Travels to Telmun are repeatedly mentioned in a group of tablets whih come patently from the archives of the temple of the goddess Ningal and list votive offerngs, incoming tithe, etc. The contexts suggest that returning sailors were wont to offer the deity in gratitude a share of their goods. In UET V 526 we read of a small amount of gold, copper and copper utensils characterized as 'tithe of the goddess Ningal from an expedition to Telmun and (from) single persons having gone (there) on their own', during the first 3 months of the year. UET V 292... listing of merchandise is more extensie; besides' red' gold, copper, lapiz lazuli in lumps, various stone beads, ivory-inlaid tables, et., we find also 'fish-eyes'--perhaps pearls. (The meaing 'pearl' for IGI.HA has been proposed by R.C. Thompson (1936y: 53, n2) on the basis of UET V... The appearance of rather numerous references to IGI.HA in Ur and especialy in connection with imports from Tilmun must be considered an argument in favor of an interpretation which is not based on philological evidence. The lack of archaeological proof for the use of pearls is of course an important arguent against the identification but its value is somewhat diminished when one considers that no ivory object has been found in Ur although the texts report on ivory as raw material as well as on ivory objects.) ... UET 78, recording ivory combs, eye-paint and certain kinds of wood, not to mention designations which we fail to understand... UET V 367: '2 mina of silver (the value of): 5 gur of oil (and of) 30 garments for an expedition to Telmun to buy (there) copper, (as the) capital for a partnership, L. and N. have borrowed from U. After safe termination of the voyage, he (the creditor) will not recognize commercial losses (incurred by the debtor); they (the debtors) hae agree to satisfy U (the creditor) with 4 mina of copper for each shel of silver as a just (price(?)].'..babtum must denote some kind of customs or dues imposed on the merchants by the city administration... all extant Old and Neo-Babylonian contracts on partnership reserve for the tamkarum not only the invested capital (plus interest) but also an equal share of the profit yielded by the business venture... The complex legal relationship between the investing and the travelling merchant has created a number of loan types of which at least two are mentioned in the Code of Hammurabi. One of them uses the characteric term tadmiqtu. We encounter this word in the paragraphs 102-103 of the Code and in a few documents of that period... UET V 428: '5 shekels of silver as a tadmiqtu-loan PN1 has borrowed from PN2. He will return the silver at a moment (yet) to be determined (?) (This) he has sworn by the life of the king.' The specific designation of the loans as tadmiqtu 'favor, kindness' (in Sumerian: KA.sa 'friendly word') should not, in spite of the obvious etymology of these terms in both languages, induce us to presume that this business transaction was not as completely under the sway of the laws of economic life as any other loan... As to the main object of the Telmun trade, the copper (termed URUDU), we obtain most of the evidence from the letters (UET V 22,29, 71 and 81) addressed to a certain Ea-na_s.ir, a travelling merchant and importer of Telmun copper. The metal came in large quantities (UET V 796 mentions more than 13,000 minaz of copper according to the weight standard of Telmun) and often in ingots termed gubarum which weighed up to 4 talents each (UET V 678). The ingots are sometimes qualified as damqu(UET V 22,81) as is also the copper itself (UET V 20 wariam la damqam, but wariam dummuqam in UET V 5 and 6). The quoted passages do not entitle us to speak of refining of copper, because Ea-na_s.ir was not a coppersmith but a merchant and because the meaning of damqum as well as dummuqum as 'good (in quality)' is borned out by such letter passages as UET V 5:28 or 22: 10-13 ('show him 15 ingots so that he may select 6 damqu ingots' ... UET V 81, lines 33-39: 'I myself gave on account of you 19 talents of copper to the palace and S'umi-abum gave (likewise) 18 talents of copper, apart from the sealed document which we both handed over to the temple of Shamash.'... Ea-na_s.ir is supposed to have imported a large copper kettle (UET V 5:25)... UET V 428: '1 mina of...silver, 1/2 mina of... silver to buy (precious stones), 'fish-eyes' and other merchandise on an expedition to Telmun, PN2 has borrowed from PN1...'... ivory as raw material (UET V 546) as well as finished ivory objects have been imported from Telmun. Among the latter we find exactly the same objects which we know so well from the dowry inventories, etc. of the Amarna letters: ivory combs (UET V 292, 678), breast plates (UET V 279), boxes (UET V 795), inlaid pieces of furniture (UET 292) and spoons (UET V 795)... Southern Mesopotamia had to rely exclusively upon ivory imported from the East, to be exact: via Telmun... we have from Mohenjodaro actual ivory combs... UET V 82 refers to the karum as a locality in which business accounts have been settled, which in Old-Babylonian practice is normally done in the temple of Shamash... A certain Lu-En-li_l-la_ is said in UET III 1689 (Ibbi-Sin, 4th year) to have received large amounts of garments and wool from the storehouse of the temple of Nanna in order to buy copper in Makkan (nig.s'am.marudu Ma.gan ki, literally: equivalent for buying copper in M.)... When Sargon of Agade proudly proclaims (Legrain 1923: 208f., col. v-vi) that ships from or destined for Meluhha, Makkan and Telmun were moored in the harbor which was situated outside of his capital, this obviously proves the existence of flourishing commercial relations with the East... We even know the name of a person, a native of 'Great-Makkan' i.e. Ur-Nammu (UET III 1193). In the period, Makkan-- 'the country of mines' seems to have been the only importer of copper... After the collapse of the Dynasty of Ur, Telmun replaces Makkan in the Eastern trade of the city... Telmun, as against Makkan, seems never to have completely lost contact with Mesopotamia... Telmun had lost contact with the mining centers of Makkan and with those regions which supplied it with stone and timber, etc. some time between the fall of the Dynasty of Larsa and the decline of power of the Hammurabi Dynasty... It turned

again into an island famous only for its agricultural products, its sweet water, etc. Copper, precious stones, and rare woods have now to come to Southern Mesopotamia either over the mountain ranges and from the West along the river routes... Sometime in the second half of the 2nd millennium B.C., Telmun seems to have come in closer contact with the rulers of Southern Babylonia (Goetze 1952)... We are fortunate indeed to have three letters at our disposal, two written by Assurbanipal's general Bel-ibni mentioning Hundaru, king of Telmun, and one written by Assurbanipal and addressed to Hundaru. The details of the dealings of the king of Telmun in his fight for survival are of little interest in the present context, far more revealing is the mention of metal (bronze), precious woods and 'kohl' i.e. eye-paint in these letters. We read of great amounts of kohl, 26 talent of bronze, numerous copper and bronze objects, of sticks of precious wood as part of the booty taken from Telmun, while another speaks of the tribute of Telmun mentioning, at the same time, bronze, perfumes and likewise 'sticks' of precious wood offered by merchants from Bit-Naialu... a passage of the inscription KAH 122 of Sennacherib which describes the tools of the crew of corvee-workers sent from Telmun to Babylon to assist the Assyrian king to tear down the city. Their tools are characterized as follows: 'bronze spades and bronze pikes, tools which are the (characteristic) product of their (native) country.' Thus, it becomes evident that Telmun has again access to the copper mines of Makkan, to the spices, perfumes and rare woods of the East... Assurbanipal's inscription in the temple of Ishtar in Niniveh mentions another island--beyond Telmun--: '[x-y]-i-lum, king of the [ ]-people who resides in Hazmani which is an island alongside Telmun' whose messengers had to travel a long way across the sea and overland to Assyria. "(A.Leo Oppenheim, The Seafaring Merchants of Ur, *Journal of the American Oriental Society*, Vol. 74, 1954, pp. 6-17).
See Kyzyl Kum which was an area of copper mines in Central Asia
Rigveda: references to metalsmithy

Dialects of the Mleccha

Copper-smelting had to occur on the outskirts of a village. Hence, the semantic equivalence of milakkha as copper.

Mleccha in Pali is milakkha or milakkhu to describe those who dwell on the outskirts of a village. (Shendge, Malati, 1977, *The civilized demons: the Harappans in Rigveda*, *Rigveda*, Abhinav Publications). A milakkhu is disconnected from va_c and does not speak Vedic; he spoke Prakrt. " *na a_rya_ mlecchanti bha_s.a_bhir ma_yaya_ na caranty uta:* aryas do not speak with crude dialects like mlecchas, nor do they behave with duplicity (MBh. 2.53.8). a dear friend of Vidura who was a professional excavator is sent by Vidura to help the Pa_n.d.avas in confinement; this friend of Vidura has a conversation with Yudhisthira, the eldest Pa_n.d.ava: "*kr.s.n.apakse caturdasyam ratrav asya purocanah, bhavanasya tava dvari pradasyati hutasanam, matra saha pradagdhavyah pa_n.d.avah purus.ars.abhah, iti vyavasitam partha dha_rtara_s.t.ra_sya me šrutam, kincic ca vidurenkoto mleccha-vacasi pa_n.d.ava, tyayca tat tathety uktam etad visvsa ka_ran.am*: on the fourteenth evening of the dark fortnight, Purocana will put fire in the door of your house. 'The Pandavas are leaders of the people, and they are to be burned to death with their mother.' This, Pa_rtha (Yudhis.t.ira), is the determined plan of Dhr.tara_s.t.ra's son, as I have heard it. When you were leaving the city, Vidura spoke a few words to you in the dialect of the mlecchas, and you replied to him, 'So be it'. I say this to gain your trust.(*MBh.* 1.135.4-6). This passage shows that there were two Aryans distinguished by language and ethnicity, Yudhis.t.ra and Vidura. Both are aryas, who could speak mlecchas' language; Dhr.tara_s.t.ra and his people are NOT aryas only because of their behaviour.

Melakkha, island-dwellers

According to the great epic, Mlecchas lived on islands: "*sa sarva_n mleccha nr.patin sa_gara dvi_pa va_sinah, aram a_ha_rym sa ratna_ni vividha_ni ca, andana aguru vastra_n.i man.i muktam anuttamam, ka_canam rajatam vajram vidrumam ca maha_ dhanam:* (Bhima) arranged for all the mleccha kings, who dwell on the ocean islands, to bring varieties of gems, sandalwood, aloe, garments, and incomparable jewels and pearls, gold, silver, diamonds, and extremely valuable coral… great wealth." (*MBh.*2.27.25-26). A series of articles and counters had appeared in the *Journal of the Economic and social history of the Orient,* Vol.XXI, Pt.II, Elizabeth C.L. During Caspers and A. Govindankutty countering R.Thapar's dravidian hypothesis for the locations of Meluhha, Dilmun and Makan; Thapar's A Possible identification of Meluhha, Dilmun, and Makan appeared in the journal Vol. XVIII, Part I locating these on India's west coast. Bh. Krishnamurthy defended Thapar on linguistic grounds in Vol. XXVI, Pt. II: *mel-u-kku =3D highland, west; *teLmaN (=3D pure earth) ~ dilmun; *makant =3D male child (Skt. vi_ra =3D male offspring. [cf. K. Karttunen (1989). India in Early Greek Literature. Helsinki, Finnish Oriental Society. *Studia Orientalia.* Vol. 65. 293 pages. ISBN 951-9380-10-8, pp. 11 ff et passim. Asko Parpola (1975a). Isolation and tentative interpretation of a toponym in the Harappan inscriptions. Le dechiffrement des ecritures et des langues. *Colloque du XXXIXe congres des orientalistes*, Paris Juillet 1973. Paris, Le dechiffrement des ecritures et des langues. Colloque du XXXIXe congres des orientalistes, Paris Juillet 1973. 121-143 and Asko Parpola (1975b). "India's Name in Early Foreign Sources." *Sri Venkateswara University Oriental Journal*, Tirupati, 18: 9-19.]

Mleccha trade was first mentioned by Sargon of Akkad (Mesopotamia 2370 B.C.) who stated that boats from Dilmun, Magan and Meluhha came to the quay of Akkad (Hirsch, H., 1963, Die Inschriften der Konige Von Agade, *Afo*, 20, pp. 37-38; Leemans, W.F., 1960, *Foreign Trade in the Old Babylonian Period*, p. 164; Oppenheim, A.L., 1954, The seafaring merchants of Ur, *JAOS*, 74, pp. 6-17). The Mesopotamian imports from Meluhha were: woods, copper (ayas), gold, silver, carnelina, cotton. Gudea sent expeditions in 2200 B.C. to Makkan and Meluhha in search of hard wood. Seal impression with the cotton cloth from Umma (Scheil, V., 1925, Un Nouvea Sceau Hindou Pseudo-Sumerian, *RA*, 22/3, pp. 55-56) and cotton cloth piece stuck to the base of a silver vase from Mohenjodaro (Wheeler, R.E.M., 1965, *Indus Civilization*) are indicative evidence. Babylonian and Greek names for cotton were: sind, sindon. This is an apparent reference to the cotton produced in the black cotton soils of Sind and Gujarat.

Milakku, Meluhha and copper

"Gordon Childe refers to the 'relatively large amount of social labour' expended in the extraction and distribution of copper and tin', the possession of which, in the form of bronze weaponry, 'consolidated the positions of war-chiefs and conquering aristocracies' (Childe 1941: 133)... With the publication of J.D. Muhly's monumental *Copper and Tin* in 1973 (Muhly 1973: 155-535; cf. 1976: 77-136) an enormous amount of data on copper previously scattered throughout the scholarly literature became easily accessible... cuneiform texts consistently distinguish refined (urudu-luh-ha) [cf. loha = red, later metal (Skt.)] from unrefined copper (urudu) strongly suggests that it was matte (impure mixture of copper and copper sulphide) and not refined copper that was often imported into the country. Old Assyrian texts concerned with the import of copper from Anatolia distinguishurudu from urudu-sig, the latter term appearing when written phonetically as dammuqum, 'fine, good' (CAD D: 180, s.v. dummuqu), and this suggests that it is not just 'fine quality' but actually 'refined' copper that is in question... TIN. In antiquity tin (Sum. nagga/[AN.NA], Akk. annaku) was important, not in its own right, but as an additive to copper in the production of the alloy bronze (Sum. sabar, Akk. siparru) (Joannes 1993: 97-8)... In some cases, ancient recipes call for a ratio of tin to copper as high as 1: 6 or 16.6 per cent, while other texts speak of a 1:8 ratio or 12.5 per cent (Joannes 1993: 104)... 'there is little or no tin bronze' in Western Asia before c. 3000 B.C. (Muhly 1977: 76; cf. Muhly 1983:9). The presence of at least four tin-bronzes in the Early Dynastic I period... Y-Cemetery at Kish signals the first appearance of tin-bronze in southern Mesopotamia... arsenical copper continued in use at sites like Tepe Gawra, Fara, Kheit Qasim and Ur (Muhly 1993: 129). By the time of the Royal Cemetery at Ur (Early Dynastic IIIa), according to M.Muller-Karpe, 'tin-bronze had become the dominant alloy' (Muller-Karpe 1991: 111) in Southern Mesopotamia... Gudea of Lagash says he received tin from Meluhha... and in the Old Babylonian period it was imported to Mari from Elam...

Abhidha_na Cinta_man.i of Hemachandra states that mlecchaand mleccha-mukha are two of the twelve names for copper: ta_mram (IV.105-6: ta_mram mlecchamukham s'ulvam rakt tam dvas.t.amudumbaram; mlecchas'a_varabheda_khyam markata_syam kani_yasam; brahmavarddhanam varis.t.ham si_santu si_sapatrakam). Theraga_tha_ in Pali refers to a banner which was dyed the colour of copper: milakkhurajanam (The Thera andTheriga_tha_, PTS, verse 965: milakkhurajanam rattam garahanta_ sakam dhajam; tithiya_nam dhajam keci dha_ressanty avada_takam; K.R.Norman, tr., Theraga_tha_: Finding fault with their own banner which is dyed the colour of copper, some will wear the white banner of sectarians).[cf. Asko and Simo Parpola, On the relationship of the Sumerian Toponym Meluhha and Sanskrit Mleccha, *Studia Orientalia,* vol. 46, 1975, pp. 205-38).

(a) (b)

Seals with identical texts from (a) Kish (IM 1822); cf. Mackay 1925 and (b) Mohenjodaro (M-228); cf. Parpola, 1994, p. 132.

Harp-player of Sumer, from a plaque of Khafaje (After Heras, 1953, p. 182).

See Sign 311 of the script: 

Hieroglyph: *tambura* 'harp'; rebus: *tambra* 'copper'.

Clay tag from Umma, Iraq; seal impression on obverse; cloth impression on reverse (Ashmolean Museum, Oxford; cf. Parpola, 1994, p. 113).

Seal inscribed; Shortugai; Jarrige, 1984, Fig. 126 Hieroglyph: baḍhia = a castrated boar, a hog (Santali) baḍhi 'a caste who work both wood and iron' Hieroglyphs: kolmo 'three' kolmo 'rice plant' Rebus: kolami 'smithy, forge'.

'Keys' inherent in the inscriptions

The principal key is the copper tablet inscriptions which use some 'recurrent' hieroglyphics. The second key provided by these copper tablet inscriptions is the invention by the fire-worker/metal-smith of 'signs' which represent pictorials.
For example, the 'antelope' pictorial is represented by a 'sign' (Sign 184). A 'kneeling adorant' pictorial is represented by a number of 'signs' (Signs 45 to 48)

Sign 48: backbone: kaṇṭa 'backbone, podex, penis' Pa. piṭṭhi -- kaṇṭaka -- m. ' bone of the spine '; Gy. eur. kanro m. ' penis ' (or < káṇṭaka --); Tir. mar -- kaṇḍḗ ' back (of the body) '; S. kaṇḍo m. ' back ', L. kaṇḍ f., kaṇḍā m. ' backbone ', awāṇ. kaṇḍ, °ḍī ' back '; P. kaṇḍ f. ' back, pubes '; WPah. bhal. kaṇṭ f. ' syphilis '; N. kaṇḍo ' buttock, rump, anus ', kaṇḍeulo ' small of the back '; B. kā̃ṭ ' clitoris '; Or. kaṇṭi ' handle of a plough '; H. kā̃ṭā m. ' spine ', G. kā̃ṭɔ m., M. kā̃ṭā m.; Si. äṭa -- kaṭuva ' bone ', piṭa -- k° ' backbone '. 2. Pk. kaṁḍa -- m. ' backbone '.3. Pk. karaṁḍa -- m.n. ' bone shaped like a bamboo ', karaṁḍuya -- n. ' backbone '.(CDIAL 2670) Rebus: See - *khaṇḍ* in *lokhaṇḍ* (overflowing pot) 'metal tools, pots and pans, metalware' (Marathi). See:- *kāṇḍa* in: अयस्--काण्ड [p= 85,1] m. n. " a quantity of iron " or " excellent iron " , (g. कस्का*दि q.v.)(Panini. Monier-Williams)

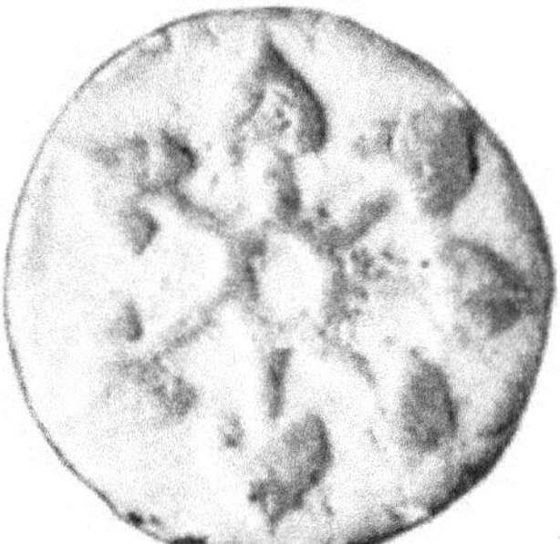

Harappa. H 243B Hieroglyphs: Hieroglyph: *loa* 'ficus religiosa' Rebus: *loh* 'copper' Hieroglyh: 'four': *gaNDa* Rebus: *kanda* 'fire-altar' Hieroglyph: *kolmo* 'three' Rebus: *kolami*'smithy,forge'. The hieroglyph multiplex meluhha cipher is read as plaintext Prakritam: *lokhaṇḍa kolami* 'metalware smithy,forge'.

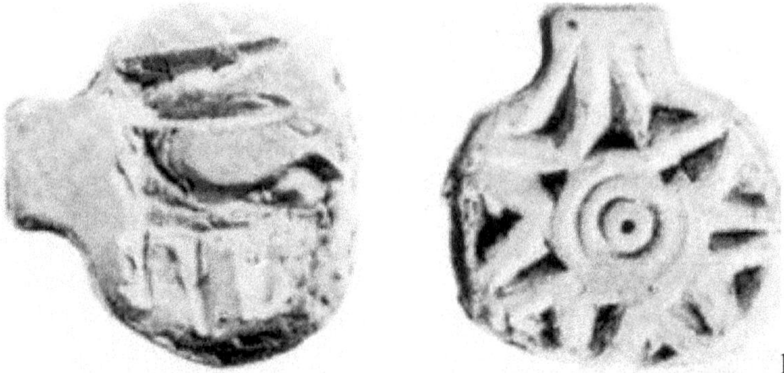

h349 A,B

Hieroglyphs: antelope, star, dotted circle. Hieroglyph: *meḍha* 'polar star' (Marathi). Rebus: *meḍ* (Ho.); *mẽṛhet* 'iron' (Munda.Ho.) Hieroglyph: kandi (pl. -l) beads, necklace (Pa.); kanti (pl. -l) bead, (pl.) necklace; kandit. bead (Ga.)(DEDR 1215). Rebus: लोहकारकन्दुः f. a blacksmith's smelting furnace (Grierson Kashmiri) *miṇḍāl* 'markhor' (Tōrwālī) Rebus: *meḍ* (Ho.); *mẽṛhet* 'iron' (Munda.Ho.)

Concentric or dotted circles hieroglyphs

Pk-30A, E

h 362-B, C

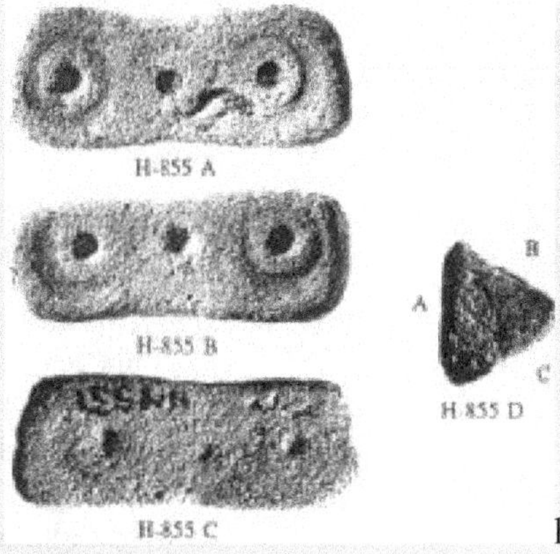

h 855 A,B,C,D

Rebus-metonymy renderings of hieroglyph multiplexes as hypertexts: dula 'pair' Rebus: dul 'cast metal'. Hieroglyph: kandi (pl. -l) beads, necklace (Pa.); kanti (pl. -l) bead, (pl.) necklace; kandit. bead (Ga.)(DEDR 1215). Rebus: लोहकारकन्दुः f. a blacksmith's smelting furnace (Grierson Kashmiri) Hieroglyph: baṭa = rimless pot (Kannada) Rebus: baṭa = a kind of iron (G .) S. baṭhu m. 'large pot in which grain is parched, large cooking fire', baṭhī f. 'distilling furnace'; L. bhaṭṭh m. 'grain—parcher's oven', bhaṭṭhī f. 'kiln, distillery', awāṇ. bhaṭh; P. bhaṭṭh m., °ṭhī f. 'furnace', bhaṭṭhā m. 'kiln'(CDIAL 9656).

The hieroglyph multiplex on Mohenjo-daro Seal m-352 can be exlained in the context of deciphered dotted circles: The + shaped structure is a fire-altar; the dotted blobs surrounding the central dotted circle denote ingots (like crucible steel ingots). *kanda* 'fire-altar'; Hieroglyph: 'kernel': *gōṭṭa ' something round '. [Cf. guḍá -- 1. -- In sense ' fruit, kernel ' cert. ← Drav., cf. Tam. koṭṭai ' nut, kernel ', Kan. goraṭe &c. listed DED 1722]K. goṭh f., dat. °ṭi f. ' chequer or chess or dice board '(CDIAL 4271) Rebus: lump of silver: G. goṭ m. ' cloud of smoke ', °ṭɔ m. ' kernel of coconut, nosegay ', °ṭī f. ' lump of silver; P. goṭṭā ' gold or silver lace ', H. goṭā m. ' edging of such ' (→ K. goṭa m. ' edging of gold braid ', S. goṭo m. ' gold or silver lace '); M. goṭ ' hem of a garment, metal wristlet '(CDIAL 4271). Rebus: खोट (p. 212) [khōṭa] *f* A mass of metal (unwrought or of old metal melted down); an ingot or wedge. (Marathi)

The third key is the technique of ligaturing adopted by the fire-worker/metal-smith, not only for the pictorials but also for the signs yielding, for example, the so-called 'fabulous animals' and a number of ligatured signs such as the 'water-carrier' sign ligatured with 'jar' sign. The ligaturing technique is exemplified by the sign 'svastika'.

Working in iron and zinc: kol 'working in iron' sattva 'zinc': m1356 Hieroglyph: *Ta.* kōlam beauty, colour, form, shape, costume, attire as worn by actors, ornament. *Ma.* kōlam form, figure (chiefly of masks, dresses); idol, body, beauty. *Ka.* kōla ornament, decoration, form, figure (chiefly of masks, dresses, etc.)(DEDR 2240) Rebus: *Ta.* kol working in iron, blacksmith; kollan̠ blacksmith. *Ma.* kollan blacksmith, artificer. *Ko.* kole·l smithy, temple in Kota village. *To.* kwala·l Kota smithy. *Ka.* kolime, kolume, kulame, kulime, kulume, kulme fire-pit, furnace; (Bell.; U.P.U.) konimi blacksmith (Gowda) kolla id. *Koḍ.* kollë blacksmith. *Te.* kolimi furnace. *Go.* (SR.) kollusānā to mend implements; (Ph.) kolstānā, kulsānā to forge; (Tr.) kōlstānā to repair (of ploughshares); (SR.) kolmi smithy (*Voc.* 948). *Kuwi* (F.) kolhali to forge.(DEDR 2133).

Allograph: twisted rope or endless knot:

meṛhao = v.a.m. entwine itself; wind round, wrap round roll up (Santali); maṛhnā cover, encase (Hindi) (Santali.lex.Bodding) Rebus: *meḍ* 'iron' (Mu.Ho.) mẽṛh t iron; ispat m. = steel; dul m. = cast iron (Mu.) meṛed-bica = iron stone ore, in contrast to bali-bica, iron sand ore (Munda) *mẽṛhẽt*'iron'; *mẽṛhẽt icena*'the iron is rusty';*ispat mẽṛhẽt*'steel', *dul mẽṛhẽt*'cast iron'; *mẽṛhẽt khaṇḍa*'iron implements' (Santali) *meḍ.* (Ho.)(Santali.lex.Bodding) *meṛed, mṛed, mṛd* iron; enga meṛed soft iron; *sanḍi meṛed* hard iron;*ispāt meṛed* steel; *dul meṛed* cast iron; *i meṛed* rusty iron, also the iron of which weights are cast; *bica meṛed* iron extracted from stone ore; *bali meṛed* iron extracted from sand ore (Mu.lex.)

měď (copper)(Czech) mid′ (copper, cuprum, orichalc)(Ukrainian) med′ (copper, cuprum, Cu), mednyy (copper, cupreous, brassy, brazen, brass), omednyat′ (copper, coppering), sul′fatmedi (Copper), politseyskiy (policeman, constable, peeler, policemen, redcap), pokryvat′ med′yu (copper), payal′nik (soldering iron, copper, soldering pen, soldering-iron), mednyy kotel (copper), medno-krasnyy (copper), mednaya moneta (copper). медь (copper, cuprum, Cu), медный (copper, cupreous, brassy, brazen, brass), омеднять (copper, coppering), Сульфатмеди (Copper), полицейский (policeman, constable, peeler, policemen, redcap), покрывать медью (copper), паяльник (soldering iron, copper, soldering pen, soldering-iron), медный котел (copper), медно-красный (copper), медная монета (copper).

This sign is used like a 'sign' and also like a 'pictorial' in scores of inscriptions. Another dominant hieroglyph is the 'dotted circle' which is not identified as a 'sign' in the Parpola and Mahadevan concordances. These signs, 'svastika' and 'dotted circle', constitute the fourth key.

jasta 'zinc' is cognate with *satthia* 'the **svastika** glyph'.

The graphemes of the script are vividly hieroglyphic as seen in many signs.
The sign list in a perspective snapshot presents a number of variants and ligatures which reinforce the hieroglyphic nature of the sign orthography.
Objects containing the inscriptions with these 'keys' or recurrent signs are clustered together in a series of hundreds of snapshots. An analysis of the types of objects used to convey the inscriptions is provided in the thousands of pages and images of the entire corpus of inscriptions documented in this website. (For example, seals, tablets in bas-relief, miniature incised tablets, copper tablets, ivory objects, bangle fragments, Kotda (Dholavira) monumental sign-board, pottery incisions, hieroglyphs of Mesopotamian finds). These snapshots are presented in the series of inscription clusters. (Note that these inscription clusters are sequenced not by sign pairs or a Sign number sequence but are 'clustered' by the keys provided by one or more dominant signs in an inscription set.)

Numerous studies of the inscriptions have been made during the past decades, including those by a Russian team under Yuri Knorozov and a Scandinavian group led by Asko Parpola. A concordance has been prepared by Iravatham Mahadevan. Parpola and associates (with financial support from UNESCO) have so far produced 3 volumes of photographic corpus.

For the trade with Mesopotamia there is both literary and archaeological evidence. The Harappan seals were evidently used to seal bundles of merchandise, as clay seal impressions with cord or sack marks on the reverse side testify. The presence of a number of Indus seals at Ur and other Mesopotamian cities and the discovery of a "Persian Gulf" type of seal at Lothal--otherwise known from the Persian Gulf ports of Bahrain (ancient Dilmun, or Telmun) and Faylahkah, as well as from Mesopotamia-- provide convincing corroboration of the sea trade suggested by the Lothal dock. Timber and precious woods, ivory, lapis lazuli, gold, and luxury goods such as carnelian beads, pearls, and shell and bone inlays, including the distinctly Indian kidney shape, were among the goods sent to Mesopotamia in exchange for silver, tin, woolen textiles, and grains and other foods. Copper ingots appear to have been imported to Lothal from Magan (possibly Oman, the Mahran region, or southeastern Iran). Other possible trade items include products originating exclusively in each respective region, such as bitumen, occurring naturally in Mesopotamia; and cotton textiles and chickens, major products of the Indus region not native to Mesopotamia.

Mesopotamian trade documents, lists of goods, and official inscriptions mentioning Meluhha (the ancient Akkadian name for the Indus region) supplement Harappan seals and archaeological finds. Literary references to Meluhhan trade date from the Akkadian, Ur III, and Isin- Larsa Periods (i.e., c. 2350-1800 BC), but as texts and archaeological data indicate, the trade probably started in the Early Dynastic Period (c. 2600 BC). During the Akkadian Period, Meluhhan vessels sailed directly to Mesopotamian ports, but by the Isin-Larsa Period, Dilmun (modern Bahrain) was the entrepot for Meluhhan and Mesopotamian traders. By the subsequent Old Babylonian period, trade between the two cultures evidently had ceased entirely.

Carts in contemporary Mesopotamia also did not use spoked wheels.

[Copper model of a chariot with four onagers harnessed abreast, from Tell Agrab, Mesopotamia; 3rd. millennium BC; the stand has been removed in the top view presented on the left.] In Mesopotamia, the under-carriage consisted (to judge from those of the hearses foundat Kish and Ur) of a single plank, 45 to 56 cm. wide, perhaps attached to the axle-tree by straps; perhaps, the axle turned with the wheels. In the case of four-wheeled wagons there is no evidence at all that the front axle was an independent pivoted bogie. Sumerians employed the onager (*Equus onager* Pallas), yoked in the manner of oxen to draw war chariots and passenger vehicles. Note the quiver with spears carried on the wagon and vanquished soldier crushed under the onagers. "It is most unlikely that horses were first domesticated or yoked to chariots in Mesopotamia, for the wild equid to be expected in that area was the onager, which had in fact been tamed there by 3000 BC. It is true that a single pictographic tablet of about that date contains the sign, compounded of 'ass' and 'mountain', that a thousand years later was to be regular cuneiform ideogram for 'horse'... Wild horses (*Equus caballus*)--essentially steppe dwellers-- have existed in northern Eurasia... The earliest convincing representations of equids drawing cars with spoked wheels occur on cylinder-seals from Hissar in north-east Persia (2000+-200 BC) and from Cappadocia (1950-1850 BC). There are written references to horse-breeding at Chagar Bazar on the Khabur by 1800 BC..." (V.Gordon Childe, 1954, Wheeled Vehicles, in: Singer et al, opcit, pp. 718ff.) [cf. Sharma's notes on the horse bones (*Equus Caballus*] found in Surkotada, in a domesticated setting, Sarasvati-Sindhu valley.]

There is evidence of a substrate language of anient Sumer; this language could be located in India in the contemporaneous Sarasvati-Sindhu civilization ca. 2500 B.C.

Many cylinder seals were used in trading moveable property items of the Mesopotamian civilization. [Note that some cylinder seals with the typical (Indus) script pictorials and signs have also been found in the sites of the Sarasvati-Sindhu civilization.]

Clay tablets were used for accounting, literary, administrative documents. [Indian historical tradition attests to the use of copper plates for conveyancing property rights. It is notable that some inscriptions are inscribed on copper tablets. So far, no other civilization has recorded such use of copper plates as recording devices for economic transactions.]

We start with an overview of the Mesopotamian civilization.

Millennia ago the fertile low lands in the river basins of Euphrates and Tigris were the home land of a rich and complex society. These civilizations were saved from oblivion by the unexpected discovery in the previous century of complete libraries in the archeological remains. Thousands of clay tablets, written in a cuneiform writing system, are buried deep under the ruins of ancient cities, when they were sacked and set into fire. The clay tablets, usually only sun-dried and stored on (inflammable) wooden shelves, are often inadvertently baked while a city was destroyed and treasures were removed. Clay was not valuable to treasure hunters and robbers in later times and clay tablets (at least until the 19th century CE) were left untouched and thus saved for eternity.

The branch of science dealing with the study of ancient civilizations in the Near East is called Assyriology, named after an Assyrian empire uncovered by the first archeological excavations.

Mesopotamia. The word 'Mesopotamia' is in origin a Greek name (*mesos* 'middle' and *potamos* 'river', so 'land between the rivers'). The name is used for the area watered by the Euphrates and Tigris and its tributaries, roughly comprising modern Irak and part of Syria. South of modern Bagdad, the alluvial plains of the rivers were called the land of Sumer and Akkad in the third millennium. Sumer is the most southern part, while the land of Akkad is the area around modern Bagdad, where the Euphrates and Tigris are close to each other. In the second millennium both regions together are called Babylonia, a mostly flat country.

Neighboring regions. The region roughly containing the Asian part of modern Turkey are referred to as Anatolia. Modern Iran is roughly equivalent to Persia and including in its southwestern part ancient Elam.

The ruins of many famous ancient cities, like Eridu, Ur, Nippur and Kish are now far from the river, but were in the past situated at the river banks.

Agriculture. After 8000 BCE Near Eastern environments become substantially more attractive for human settlements. The Atlanticum is the period in which agriculture developed in the Near East, around the Nile in Egypt and in the Indus valley in India.

If the Sumerians aren't the ones who actually invented writing than they are at least responsible for quickly adopting and expanding the invention to their economic needs (the first tablets are predominantly economic in nature).

Sumerian has no known relation to any other language. There seems to be a remote relationship with Dravidian languages (like spoken by the Tamils, now in the south of India). There is evidence that the Dravidian languages were spoken in the north of India, being displaced by the arrival of the Indo-European invaders around 1500 BCE. Because of the term 'the black-headed ones', sag.gi$_6$.ga it is possible (but far from proven) that the Sumerians are an early branch of one of the people now living in southern India.

Sumerian/Elamite inventions: Cylinder seals (French *Sceaux-cylindres*, German *Zylindersiegel*) are small (2-6 cm) cylinder-shaped stones carved with a decorative design in intaglio (engraved). Cylinder seals are a typical Sumerian invention. Such seals were also used in the Sarasvati-Sindhu civilization. The cylinder was roled over wet clay to mark or identify clay tablets, envelopes, ceramics and bricks. It so covers an area as large as desired, an advantage over earlier stamp seals. Its use and spread coincides with the use of clay tablets, starting at the end of the 4th millennium up to the end of the first millennium. After this time stamp seals are used again.

Purpose. The seals are needed as signature, confirmation of receipt, or to mark clay tablets and building blocks. The invention fits with the needs caused by the general development of city states.

substrate languages. A language (in particular as it appears in proper names and geographical names) may show signs of so called substrate languages (like the influence of Celtic on ancient Gaul; compare some Indian geographical names in the US attesting the original inhabitants). Some professional names and agricultural implements in Sumerian show that agriculture and the economic use of metals existed before the arrival of the Sumerians.

Sumerian words with a pre-Sumerian origin are:

- professional names such as simug 'blacksmith' and tibira 'copper smith', 'metal-manifacturer' are not in origin Sumerian words.
- agricultural terms, like engar 'farmer', apin 'plow' and absin 'furrow', are neither of Sumerian origin.
- craftsman like nangar 'carpenter', a:gab 'leather worker'
- religious terms like sanga 'priest'
- some of the most ancient cities, like Kish, have names that are not Sumerian in origin.

These words must have been loan words from a substrate language. The words show how far the division in labor had progressed even before the Sumerians arrived.

In texts from the 19th century BCE, it appears that trade was performed in a professional, capitalistic way (at least during a period of almost a century in the Old Assyrian period):

barter by boat over the Euphrates and the Persian Golf and with regular caravans by donkeys to Anatolia (modern Turkey).

Merchandise. Apart from cereals the inhabitants of Mesopotamia themselves had little to offer. Cereals were indeed exported but was too bulky for donkey transport over long distances. Imported material from elsewhere were again exported. Like tin, an important metal for bronze, that in those times probably came out of Afghanistan (although there are many Tin-routes). It was exported to Anatolia, a major center of metal industry, where in extensive forests wood was abundantly available to fuel the furnaces. Other merchandise were dates, sesame oil and in particular craft materials. Babylonia had an extensive wool industry. Coupons of 4 by 4.5 meter were in the 19th century BCE transported by the hundreds. From Anatolia silver and gold was imported.

Dominique Collon, 'First Impressions, cylinder seals in the Ancient Near East', British Museum Publications, London, 1987, ISBN 0-7141-1121-X.

Decipherment: internal evidence (structure and form)

Analyses and Method
The decipherment problem
A major problem in establishing the continuity of the Indian civilization beyond ca. 1300 BCE is the as yet unresolved problem of the decipherment of the inscriptions of the Sarasvati-Sindhu civilization.

Indian languages constitute the core legacy of the linguistic area of this civilization.

Conclusions

It would appear that many inscriptions were descriptions of weapons and metalwork catalogues of artifacts made by the metal-/fire-workers of the bronze-age civilization, which matured ca. 3000 BCE.

Six Rosetta stones of Indus Script validate the Indus Script Cipher. A seventh hints at the underlying language of the cipher: Meluhha (cognate mleccha). Several hundred Rosetta stones are Punch-marked coins from ca. 6th cent. BCE which display Indus Script hieroglyphs together with Kharoṣṭhī and Brāhmī syllabic writing.

The Sarasvati and Sindhu rivers in Northwest India sustained this civilization and the continuity of the Indian civilization into historical periods is confirmed by the underlying semantic unity of the Indian languages.

The fire-workers of the civilization produced the inscriptions related principally to the bronze-age artefacts, principally of weapons.

The fire-workers of the Rigveda worked on one mineral: electrum (soma).
The Sarasvati river (which nurtured the bronze-age civilization) is adored in the Rigveda.

The desiccation of the Sarasvati river (ca. 1700-1300 B.C.) led to the migrations of populations away from the banks of this river and principally eastwards and southwards.

The fire-workers of the Sarasvati-Sindhu civilization who worked with minerals and the Rigvedic peoples who specialized in processing one mineral, electrum or soma, migrated away from the Sarasvati river due to the desiccation of the river.

This leads to the formulation of two hypotheses:

A cooperative society and a continuous culture had existed right from the chalcolithic-age through the bronze-age to the historical periods on the Sarasvati-Sindhu doab and the rest of India.

A *lingua franca* had emerged in the doab ca. 3000 B.C. with intense interaction and resultant cross-borrowings of lexemes of an expansive contact zone (from Tigris-Euphrates to Ganga, from the Caucus mountains to the Gulf of Khambat, from Kashmir to Kanyakumari) constituting the Sarasvati-Sindhu doab and the rest of India as an Indian Linguistic Area (*sprachbund*).

The formulation of these hypotheses is a plea for unravelling further the as yet untold story of the formation of Indian languages as an exercise in general semantics.

Signs on an armoury (*jīnas'ālā*)

Ten signs presented on a monolithic sign-board of Dholavira (Kotda):

Dholavira (Kotda) on Kadir island, Kutch, Gujarat22; 10 signs inscription found near the western chamber of the northern gate of the citadel high mound (Bisht, 1991: 81, Pl. IX); each sign is 37 cm. high and 25 to 27 cm. wide and made of pieces of white crystalline rock; the signs were apparently inlaid in a wooden plank ca. 3 m. long; maybe, the plank was mounted on the facade of the gate to command the view of the entire cityscape. Ten signs are read from left to right. The 'spoked circle' sign seems to be the divider of the three-part message.

Method

A simple step is attempted and presented.

The pictorials in inscriptions on media unearthed in archaeological excavations (and taken from the exquisite corpuses of Mahadevan and Parpola) are tagged to the morphemes of the languages of the sub-continent.

Using the rebus principle, homonyms with substantive meanings are identified: such as the tools of jeweller-smithy, turner, silver-trader.

Engraved shell plaques, Telloh, 3rd millennium B.C. (London)[Note the trident, spears and the lion biting into the neck of the one-horned bull]

Animals depicted on a gaming board (Mesopotamia)

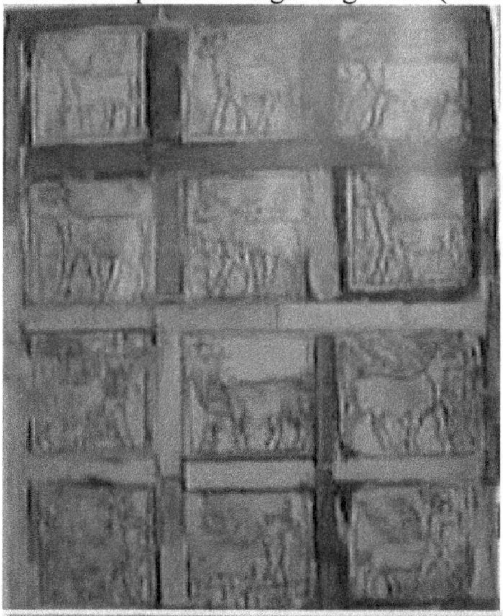

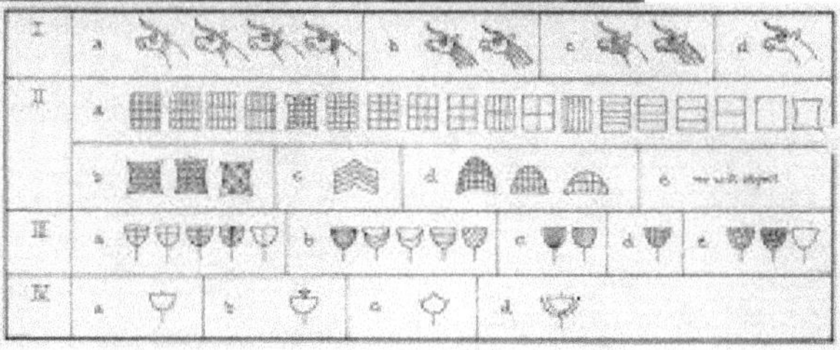

Group 1: hatched face animal (with zig-zag or straight cage on the standard) is associated with the north, around Harappa and the Sarasvati river

Group 2: (with collared necks and straight cage on the standard) is found in the south, around Mohenjodaro

cf. Rissman, 1989: 168.

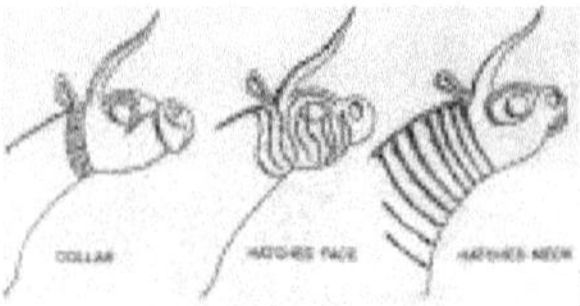
Decorations on the head and neck of the 'unicorn'

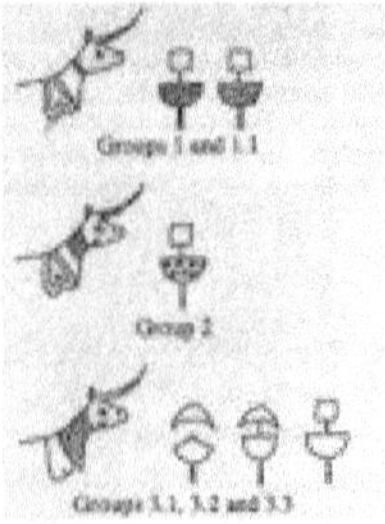
Three groups of 'unicorn' seals; cf. Franke-Vogt 1992: fig. 13.3

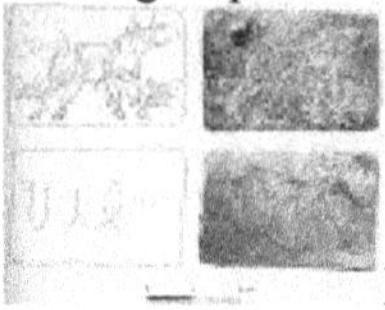
Inscribed copper tablet DK 11307 Mohenjodaro. Conjoined bovids (with 'unicorn' stripes on the face) with two 'altars' in front. Four signs on reverse. (Jansen and Urban, 1987, p. 71). [The stylised pannier on the bovids is an indicator that a 'unicorn' (ibex/urus) is depicted with two horns. The 'altars' may be 'troughs' which normally appear in front of other animal pictorials such as the bison, tiger, elephant or rhinoceros.]

Cylinder seal; Louvre, ca. 3000 B.CCylinder seal; Louvre, ca. 3000 B.C. (Sumerian seal from Jemdet Nasr showing 13 'unicorns'; cf. Heras, 1953, p. 220).

Standard of Ur depicting the one-horned bull and other scenes.

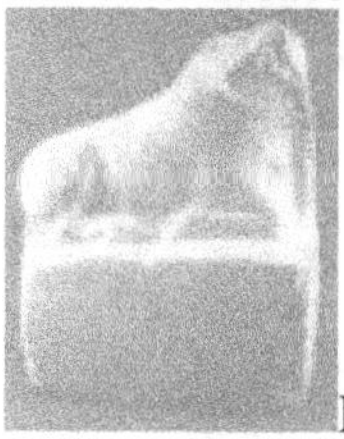
Ram's body and the elephant's trunk; SD 1109; Stone statue; Mohenjodaro Museum 430 (H 25.5cm; L: 19.5 cm; B: 13 cm.)

Sind Ibex (*Capra aegagru, Erxleben* or *Capra hircus*, L.);Yellow limestone statue; U 81036; Mohenjodaro Museum (H: 16.5 cm.; L: 22 cm; B: 12.3 cm.) [loc. cit.Jansen and Urban, 1987, p. 67].

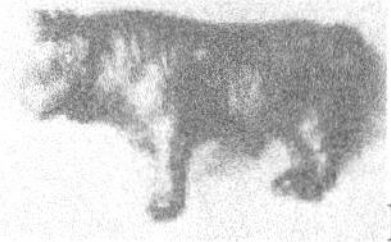
Kalibangan: copper bull (ca. 2300 to 1750 B.C., Period II); Pl. XXV, Possehl, ed., 1979, *Ancient Cities of the Indus*.

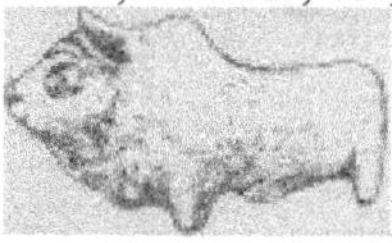
Mehrgarh; stone bull, Period I, Neolithic (5378+/- 290 and 5182+/-80 B.C.); Jarrige, Jean Francois, Towns and Villages of Hill and Plain, in *Frontiers of the Indus Civilization*, 1984, Fig. 33.3

Inlay of a bull; Tell El-obeid, ca. 3300 B.C.

Bull-god and goddess, Susa, 2nd millennium B.C. (Paris) [Note the high quiver holding 5 spears indicating a hieroglyphic semantic link between the bull icon and weapons]. There are ligatured pictorials on the seals and tablets of the Sarasvati Sindhu civilization depicting a horned person with hoofs and tail.

Hieroglyph: *khōli* f. ' quiver ' (Samskritam) P. *khol* f. ' sheath, case '; Ku. *khol* ' covering '; N. *khol* ' sheath ', B. *khol*, °*lā*; Or. *khoḷi* ' quiver ', °*ḷā* ' sheath ', H. *khol* (CDIAL 3944) Rebus: kol 'kolhe smelters'; 'working in iron'. Hieroglyph: barad, barat 'ox' Rebus: भरत (p. 603) [bharata] n A factitious metal compounded of copper, pewter, tin &c. (Marathi)

From the Babylon of Nebuchadnezzar Dr. Koldewey recovered the magnificent Ishtar Gate. It has been restored and erected in the Berlin Museum. Note the depiction of the one-horned bull.

Mating scenes

Moulded tablet, Mohenjodaro (M489B); a standing human couple in sexual intercourse (*a tergo*); two goats eating leaves from a tree; a cock (hen?); a three-headed animal.

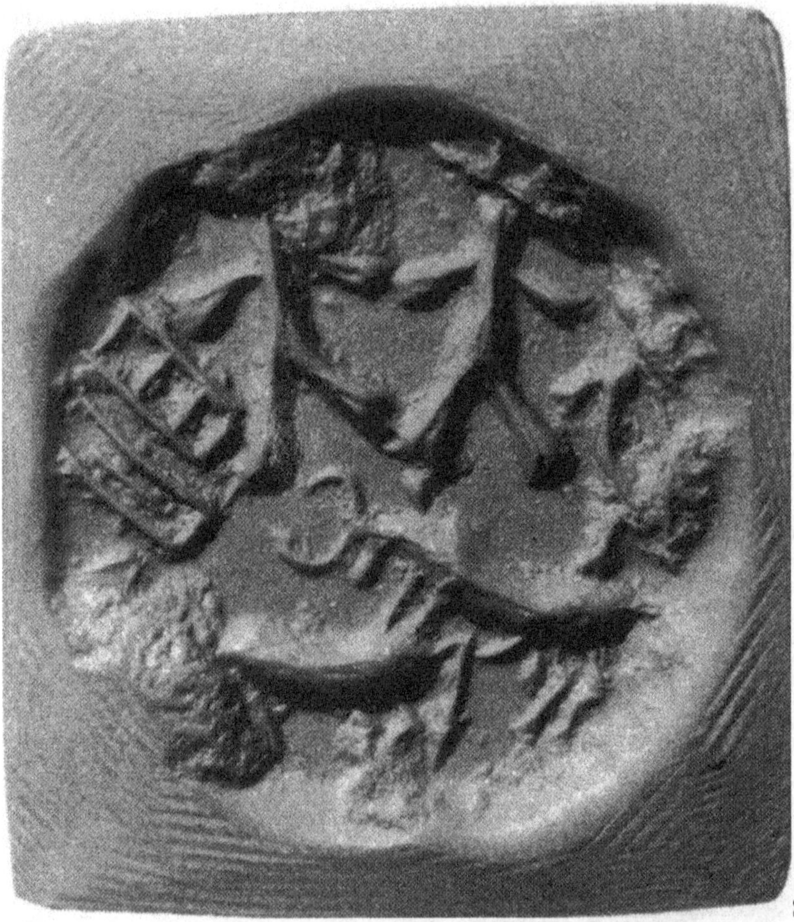

Seal impression (BM 123059), from an antique dealer, Baghdad; script and motif of a bull mating with a cow; cf. Gadd 1932: no.18; Parpola, 1994, p.219.

Hieroglyph: *saṅghā*, *saṅgā* copulation (of animals) (Or.); rebus: *sangaDa* 'turner's lathe'. *Dula* 'pair' Rebus; *dul* 'cast metal' meD 'body' Rebus: *meD* 'iron'Hieroglyph: *kāmsako, kāmsiyo* = a large sized comb (G.) Rebus: *kaṁsa* bronze'; *kā̃sāri* 'pewterer'. Alternative: Hieroglyph: *khareḍo* = a currycomb Rebus: *kharādī* ' turner'.

m1162. Mohenjo-daro seal with the same hieroglyph which appears on Kanmer circular tablets.  Glyph 33. Text 2068 *kāmsako, kāmsiyo* = a large sized comb (G.)

Rebus: *kaṁsa* bronze'; *kā̃sāri* 'pewterer' (Bengali) *kāḍ* 2 काड़ a man's length, the stature of a man (as a measure of length) Rebus: *kāḍ* 'stone'. *ibha* 'elephant'

Rebus: *ibbo* 'merchant'. *ib* 'iron'.

m1162 Text 2058 Ligatured glyph of three sememes: 1. *meḍ* 'body'(Mu.); rebus: 'iron' (Ho.); *kāḍ* 2 काड़ a man's length, the stature of a man (as a measure of length); rebus: *kāḍ* 'stone';Ga. (Oll.) *kanḍ* , (S.) *kanḍu (pl. kanḍkil)* stone; 2. *aḍar* 'harrow'; rebus: *aduru* 'native metal'. *ibha* 'elephant'; rebus: *ibbo* 'merchant' (Gujarati)

kā̃ḍ reed Rebus: *kāṇḍa* 'tools, pots and pans, metal-ware' Ku. *lokhaṛ* 'iron tools '; H. *lokhaṇḍ* m. ' iron tools, pots and pans '; G. *lokhā̃ḍ* n. 'tools, iron, ironware'; M. *lokhā̃ḍ* n. ' iron '(CDIAL 11171).

kāmsako, kāmsiyo = a large sized comb (G.) Rebus: *kaṁsa*= bronze (Te.) *kā̃sāri* 'pewterer' (Bengali) kãsārī; H. kasārī m. ' maker of brass pots' (Or.) Rebus: kaṁsá1 m. ' metal cup ' AV., m.n. ' bell -- metal ' Pat. as in S., but would in Pa. Pk. and most NIA. lggs. collide with kā´ṁsya -- to which L. P. testify and under which the remaining forms for the metal are listed. 2. *kaṁsikā -- .1. Pa. kaṁsa -- m. ' bronze dish '; S. kañjho m. ' bellmetal '; A. kā̃h ' gong '; Or. kā̃sā ' big pot of bell -- metal '; OMarw. kāso(= kā̃ -- ?) m. ' bell -- metal tray for food, food '; G. kā̃sā m. pl. '

cymbals '; -- perh. Woṭ. kasṓṭ m. ' metal pot ' Buddruss Woṭ 109. 2. Pk. kaṁsiā -- f. ' a kind of musical instrument '; A. kā̃hi ' bell -- metal dish '; G. kā̃śī f. ' bell -- metal cymbal ',kā̃śiyɔ m. 'open bellmetal pan' kā´ṁsya -- ; -- *kaṁsāvatī -- ? Addenda: kaṁsá -- 1: A. kā̃h also ' gong ' or < kā´ṁsya – (CDIAL 2576). kāṁsya ' made of bell -- metal ' KātyŚr., n. ' bell -- metal ' Yājñ., ' cup of bell -- metal ' MBh., aka -- n. ' bell -- metal '. 2. *kāṁsiya -- .[kaṁsá -- 1] 1. Pa. kaṁsa -- m. (?) ' bronze ', Pk. kaṁsa -- , kāsa -- n. ' bell -- metal, drinking vessel, cymbal '; L. (Jukes) kā̃jāadj. ' of metal ', awāṇ. kāsā ' jar ' (← E with -- s-- , not ñj); N. kā̃so ' bronze, pewter, white metal ', kas -- kuṭ ' metal alloy '; A. kā̃h' bell -- metal ', B. kā̃sā, Or. kãsā, Bi. kā̃sā; Bhoj. kā̃s ' bell -- metal ',kā̃sā ' base metal '; H. kās, kā̃sā m. ' bell -- metal ', G.kā̃sũ n., M. kā̃sẽ n.; Ko. kā̃śẽ n. ' bronze '; Si. kasa ' bell -- metal '. 2. L. kā̃ihā̃ m. ' bell -- metal ', P. kā̃ssī, kā̃sī f., H. kā̃sīf.*kāṁsyakara -- , kāṁsyakāra -- , *kāṁsyakuṇḍikā -- , kāṁsyatāla -- , *kāṁsyabhāṇḍa -- .Addenda: kāṁsya -- : A. kā̃h also ' gong ', or < kaṁsá -- . (CDIAL 2987).*kāṁsyakara ' worker in bell -- metal '. [See next: kāṁsya -- , kará -- 1] L. awāṇ. kasērā ' metal worker ', P. kaserā m. ' worker in pewter ' (both ← E with -- s --); N. kasero ' maker of brass pots '; Bi. H. kaserā m. ' worker in pewter '. (CDIAL 2988). kāṁsyakāra m. ' worker in bell -- metal or brass ' Yājñ. com., kaṁsakāra -- m. BrahmavP. [kā´ṁsya -- , kāra -- 1] N. kasār ' maker of brass pots '; A. kãhār ' worker in bell -- metal '; B. kā̃sāri ' pewterer, brazier, coppersmith ', Or. kãsārī; H. kasārī m. ' maker of brass pots '; G.kãsārɔ, kas m. ' coppersmith '; M. kā̃sār, kās m. ' worker in white metal ', kāsārḍā m. ' contemptuous term for the same '. (CDIAL 2989).

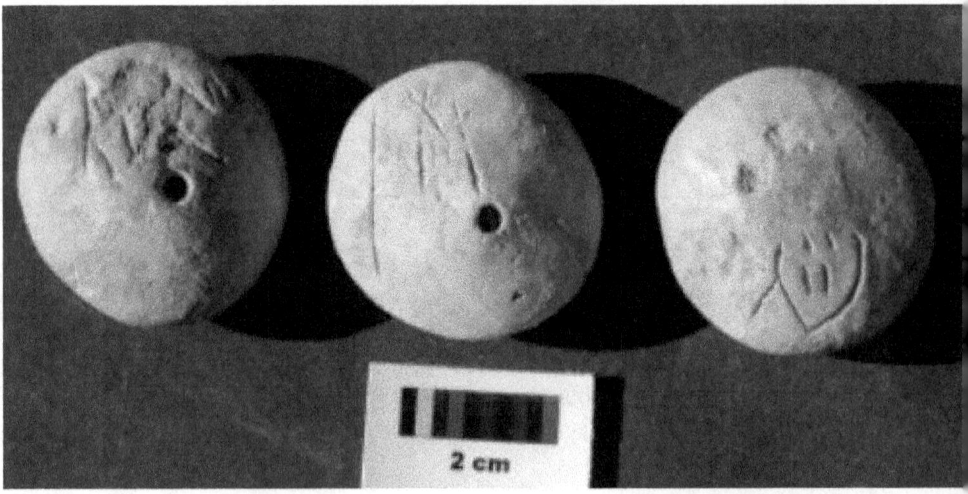

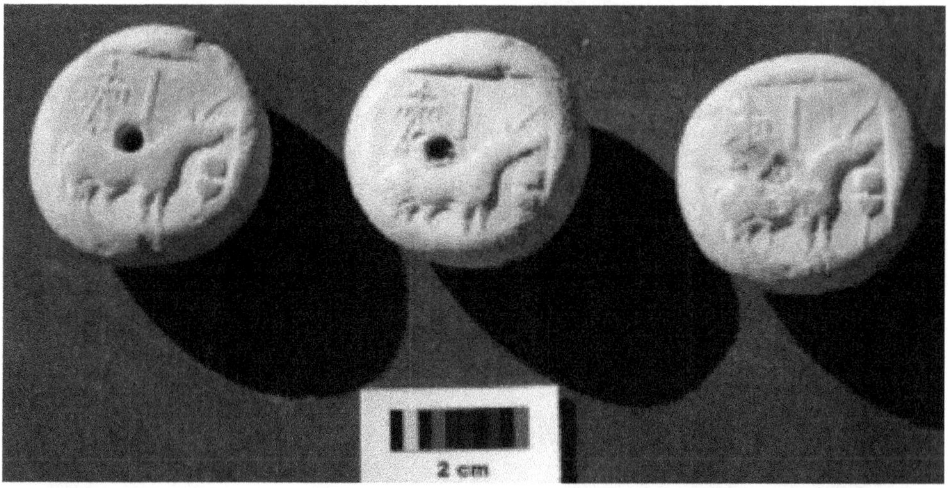

After Figures 12 and 13 in: Kharakwal, JS, YS Rawat, T. Osada, LC Patel, Hanmukh Seth, Rajesh Meena, S. Meena, KP Singh, & A. Hussain, Kanmer: a multicultural site in Kachchh, Gujarat, India, pp.355-376)

Rebus readings of Meluhha hieroglyphs:

koḍa ‘one’(Santali) Rebus: *koḍ* ‘artisan’s workshop’. *kõda* ‘young bull-calf’. Rebus: *kũdār ‘turner’. sangaḍa* ‘lathe, furnace’. Rebus: *samgara* ‘living in the same house, guild’. Hence, smith guild.

kāmsako, kāmsiyo = a large sized comb (G.) Rebus: *kaṁsa* 'bronze' (Te.) [See Meluhha glosses given below.]
mēd ‘body’ (Kur.)(DEDR 5099); meḍ ‘iron’ (Ho.) *kāḍ* 2 काड़ a man's length, the stature of a man (as a measure of length); rebus*: kāḍ* ‘stone’; Ga. (Oll.) *kanḍ* , (S.) *kanḍu (pl. kanḍkil)* id.

'The perforations may have been used for inserting some kind of thread perhaps to hang it on the neck.' Three terracotta seal impressions all with perfoations (dia 4.15 mm) off center. Stamped by a squarish seal with a unicorn motif and two Indus hieroglyphs on top. All the three seal impressions have the same motif and hieroglyphs.

On the reverse, each one has a different picture or symbol (Kharakwal et al 2009: 147-163). These are comparable to the following Meluhha hieroglyphs:

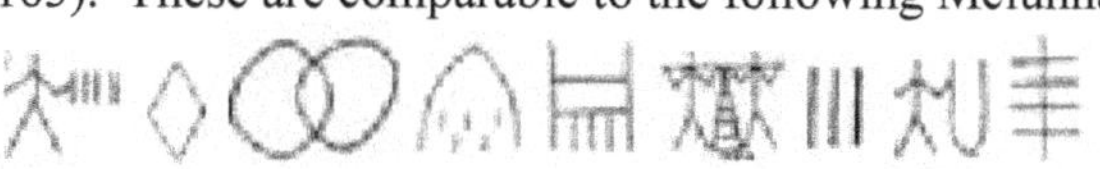

Broken clay circular sealing. 2.05cmX2.03cmX0.90cm Wt. 2.7 g. Unicorn motif with three hieroglyphs. Comparable to Seal H156A, impression H156a (Harappa)

 Hieroglyphs

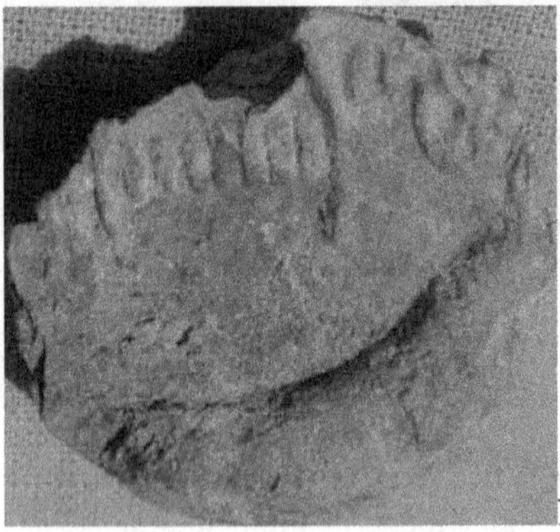

No. 06-1054 (Kanmer)

No 09-1997 Squarish steatite button seal. 1.06cm X 1.10cm X 0.48 cm Wt. 0.4 g; perforated knob on reverse. Goat with short tail standing facing left.

Two hieroglyphs: 

Mineral workshop

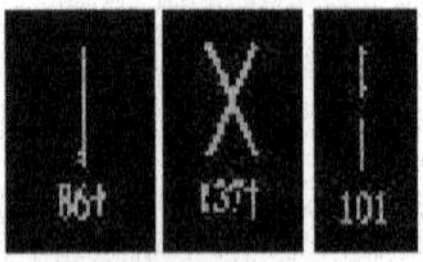

dātu = cross (Te.); dhatu = mineral (Santali)

sal stake, spike, splinter, thorn, difficulty (H.) Rebus: sal 'workshop' (H.)
kod. 'one' (Santali); rebus: kod. 'workshop' (G.)

Furnace workshop

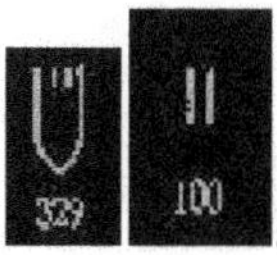

aṭar 'splinter' (Ma.); aḍaruni 'to crack' (Tu.) aduru 'native metal (Ka.)
baṭa = a kind of iron (G .) **baṭa** = rimless pot (Kannada)
S. baṭhu m. 'large pot in which grain is parched, large cooking fire', baṭhī f. 'distilling furnace'; L. bhaṭṭh m. 'grain—parcher's oven', bhaṭṭhī f. 'kiln, distillery', awāṇ. bhaṭh; P. bhaṭṭh m., °ṭhī f. 'furnace', bhaṭṭhā m. 'kiln'; S. bhaṭṭhī keṇī 'distil (spirits)'. (CDIAL 9656)

Metal workshop

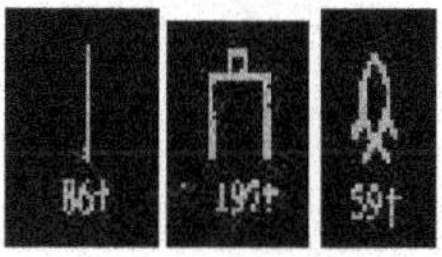
ayo, hako 'fish'; a~s = scales of fish (Santali); rebus: aya = iron (G.); ayah, ayas = metal (Skt.)
sal stake, spike, splinter, thorn, difficulty (H.) Rebus: sal 'workshop' (H.)
kod. 'one' (Santali); rebus: kod. 'workshop' (G.)

Decoding of the identical inscription on the three tablets of Kanmer.

Glyph: One long linear stroke. koḍa 'one' (Santali) Rebus: koḍ 'artisan's workshop' (Kuwi) Glyph: meḍ 'body' (Mu.) Rebus: meḍ 'iron' (Ho.) Ligatured glyph : aḍar 'harrow' Rebus: aduru 'native metal' (Kannada). Thus the glyphs can be read rebus. Glyph: koḍiyum 'heifer' (G.) Rebus: koḍ 'workshop (Kuwi) Glyph: sangaḍa 'lathe' (Marathi) Rebus 1: Rebus 2: sangaḍa 'association' (guild). Rebus 2: sangatarāsu 'stone cutter' (Telugu). The output of the lapidaries is thus described by the three tablets: *aduru meḍ sangaḍa koḍ* 'iron, native metal guild workshop'.

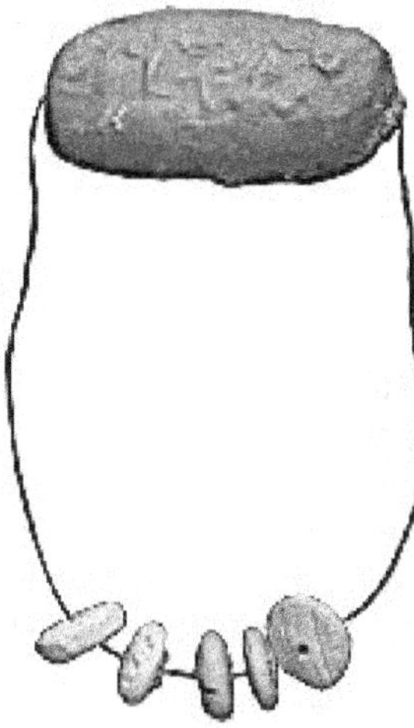

Seal. Kanmer.

Epigraph

Elephant glyph: ibha 'elephant' (Skt.) Rebus: ib 'iron' (Santali) ibbo 'merchant' (Gujarati)

Metal
ayo 'fish' (Mu.); *kaṇḍa* 'arrow'; *kaṇḍa, kāṇḍa, kāḍe* = an arrow (Ka.) *kāṇḍ kāṇ kōṇ, ko~_, ka~_ṛ* arrow (Pas'.);*ka~_ḍī* arrow (G.) Cf. *kaṇṭam* 'arrow' (Ta.)
Rebus: *ayaskāṇḍa* "a quantity of iron, excellent iron" (Pāṇ gaṇ)
Workshop
sal "stake, spike, splinter, thorn, difficulty" (H.);
Rebus: *sal* 'workshop' (Santali); *śāla* id. (Skt.)

Turner
kundau, *kundhi* corner (Santali) *kuṇḍa* corner (S.): *khoṇḍ* square (Santali) ***khuṇṭa**2 ' corner '. 2. ***kuṇṭa -- 2.** [Cf. *khōñca --] 1. Phal. *khun* ' corner '; H. *khũṭ* m. ' corner, direction ' (→ P. *khũṭ* f. ' corner, side '); G. *khũṭṛī* f. ' angle '. <-> X kōṇa -- : G. *khuṇ* f., *khūˇṇɔ* m. ' corner '. 2. S. *kuṇḍa* f. ' corner '; P. *kũṭ* f. ' corner, side ' (← H.).(CDIAL 3898).

ಕೊಣ್ಡ kŏṇḍa. Tbh. of ಕುಣ್ಡ (Śmd. 355; Abh. P. 10, after 183; My.). — ಕೊಣ್ಡಪ್ಪ. -ಅಪ್ಪ. N. among Brâhmaṇas (S. Mhr.). — ಕೊಣ್ಡಬಣ್ಡಿ. A cart used at the kŏṇḍa feast (My.). — ಕೊಣ್ಡಹಬ್ಬ. A feast in honor of Vîrabhadra at which Liṅgavantas carry an idol of Vîrabhadra and dance with it on live coals in a pit (My.).

ಕುಣ್ಡ kuṇḍa. = ಕೊಣ್ಡ. A hole in the ground, a pit. 2, a *pot* (ಮಡು, ಕುಪ್ಪ, etc. Mr. 209; see B. 3, 80). 3, a pool,

Allograph: kunta 'lance, spear' (Kannada)

Rebus: **kunda**1 m. ' a turner's lathe ' lex. [Cf. *cunda -- 1] N. *kũdnu* ' to shape smoothly, smoothe, carve, hew ', *kũduwā* ' smoothly shaped '; A. *kund* ' lathe ', *kundiba* ' to turn and smooth in a lathe ', *kundowā* ' smoothed and rounded '; B. *kũd* ' lathe ', *kũdā*, *kõdā* ' to turn in a lathe '; Or. *kūˇnda* ' lathe ', *kũdibā*, *kũd*° ' to turn ' (→ Drav. Kur. *kũd* ' lathe '); Bi.*kund* ' brassfounder's lathe '; H. *kunnā* ' to shape on a lathe ', *kuniyā* m. ' turner ', *kunwā* m. (CDIAL 3295). **kundakara** m. ' turner ' W. [Cf. *cundakāra -- : kunda -- 1, kará -- 1] A. *kundār*, B. *kũdār*, °*ri*, Or. *kundāru*; H. *kũderā* m. ' one who works a lathe, one who scrapes ', °*rī* f., *kũdernā* ' to scrape, plane, round on a lathe '.(CDIAL 3297). ***Ta.* kuntaṉam** interspace for setting gems in a jewel; fine gold (<

Te.). ***Ka.*** **kundaṇa** setting a precious stone in fine gold; fine gold; **kundana** fine gold.***Tu.*** **kundaṇa** pure gold. ***Te.*** **kundanamu** fine gold used in very thin foils in setting precious stones; setting precious stones with fine gold. (DEDR 1725).

Ka. **kunda** a pillar of bricks, etc. ***Tu.*** **kunda** pillar, post. ***Te.*** **kunda** id. ***Malt.*** **kunda** block, log. ? Cf. Ta. **kantu** pillar, post.(DEDR 1723). ***கற்கந்து*** *kaṟ-kantu* , *n.* < கல் +. Stone pillar; கற்றூண். கற்கந்தும் எய்ப்போத்தும் . . . அனை யார் (இறை. 2, உரை, 27).

Seal impression, Chanhujo-daro; bison bull (*Bos gaurus*) about to trample a person (have intercourse with a priestess?) lying on the ground. After Mackay 1943: pl. 51:13.

Spearing a buffalo and a bull

Spearing a buffalo/bull; a naked man lifts one of his feet onto the head of the buffalo and attacks it with a spear; (a) seal impression, Mohenjodaro (DK 8165); after Mackay 1938: pl.88, no.279; (b) moulded terracotta tablet, Mohenjodaro (DK 4547), in front of a tree;

three persons stand near the tree; (c) one side of a moulded triangular prism, Mohenjodaro (M492C); a snake with expanded hood is behind the short-horned bull which is attacked by a man with a spear, with one foot on the muzzle of the bull (cf. Mahadevan, 1977, p. 809).

Hieroglyph: *rāngo* 'water buffalo bull' (Ku.N.)(CDIAL 10559)
Rebus: *rango* 'pewter'. *ranga, rang* pewter is an alloy of tin, lead, and antimony (anjana) (Santali). Hieroglyph: *kol* 'to kill' Rebus: *kol* 'working in iron' (Tamil)

Hieroglyph: कोलणें [*kōlaṇēṃ*] v c To strike the विटी in the hole कोली with the bat or दांडू. (In the game of विटीदांडू). कोलून मारणें To kick up the heels of (Marathi) *kolsa* = to kick the foot forward (Santali) Rebus: *kol* 'kolhe smelter'; *kolle* 'blacksmith'; *kolami* 'smithy, forge'; kol 'working in iron'.

Hieroglyph: kole.l 'temple' Rebus: kole.l 'smithy'.

Fish signs

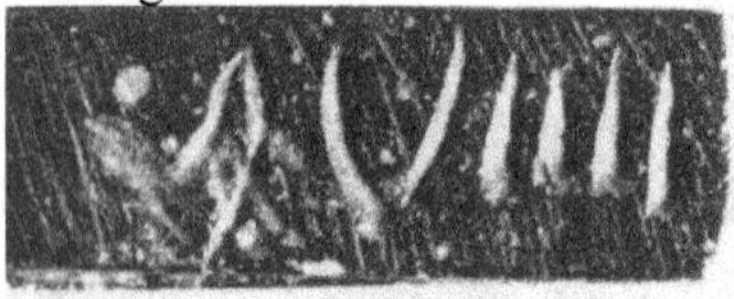

Fish on miniature tablets, Harappa (a) H-302; (b) 3452; after Vats 1940: II, 452 B. Parpola, 1994, p. 194. Rebus-metonymy cipher of Meluhha: *bhāṛ ayas kāṇḍa*, 'furnace metalware, excellent iron.'

Fish-shaped tablet (3428), Harappa with incised text; eye is a dotted circle; after Vats 1940: II, pl. 95, no.428; Parpola, 1994, p. 194. Hieroglyph: gaNDa 'four' Rebus: kanda 'fire-altar'. Hieroglyph: baTa 'wide-mouthed pot' Rebus: *bhāṛ* m. 'iron oven, fire, furnace ' (Kumaoni)(CDIAL 9684) Hieroglyph: Aya 'fish' Rebus: aya 'iron' (Gujarati); ayas 'metal' (Rigveda) Hieroglyph: WPah. bhal. *kān* n. ' arrow ', jaun. *kā̃ḍ*; N. *kā̃ṛ* ' arrow ', *kā̃ṛo* ' rafter '; A. *kā̃r* ' arrow '; B. *kā̃ṛ* ' arrow ',(CDIAL 3023) Rebus: *khā̃ḍā* 'pots, pans, tools, metalware' (Marathi)

h872b tablet in bas-relief; alligator catching a fish in its jaws.

h884A

h884B

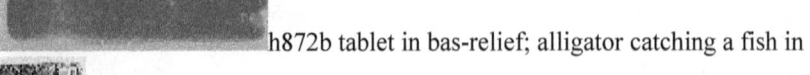

h884 incised tablet with a fish depicted on one side (B).

Fish signs (and variants) seem to be differentiated from, perhaps a loop of threads formed on a loom or loose fringes of a garment. This may be seen from the seal M-9 which contains the sign  Sign 180

Hieroglyph: sangaD 'lathe' Rebus: sangAta 'guild' Hieroglyph: खोंड (p. 216) [khōṇḍa] *m* A young bull, a bullcalf (Marathi) Rebus: khōṇḍar 'turner' (Bengali)

Hieroglyph: kolom 'three' Rebus: kolami 'smithy, forge' PLUS karNika 'rim of jar' Rebus: karNI 'supercargo'; karNIka 'scribe'.

Hieroglyph: P. goṭṭā ' gold or silver lace ', H. goṭā m. ' edging of such ' (→ K. goṭa m. ' edging of gold braid ', S. goṭo m. ' gold or silver lace '); M. goṭ ' hem of a garment '. (CDIAL 4271) गोटा [gōṭā] A narrow fillet of brocade. Rebus: गोटी [gōṭī] f (Dim. of गोटा) A lump of silver: as obtained by melting down lace or fringe. (Marathi) go°ṭī f. ' lump of silver' (Gujarati); M. goṭ ' metal wristlet '. (CDIAL 4271)

Hieroglyph: koDa 'one' Rebus: koD 'workshop'

Signs 180, 181 have variants.

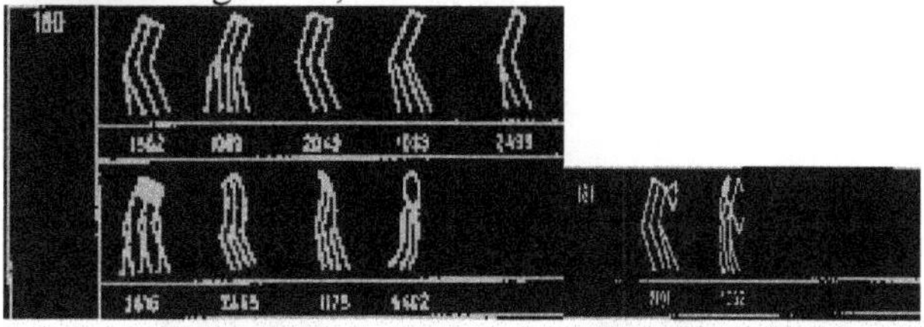

Dotted Circles

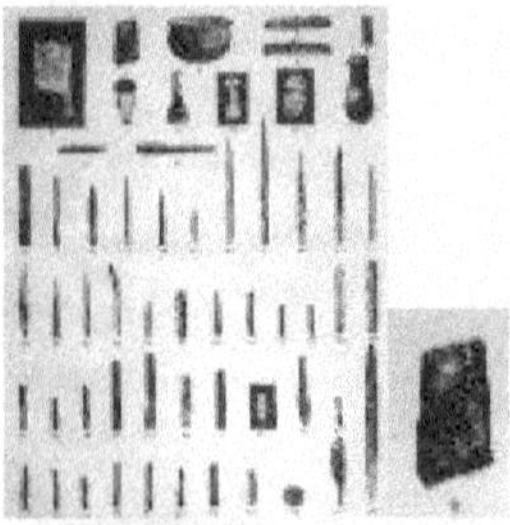

Ivory and bone objects, Harappa (After Vats, Pl.CXIX).No.6 is an ivory comb fragment with one preserved tooth and ornamented with double incised circles (3.8 in. long). No.1 is another comb fragment, also with dotted circles. Nos. 13, 15, 16 are kohl sticks. Nos. 12, 17 to 29 are hair pins, needles and awls. Nos. 3-t, 30-41, 43 and 45-54 are balusters which could have been used as dice or for casting in any game of chance.

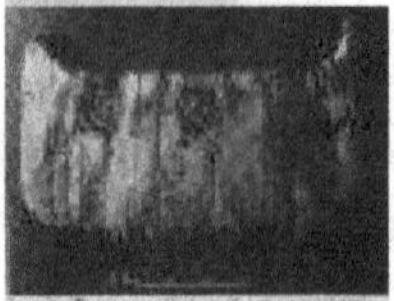

Kalibangan, Ivory comb with three dotted circles; Kalibangan, Period II; Thapar 1979, Pl.XXVII, in: *Ancient Cities of the Indus.*

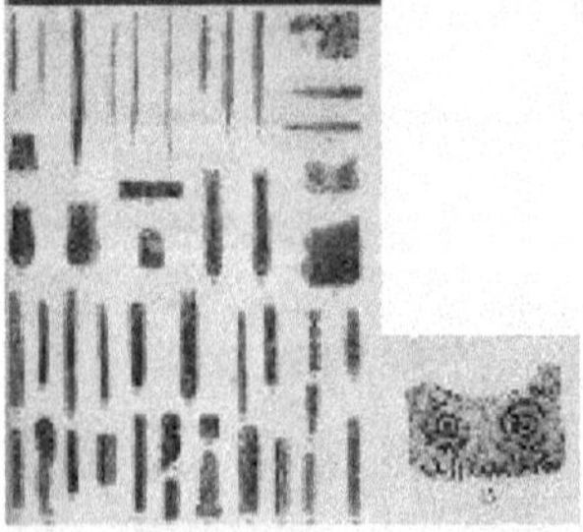

Ivory bone objects, needles, awls, handles, Mohenjodaro No.13 ivory comb fragment; Nos. 22 to 45 ivory objects: all with dotted circles inscribed (After Marshall, Pl. CXXXII).

(S. Kalyanaraman, 2010, The Bronze Age Writing System of Sarasvati Hieroglyphics as Evidenced by Two “Rosetta Stones” - Decoding Indus script as repertoire of the mints/smithy/mine-workers of Meluhha, Journal of Indo-Judaic Studies, Number 11, pp. 47–74) Excerpts from submitted monograph:

Bronze age and writing system of Sarasvati hieroglyphs evidenced by two ‘rosetta stones’ Decoding Indus script

Dr. S. Kalyanaraman, Sarasvati Research Centre

Two ‘rosetta stones’ of the bronze age writing system are the two pure tin ingots discovered in a shipwreck in Haifa. This monograph reads the epigraphs incised on the ingots as hieroglyphs, depicting the nature of the property item: metallic tin (**ranku dhaatu**) read rebus in mleccha (meluhha, melukkha), the lingua franca of the bronze age civilization linguistic area. India as a linguistic area is well-argued by Emeneau (Emeneau 1956: 3-16; Emeneau 1974: 92-134)

The epigraphs on the tin ingots have been deciphered as related to ranku “antelope”, “liquid measure”; read rebus: ranku 'tin'.

Tin from Meluhha; Mleccha as a language

"Tin from 'Meluhha'...According to the Larsa texts, merchants were there (in Mari and Larsa) to purchase copper and tin: the copper came from Magan in Oman, via Tilmun (Bahrain), but the origin of the tin is left in question. Tin mines in north-west Iran or the Transcaucasus are highly unlikely. Fortunately, there is evidence for another tin source in texts from Lagash. Lagash, about 50 km east of Larsa, was of minor importance except under the governorship of Gudea (ca. 2143-2124 BC). His inscriptions indicate extensive trade: gold from Cilicia in Anatolia, marble from Amurra in Syria, and cedar wood from the Amanus Mountains between these two countries, while up through the Persian Gulf or 'Southern Sea' came more timber, porphyry (strictly a purplish rock), lapis lazuli and tin. (Mulhy 1973: 404).

Tin used in Indus Valley civilization is well attested. (Muhly 1985: 283; Stech and Pigott 1986: 43-4). Gudea c. 2100 BC, identified Meluhha as the source of his tin (Falkenstein 1966: i.48: Cylinder B: XIV). "...tin may well often have travelled by sea up the Gulf from distribution centres in the Indus Valley. In the Old Babylonian period tin was shipped through Dilmun (Leemans 1960: 35)... It is now known that Afghanistan has two zones of tin mineralization. One embraces much of eastern Afghanistan from south of Kandahar to Badakshan in the north-east corner of the country; the other lies to the west and extends from Seistan north towards Herat (Cleuziou and Berthoud 1982), the valley of the Sarkar river, where the hills are granitic. Here tin appears commonly as cassiterite, frequently associated with copper, gold, and lead, and in quantities sufficient to attract attention in antiquity. Bronzes at Mundigak, and the controversial Snake Cave artefacts, indicate local use of bronze by at least the third millennium BCE (Shaffer 1978: 89, 115, 144). A number of scholars have pointed out the possibility that tin arrived with gold and lapis lazuli in Sumer through the same trade network, linking Afghanistan with the head of the Gulf, both by land and sea (Stech and Pigott 1986: 41-4)." (Moorey, 1994: 298-299).

"There is an extensive belt of placer deposits in the Malay peninsula which stretches over a distance of 1000 miles. The location of the early tin mines is lost to history, but the first documented use of tin seems to be in Mesopotamia, followed soon by Egypt. The tin probably came in through the Persian Gulf, or down what would later be the Silk Route. Some tin has been found in central Africa, and could have supplied a small amount to Egypt. However, the earliest needs for the mineral must have been met by Indian sources, the material being carried westward by migrations from southern and eastern Asia toward the Mediterranean area or from nearby sources." (Web resource: ancientroute.com)

"...More recent archaeological researches in East Arabia have brought to light many finds which are related to the presence of Indus valley people. In the settlements of Hili 8 and Maysar-1, both of which have been investigated, Indus valley pottery is frequently found. Seals with Indus valley script and typical iconography indicate influences in Makkan down to the level of business organization. Marks identifying pottery in Makkan were taken from those used in the Indus valley, including the use of the signs on pottery used in the Indus valley. The discovery of a sea-port-- which may be ascribed to the Harappans-- at Ra's al-Junayz on Oman's east coast by an Italian expedition would seem to indicate that trade routes should be viewed in a more differentiated fashion than has been done up to now." [Sege Cleuziou 1978/79, 30ff.; Gerd Weisgerber 1980: 62-110; Gerd Weisgerber, 1981; Tosi, 1982; Gerd Weisgerber 1986: 135-142. [Simo Parpola et al 1977: 129-165: 'If the tablets and their sealed envelopes had not been found, in fact, we might never have suspected the existence of a merchant colony.' (Ozguc 1962).

This is rebus for: melukka copper (Pali) [cf.Meluhhan interpreter shown on a cylinder seal; the Meluhhan is shown carrying a goat on his hands (Figure 1)]

Figure 1 Shu-ilishu's Akkadian cylinder seal (showing Meluhhan sea-faring merchant)

The antelope carried by the bearded Me-lah-ha on an Akkadian cylinder seal may be a

phonetic determinant: mel.aka or mr..eka (Telugu)(melu-hha; also, melech, 'king'; plural form, 'melechim'). [cf. Melech Hamashiah: King Messiah; Akad: {Akkad} A city in Mesopotamia (now Iraq) which was part of Nimrod's kingdom, founded by Melech Sargon around 2350 BCE Genesis 10:10.

On some glyphs, the antelope is held by its neck (med.a or melkhaa) (Figure 2):

Figure 2 Ur seal (showing a person holding an antelope by its neck)

Two figures carry between them a vase, and one presents a goat-like animal (not an antelope) which he holds by the neck. Human figures wear early Sumerian garments of fleece.

melkha_ throat, neck (Kur.); melque throat (Malt.)(DEDR: 5080). This glyph of holding by the throat of the animal is a phonetic determinant of the animal itself: me_lh goat (Br.); mr..e_ka (Te.); meque to bleat (Malt.); me_ke she-goat (Ka.); goat (Nk.) me~_ka, me_ka goat (Te.); me.ke (Kol.); me_ge goat (Ga.); meka_, me_ka (Go.); me_xna_ to call, hail (Kur.)(DEDR: 5087). med.a = neck (Te.lex.) met.e = the throat (Ka.); men-n.a, men-n-i (Ta.); menne (Ma.); mid.ar-u = the neck, the throat (Ta.Ma.); met.regat.t.u = a swelling of the glands of the throat (Ka.lex.) [The dotted circle connoting the eye: khan:gar 'full of holes'; rebus: kan:gar 'furnace']

Jayaswal notes that mleccha was the Samskr.tam representation of Hebrew melekh meaning, 'king' and that the utterance: he lavah! he lavah! in the S'atapatha Bra_hman.a was a specimen of mleccha speech; that this speech is cognate with Hebrew e_loa_h (plural e_lo_him) meaning, 'God' (Jayaswal 1914: 719). For the specimen of mleccha speech, an alternative explanation is provided in Maha_bha_s.ya with a variation, helayo helayo; Sa_yan.a_ca_rya notes that the specimen of Asura/mleccha speech is a variant of he 'rayo, he 'raya meaning, 'O the (spiteful) enemies', explained by the asuras' inability to pronounce the sounds, - r- and –y-. (Chatterjee 1957: 10-11). The word me-la-hha may also be cognate with: mer.h, med.h, 'copper merchant'. Another example of a substrate term: Sumerian tibira, tabira (Akkadian. LU2 URUDU-NAGAR =. "[person] copper-carpenter"); a word indicating borrowing from a substrate. In Pkt. tambira = copper. According to Gernot Wilhelm, the Hurrian version of tabira is: tab-li 'copper founder'; tab-iri 'the one who has cast (copper)'.

The city-state of Lagash (ca. 2060: king Shulgi) records a toponym about the presence of a 'Melukkhan village'. (Parpola 1975: 46). The word 'Melukkha' also appears, occasionally, as a personal name in cuneiform texts of the Old Akkadian and Ur III periods. Seals of the Indian civilization have been found in Mesopotamia and Iran at Kish (modern Tell Ingharra), Ur, Tell Asmar, Nippur (modern Nuffar), and Susa; a shard with an inscription has been found at Ras al-Junayz, the southeastern extremity of the Oman Peninsula; seal impressions of the civilization have been found at Umma (Tell Jokha) and Tepe Yahya; pottery of the civilization has been found at Ras al-Junayz, Asimah, Maysar, Hili 8, Tell Abraq -- in Oman and United Arab Emirates. Susa, Qalat al-Bahrain, Shimal (Ras al-Khaimah) and Tell Abraq (Umm al-Qaiwain) -- sites around the Arabian Gulf -- have yielded cubical weights of banded chert (unit weight: 13.63 grams) which are the hall-mark of the civilization.

Mleccha trade was first mentioned by Sargon of Akkad (Mesopotamia 2370 B.C.) who stated that boats from Dilmun, Magan and Meluhha came to the quay of Akkad (Hirsch, 1963: 37-38; Leemans 1960: 164; Oppenheim 1954: 6-17). The Mesopotamian imports from Meluhha were: woods, copper (ayas), gold, silver, carnelina, cotton. Gudea sent expeditions in 2200 B.C. to Makkan and Meluhha in search of hard wood. Seal impressions (?) with the cotton cloth from Umma (Scheil 1925: 55-56) and a cotton cloth piece stuck to the base of a silver vase from Mohenjodaro (Wheeler 1965) are indicative evidence. Babylonian and Greek names for cotton were: sind, sindon. This is an apparent reference to the cotton produced in the black cotton soils of Sind and Gujarat. Ca. 2150-

2000 BC, ivory from Meluhha is mentioned in connection with ivory bird figurines (Oppenheim 1954: II, 15 n.24).

Lipshur litanies state: 'Melukkha...is the land of carnelian' (Sumerian NA4.GUG, Akkadian sa_mtu). In the 17th century BC, the Neo-Assyrian king Esarhaddon called himself, 'king of the kings of Dilmun, Magan, and Melukkha'. The Sumerian myth Enki and the World Order has Enki exclaiming: 'Let the magilum-boats of Melukkha transport gold and silver for exchange!' Enki and Ninkhursag (lines 1-9, Tr. by B. Alster) has references to the products of Melukkha: 'The land Tukrish shall transport gold from Kharali, lapis lazuli, and bright...to you. The land Melukkha shall bring carnelian, desirable and precious, sissoo-wood from Magan, excellent mangroves, on big-ships! The land Markhashi will (bring) precious stones, dus'ia-stones, (to hand) on the breast, mighty, diorite-stones, u-stones, s'umin-stones to you!' [The cuneiform characters meluh-ha should be read with an alternative phonetic value: me-lah-ha. (Parpola et al 1970: 37); me-la_h-ha are a clan from a Sindhi tribe known as Mohaana.]

'Melukkha' is cognate with Pali 'milakkha' or Sanskrit 'mleccha'. In Pali, 'milakkha' also means, 'copper'. In Sanskrit, 'mleccha-mukha' means 'copper'.

An opinion is that during the pre-Harappan and Harappan periods, the main supply of tin was from the western regions: Khorasan and the area between Bukhara and Samarkand (Chakrabarti 1979: 61-74). The ancient tin mines in the Kara Dagh District in NW Iran and in the modern Afghan-Iranian Seistan could have been possible sources. Harappan metal-smiths used to conserve tin by storing and re-using scrap pieces of bronze, making low-tin alloys and substituting tin by arsenic. It is possible that some of the imported tin (like lapis lazuli) was exported to Mesopotamia.

Melakkha, islanddwellers

According to the great epic, Mlecchas lived on islands: "sa sarva_n mleccha nr.patin sa_gara dvi_pa va_sinah, aram a_ha_ryàm àsa ratna_ni vividha_ni ca, andana aguru vastra_n.i man.i muktam anuttamam, ka_ñcanam rajatam vajram vidrumam ca maha_ dhanam: (Bhima) arranged for all the mleccha kings, who dwell on the ocean islands, to bring varieties of gems, sandalwood, aloe, garments, and incomparable jewels and pearls, gold, silver, diamonds, and extremely valuable coral… great wealth." (*MBh.* 1933-1966: 2.27.25-26).

According to Geiger and Kern, the Pali term, mila_ca meaning 'forest dweller' was the original variant of milakkha and was used in Jatakas and Digha Nikaya (Wilhelm 1956: 524).This term, mleccha, should be differentiated from another term, paashanda, who were opposed to the doctrines of the times. There is no indication whatsoever in any text that mleccha were paashanda; the mleccha were in fact an integral and a dominant part of the community called in the Rigveda Bharatam janam – the people of the nation of Bharata (RV 3.53.12). Similarly, there is no indication whatsoever that mleccha were a distinct linguistic entity. The only differentiation indicated in the early texts that mleccha is 'unrefined' speech, that is, the lingua franca (as distinct from the dialects used in mantra-s or Samskrtam).

Thus mleccha is a reference to a common dialect, the spoken tongue in the Indic language family.

What distinguished mleccha and arya, when used in reference to language-speakers or dialect-speakers, were only places of habitation, norms of behaviour and dialectical variations in parole (ordinary spoken language) juxtaposed to grammatically 'correct' Samskr.tam or inscriptional Prakrits or Pali.

Mleccha in Sanskrit is milakkha or milakkhu in Pali, and the term describes those who dwell on the outskirts of a village. (Shendge 1977).

Meluhha is the region where Indian languages, such as mleccha (cognate, melukkha, meluhha) were spoken; Mahabharata attests, in the context of a cryptographic reference, that Vidura and Yudhishthira spoke in mleccha.

A milakkhu is disconnected from vaac [refined speech, for e.g. as Samskr.tam, as distinguished from the natural (spoken dialect or lingua franca) Prakrt] and does not speak Vedic; he spoke Prakrt. "na a_rya_ mlecchanti bhaashaabhir maayayaa na caranty uta: aryas do not speak with crude dialects like mlecchas, nor do they behave with duplicity (MBh. 2.53.8). A dear friend of Vidura who was a professional excavator is sent by Vidura to help the Pandavas in confinement; this friend of Vidura has a conversation with Yudhisthira, the eldest Pandava: "krishnapakse caturdasyàm ràtràv asya purocanah, bhavanasya tava dvàri pradàsyati hutàsanam, màtrà saha pradagdhavyàh pandavàh purusharshabhàh, iti vyavasitam pàrtha dhaartaraashtraasya me šrutam, kiñcic ca vidurenkoto mleccha-vàcàsi pandava, tyayà ca tat tathety uktam etad visvàsa ka_ran.am: on the fourteenth evening of the dark fortnight, Purocana will put fire in the door of your house. 'The Pandavas are leaders of the people, and they are to be burned to death with their mother.' This, Paartha (Yudhishtira), is the determined plan of Dhr.tara_s.t.ra's son, as I have heard it. When you were leaving the city, Vidura spoke a few words to you in the dialect of the mlecchas, and you replied to him, 'So be it'. I say this to gain your trust. This passage shows that there were two Arya-s distinguished by language group, Yudhis.t.ra and Vidura. Both are aryas, who could speak mleccha language (mleccha vaacasi); Dhrtaraashtra and his people (who could also speak mleccha) are NOT arya (respected persons) only because of their behaviour.

Find-spot of the first two 'rosetta stones'

At the port of Dor, south of Haifa, fisherfolk had raised about 7 tonnes of copper and tin ingots in the 1970's. In 1976 two ingots were found in a shipwreck in the sea near this Phoenician port. Ingot 1 and Ingot 2; Museum of Ancient Art, Municipal Corporation of Haifa.

The following picture of these two ingots incised with epigraphs was published in 1977 (Muhly 1977). Muhly notes: "... copper is likely to be a local product; the tin was almost always an import... There is certainly no tin on Cyprus, so at best the ingots could have been transhipped from that island. How did they then find their way to Haifa? Are we dealing with a ship en route from Cyprus, perhaps to Egypt which ran into trouble and sank off the coast of Haifa? If so, that certainly rules out Egypt as a source of tin. Ingots of tin are rare before Roman times and, in the eastern Mediterranean, unknown from any period. What the ingots do demonstrate is that metallic tin was in use during the Late Bronze Age...rather extensive use of metallic tin in the ancient eastern Mediterranean, which will probably come as a surprise to many people." (Muhly 1976: 47). We do not know where the tin ingots were moulded, and where the epigraphs were incised, but it is possible to read the epigraphs using references to cryptography in Mahabharata and *mlecchita vikalpa* 'cryptography' mentioned by Vātsyāyana in *vidyaa samuddes'ah* (objective of education or acquisition of knowledge in 64 arts).

In the old Akkadian period, the ingots of tin are called s'uqlu and weigh about 25 kg. The two ingots found at Haifa weigh about 5 kg. each.

To what period the two ingots belonged is uncertain. Some conjectures are that they could have come from Ugarit or Cyprus; these conjectures are questionable. The glyphs incised on the ingots DO NOT resemble Cypro-Minoan symbols used in Cyprus or Hittite hieroglyphs used in Ugarit or Cretan hieroglyphs ca. 1500 to 1100 BC.
One possibility is that they were weighed at Ugarit and stamped as they travelled through the long overland caravan route right up to the western end. [Anon. 1980: 1-2; Maddin et al 1977: 35-47] .

Figure 3. Two tin ingots found in a shipwreck in Haifa.

Figure 4. Three incised hieroglyphs on the tin ingots (zoomed)

The epigraphs inscised on the tin ingots are Sarasvati hieroglyphs of mleccha (meluhha) language which is part of the Indic language family. (These are called 'Sarasvati hieroglyphs' because, about 80% of the archaeological sites of the so-called Indus Valley civilization are on the banks of this Vedic river). The epigraphs 'certify' the metal as ranku, 'tin' (moulded out of) bat.a, a furnace; ranku is represented by two homonys: antelope, liquid-measure both phonetically read as ranku. bat.a is represented by X glyph, bat.a is a homonym meaning 'road'. [An alternative is to read this glyph as daat.u 'cross' (Telugu); rebus: dhaatu 'mineral' (Skt.)] Thus, both the epigraphs connote 'tin (out of) furnace'. The two tin ingots become the two 'rosetta stones' validating the decipherment of sarasvati hieroglyphs (so-called Indus script) as the repertoire of a smithy/metalsmith-merchant engaged in the bronze-age trade of minerals, metals and alloys and using types of furnaces/smelters.
This pictograph which magnifies the writing on (?) tin ingot 1, clearly refers to an antelope as depicted on the Mohenjodaro copper plate inscription: (m-516b shown).
The three signs zoomed-in in the illustrations, have parallels in the inscriptions of the civilization; in m-1336 the 'antelope' pictograph appears together with the 'liquid-

measure' pictograph; X sign occurs on many inscriptions with many variants elaborating it as a junction of two roads:

Figure 5.Seal m-1336a

Figure 6 Text on Seal m-1336a 2515 (Mahadevan)

Figure 7 Seal m-1341

Figure 8 Text of Seal m-1341 2092

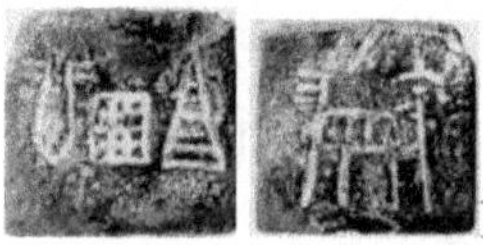
Figure 9 Two sides of tablet: m0516 (copper plate)

3398 Figure 10 Text of tablet m0516

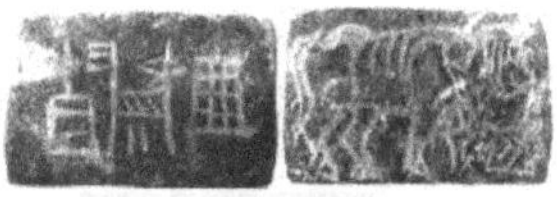
Figure 11 Two sides of tablet m-0522 (copper plate)

Figure 12 Text of tablet m-0522 3378

(Note: Figures 9 and 10, m0516 and m-522 are copper plates; on Figure 9, m0516 side A of the copper plate shows the antelope glyph; on Figure 10, m0522 side B the antelope glyph becomes a middle segment of a three-glyph epigraph. This is a clear demonstration of the continuum of the so-called field symbols or pictorial motifs and the so-called sigs of the so-called Indus script. Both the ‘pictorial motifs or field symbols’ and ‘signs’, a bi-partite categorization used in the corpuses of Parpola and Mahadevan, are hieroglyphs).

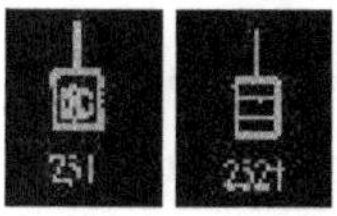

Figure 13. Signs 251, 252. ran:ku ‘liquid measure (Mundari)

Figure 14. Sign 249 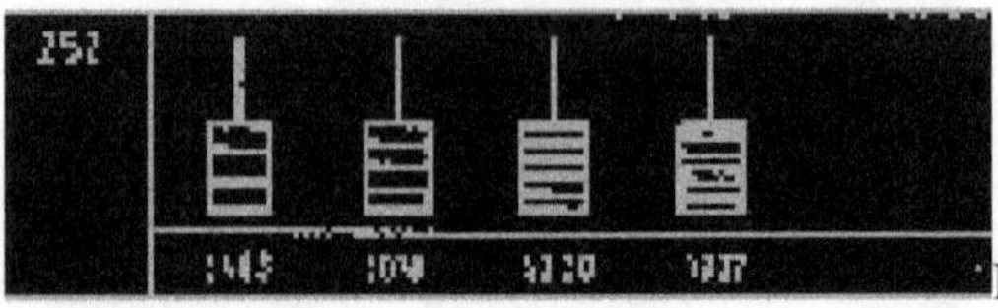

Figure 15 Sign 252 and variants The ‘liquid measure’ glyph may be seen to be a liquid measure by the orthographic styles shown on Sign Variants of Sign 252 with part filling of the liquid measuring container (with a handle).

The hieroglyphs may be read:

Figure 16. Sign 184 ran:ku ‘antelope’. Read rebus, the hieroglyphs connote ran:ku ‘tin’.

Sign 182 (See Figure 17) is a stylized glyph denoting a ram or antelope: tagar (Skt.); rebus: takaram ‘tin’ (Ta.)

That the ‘antelope’ sign is a derivative from the ‘antelope’ glyph is seen from the Sign Variants of Signs 182 to 184

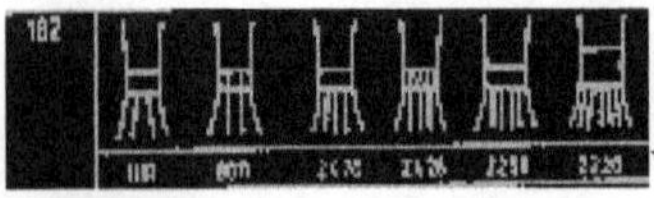

V182 

V184 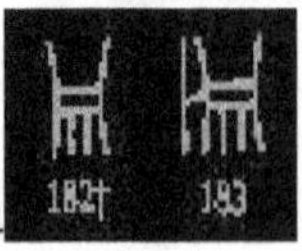

Figure 17. Sign 182, 183, 184 and variants

The sign 182 is repeatedly used on a copper plate epigraphs and substitutes for an ‘antelope’ glyph.

Liquid measure: ran:ku; rebus: ran:ku = tin; rebus: ran:ku = antelope. Thus both liquid measure glyph and antelope glyphs are graphonyms (graphically denoting the same rebus substantive: ran:ku, ‘tin’. Both the glyphs may be decoded as denoting ‘tin’ (ore) to describe the nature of the ingots being moved on the ships to Haifa and to Cape Gelidonya.

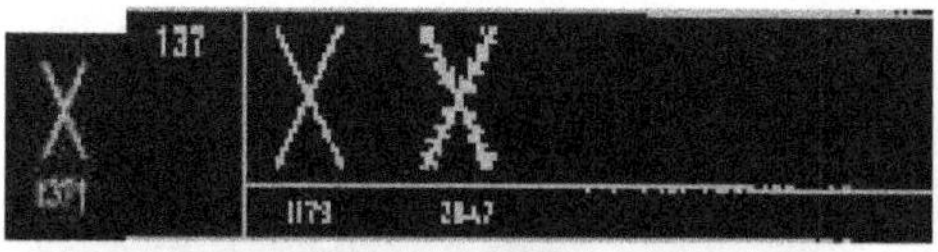

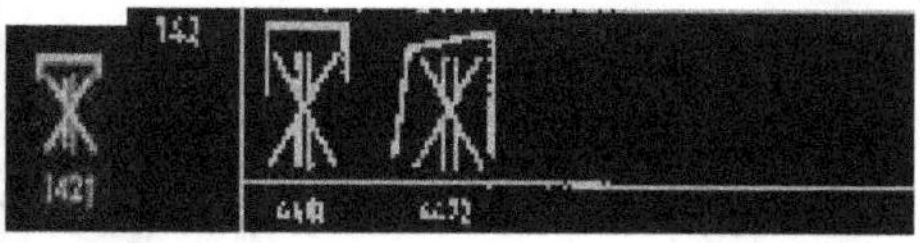

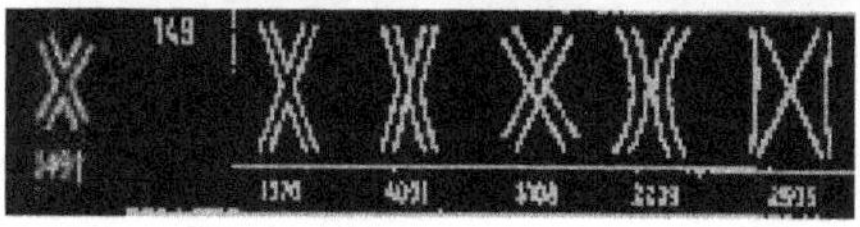

Figure 18 Sign 137, 142, 149 and variants

This glyph could connote the junction of two roads: bat.a means 'road'; rebus: bat.a means 'furnace, smelter'. An alternative interpretation for the X glyph and its variants, is possible, again in Indic family of languages. X may refer, rebus, to dha_tu 'mineral'. ta_tu = powder, dust, pollen (Ta.); to.0 = powdery, soft (of flour or powdered chillies)(To.). There is a possibility that the early semant. Of 'dha_tu' was cassiterite, powdery tin mineral.

If X glyph connotes a cross over: daant.u = cross over; da.t.- (da.t.-t-) to cross (Kol.); daat.isu – to cause to pass over (Ka.); da.t.- (da.t.y-) to cross (mark, stream, mountain, road)(Ko.); ta_t.t.uka to get over or through (Ma.); ta_n.t.u = to cross, surpass (Ta.)(DEDR 3158). In RV 6.044.23 the term used is: tridhaatu divi rocaneshu = 'three-fold amritam hidden in heaven' is the metaphor; and in RV 8.044.12 the term is: tridhaatunaa s'armanaa.

In addition to the glyphs of antelope and liquid-measure to read rebus: ranku 'tin', there is another homonymous lexeme which also refers to tin:

r-an:ku, ran:ku = fornication, adultery (Te.lex.) This semantics explains the extraordinary glyptics employed on many epigraphs, showing the sexual act.

Figure 19 A bull mating with a cow. Seal impression .

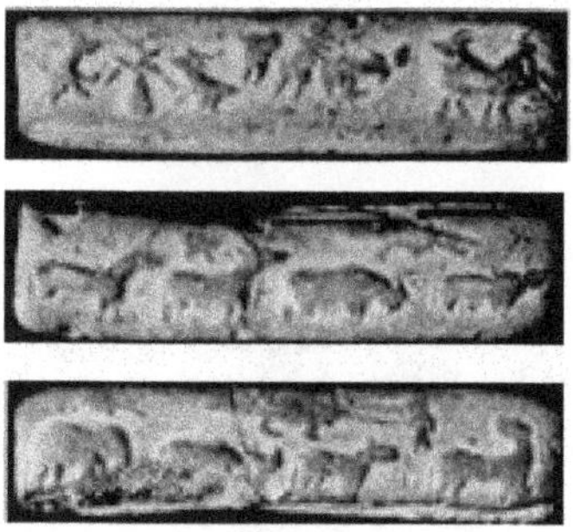

Figure 20 One side of a prism tablet m-0489. A standing human couple mating (a tergo).

A writing system called mlecchita vikalpa

The mleccha-speaking artisans invented

alloying of metals and a writing system. Like the postman in *Father Brown*, the linguistic area of India circa 5500 years ago has gone unnoticed simply because it is all around us, as a dialectical continuum stretching from Kanyakumari to Kashmir, from Dholavira to Dacca. The prehistory of the civilization is also all around us emphasizing the cultural continuity for over 5500 years to the present day. Our ancestral postmen have delivered the messages in emphatic glyphs constituting over 3,000 epigraphs anchored on lexemes of the linguistic area of the civilization. The substratum language was mleccha! We had somehow not noticed the postmen for the last 150 years, ever since the first seal was discovered close to the banks of River Sarasvati. It is possible to identify both the mleccha messenger and the mleccha messages. To quote, Tolka_ppiyam, **"ellaac collum porul kur-ittanave_"** (Tol. Col. Peya. 1), i.e. all words are semantic indicators. Hence, the use of rebus to denote *res* 'things'.

A remarkable link between the invention of alloying and the birth of the art of writing has been noted: "The Early Bronze Age of the 3rd millennium B.C. saw the first development of a truly international age of metallurgy... The question is, of course, why all this took place in the 3rd millennium B.C. It seems to me that any attempt to explain why things suddenly took off about 3000 B.C. has to explain the most important development, the birth of the art of writing... As for the concept of a Bronze Age one of the most significant events in the 3rd millennium was the development of true tin-bronze alongside an arsenical alloy of copper..." (Muhly 1973a: 221f.)

Justification for the use of rebus method

Hieroglyphs are pictograms used to represent phonograms (syllabic sounds or word sounds). Hieroglyphs use pictorial symbols to connote, as rebus, individual sounds of the spoken language. The word, 'rebus' is an ablative plural of *res* 'thing' and means 'of or by things' derived from the phrase: *nōn verbīs sed rébus"* meaning "not by words but by things". An example illustrates the rebus principle. The sounds in the sentence, "I can see you" can be written down by using the pictographs of "eye - can – sea – ewe". (Web source: Wikipedia).

Using the rebus principle, homonyms with substantive meanings are identified: such as the tools of jeweller-smithy, turner, miner, smith, metals-trader, mint. (A homonym is one of a group of words that share the same spelling and the same pronunciation but have different meanings.)

Two categories of lexemes are collated:

words which are adaptable for hieroglyphic representation ('image' words);

words related to the artefacts of the bronze-age civilization ('tool or product' words).

[A word links tightly together one or more morphemes and is a unit of language which carries meaning.]

Demonstrating the hieroglyptic nature of the writing system of Indus script

Figure 21 Relief spinner Louvre Museum Sb2834.jpg Elamite epigraph of Susa kut.he = leg of bedstead or chair (Santali.lex.) Rebus: kut.hi 'a furnace for smelting iron ore to smelt iron'; *kolheko kut.hieda* koles smelt iron (Santali) kol 'tiger' (Santali) [cf.tiger's legs of the bedstead] bed.a hako 'fish' (Santali) Rebus: bed.a 'either of the sides of a hearth' (G.) bhin.d.a a lump, applied especially to the mass of iron taken from the smelting furnace (Santali)

[Early form of hako is 'ayo'; rebus: ayas 'metal'] Six: bat.a (G.); Rebus: bat.a 'furnace'.

Figure 22 Seal impression showing female water-carrier Water carrier with a skin (or pot?) hung on each end of the yoke across his shoulders and another one below the crook of his left arm; the vessel on the right end of his yoke is over a receptacle for the water; a star on either side of the head (denoting supernatural?). The two celestial objects depicted on either side of the water-carrier's head can be interpreted as a phonetic determinant: kol. 'planet'. The whole object is enclosed by 'parenthesis' marks. The parenthesis is perhaps a way of splitting the ellipse (Hunter 1932: 476). kut.i = a woman water-carrier (Te.) kut.i = to drink; drinking, beverage (Ta.); drinking, water drunk after meals (Ma.); kud.t- to drink (To.); kud.i to drink; drinking (Ka.); kud.i to drink (Kod.); kud.i right, right hand (Te.); kut.i_ intoxicating liquor (Skt.)(DEDR 1654). Rebus: kut.hi 'a furnace for smelting iron ore to smelt iron'; *kolheko kut.hieda* koles smelt iron (Santali) kaca kupi 'scorpion' (Santali) Rebus kacc = iron (Go.)

Hunter calls it an unmistakable example of an 'hieroglyphic' seal. enclosure Signs of the field: ( )

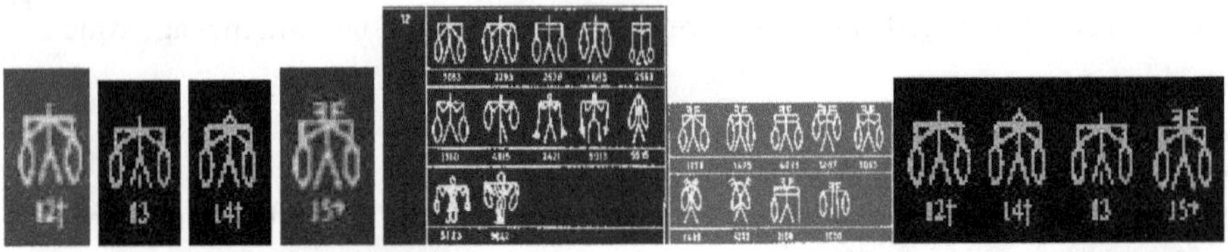

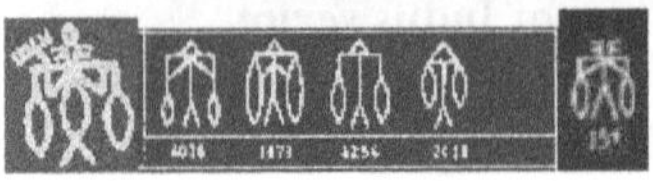

Figure 22 Signs 12, 13, 14, 15 and 342

Sign 12 (80) is a ligature of kan.d.a kanka 'rim of pot' + kut.i 'water carrier'. Rebus: kan.d.a kanka 'altar for copper' + kut.hi 'metal furnace'. *ke~r.e~ ko~r.e~* an aboriginal tribe who work in brass and bell-metal (Santali)

Sign 15 is a ligature of Sign 12 and Sign 342  Thus, Sign 15 can be orthographically read as: kut.i = woman water-carrier (Telugu); khan.d.a kanka = rim of a jar. The rebus representation, i.e. homonyms could be: kanaka = gold; kolhe = smelters of iron. Kut.hi 'smelter' (Santali)]

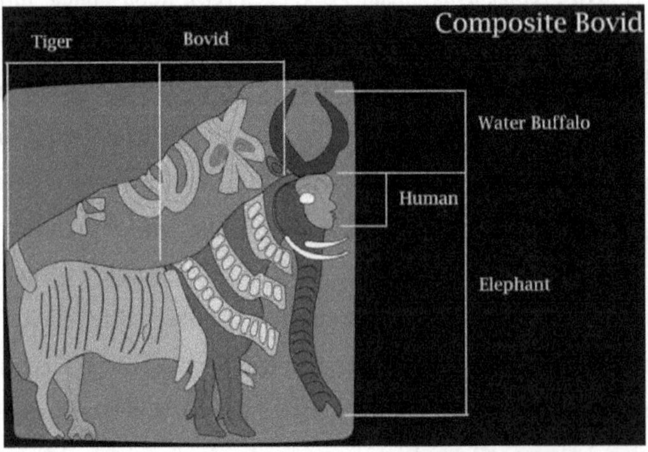

Figure 23: Composite bovid, ligatured components (the elements in the face shown on Seal m-304 is evidenced by zoomed-in pictorial motifs from other seals).Elements in m-304 face (Huntington 2007): two profile faces, bovine ears. Probable bristles like the bristles on a tiger's mane. The face profiles do not match with other faces profiled on other inscribed objects. The profiles of two faces however, can be

compared the profile of human face shown on this seal of a composite animal (elements: human, tiger, tiger's mane, markhor horns). Many such hieroglyphs are discussed in detail, in a series of ebooks/webpages at the portal (Kalyanaraman 2008)

Mlecchita vikalpa is one of the 64 arts to be learnt by youth. This, together with **des'a bhaashaa jnaana** and **akshara mushthika kathanam** (language and communication systems using mudra-s, that is, fingers and wrists) constitute three language-and-writing system-related arts according to vidyaasamuddes'a s'loka (verse detailing the objective of learning the arts) in Vātsyāyana's *Kāmasutra.* Manu notes: **mleccha vaacas caaryavaacas ca sarve te dasyavah smritaah** (trans. Mleccha dialect speakers and arya dialect speakers all are remembered as dasyu) (*Manu Smriti* 10.45).

It cannot be mere coincidence that over 100 pictorial motifs and over 400 signs can all be related rebus using mleccha (meluhha) dialect of the Indian linguistic area (Emeneau 1956: 3-16; Emeneau 1974: 92-134) to the repertoire of a mint/smithy listing property items: minerals, metals, alloys, furnaces and mine/smithy professionals.

References

Anon., 1980, Ingots from wrecked ship may help to solve ancient mystery, *Inst. Archaeo-Metallurgical Studies Newsletter,* No. 1, 1-2

Chakrabari, D.K., 1979, The problem of tin in early India--a preliminary survey, in: *Man and Environment,* Vol. 3, pp. 61-74

Chatterjee, K.C., 1957, *Patanjali's Mahabhah.ya*, Calcutta. A. Mukherjee & Co.

Cleuziou, S., 1978-79, Preliminary report on the second and third excavation campaigns at Hili 8, Archaeology in the United Arab Emirates, vol. 2/3, 30ff.

Cleuziou, S., and Berthoud, Th., 1982, Early tin in the Near East: a reassessment in the light of new evidence from western Afghanistan, *Expedition*, 25.

DEDR, 1984, Burrow, T. and Emeneau, M.B. (eds). *A Dravidian Etymological Dictionary Revised,* 2nd edn., eds., Oxford

Emeneau, M.B., 1956, India as a linguistic area, *Lang.* 32, 3-16

Emeneau, M.B., 1974, The Indian linguistic area revisited, *CCSAL*, 92-134

Falkenstein, A., Wahrsagung' in der sumerischen Ueberlieferung, *CRRA* 14: 55-56

Gadd, 1932, *PBA* 18

Hirsch, H., 1963, Die Inschriften der Konige Von Agade, *Afo*, 20, pp. 37-38

Hunter, G.R., 1932, Mohenjodaro--Indus Epigraphy *JRAS*, 476

Jayaswal, KP, 1914, 'Kleine Mitteilungen', *Zeitschrift der Deutschen Morgenlandischen Gesellschraft,*, vol. LXXII, p. 719

Kalyanaraman, S., 2008, Web resource on decoding Indus script (including Epigraphica Sarasvati or corpus of Indus script inscriptions) http://sites.google.com/site/kalyan97

Leemans, W.F., 1960, Foreign trade in the old Babylonian period as revealed by texts from southern Mesopotamia, Leiden

Maddin, R., T.S. Wheeler and J. Muhly, 1977, Tin in the ancient Near East: old questions and new finds, *Expedition*, 19, 35-47

Mahadevan, I., 1977, *Indus Script*, Delhi, Archaeological Survey of India

MBh., 1933-1966, *Mahabhrata* critical edition, Poona, Bhandarkar Oriental Institute

Moorey, P.R.S., 1994, *Ancient Mesopotamian Materials and Industries,* Oxford, Clarendon Press

J.D. Muhly, 1973a, Copper and Tin, Conn.: Archon., Hamden; *Transactions of Connecticut Academy of Arts and Sciences*, vol. 43

Muhly, J.D., 1973b, Tin trade routes of the Bronze Age, *Scientific American*, 1973, 61, 404-13

Muhly, J.D., 1976, *Copper and Tin, Hamden*, Archon Books.

Muhly, J.D., 1977, New evidence for sources of and trade in bronze age tin, in: Alan D. Franklin, Jacqueline S. Olin, and Theodore A. Wertime, *The Search for Ancient Tin*, Seminar organized by Theodore A. Wertime and held at the Smithsonian Institution and the National Bureau of Standards, Washington, D.C., March 14-15, 1977

Muhly, J.D., 1985, Sources of tin and the beginnings of bronze metallurgy, *AJA* 89: 275-291

Oppenheim, A.L., 1954, The seafaring merchants of Ur, *JAOS*, 74, pp. 6-17

Ozguc, T., 1962, An Assyrian trading outpost, *Scientific American*, 1962, 97 ff.

Parpola, Asko, S. Koskenniemi, S. Parpola and P. Aalto, 1970, *Decipherment of the Proto Dravidian Inscriptions of the Indus Valley,* no. 3, Copenhagen

Parpola A. and S. Parpola, 1975, On the relationship of the Sumerian Toponym Meluhha and Sanskrit Mleccha, *Studia Orientalia* 46

Parpola, Simo, Asko Parpola and Robert H. Brunswig, 1977, The Meluhha village. evidence of acculturation of Harappan traders in the later third millennium

Mesopotamia?, *Journal of the Economic and Political History of the Orient*, vol. 20, 129-165

Parpola, A. et al, 1987, Corpus of Indus seals and inscriptions, Vol. 1 Collections in India, Helsinki: Suomalainen Tiedeakatemia

Parpola,. A. et al, 1991, Corpus of Indus seals and inscriptions, Vol. 2 Collections in Pakistan, Helsinki: Suomalainen Tiedeakatemia.

Porada, E., 1971, Remarks on seals found in the Gulf States. *Artibus Asiae* 33 (4): 331-7: pl.9, Figure 5

RV. *Rigveda*, 1896, tr. By Ralph TH Griffith.

Scheil, V., 1925, Un Nouvea Sceau Hindou Pseudo-Sumerian, *RA*, 22/3, pp. 55-56)

Shaffer, J.G., 1978, *Prehistoric Baluchistan: With Excavation Report on Said Qala Tepe.* Delhi: B.R.Publishing Corp

Shendge, Malati, 1977, *The civilized demons: the Harappans in Rigved*a, Abhinav Publications

Stech, T. and Pigott, V.C.,1986, The Metals Trade in Southwest Asia in the Third Millennium B. C., *Iraq,* 48: 39-64.

Tol.Col. Tolkaappiyam Collakaraati, a Tamil work of grammar of ca 3rd century BCE to 10th cent. CE Full text on web address:
http://www.tamil.net/projectmadurai/pub/pm0100/tolkap.pdf

Tosi, M., 1982. *A possible Harappan Seaport in Eastern Arabia: Ra's Al Junayz in the Sultanate of Oman*, paper read at the 1st International Conference on Pakistan Archaeology, Peshawar

Web resource:

ancientroute.com http://www.ancientroute.com/resource/metal/tin.htm

Wikipedia http://en.wikipedia.org/wiki/Rebus

Weisgerber, G., 1980, '...und Kupfer in Oman', *Der Anschnitt*, vol. 32, 1980, 62-110

Weisgerber, G., 1981, *Makkan and Meluhha- 3rd millennium copper production in Oman and evidence of contact with the Indus valley*, Paper read in Cambridge 1981 and to appear in South Asia Archaeology 1981

Weisgerber, G., 1986, Dilmun--a trading entrepot; evidence from historical and archaeological sources, 135-142 in: Shaikha Haya Ali Al Khalifa and Michael Rice (eds.) *Bahrain through the ages: the archaeology*, London, KPI.
Wheeler, R.E.M., 1965, *Indus Civilization*, Cambridge, Cambridge University Press
Wilhelm, Geiger, 1956, Jataka, XIV, 486; XVII, 524; Pali Literature and Language, tr. BK Ghosh, Calcutta.

Figures

Figure 1 Shu-ilishu's Akkadian cylinder seal (showing Meluhhan sea-faring merchant) Source: de Clercq, Louis. *Collection de Clercq: Catalogue Méthodique et Raisonné: Antiquités Assyriennes, Cylindres Orientauz, Cachets, Briques, Bronzes, Bas-Reliefs, Etc.* Paris: E. Leroux, 1888. Shu ilishu is stated to be a translator of the Meluhhan language on this cylinder seal.
Figure 2 Ur seal (showing a person holding an antelope by its neck) urseal8Seal; BM 118704; U. 6020 (Gadd 1932: 9-10) PBA 18 (1932; pl. II, no.8)
Figure 3. Two tin ingots found in a shipwreck in Haifa.
Figure 4. Three incised hieroglyphs on the tin ingots (zoomed)
Figure 5. Seal m-1336a (Referenced in Parpola, *Corpus of Indus inscriptions*)
Figure 6. Text on seal m-1336a 2515 (Referenced in Mahadevan, *Indus Script*)
Figure 7 Seal m-1341 Referenced in Parpola, *Corpus of Indus inscriptions*)
Figure 8 Text of Seal m-1341 (Referenced in Mahadevan, *Indus Script*)
Figure 9 Two sides of tablet: m0516 (copper plate) (Referenced in Parpola, *Corpus of Indus inscriptions*)
Figure 10 Text of tablet m0516 (Referenced in Mahadevan, *Indus Script*)
Figure 11 Two sides of tablet m-0522 (copper plate) (Referenced in Parpola, *Corpus of Indus inscriptions*)
Figure 12 Text of tablet m-0522 3378 (Referenced in Mahadevan, *Indus Script*)
Figure 13. Signs 251, 252 (Referenced in Mahadevan, *Indus Script*)
Figure 13. Signs 251, 252. (Referenced in Mahadevan, *Indus Script*)
Figure 14. Sign 249 (Referenced in Mahadevan, *Indus Script*)
Figure 15 Sign 252 and variants (Referenced in Mahadevan, *Indus Script*)
Figure 16. Sign 184 (Referenced in Mahadevan, *Indus Script*)
Figure 17. Sign 182, 183, 184 and variants (Referenced in Mahadevan, *Indus Script*)

Figure 18 Sign 137, 142, 149 and variants (Referenced in Mahadevan, *Indus Script*)
Figure 19 A bull mating with a cow. Seal impression (BM 123059). From an antique dealer in Baghdad. (Cf. Gadd 1932: no. 18).
Figure 20 One side of a prism tablet m-0489. (Tablet from Mohenjodaro; Referenced in Parpola, *Corpus of Indus inscriptions*
Figure 21 Relief spinner. Louvre Museum collection Sb2834.jpg Web source: http://upload.wikimedia.org/wikipedia/commons/d/d5/Relief_spinner_Louvre_Sb2834.jpg
Figure 22 Seal impression showing female water-carrier Ur (Upenn; U.16747)); [Edith Porada, 1971, Remarks on seals found in the Gulf States. *Artibus Asiae* 33 (4): 331-7: pl.9, Figure 5]

Figure 22 Signs 12, 13, 14, 15 and 342 (Referenced in Mahadevan, *Indus Script*)
Figure 23: Composite bovid, ligatured components (the elements in the face shown on Seal m-304 is evidenced by zoomed-in pictorial motifs from other seals).Web resource: http://kaladarshan.arts.ohio-state.edu/Projects/Iconographic%20Discussions/harrapan%20seals/Harappan%20Seals.pdf)

Conclusions

A brief overview on the method of Indus Script decipherment. The cipher is rebus-metonymy layered Meluhha (mleccha speech). Signs and pictorials are hieroglyph multiplexes of Indian sprachbund of Bronze Age Ancient Near East. The language of the writing system is Prakritam. Indus Script Corpora surveyed as catalogus catalogorum of metalwork include c. 7000 inscriptions along the Maritime Tin Road from Hanoi, Vietnam to Haifa, Israel.

Meluhha people who created the Sheffield of Ancient Near East in Chanhu-daro, invented and used writing in the River Valleys of Sarasvati, Indus (Sindhu) rivers and Indo-Iran borderlands.

An ancient document Rigveda refers to these people as Bhāratam Janam who lived on the banks of Rivers Sarasvati and Sindhu. They mediated the maritime trade of tin from the Tin Belt of the world in Ancient Far East. Meluhha settlements are attested in cuneiform texts. A cylinder seal of Shu-ilishu points to an Akkadian translator needed to transact with the Meluhhan seafaring merchant. The discovery of two pure tin ingots in a shipwreck in Haifa points to the links with the Nahal Mishmar cire perdue artifacts.

The continuum of the writing system is evident on hundreds of hieroglyphs of the Indus Script which continue to signify metalwork on early punch-marked coins with Kharoṣṭhī and Brāhmī syllabic scripts used conjointly. Inscriptions signify metalwork catalogues on copper plates. Such inscriptions point to the possibility of printing such copper plates on tree-barks or other media for dissemination of artisans' messages.

The unique hypertext formats of Indus Script Corpora provide a framework for improved cyber security and advanced encryption systems with multi-layered hieroglyph multiplexes. Successful decipherment points to the need for re-evaluating the formation and evolution of Ancient Indian languages. Austro-asiatic, Indo-Aryan and Dravidian speakers seem to have formed an Indian sprachbund (speech union) during the early Bronze Age as evidenced by the many metalwork glosses present in all these language streams.

The presence of Sivalinga in Harappa and of over 80% of the archaeological settlements on the banks of Vedic River Sarasvati, the tradition of wearing sindhur (vermilion) at the parting of the hair by married women, celebration of marriages wearing turbinella pyrum (sankha, conch-shell) bangles, persons seated in penance yoga postures attest to the continuum of Sarasvati-Sindhu Civilization into the historical periods of ancient India. What Geoerge Coedes calls in his work Histoire ancienne des états hindouises d'Extrême Orient,1944 (English trs Hinduised States of Far East) is an attestation of the dharma-dhamma as the founding principles of state formation in India and in the Far East. Further researchers into the Maritime Tin Road from Hanoi, Vietnam exemplified by Dong Son Bronze Drums and the 3rd millennium BCE Bronze Age site of Bon Chiang will be significant contributions to archaeometallurgical studies to further evaluate the nature of the tin-bronze revolution achieved from 3rd millennium BCE.

The contours of the Indian sprachbund (speech union) have to be further outlined by comparative and historical studies in Indo-European linguistics and Chandas of Vedic times in relation to mleccha (meluhha) speech or vaak. The presence of ancu of Tocharian as a cognate of ams'u (synonym of Soma) in Rigveda points to the oral transmissions of knowledge systems and Vedic heritage across Eurasia. The narrative of Soma has not yet been fully told; it is clear that Soma is in nuce in the ancient human document, the Rigveda.

Peacock, pine cone, fish are Meluhha hieroglyphs. These hieroglyphs signify one category of life during Bronze Age: metalwork.

Pine cone and peacocks in bronze and fish are Meluhha hieroglyphs like Indus Script Cipher. They belong to kole.l 'smithy, temple' (Kota).

See: https://www.academia.edu/12804348/Two_bronze_peacocks_11_ft._high_bronze_pine_cone_at_Vatican_are_Meluhha_hieroglyphs_metalwork_catalogues._Archaemetallurgical_analyses_by_Vatican_suggested

What is described as a "pinecone" at the small museum at Arbeia (South Shields, near Newcastle-upon-Tyne, U.K.), which was

found in Romano-British context.
https://aediculaantinoi.wordpress.com/2012/04/06/megalensia-the-third-day/

See: http://bharatkalyan97.blogspot.in/2015/05/rigveda-soma-not-herb-not-drink-but.html A tree associated with smelter and linga from Bhuteshwar, Mathura Museum. Architectural fragment with relief showing winged dwarfs (or gaNa) worshipping with flower garlands, Siva Linga. Bhuteshwar, ca. 2nd cent BCE. Lingam is on a platform with wall under a pipal tree encircled by railing. (Srivastava, AK, 1999, Catalogue of Saiva sculptures in Government Museum, Mathura: 47, GMM 52.3625) The tree is a phonetic determinant of the smelter indicated by the railing around the linga: **kuṭa**, *°ṭi* -- , *°ṭha* -- 3, *°ṭhi* -- m. ' tree ' Rebus: *kuṭhi* 'smelter'. ***kuṭa,*** *°ṭi* -- , *°ṭha* -- 3, *°ṭhi* -- m. ' tree ' lex., *°ṭaka* -- m. ' a kind of tree ' Kauś.Pk. *kuḍa* -- m. ' tree '; Paš. lauṛ. *kuṛā'* ' tree ', dar. *kaṛék* ' **tree**, oak ' ~ Par. *kōṛ* ' stick ' IIFL iii 3, 98. (CDIAL 3228). See:
http://bharatkalyan97.blogspot.in/2015/05/worship-of-siva-linga-is-cultural-bond.html

This museum artifact is comparable to the monumental 6 ft. tall inscribed stone linga discovered in Candi Sukuh as the sacred, venerated pillar of light, described in Atharva Veda Stambha Sukta.

Candi Cetho. Lingga shows a pair of balls at the top of the penis -- to be read rebus as Meluhha hieroglyph composition: lo-khaNDa, penis + 4 balls; Rebus: iron, metalware. The four balls of the penis are also clearly shown on a 6 ft. tall linga inscribed with 1. a sword; and 2. inscription in Javanese, referring to 'inauguration of the holy ganggasudhi...'

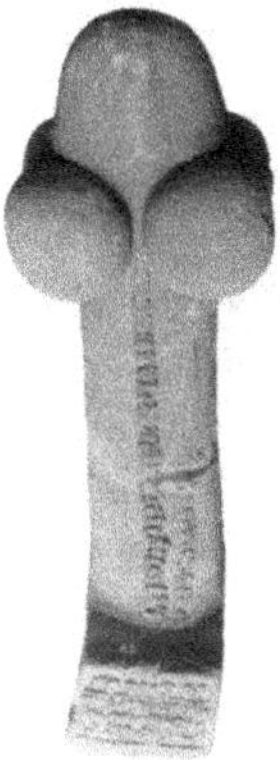

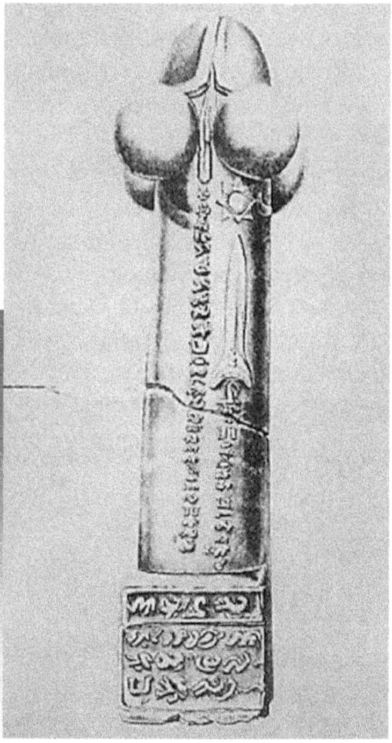

See: http://bharatkalyan97.blogspot.in/2015/01/sekkizhar-periya-puranam-candi-sukuh.html Histoire ancienne des Etats hindouises along the Tin Road from Haifa to Hanoi. NaMo, Obama, announce United Indian Ocean States.

lo 'penis' Rebus: loh 'copper, metal'

Hieroglyphs: gaṇḍa 'swelling' gaṇḍa 'four' gaṇḍa 'sword'
Rebus: kāṇḍa 'tools, pots and pans and metal-ware' (Marathi)

Together, hieroglyphs: lo + gaṇḍa. Rebus: लोखंड [lōkhaṇḍa] 'metalwork'

Metaphor: Sh. K.ḍoḍ. *lō* m. ' light, dawn '; L. awāṇ. *lō* ' light '; P. *lo* f. ' light, dawn, power of seeing, consideration '; WPah. bhal. ***lo*** f. ' light (e.g. of moon) '.(CDIAL 11120). + *kaṇṭa* 'manliness'. Metaphorical rendering of the effulgence (sun and moon) associated with the pillar of light yielding the imagery of an representation of a fiery pillar with unfathomable beginning, unreachable end, thus of infniity of Mahadeva representing the paramaatman for the aatman in search of nihs'reyas (moksha), from Being to Becoming, the way earth and stones transmute into metal in the smelter and smithy, kole.l 'smithy, temple'.

Bharatiyo, 'metalcasters' (Gujarati) are awestruck by this parallel with the cosmic energy replicated in the energies of the smelter, fire-altar and smithy. Hence, the veneration of the linga + 4 spheres as the essence of every phenomenon on cosmos, on the globe, of the world. These hieroglyphs and related metaphors thus yield the gestalt of Bharatiyo, 'metalcasters' (Meluhha). This enduring metaphor finds expression in sculptures on many Hindu temples of Eurasia.

The gloss *gaṇḍu* 'manliness' (Kannada); 'bravery, strength' (Telugu) is a synonym of the expression on Candi Suku linga inscription: 'sign of masculinity is the essence of the world'. Thus, the gloss *lokhaṇḍa* which is a direct Meluhha speech form related to the hieroglyph composition on Candi Suku inscription is the sign of masculinity. The rebus renderings of khandoba or kandariya mahadeva are elucidations of the rebus gloss: *kaṇḍa, 'mahadeva S'iva or mahes'vara.'* The hieroglyphs deployed on the 1.82m. tall stone sculpture of linga with the inscription and hieroglyphs of sword, sun, moon and four balls deployed just below the tip of the phallus are thus explained as Meluhha speech: *lokhaṇḍa*. The rebus rendering of the phrase is: *lo* 'light' and *kaṇṭa* 'manliness'. These attributes constitute the effulgence of the linga as the fiery pillar, *skhamba* venerated in Atharva Veda Skhamba sukta as the cosmic effulgence as the cosmic essence.

gaṇḍa -- m. ' four' (Munda) गंडा[gaṇḍā] m An aggregate of four (cowries or pice). (Marathi) <ganDa>(P) {NUM} ``^four''. Syn. <cari>(LS4), <hunja-mi>(D). *Sa., Mu.<ganDa> `id.', H.<gA~Da> `a group of four cowries'. %10591. #10511.<ganDa-mi>(KM) {NUM} ``^four''. |<-mi> `one'. %10600. #10520. Ju<ganDa>(P) {NUM} ``^four''. gaṇḍaka m. ' a coin worth four cowries ' lex., ' method of counting by fours '

W. [← Mu. Przyluski RoczOrj iv 234]S. gaṇḍho m. ' four in counting '; P. gaṇḍā m. ' four cowries '; B. Or. H. gaṇḍā m. ' a group of four, four cowries '; M. gaṇḍā m. ' aggregate of four cowries or pice '.(CDIAL 4001)

gaṇḍa -- m. 'swelling, boil, abscess'(Pali)

Rebus: kaṇḍ 'fire-altar' (Santali) kāṇḍa 'tools, pots and pans and metal-ware' (Marathi) खंडा [khaṇḍā] m A sort of sword. It is straight and twoedged. खांडा [khāṇḍā] m A kind of sword, straight, broad-bladed, two-edged, and round-ended.खांडाईत [khāṇḍāīta] a Armed with the sword called खांडा. (Marathi)

लोखंड [lōkhaṇḍa] n (लोह S) Iron.लोखंडकाम [lōkhaṇḍakāma] n Iron work; that portion (of a building, machine &c.) which consists of iron. 2 The business of an ironsmith. लोखंडी [lōkhaṇḍī] a (लोखंड) Composed of iron; relating to iron.

http://bharatkalyan97.blogspot.in/2015/01/significance-of-linga-and-4-spheres-on.html

``^penis":So. *laj*(R) - *lij* - *la'a'j* - *laJ*/ *laj* - *kaD* `penis'.

Sa. *li'j* `penis, esp. of small boys'.
Sa. *lO'j* `penis'.Mu. *lOe'j* ~ *lOGgE'j* `penis'. ! *lO'j*Ho *loe* `penis'Ku. *la:j* `penis'.
@(C289) ``^penis":Sa. *lOj* `penis'.Mu. *lOj* `penis'.KW *lOj*@(M084) (Munda etyma)

Rebus: lo 'copper' **lōhá** ' red, copper -- coloured ' ŚrS., ' made of copper ' ŚBr., m.n. ' **copper** ' VS., MBh. [*rudh --] Pa. *lōha* -- m. ' metal, esp. copper or bronze '; Pk. *lōha* -- m. ' iron ', Gy. pal. *li°*, *lihi*, obl. *elhás*, as. *loa* JGLS new ser. ii 258; Wg. (Lumsden) "*loa*" ' steel '; Kho. *loh* ' copper '; S. *lohu* m. ' iron ', L. *lohā* m., awāṇ. *lō`ā*, P. *lohā* m. (→ K.rām. ḍoḍ. *lohā*), WPah.bhad. *lɔ̃un*., bhal. *lòtilde;* n., pāḍ. jaun. *lōh*, paṅ. *luhā*, cur. cam. *lohā*, Ku. *luwā*, N. *lohu*, *°hā*, A. *lo*, B. *lo*, *no*, Or. *lohā*, *luhā*, Mth. *loh*, Bhoj. *lohā*, Aw.lakh. *lōh*, H. *loh*, *lohā* m., G. M. *loh* n.; Si. *loho*, *lō* ' metal, ore, iron '; Md. *ratu* -- *lō* ' copper '. WPah.kṭg. (kc.) *lóɔ* ' iron ', J. *lohā* m., Garh. *loho*; Md. *lō* ' metal '.(CDIAL 11158)
http://bharatkalyan97.blogspot.in/2015/01/meluhha-hieroglyphs-and-candi-sukuh.html

Hieroglyph: kanda m. bulbous root (Samskritam) Ash. piċ-- kandə ' pine ' Rebus:lo-khāṇḍa 'tools, pots and pans, **metal**-ware'. लोखंड [**lōkhaṇḍa**] 'metalwork' Rebus: loh 'copper, iron, **metal**' (Indian sprachbund, **Meluhha**).

Hieroglyphs of a spinner bas-relief fragment from Susa dated to 8th cent. BCE (now in Louvre Museum) are identified. The Elamite lady spinner bas-relief is a composition of hieroglyphs depicting a guild of wheelwrights or 'smithy of nations' (harosheth hagoyim). The hieroglyphs are read rebus using lexemes of Indian sprachbund given the archeological evidence of Meluhha settlers in Susa.

Figure1. Susa spinner bas-relief fragment. Source:
http://fr.wikipedia.org/wiki/Fichier:Relief_spinner_Louvre_Sb2834.jpg
http://www.louvre.fr/en/oeuvre-notices/spinner

H. 9 cm. W. 13 cm. Bituminous stone, a matte, black sedimentary rock. With her arms full of bracelets, the spinner holding a spindle is seated on a stool with tiger-paw legs. Elegantly coiffed, her hair is pulled back in a bun and held in place with a headscarf crossed around her head. Behind the spinner is an attendant holding a square wickerwork(?) fan. In front is a table with tiger-paw legs, a fish with six bun ingots. Susa. Neo-elamite period. 8th to 6th century BCE. The bas-relief was first cited in J, de Morgan's Memoires de la Delegation en Perse, 1900, vol. i. plate xi Ernest Leroux. Paris. Current location: Louvre Museum Sb2834 Near Eastern antiquities, Richelieu, ground floor, room 11.

The fish on a stool in front of the spinner with head-wrap can be read rebus for key hieroglyphs:

khuṭo 'leg, foot'. khũṭ 'community, guild' (Santali)
kāti 'spinner' rebus: 'wheelwright.'
vēṭha'head-wrap'. Rebus: veṭa , veṭha, veṇṭhe 'a small territorial unit'.
sãi kol ayas kāṇḍa baṭa 'friend+tiger+fish+stool+six' rebus: association (of) iron-workers' metal stone ore kiln.

The Elamite lady spinner bas-relief is a composition of hieroglyphs depicting a guild of wheelwrights or 'smithy of nations' (harosheth hagoyim).

1. Six bun ingots. bhaṭa 'six' (Gujarati). Rebus: bhaṭa 'furnace' (Gujarati.Santali)
2. ayo 'fish' (Munda). Rebus: ayas 'metal' (Sanskrit) aya 'metal' (Gujarati)
3. kātī 'spinner' (G.) kātī 'woman who spins thread' (Hindi). Rebus: khātī 'wheelwright'

(Hindi). kāṭi = fireplace in the form of a long ditch (Ta.Skt.Vedic) kāṭya = being in a hole (VS. XVI.37); kāṭ a hole, depth (RV. i. 106.6) khāḍ a ditch, a trench; khāḍ o khaiyo several pits and ditches (G.) khaṇḍrun: 'pit (furnace)' (Santali) kaḍaio 'turner' (Gujarati)
4. kola 'woman' (Nahali). Rebus: kolami 'smithy' (Te.)
5. Tiger's paws. kola 'tiger' (Telugu); kola 'tiger, jackal' (Kon.). Rebus: kol 'working in iron' (Tamil) Glyph: 'hoof': Kumaon. khuṭo 'leg, foot', °ṭī 'goat's leg'; Nepalese. khuṭo 'leg, foot'(CDIAL 3894). S. khuṛī f. 'heel'; WPah. paṅ. khūṛ 'foot'. (CDIAL 3906). Rebus: khũṭ 'community, guild' (Santali)
6. Kur. kaṇḍō a stool. Malt. kanḍo stool, seat. (DEDR 1179) Rebus: kaṇḍ 'fire-altar, furnace' (Santali) kāṇḍa 'stone ore'.
7. meḍhi, miḍhī, meṇḍhī = a plait in a woman's hair; a plaited or twisted strand of hair (P.) Rebus: meḍ 'iron' (Ho.)
8. 'scarf' glyph: dhaṭu m. (also dhaṭhu) m. 'scarf' (Wpah.) (CDIAL 6707) Rebus: dhatu 'minerals' (Santali)
9. Glyph 'friend': Assamese. xaï 'friend', xaiyā 'partner in a game'; Sinhala. saha 'friend' (< nom. sákhā or < sahāya -- ?). sákhi (nom. sg. sákhā) m. 'friend' RigVeda. 2. sakhī -- f. 'woman's confidante' (Sanskrit), 'a mistress' VarBrS. 1. Pali. sakhā nom. sg. m. 'friend', Prakrit. sahi -- m.; Nepalese. saiyā̃ 'lover, paramour, friend' (or < svāmín --); 2. Pali. sakhī -- , sakhikā -- f. 'woman's female friend', Prakrit. sahī -- , °hiā -- f., Bengali. sai, Oriya. sahi, saï, Hindi. poet. saïyo f., Gujarati. saï f., Marathi. say, saī f. -- Ext. -- ḍ -- : OldMarwari. sahalaṛī f. 'woman's female friend'; -- -- r -- : Gujarati. sahiyar, saiyar f.; -- -- ll -- (cf. sakhila --): Sindhi. Lahnda. Punjabi. sahelī f. woman's female friend', N. saheli, B. saylā, OAw. sahelī f.; H. sahelī f. ' id., maidservant, concubine'; OldMarwari. sahalī, sahelī 'woman's female friend', OldGujarati. sahīlī f., Marathi. sahelī f. (CDIAL 13074). Apabhramśa. sāhi 'master'-- m.; Gypsy. pal. saúi ' owner, master ', Sindhi. sā̃ī˜ m., Lahnda. sā̃i, mult. (as term of address) sā̃i; Punjabi. sāī˜, sāīyā̃ m. 'master, husband'; Nepalese. saiyā̃ 'lover, paramour, friend' (or < sákhi --); Bengali. sā̃i 'master', (used by boys in play) cā̃i; Oriya. sāī̃ 'lord, king, deity'; Maithili. (ETirhut) saī̃ẽ 'husband (among lower classes)', (SBhagalpur) sā̃ī 'husband (as addressed by wife)'; Bhojpuri. sāī˜ 'God'; OldAwadhi. sāīṁ m. 'lord, master , lakh. sāī 'saint'; Hindi. sā̃ī m. 'master, husband, God, religious mendicant'; Gujarti. sā̃ī m. 'faqir', sā̃ 'term of respectful address'; Marathi. sāī 'title of respect, term of address'; Sinhala. sāmi -- yā, hä° 'husband', himi -- yā 'master, owner, husband' (Perh. in Marathi. -- s affix to names of relationship (see śrī -- Add.). WPahari.poet. saī̃ m. (obl. saī̃) ' friend, lover, paramour '. (CDIAL 13930). Rebus: 'association': Oriya. sāhi, sāi ' part of town inhabited by people of one caste or tribe '; sākhiya (metr.), sākhyá -- n. ' association, party ' RigVeda., 'friendship' Mahāv. [sákhi] Pa. sakhya -- n. ' friendship ' (< sākhyá -- ? -- acc. sg. n. sakkhi and sakkhī -- f. from doublet sakhyaṁ ~ *sākhiya: cf. type sāmagrī -- ~ sāmagrya --) (CDIAL 13323). 10. Glyph: 'head-wrap': veṭha [fr. viṣṭ, veṣṭ] wrap, in sīsa° head-- wrap, turban M i.244; S iv.56. (Pali) Prakrit. veṭṭhaṇa -- n. 'wrapping', °aga -- n. 'turban' (CDIAL 12131). vēṣṭá m. 'band, noose' 'enclosure' (Sanskrit), °aka- m. 'fence', n. 'turban' lex. [√vēṣṭ] Marathi.

veṭh, vēṭh, veṭ, vēṭ m.f. 'roll, turn of a rope'; Sinhala. veṭya 'enclosure'; -- Pali. sīsa -- vēṭha -- m. 'head -- wrap',vēṭhaka -- 'surrounding'; Prakrit. vēḍha -- m. 'wrap'; Sindhi. veṛhu m. 'encircling'(CDIAL 12130). Rebus: 'territorial unit': veṭa , veṭha, veṇṭhe 'a small territorial unit' (Ka.IE8-4) (Pali) Assamese. Beran 'act of surrounding'; Oriya. beṛhaṇa, °ṇi 'girth, circumference, fencing, small cloth worn by woman'. (CDIAL 12131). Pushto: باړه bāraʻh, s.f. (3rd) 'A fortification, defence, rampart, a ditch, palisade, an entrenchment, a breastwork'. Pl. ې ey. (Pushto). Prakrit. vēḍha -- m. 'wrap'; S. veṛhu m. 'encircling'; Lahnda. veṛh, vehṛ m. 'fencing, enclosure in jungle with a hedge, (Ju.) blockade', veṛhā,vehṛā m. 'courtyard, (Ju.) enclosure containing many houses'; Punjabi. veṛhā, be° m. 'enclosure, courtyard'; Kumaon. beṛo 'circle or band (of people)' WesternPahari.kṭg. beṛɔ m. palace', Assamese. also berā ' fence, enclosure ' (CDIAL 12130). Hindi. beṛhnā ' to enclose, surround '; Marathi. veḍhṇẽ 'to twist, surround'; (CDIAL 12132). kharoṣṭhī 'blacksmith lip, carving' and harosheth 'smithy' kharoṣṭī the name of a script in ancient India from ca. 5th century BCE is a term cognate with harosheth hagoyim of the Old Bible. kharoṣṭhī (khar + oṣṭa 'blacksmith + lip' or khar + uṣṭa – 'blacksmith' + 'settled') is a syllabic writing system of the region where Indian hieroglyphs were used as evidenced by Indus Script corpora. The word –goy- in hagoyim is cognate with goy 'gotra, clan' (Prakrit). (Details in S. Kalyanaraman, 2012, Indian Hieroglyphs). gōtrá n. ' cowpen, enclosure ' RigVeda., ' family, clan '1. Pali. gotta -- n. ' clan ', Prakrit. gotta -- , gutta -- , amg. gōya -- n.(CDIAL 4279).

http://tinyurl.com/79nm28f Etymology of harosheth is variously elucidated, while it is linked to 'chariot-making in a smithy of nations'.

http://en.wikipedia.org/wiki/Harosheth_Haggoyim.

Harosheth Hebrew: הגויים חרושת; is pronounced khar-o-sheth? Most likely, (haroshet) a noun meaning a carving. Hence, kharoṣṭhī came to represent a 'carving, engraving' art, i.e. a writing system. Harosheth-hagoyim See: Haroshet [Carving]; a forest; agriculture; workmanship; harsha [Artifice: deviser: secret work]; workmanship; a wood http://tinyurl.com/d7be2qh Cognate with haroshet: karṣá m. ' dragging ' Pāṇ., ' agriculture ' Āp.(CDIAL 2905). karṣaṇa n. ' tugging, ploughing, hurting ' Manu (Sanskrit), ' cultivated land ' MBh. [kárṣati, √kṛṣ] Prakrit. karisaṇa -- n. ' pulling, ploughing '; Gujarati. karsaṇ n. ' cultivation, ploughing '; OldGujarati. karasaṇī m. ' cultivator ', Gujarati. karasṇī m. -- See *kṛṣaṇa -- .(CDIAL 2907). Harosheth-hagoyim is the home of general Sisera, who was killed by Jael during the war of Naphtali and Zebulun against Jabin, king of Hazor in Canaan (Judges 4:2). The lead players of this war are the general Barak and the judge Deborah. The name Harosheth-hagoyim obviously consists of two parts. The first part is derived from the root , which HAW Theological Wordbook of the Old Testament treats as four separate roots (harash I, II, III, & IV). The verb (harash I) means to engrave or plough. HAW Theological Wordbook of the Old Testament reads, "The basic idea is cutting into some material, e.g. engraving metal or plowing soil." Derivatives of this verb are: (harash), meaning engraver; (haroshet) a noun meaning a carving. This word is equal to the first part of the name Harosheth-hagoyim; (harish), meaning plowing or plowing time; (maharesha) meaning ploughshare; (harishi), a word which is only used in Jona 4:8 to indicate a certain characteristic of the sun - vehement (King James) or scorching (NIV). The verb (harash II) most commonly denotes refraining from speech or response, either because one is deaf or mute, or because one doesn't want to respond. None of the sources indicates a relation with the previous root, and perhaps there is none, but on the other hand, perhaps deafness was regarded in Biblical as either being marked or else cut or cut off. The noun (horesh) from root (hrsh III) occurs only in Isaiah 17:9 and has to do with a wood or forest. The noun (heresh) from root (hrsh IV) occurs only in Isaiah 3:3 and probably means magical art or expert enchanter, or something along those lines. The second part of the name, hagoyim, comes from the definite article (ha plus the common word (goy) meaning nation, people, gentile. This word comes from the assumed root (gwh), which is not translated but which seems to denote things that are surpassed or left behind. Other derivatives are: (gaw a and gew), meaning back, as in "cast behind the back," i.e. put out of mind (1 Kings 14:9, Nehemiah 9:26, Isaiah 38:17); (gewiya), meaning body, either dead or alive (Genesis 47:18, Judges 14:8, Daniel 10:6). The meaning of the name Harosheth-hagoyim can be found as any combination of the above. NOBS Study Bible Name List reads Carving Of The Nations, but equally valid would be Silence Of The Gentiles or Engraving Of What's Abandoned. Jones' Dictionary of Old Testament Proper Names reads Manufactory for Harosheth and "of the Gentiles" for Hagoyim. http://www.abarim-publications.com/Meaning/Harosheth.html Judges 4:13 And Sisera gathered together all his chariots, even nine hundred chariots of iron, and all the people that were with him, from Harosheth-goiim, unto the brook Kishon. Variant: harosheth hagoyim 'smithy of nations'. Cognate with kharoṣṭhī goy, 'blacksmith's lip clan' खरोष्टी kharōṣṭī , 'A kind of alphabet; Lv.1.29'. Often, there is an alternative (perhaps, erroneous) transliteration as kharōṣṭhī. The compound is composed of: khar + ōṣṭī (or, उष्ट mfn. 'burnt' (CDIAL 2386); uṣṭa -- 'settled' (Sanskrit) (CDIAL 2385) ṓṣṭha m. ' lip ' RigVeda. Pali. oṭṭha -- m., Prakrit. oṭṭha -- , uṭ°, hoṭṭha -- , huṭ° m., Gypsy. pal. ōšt, eur. vušt m.; Kashmiri. wuṭh, dat. °ṭhas m. 'lip'; Lahnda. hoṭh m., Punjabi. hoṭh, hõṭh m., WesternPahari. bhal. oṭh m., jaun. hōṭh, Kumaon. ū̃ṭh, gng. ōṭh, Nepalese. oṭh, Assamese. ō̃ṭh, MiddleBengali. Oriya. oṭha, Maithili. Bhojpuri. oṭh, Awadhi. lakh. ō̃ṭh, hō̃ṭh, Hindi. oṭh, õṭh, hoṭh, hõṭhm., Gujarati. oṭh, hoṭh m., Marathi. oṭh, õṭh, hoṭ m., Sinhala. oṭa.WesternPahari.poet. oṭhḷu m. 'lip', hoṭṛu, kṭg. hóṭṭh, kc. ōṭh, Garhwali. hoṭh, hō̃ṭ. (CDIAL 2563). utaṭu 'lip' (Tamil). In the context of use of the term kharōṣṭī for a writing system, it is apposite to interpret the compound as composed of khar + ōṣṭī 'blacksmith + lip'. "The Kharoṣṭhī scrolls, the oldest collection of Buddhist manuscripts in the world, are radiocarbon-dated by the Australian Nuclear Science and Technology Organisation (ANSTO). The group confirms the initial dating of the Senior manuscripts to 130-250 CE and the Schøyen manuscripts

to between the 1st and 5th centuries CE."
http://en.wikipedia.org/wiki/2006_in_archaeology "The Kharoṣṭhī script is an ancient Indic script used by the Gandhara culture of ancient Northwest South Asia(primarily modern-day Afghanistan and Pakistan) to write the Gāndhārī language (a dialect of Prakrit) and the Sanskrit language. An abugida (or "alphasyllabary"), it was in use from the middle of the 3rd century BCE until it died out in its homeland around the 3rd century CE. It was also in use in Kushan, Sogdiana (see Issyk kurgan) and along the Silk Road where there is some evidence it may have survived until the 7th century in the remote way stations of Khotan and Niya...As preserved in Sanskrit documents the alphabet runs: a ra pa ca na la da ba ḍa ṣa va ta ya ṣṭa ka sa ma ga stha ja śva dha śa kha kṣa sta jñā rtha (or ha) bha cha sma hva tsa gha ṭha ṇa pha ska ysa śca ṭa ḍha ..."
http://en.wikipedia.org/wiki/Kharosthi

The bas-relief fragment of Susa contains hieroglyphs which are read from the lexemes of Indian sprachbund. The message is that the speakers are a guild of iron (metal, kol) stone ore (ayaskāṇḍa) workers belonging to the clan (association, saī) of wheelwrights (kātī). The glosses are of mleccha (meluhha), confirming the Indian hieroglyphic tradition evidenced by Indus script corpora. The Susa bas-relief fragment was written in an area which also used cuneiform syllabic script just as Indus script hieroglyphs continued to be used together with kharoṣṭhī syllabic script from ca. 5th cent. BCE in the Indus script corpora area. Apparently, cuneiform was used to denote syllables of names, while the hieroglyphs denoted the professions and artisanal competence or repertoire of metal and mineral resources used using glosses from Indian sprachbund. It is likely that most of the animals such as antelopes, on cylinder seals of the interaction area (Mesopotamia, in particular) were not mere artistic devices but were hieroglyphs representing professions and descriptive attributes of metalwork catalogues.

The decipherment of Indus Script reinforces the essential semantic unity of all ancient languages of India and the common cultural thread of dharma-dhamma which runs through the historical narratives of Bhāratam Janam.

agate, 184, 186, 192
Akkadian, 45, 79, 118, 127, 153, 194, 229, 253, 254, 255, 257, 270
alligator, 26, 42, 93, 248
allograph, 20, 62
alloy, 28, 30, 31, 32, 33, 38, 56, 58, 69, 76, 78, 92, 94, 96, 98, 110, 119, 120, 127, 133, 138, 141, 151, 161, 167, 168, 172, 175, 182, 211, 212, 222, 242, 248
alloying, 135, 175
Amri, 215
angle, 7, 36, 115, 120, 246
antelope, 22, 23, 24, 42, 43, 44, 47, 84, 92, 114, 123, 133, 134, 154, 163, 207, 225, 226, 251, 253, 258, 259, 260, 261
Arabia, 252
Arabian Gulf, 254
archer, 35, 80, 91, 123
arrow, 7, 19, 21, 39, 40, 54, 68, 69, 70, 91, 109, 173, 179, 181, 246, 248
arsenic, 255
artifact, 95, 97, 110, 153, 169, 272
artifacts, 51, 108, 125, 135, 159, 164, 168, 169, 170, 171, 270
artisan, 24, 62, 69, 72, 114, 115, 118, 136, 148, 167, 169, 243, 245
artisan guild, 148
artisan guilds, 148
awl, 116, 181
axe, 9, 10, 23, 41, 47, 52, 165, 173, 177, 180, 198, 199, 209, 217
ayas, 16, 17, 21, 28, 30, 32, 33, 34, 37, 41, 42, 58, 60, 70, 85, 92, 96, 151, 221, 245, 248
ayo, 41, 42, 69, 151, 245, 246
backbone, 8, 30, 32, 58, 68, 76, 225
Bahrain, 251, 252, 254, 268
Banawali, 40, 44, 48
bangle, 175, 182, 229
baran, 30, 58, 76
bat, 15, 127, 248
bead, 37, 60, 61, 172, 184, 186, 187, 194, 226, 227
beads, 10, 54, 61, 62, 118, 128, 135, 171, 172, 184, 185, 186, 187, 193, 216, 218, 226, 227, 229
bed, 263
bell-metal, 110, 140
belt, 252
Bha_rata, 256
bha_s.a_, 256
Bhirrana, 127, 128
bird, 37, 55, 56
Bisht, 40, 117, 234
bison, 16, 22, 23, 26, 27, 62, 66, 102, 109, 149, 236, 247
blacksmith, 26, 28, 29, 33, 44, 61, 62, 72, 74, 75, 86, 87, 91, 93, 94, 95, 97, 104, 105, 107, 109, 110, 111, 115, 121, 127, 133, 150, 168, 226, 227, 228, 232, 248
boar, 68, 134, 173, 224
boat, 20, 56, 64, 82, 97, 215, 218, 233
body, 8, 27, 30, 31, 32, 37, 38, 52, 54, 63, 64, 78, 79, 96, 98, 101, 102, 103, 104, 106, 109, 119, 122, 124, 128, 133, 200, 204, 214, 225, 228, 237, 240, 241, 243, 245
bos gaurus, 69, 171
bos indicus, 73, 95, 97, 109, 113, 133
bovine, 7, 25, 27, 109
bracelet, 184, 185

branch, 25, 64, 89, 92, 95, 98, 110, 121, 127, 160, 165, 231, 232
brass, 16, 28, 31, 36, 79, 91, 100, 110, 121, 133, 141, 212, 228, 241, 264
bronze, 9, 40, 47, 51, 52, 62, 79, 87, 118, 119, 127, 128, 134, 136, 141, 150, 151, 172, 173, 175, 180, 181, 182, 187, 199, 201, 203, 206, 207, 209, 212, 215, 220, 222, 233, 234, 240, 241, 243, 252, 255, 257, 258, 263, 266, 271, 275
buffalo, 25, 26, 27, 69, 90, 91, 149, 247, 248
bull, 16, 22, 23, 24, 26, 27, 40, 55, 56, 57, 58, 59, 60, 61, 65, 66, 69, 70, 74, 75, 84, 92, 94, 104, 109, 114, 120, 128, 132, 133, 136, 138, 149, 155, 208, 235, 237, 238, 239, 240, 243, 247, 248, 249, 261, 269
bullcalf, 40, 56, 65, 104, 136, 249
Campbell, 100
canal, 100, 113
caravan, 258
carnelian, 172, 185, 186, 187, 192, 229, 255
carpenter, 54, 68, 215, 232, 254
cast, 9, 17, 21, 28, 29, 30, 31, 32, 33, 36, 38, 39, 56, 57, 58, 62, 69, 70, 72, 76, 77, 92, 96, 98, 100, 104, 115, 116, 121, 136, 137, 141, 157, 159, 162, 171, 174, 179, 184, 185, 201, 209, 227, 228, 240
casting, 42, 62, 70, 72, 74, 83, 133, 135, 140, 142, 172, 173, 174, 217, 250
chalcedony, 186, 192
Chanhujo-daro, 247
chert, 254
cipher, 1, 3, 108, 157, 159, 169, 171, 225, 248, 270
circumgraph, 21, 22
cire perdue, 74, 83, 135, 159, 170, 270
citadel, 40, 115, 116, 117, 118, 234
city, 253, 254, 257
cloth, 254
comb, 52, 87, 240, 241, 243, 250
community, 68, 75, 94, 133, 134, 135, 169
composite animal, 95, 97, 103, 108, 109, 110, 113, 133
conch, 91, 270
copper, 251, 252, 253, 254, 255, 257, 258, 259, 260, 264, 267
copper tablet, 25, 26, 27, 39, 40, 225, 229, 231, 236
coppersmith, 62, 219, 242
copulation, 240
corner, 21, 32, 36, 37, 38, 57, 58, 67, 115, 138, 171, 202, 246
cotton, 254
crab, 9, 37, 38, 60, 76, 115
crocodile, 22, 93, 133, 140
cubical, 254
cuneiform, 254, 255
Cunningham, 158, 170
currycomb, 21, 38, 47, 76, 240
curved, 29, 57, 81, 123, 124, 173
cylinder seal, 253
cypher, 54, 116, 118
dagger, 10, 124, 173, 200
daggers, 9, 10, 173, 174, 179, 203, 209
dance, 123, 126, 127
decoded, 95, 97, 109, 110, 148
deer, 43, 128

Dholavira, 114, 116, 117, 118, 229, 234, 262
Dilmun, 251, 252, 254, 255, 268
dotted circle, 8, 41, 52, 61, 134, 137, 205, 226, 227, 228, 248, 250, 253
Dravidian, 255, 266
drill, 61, 174
drummer, 28
Egypt, 252, 257
Egyptian, 17, 19, 116, 173
engraver, 62, 115, 175
epigraph, 52
eraka, 16, 24, 30, 33, 36, 37, 39, 52, 70, 99, 115, 116, 140, 157, 159, 161, 171
Failaka, 134
ficus religiosa, 31, 36, 74, 94, 96, 98, 116, 225
field symbol, 11, 15, 17, 18, 21, 24, 26, 33
fish, 15, 16, 19, 20, 21, 24, 26, 28, 30, 32, 33, 34, 37, 39, 40, 41, 42, 58, 60, 69, 70, 77, 91, 92, 93, 96, 109, 116, 128, 140, 151, 155, 160, 161, 174, 181, 215, 218, 245, 246, 248, 249, 263, 271
fishes, 25, 33
forge, 8, 10, 20, 21, 26, 28, 30, 31, 32, 34, 36, 37, 38, 39, 43, 44, 47, 56, 57, 58, 59, 60, 62, 67, 68, 69, 70, 76, 78, 86, 87, 90, 95, 97, 104, 110, 120, 136, 138, 150, 160, 205, 224, 225, 228, 248, 249
frog, 8, 35, 82, 99
gimlet, 136
gloss, 52, 73, 74, 75, 77, 79, 80, 93, 95, 97, 105, 107, 111, 159, 171, 274
glosses, 73, 74, 79, 80, 93, 159, 169, 171, 243, 270
glyph, 47, 51, 52, 62, 72, 91, 94, 95, 96, 97, 108, 109, 110, 127, 133, 140, 149, 205, 229, 241, 245, 246
glyptic, 114
goat, 25, 44, 45, 82, 96, 98, 106, 123, 124, 133, 137, 160, 253
goats, 44, 96, 98, 202, 207, 239
goblet, 199
gold, 10, 16, 54, 60, 63, 72, 77, 80, 91, 96, 98, 135, 142, 172, 173, 174, 175, 181, 184, 185, 186, 187, 189, 199, 209, 211, 214, 216, 218, 221, 227, 229, 233, 246, 249, 251, 252, 254, 255, 264
grapheme, 19, 27, 28
guild, 20, 57, 68, 72, 94, 96, 122, 132, 133, 134, 136, 169, 243, 245, 249
Gujarat, 254
Haifa, 47, 114, 141, 270, 274
harrow, 29, 32, 34, 37, 38, 39, 63, 205, 241, 245
hearth, 263
heifer, 62, 110, 133, 136, 245
Heras, 26, 223, 236
hieroglyph, 3, 17, 23, 24, 30, 32, 33, 39, 41, 43, 45, 49, 52, 56, 68, 70, 74, 76, 77, 78, 93, 95, 97, 100, 102, 104, 108, 111, 114, 116, 127, 150, 155, 160, 163, 164, 169, 225, 227, 228, 241, 270, 273, 274
hieroglyphic, 19, 50, 159, 171, 229, 238
hill, 18, 29, 123, 165
homophone, 17
horn, 15, 61, 62, 64, 76, 81, 91, 94, 95, 96, 98, 110, 123, 124, 127, 153, 174, 244, 245, 246

horns, 7, 23, 25, 26, 27, 42, 64, 81, 90, 95, 97, 101, 102, 103, 106, 109, 110, 124, 128, 157, 202, 236
Hunter, 19, 80
ibex, 236
incised, 257, 258
ingot, 59, 60, 78, 87, 94, 95, 98, 100, 105, 107, 108, 121, 159, 162, 163, 169, 227, 258
inscription, 254, 258
intercourse, 239, 247
inventory, 135
iron, 8, 9, 16, 17, 21, 24, 26, 28, 30, 31, 32, 33, 34, 35, 36, 37, 38, 39, 40, 41, 42, 44, 56, 57, 58, 60, 61, 62, 63, 67, 69, 70, 72, 73, 74, 75, 76, 77, 78, 79, 80, 84, 85, 86, 87, 91, 92, 93, 94, 95, 96, 97, 100, 104, 105, 107, 109, 110, 111, 118, 120, 121, 126, 127, 133, 134, 138, 140, 142, 147, 148, 149, 150, 151, 156, 160, 162, 163, 166, 167, 174, 224, 225, 226, 227, 228, 239, 240, 241, 243, 245, 246, 248, 273, 275
iron ore, 77, 78
ironsmith, 62, 74, 275
ivory, 255
jackal, 95, 98, 109, 120
jar, 16, 19, 21, 22, 33, 34, 35, 56, 59, 62, 83, 96, 120, 148, 174, 178, 179, 180, 183, 227, 242, 249
joined, 26, 64, 104, 114, 132, 133, 137, 175
Kalyanaraman, 1, 3
kamaḍha, 9, 76, 116
Kanmer, 241, 243, 244, 245
Kashmir, 262
kharoṣṭī, 115
Kish, 213, 215, 222, 223, 230, 231, 232, 254
kũdār, 21, 32, 57, 58, 59, 60, 66, 67
kundau, 246
ladder, 20, 95, 132
language, 251, 256, 257, 258, 262, 263
languages, 256, 261
lapidaries, 61, 114, 159, 171, 245
lapidary, 62, 115, 159, 170
lapis lazuli, 10, 211, 212, 214, 216, 229, 251, 252, 255
lead, 252
ligature, 35, 36, 37, 76, 95, 97, 110, 127, 163
ligatured, 15, 22, 25, 26, 27, 33, 39, 42, 43, 56, 72, 76, 94, 96, 97, 100, 109, 111, 121, 160, 163, 227, 238
linear stroke, 27, 33, 38, 77, 245
linga, 272, 273, 274, 275
lion, 155, 198, 208, 214, 235
Luristan, 173, 200, 201
Magan, 251, 254, 255
Mahābhārata, 107
Mahadevan, 15, 17, 19, 21, 22, 27, 28, 33, 34, 72, 96, 97, 102, 109, 229, 234, 248, 259
makara, 42
markhor, 22, 23, 25, 26, 27, 35, 40, 41, 44, 74, 82, 94, 96, 98, 102, 104, 106, 111, 124, 226
Marshall, 175, 184, 185, 186, 187, 188, 211, 212, 213, 250
Meadow, 50
Meluhha, 3, 17, 30, 44, 45, 46, 51, 58, 68, 73, 74, 75, 76, 77, 79, 93, 114, 116, 118, 119, 120, 134, 150, 155, 157, 159, 168, 169, 171, 212, 213, 215, 218, 221, 222, 229, 243, 248, 251, 254,

256, 266, 267, 270, 271, 273, 274, 275
Meluhhan, 253
merchant, 20, 41, 44, 57, 68, 94, 97, 118, 122, 127, 133, 140, 215, 218, 241, 246, 270
merchants, 251, 266
Mesopotamia, 252, 253, 254, 255, 267
metal, 255, 258, 263, 264, 267
metals, 258, 262
metalsmith, 29, 116, 138, 209
mineral, 51, 73, 76, 77, 78, 94, 96, 104, 110, 117, 136, 140, 142, 145, 146, 159, 211, 233, 234, 244
mint, 262
mleccha, 43, 44, 52, 94, 95, 98, 100, 105, 107, 108, 110, 118, 120, 122, 127, 133, 159, 171, 220, 221, 222, 270, 271
Mleccha, 251, 254, 256, 266
Mohenjodaro, 254, 258
monkey, 133
mountain, 8, 18, 36, 56, 93, 110, 113, 123, 212, 220, 230
Munda, 8, 9, 41, 44, 77, 79, 80, 94, 99, 104, 109, 120, 121, 122, 124, 127, 148, 149, 151, 162, 226, 228, 274, 275
Mundari, 259
Narmer, 116
native metal, 29, 32, 34, 37, 38, 39, 60, 73, 74, 75, 76, 109, 110, 115, 120, 135, 138, 166, 205, 241, 245
Nausharo, 12, 204
neck, 27, 61, 62, 69, 101, 102, 103, 109, 112, 204, 235, 236, 243
Nippur, 215, 231
numeral, 43, 70, 77
offering, 25, 99, 124, 154, 158, 169
ore, 35, 37, 38, 41, 62, 73, 74, 75, 76, 77, 78, 79, 84, 86, 94, 104, 110, 115, 121, 137, 138, 140, 141, 144, 146, 166, 174, 211, 212, 228, 260, 263, 275
organization, 252
pace, 123, 127
Pakistan, 267
Pāṇini, 151
pannier, 72, 236
Parpola, 7, 10, 11, 17, 19, 20, 23, 25, 27, 41, 221, 222, 223, 224, 229, 234, 240, 248, 252, 255, 259, 266
pectoral, 155
penance, 85, 90, 102, 104, 270
Persian Gulf, 251, 252
pewter, 28, 30, 58, 69, 76, 85, 133, 239, 242, 248
phonetic, 17, 19, 43, 45, 78, 96, 98, 272
pictorial motif, 11, 17, 24, 73, 76, 111
pipal, 272
platform, 20, 82, 196, 197, 272
Pleiades, 94
portable furnace, 75, 116, 136
Possehl, 40, 237
pottery, 252, 254
Prakrit, 124
priest, 217, 232
Proto-Elamite, 43, 46
punch-marked, 157, 158, 169, 170, 270
Rakhigarhi, 56, 114, 131
ram, 23, 26, 27, 35, 40, 41, 42, 44, 52, 54, 74, 81, 95, 96, 97, 102, 104, 109, 113, 123, 124, 133, 137, 147, 260
rat, 120

rebus, 251, 253, 260, 261, 262, 263, 264
rebus method, 17, 41, 108, 109
reduplicated, 127
rhinoceros, 16, 23, 25, 26, 27, 67, 68, 90, 133, 134, 140, 236
Rigveda, 16, 37, 58, 69, 92, 93, 217, 220, 233, 248, 270, 271
rim of jar, 16, 19, 32, 34, 35, 58, 60, 96, 120, 148, 249
rimless pot, 28, 31, 33, 35, 36, 37, 39, 56, 60, 68, 70, 78, 97, 127, 227, 245
road, 33, 83, 120, 127
Sanskrit, 255, 256, 266
Santali, 263, 264
Sarasvati, 1, 2, 3, 16, 39, 48, 52, 108, 129, 203, 205, 207, 209, 230, 231, 232, 233, 234, 235, 238, 258, 262, 270
scarf, 94, 104, 109, 114, 136, 159, 160, 163, 164
scorpion, 26, 35, 74, 104, 106
scribe, 16, 19, 32, 34, 35, 56, 58, 60, 72, 96, 98, 120, 148, 149, 153, 155, 249
semantic, 17, 79, 81, 108, 114, 133, 138, 139, 148, 164, 220, 233, 238, 280
serpent, 26, 27, 41, 94, 95, 97, 101, 102, 104, 109, 110, 208
Shaffer, 252
ship, 257, 258, 265
Shortugai, 211, 212, 224
signboard, 114, 117
silver, 10, 29, 34, 38, 40, 54, 56, 60, 63, 72, 74, 76, 77, 78, 79, 80, 91, 100, 135, 158, 169, 172, 173, 174, 175, 181, 184, 186, 189, 209, 211, 213, 216, 218, 221, 227, 229, 233, 234, 249
Sindhi, 255
smelter, 28, 33, 34, 35, 70, 86, 87, 91, 104, 121, 134, 160, 162, 248, 272, 274
smelting, 61, 72, 73, 75, 78, 86, 91, 94, 97, 100, 105, 107, 135, 142, 146, 162, 172, 211, 220, 226, 227
smith, 33, 42, 72, 80, 86, 87, 91, 96, 109, 138, 174, 215, 225, 227, 232, 243
smiths, 72, 134, 174, 175
smithy, 10, 20, 21, 26, 28, 30, 31, 32, 34, 36, 37, 38, 39, 43, 44, 47, 56, 57, 58, 59, 60, 61, 62, 67, 68, 70, 76, 78, 86, 87, 90, 95, 97, 104, 108, 109, 114, 115, 118, 120, 122, 126, 133, 134, 138, 150, 159, 160, 161, 171, 205, 224, 225, 228, 234, 248, 249, 262, 271, 274
spade, 77, 113
spear, 7, 124, 179, 181, 209, 213, 246, 247
splinter, 7, 32, 33, 60, 67, 74, 83, 96, 244, 245, 246
spokes, 16, 140
sprachbund, 46, 52, 68, 93, 114, 118, 150, 159, 171, 234, 270, 271, 275
spy, 24, 33
squirrel, 57
śreṇi, 96
standard device, 61, 62, 136, 155
star, 60, 122, 156, 215, 226, 232
steel, 75, 96, 98, 104, 121, 160, 227, 228, 275
step, 123, 127, 211, 234

stone, 10, 12, 14, 29, 34, 35, 38, 39, 41, 52, 61, 73, 74, 77, 78, 86, 110, 112, 117, 120, 121, 122, 137, 140, 147, 172, 181, 187, 194, 203, 209, 213, 216, 218, 228, 237, 241, 243, 245, 247, 272, 274
stool, 94, 120
substrate, 218, 230, 232
Sumerian, 9, 10, 17, 19, 26, 49, 79, 137, 155, 157, 209, 212, 213, 214, 215, 217, 219, 221, 222, 232, 236, 253, 254, 255, 266, 267
summit, 29
Surkotada, 203, 230
Susa, 50, 118, 134, 150, 160, 238, 254, 263
svastika, 24, 28, 205, 213, 227, 229
symbols, 258, 259, 262
tablets, 252
tail, 7, 22, 23, 26, 27, 44, 60, 95, 97, 101, 102, 104, 106, 109, 110, 111, 161, 201, 204, 238, 244
Tello, 218
Telugu, 253
Tepe Yahya, 43, 44, 46, 119, 254
terracotta, 25, 39, 40, 87, 88, 128, 174, 189, 199, 203, 204, 243, 247
Theobald, 157, 158, 169, 170
tiger, 16, 23, 24, 26, 27, 28, 33, 87, 88, 90, 94, 95, 97, 101, 102, 104, 105, 106, 109, 120, 132, 133, 134, 138, 139, 140, 163, 236, 263, 264
tin, 30, 42, 43, 44, 45, 47, 51, 52, 58, 60, 69, 70, 72, 76, 80, 85, 114, 119, 125, 133, 141, 146, 147, 160, 163, 172, 175, 182, 207, 209, 212, 217, 222, 229, 233, 239, 248, 251, 257, 258, 260, 261, 265, 266, 270, 271
tin ingot, 47, 141, 270
tools, 262
trader, 40, 234
traders, 266
transport, 255
tree, 23, 25, 33, 62, 64, 72, 76, 81, 85, 87, 88, 89, 95, 98, 110, 120, 121, 123, 127, 134, 139, 159, 160, 161, 162, 170, 230, 239, 247, 270, 272
trough, 32, 34, 60, 66, 67, 68, 86, 137, 217
turner, 21, 32, 38, 47, 57, 58, 59, 60, 64, 65, 66, 67, 76, 104, 115, 116, 133, 136, 140, 234, 240, 243, 246, 249
tusk, 64, 95, 98, 110, 127
United Arab Emirates, 254, 265
upraised arm, 39, 52
Ur, 10, 11, 132, 152, 175, 189, 194, 199, 202, 209, 212, 214, 215, 218, 221, 222, 229, 230, 231, 237, 254, 266, 269
Uruk, 137, 138, 139, 163, 207
vagina, 8
Vats, 12, 13, 14, 15, 41, 175, 178, 179, 180, 181, 182, 189, 190, 191, 192, 212, 248, 250
Vātsyāyana, 52, 118
Veda, 217, 272, 274
Vedic, 29, 72, 96, 123, 136, 217, 220, 270, 271
vessel, 7, 8, 25, 32, 44, 58, 60, 68, 81, 85, 97, 120, 125, 159, 171, 175, 242
vice, 96
Vidale, 104, 106, 108
vikalpa, 1, 52, 53, 72, 108
waist-zone, 61
warehouse, 11, 59, 92

water-carrier, 34, 35, 227
weights, 27, 121, 171, 228, 254
wheel, 16, 22, 30, 33, 36, 37, 70, 115, 116, 140
Wheeler, 254, 266, 268
wide-mouthed pot, 248
wing, 161
workshop, 6, 7, 10, 26, 30, 32, 33, 58, 60, 62, 67, 69, 72, 74, 76, 78, 83, 92, 96, 115, 116, 127, 136, 174, 217, 243, 244, 245, 246, 249
writer, 134
zebu, 26, 27, 69, 70, 72, 73, 74, 75, 94, 95, 97, 101, 102, 103, 104, 106, 109, 113, 120, 132, 133, 198, 209
zinc, 24, 28, 30, 32, 58, 61, 68, 70, 76, 125, 141, 205, 228, 229

www.ingramcontent.com/pod-product-compliance
Lightning Source LLC
Chambersburg PA
CBHW060149050426
42446CB00013B/2734
9 780991 104840